KANJI NO SATORI

漢字　の　悟り

STEVE THENELL

MILLET RAIN PUBLISHING
USA

Published by Millet Rain Publishing
USA
www.milletrain.com

Text © 2015 Steve Thenell

Set in Cardo.
Principal kanji font: DynaFont DFKyoKaSho W4.

All rights reserved.
No part of this publication may be reprinted or reproduced or utilized in any form or by any electronic, mechanical, or other means, now known or hereafter invented, without permission in writing from the publisher.

While every precaution has been taken in the preparation of this book, the publisher assumes no responsibility for errors or omissions, or for damages resulting from the use of the information contained herein.

First edition, 2015

ISBN 978-0-9972223-0-2

Publisher's Cataloging-in-Publication Data

Thenell, Steve, 1968-
         Kanji no Satori
/ Steve Thenell.
             p. cm.
         English.
         Includes index.
         ISBN 978-0-9972223-0-2
         1. Japanese language -- Study and teaching.   I. Title.
         495.6—ddc21

Contents

Acknowledgments   vii
Foreword   viii
How to Use This Book   x
Style Notes   xii
Content Notes   xiii

Part 1 – Foundation

Chapter 1 – Introduction to Kanji

1.1	What are Kanji?	3
1.2	A Brief History	4
1.3	How Many Characters Are There?	5
1.4	Diving In: Our First Five Characters	5
1.5	Basic Characteristics of the Characters	6
1.6	Elements	8
1.7	Compound Words	9
1.8	The Two Major Ways to Read Characters	11
1.9	Using Kanji to Write Native Japanese Words	13
1.10	The Structure of Japanese Sentences	14
1.11	Character Etymology	16
1.12	The Characters are Primarily Phonetic	17
1.13	The Common Use Characters	18
1.14	Chapter Summary	18

Chapter 2 – Character Design and History

2.1	The Legendary Origin	21
2.2	The Spoken Language Came First	22
2.3	The First Stage: Pictographs	22
2.4	The Next Stage: Ideographs	23
2.5	Meaning Extension and Change	27
2.6	The Determinative	32
2.7	The Phonetic	36
2.8	Determinative-Phonetic Characters	40
2.9	Character Nesting	45
2.10	The Traditional Six Principles of Character Creation	47
2.11	Transformation of Character Forms	47
2.12	Character Substitution	60
2.13	*Kokuji* – 'Made in Japan' Characters	63
2.14	Side Note: Comparison with the Latin Alphabet	64
2.15	Chapter Summary	64

Chapter 3 – Learning the Characters

3.1	Myths and Misconceptions	67
3.2	What to Expect	70
3.3	Why Learning the Characters is Challenging	72
3.4	Considering Character Etymology	77
3.5	Considering Character Meaning	79
3.6	Breaking Down a Character	80
3.7	Character Quantity and Frequency of Occurrence	81
3.8	Recommended Approach to Learning Characters	86
3.9	From This Point Forward	88

Chapter 4 – Character Organization

4.1	The Radical	89
4.2	Determinative and Radical: The Differences	93
4.3	Character Regions	96
4.4	The *Jōyō Kanji*	98
4.5	The *Kyōiku Kanji*	98
4.6	The *Jinmeiyō Kanji*	99
4.7	*Hyōgaiji*	100
4.8	Chapter Summary	100

Chapter 5 – Character Usage in Depth

5.1	When Kanji Are Not Used	101
5.2	*Ateji* – Using Characters Only for Their Sound	105
5.3	*Jukujikun* – Multi-Character Special Readings	107
5.4	Counter Words	109
5.5	Prefixes and Suffixes	111
5.6	Single Character Inheriting Compound Meaning	113

Chapter 6 – Character Form in Depth

6.1	Strokes, Stroke Count, and Stroke Order	115
6.2	Side Note: Handwritten Characters	116
6.3	The *Kaisho* Calligraphic Script	117
6.4	Character Printing Styles	118
6.5	Stroke Variations	120
6.6	Element Variations	122
6.7	Variant Characters	124
6.8	Character Composition	126

Chapter 7 – The *On* Reading in Depth

7.1	*Kango*	131
7.2	Parts of Speech	132
7.3	Polite Modifiers	135
7.4	Valid *On* Readings	135
7.5	Multiple *On* Readings – Character and Phonetic	138

7.6	The Principal *On* Reading	139
7.7	Different Readings for Different Meanings	139
7.8	Causes of Multiple *On* Readings	140
7.9	Classification of *On* Readings	141
7.10	Related Readings	144
7.11	Unrelated Readings – Special Role Borrowing	150
7.12	False Phonetics	151
7.13	*On* Compound Homophones	152

Chapter 8 – The *Kun* Reading in Depth

8.1	The Sounds of Native Japanese Words	153
8.2	Word Inflection and *Okurigana*	156
8.3	Transitive and Intransitive Verbs	158
8.4	Native Japanese Compound Words	160
8.5	Multiple *Kun* Readings	162
8.6	Applying Kanji to Fixed Expressions	164
8.7	Derived Words Appear to Broaden Character Meaning	165
8.8	*Kun*-based Homophones	165
8.9	Kanji Can Hide Word Connections	166
8.10	Mostly Obsolete Word Inflections	168
8.11	*Nanori* Readings	169

Chapter 9 – Compound Words in Depth

9.1	Two-Character Compounds	171
9.2	Three- and Four-Character Compounds	174
9.3	Mixed *On* and *Kun* Compounds	175
9.4	Characteristics of Some Compound Words	175
9.5	Compound Etymologies and Meaning Change	176
9.6	Compound Reading Sound Changes	178
9.7	Special Sound Change: *Sokuon*	178
9.8	Special Sound Change: *Rendaku*	179
9.9	Special Sound Change: *Renjō*	181
9.10	Other Kinds of Special Readings	182
9.11	Compounds Built from Abbreviation	183
9.12	*Mazegaki*	184
9.13	Conversion of Native Japanese Words into *Kango*	185

Part 2 – Reference Lists

Section 1 – List of Major Determinatives	189
Section 2 – List of Phonetic Components	195
Section 3 – List of Other Components	227
Section 4 – List of Radicals	231

Appendices

A. Glossary of Key Terminology	241
B. Japanese Romanization Styles	249
C. Principles of Stroke Order	251
D. The Traditional Six Principles of Character Creation	263
E. The Origin of *Kana*	265
F. Radicals in Depth	269
G. Character Simplifications and Variant Forms	279
H. Common *Kokuji*	291
I. *Kun* Readings That Fit the Pattern of Valid *On* Readings	293
J. *Boinkōtai* Noun Inflection	297
K. Common Compounds with Special Readings	299
L. Mixed *On-Kun* Compounds	301
M. Four-Character Compounds	303
N. Semi-cursive and Cursive Scripts	307
O. Special Non-Kanji Characters	309
P. The 100 Most Common Japanese Surnames	311
Index	313
List of Book Illustrations	317
About the Author	318

Acknowledgments

I am thankful for the useful advice and assistance I received in the preparation of this book from Daniel Dupriest, Nader Ghotbi, Ed Naidich, Sam Shiffman, Joe Spector, Joe Strasser, Roger and Mariko Chouinard, and Jun Tau.

Thanks to Tim Eyre and to Dr. Ulrich Apel of Japan's National Institute of Informatics for allowing the use of Tim's Kanji Stroke Orders font, used to display the stroke order diagrams in Appendix C of the book.

Thanks also to other individuals and organizations who have made their fonts available for use in this project, including David Perry (Cardo), Paratype (PT Sans), Peter Becker (Vinta), Academia Sinica (Jiaguwen, Jinwen, and Beishida Shuowen Xiaozhuan), the Republic of China Ministry of Education (Standard Kaishu), Wang Hanzong (Li Su Medium and Shin Su Medium), Aoyagi Kouzan (Kouzan Brush Font and Kouzan Brush Font Sousyo), Arphic Technology (AR PL UKai), and cwTeX (cwTeX Ming).

And special thanks to Betty Young for all of the tremendous support she provided while I worked on the book.

Finally, I could not have assembled together all the information in this book without the tireless work of many who preceded me in the study of the characters. These people are too numerous to mention, but I am very much in their debt.

Foreword

Welcome to Kanji no Satori!

The goal of this book is to be a comprehensive guide to understanding and gaining proficiency with kanji: the Chinese characters used in the writing of the Japanese language. Notably, rather than presenting numerous tables of characters, the aim of this book is to help you build in your mind a complete foundation for the optimal learning of the characters. Once that is accomplished, then you can go on to study the individual characters using whichever study materials you prefer. In short, with this book you will learn *how to learn* the characters, in a way that you will be able to successfully retain what you have learned.

The key part of the book's approach to building that foundation is in explaining the most important underlying theory of the characters. You learn about the characters before (and as) you learn the characters themselves. When I learn something, I like to understand the 'why' behind what I am learning, rather than just memorize something blindly. In the long run, it truly helps me to retain what I have learned. This is especially true of a complicated subject such as kanji. Throughout the book, you will see plenty of explanations designed to help you achieve this kind of underlying understanding, providing answers to the 'why' questions, and taking the mystery out of kanji.

One of the biggest hurdles kanji learners face is that there are so many exceptions to rules and so many complicated aspects of the characters that it is easy to get confused. With the foundation built by this book, you can cut through much of that confusion, and much more rapidly gain proficiency with the characters. Importantly, there are lots of underlying patterns contained within the characters that many people who study them often fail to see. Being aware of these patterns can substantially reduce the required effort needed to learn the characters.

Nonetheless, mastering kanji is by no means a simple effort. It is very challenging and time-consuming regardless of which method is used to learn the characters. Even if shortcuts are used, the time investment required is immense; the amount of memorization needed is considerable. But if you start out learning in an inefficient way, achieving kanji literacy will require a substantial effort beyond what is really necessary.

While a method such as brute force rote memorization can be successful for learning the first one or two hundred characters, after that things start getting more and more complicated and confusing. If you don't have a good foundation, and a good method for mentally organizing what you have learned, continuing to learn and remember additional characters will become a greater and greater struggle.

Although it's true that different people learn more effectively with different methods, with such a complicated subject as kanji I believe that the systematic approach presented in this book is helpful for any learner hoping to achieve literacy in the Japanese language.

On some topics, this book goes into a lot of depth. Your initial reaction might be, "I don't need to know all of this just to use the characters." However, I believe that you will find that having this understanding will, in the long run, enhance your proficiency with kanji.

This book does not formally present a full set of characters, and as such is designed to be used as a companion book to other study materials. The specific information presented here is intended to be that which is most useful for a student trying to gain a basic proficiency of and comfort with the characters.

The title of this book translates into English as "the enlightenment of kanji." That's what I believe this book brings to the reader. I hope this book gives you a solid grounding in kanji, and thereby helps you to quickly clear the hurdle of kanji confusion, and begin to be able to have an enriching experience using the Japanese language.

Steve Thenell
September 2015

How to Use This Book

This book is designed to be used together with any kanji study materials in which characters are learned one by one. This book acts as a supplement to such materials.

The book is divided into two major parts: Part 1 (Foundation) and Part 2 (Reference Lists).

Part 1 provides extensive background, history, and theory about the Chinese characters to enable the reader to understand how the characters are designed, and how they are used in the modern Japanese language. This material is not just academic; it serves to create a framework in the mind of the reader so that the characters may be learned more easily.

Part 2 presents lists of reference data designed to assist with the learning and memorization of the characters.

Part 1 Breakdown

Part 1 is divided into nine chapters. The first four chapters provide the most basic, essential information. The final five chapters go into more detail on a variety of useful topics. Most important are Chapters 1 through 3:

> Chapter 1 gives a general overview of kanji and introduces the fundamental concepts regarding the use of kanji in Japanese.

> Chapter 2 explains a history of the characters, which helps you to understand the different types of characters that exist today.

> Chapter 3 discusses the challenges of learning the characters, and provides a recommended method for doing so.

Reading Order

If you really want to get started learning the characters, it's not necessary to read all of Part 1 before doing so, but all readers are encouraged to read at least the first three chapters of Part 1 before starting an in-depth study of the characters. Even if all of the concepts introduced in those chapters are not yet entirely clear, having familiarity with this background information will make studying the characters easier. After that, it's fine to launch into an in-depth study of the characters before Part 1 is finished, learning the remaining concepts of Part 1 after you have already become familiar with a number of characters.

Reviewing Part 1

After a little time, as you have gained more familiarity with the characters, it is useful to go back and review the content of Part 1.

Use of Characters in Part 1

Some actual characters will be shown and discussed in Part 1 of the book. However, this is done only to illustrate the concepts being explained, so don't go out of your way to memorize these characters at the time you study Part 1. This can wait until you begin your formal study of the characters.

Appendices

The book's appendices contain topics that are not essential for learning and using the characters, but are designed for readers who have more of an interest in the topics presented there. They also contain a lot of reference information which you may find helpful. They can be read at any time (or not at all).

Kana Syllabaries

This book assumes the reader has already attained a basic familiarity and proficiency with the *hiragana* and *katakana* syllabaries.

Application Support

Studying using computer-based flashcard methods is highly recommended. To assist with memorization, a companion app, called kanji-no-satori, is planned for development. You can find information about this app, and instructions for obtaining it when it becomes available, as well as other kanji study aid recommendations, on the book's official web page:

http://www.milletrain.com/kanjinosatori

Style Notes

Throughout this book, the Hepburn style of romanization of Japanese words is used as the default. Within the Hepburn style, there are several different ways to represent long vowels. In this book, *a*, *i*, *o*, and *u* long vowels are denoted by use of a single letter with a macron (a straight horizontal line appearing above the letter). A long *e* vowel is represented with the vowel pair *ei*. Styles of romanization are discussed in Appendix B.

Japanese terms and words used in the book are generally *italicized*. Some frequently used terms, such as the word *kanji* itself, revert to normal (non-italicized) text after repeated usage. The pair of words *on* and *kun* are exclusively written in italics throughout the book to avoid confusion with the English word 'on.'

When important terminology is first defined, each term is presented in **boldface**. All such terms are also defined in the Appendix A glossary, where the Japanese equivalents of the terms are provided. In cases where one of these terms is reintroduced in a subsequent chapter, such as for a more detailed discussion, it is placed in italics when first mentioned, or redefined, in that later chapter.

Throughout the book, Japanese words are not capitalized except for proper nouns or when starting sentences.

Chinese proper nouns, such as people and book names, are directly transliterated from Chinese into English. Therefore they may appear differently than the same words when transliterated from the Japanese language, where character pronunciations are often different from Chinese.

Content Notes

In this book some character etymologies are described. These are explanations of the origins of the characters—why they were designed the way they were. Generally speaking, it is not possible to know character origins with certainty, because they weren't documented at the time the characters were created (for most characters); that information has been mostly lost to time. In this book, wherever character etymologies are given, only those which are highly plausible and have support of character historians and researchers are mentioned. But the reader must understand that this information cannot be taken as absolute fact.

Throughout the book, many example words using the characters are given. English definitions are provided for these Japanese words, but it is simply not possible in this kind of book to give definitions that are as comprehensive and detailed as what can be found in a Japanese-English dictionary. Readers are encouraged to use the definitions in this book as references, but should understand that full, comprehensive definitions must be obtained elsewhere.

Part 1

Foundation

基

Chapter 1

Introduction to Kanji

This chapter provides a very general overview of the Chinese characters, presenting the most important things you should know as you begin to study the characters. This is just a broad explanation of the most important concepts. Don't worry if you don't understand all the details yet; most of the topics in this chapter will be explained in further detail later in the book.

1.1 What are Kanji?

Kanji are the main characters upon which the Japanese writing system is based. *Kanji* is a Japanese word. It is composed of two parts: *kan* and *ji*. In this word, the first part means 'Chinese' and the second part means 'character' (as in a character used in writing). The characters are called *kanji* because they come from and were originally created in China.

The Japanese language does not distinguish between singular and plural nouns, so the word *kanji* can be translated into English as either 'Chinese character' or 'Chinese characters,' depending on whether you are referring to one or multiple characters. Furthermore, the word *kanji* when used in English is both the singular and the plural form. Thus, when talking about more than one character, you would say, for example, 'two kanji,' not 'two kanjis.'

What makes kanji interesting and so fundamentally different from the alphabet used in English (i.e., the Latin, or Roman, alphabet) is that each character has a meaning associated with it. The Latin alphabet is a *phonetic* alphabet, wherein each character (that is, letter) merely indicates a sound. It's necessary to string these alphabetic characters together to make words that have meaning. Each individual kanji, though, contains meaning, even when used by itself.

Languages like English that use an alphabet generally have a small number of different characters used to form the words of the language. With kanji, though, there are a very large number of characters from which words are made. Sometimes words are written using only one character by itself, but more often two or more characters are used in combination to make words.

Modern Japanese is written with a mixture of kanji and two syllabaries: **hiragana** and **katakana** (and to a limited extent the Latin alphabet, as well). The syllabaries were invented in Japan. Each of the syllabaries is similar to an alphabet, but different in that each character represents a complete spoken syllable, rather than just a single sound. (This is why they are called 'syllabaries.') Unlike kanji, the characters in the hiragana and katakana syllabaries have no meaning associated with them.

Before studying kanji, it is important to already have knowledge of and some degree of proficiency with both hiragana and katakana. This book assumes the reader already has that proficiency.

1.2 A Brief History

Based on archaeological findings, it is known that kanji were in use at least as far back as 1200 BC, during China's Shang Dynasty. They were likely first created even earlier than that, but no concrete evidence to support that has yet been discovered. The set of characters in existence during the Shang Dynasty was rather different from that of today; the characters went through many changes over thousands of years before reaching the modern form.

The characters were not created all at once. In China, new characters continued to be added over thousands of years as the spoken language developed and new words were formed, requiring characters to represent them. The Japanese, who began using the characters around the fifth century AD, even created some new characters of their own to represent uniquely Japanese words, although only a very small number of these are still commonly used. In modern times, characters are still sometimes created in China, though very infrequently. In Japan, though, the set of characters in use is considered fixed; new characters are no longer added.

The use of Chinese characters in writing spread from China to numerous other Asian countries, including Korea and Vietnam, but today only the Japanese language and the various languages native to China use Chinese characters as the core of their written language. The characters have been replaced with other writing systems in the other countries which once used them, although they are still used to a limited extent in South Korea.

1.3 How Many Characters Are There?

One of the first questions asked by new students of kanji is, "How many characters are there?" The number of different, unique characters that have been created is staggeringly large: in excess of 90,000. That may seem daunting to someone just starting to learn them, but the reality is that the vast majority of these characters are obscure or obsolete, and will not ever be encountered, even once, by the average Japanese (or Chinese) person in an entire lifetime.

You won't even find all of those characters in a standard character dictionary. A typical modern Japanese kanji dictionary contains about 12,000 characters. And even many of these are rarely or never encountered by a typical reader.

That leads to the question, "How many characters do I *really* need to know?"

Before answering that question, it is important to realize that different characters are encountered with different frequencies. Some characters are so fundamental to written Japanese that they are seen many times a day as part of many different words. Others, though, are encountered only occasionally as part of one or two common words, and almost never in any other context. Some are used only in people or place names, but not in any other everyday words. Some are seen so infrequently that many Japanese people do not know them with confidence.

A reasonable standard for whether a character 'needs to be known,' then, is whether a literate Japanese person who encounters the character in writing would be expected to be familiar with it. Roughly between 2500 and 3000 characters meet this standard.

So should you learn this many characters up front before learning the Japanese language?

Absolutely not. For a new learner of Japanese, many of the less frequently encountered characters are of little use. They are not likely to be encountered at all in reading material that a beginner would read, and trying to memorize them in the early stages of learning Japanese would be a difficult task and would inevitably result in confusion and the need to relearn them later on.

Instead, it is better to learn the most commonly used characters first, together with learning the Japanese language itself, and then gradually increase the number of characters studied, as your Japanese language ability develops. This is how Japanese children learn, and it is a method that makes sense for adults, as well.

Chapter 3 presents a more detailed discussion of the challenges and strategies of learning the characters. For now, though, let's start looking at some of them.

1.4 Diving In: Our First Five Characters

As the various concepts about kanji are explained here in Part 1 of the book, it's nice to have some characters to refer to.

Here are the first five characters we will examine:

木　火　土　金　水

These characters were chosen for the first five because they are all very common characters that you will see often and learn quickly, and they are all among the first set of characters learned by Japanese schoolchildren. They also share an interesting relationship: they represent the 'five phases' (sometimes called 'five elements') of ancient Chinese philosophy: wood, fire, earth, metal, and water, as shown below.

木　　　火　　　土　　　金　　　水
wood　　fire　　earth　　metal　　water

These and other characters will be shown throughout Part 1 of the book to help explain the topics presented. But there's no need to carefully study or memorize these five or any other characters at this time.

1.5 Basic Characteristics of the Characters

All kanji have the following three basic characteristics:

- Form

The **form** of a character is simply the way it is written, including the shape and orientation of the lines that make up the character.

The forms of some of the oldest characters are based on drawings of the objects they represent. For example, the 'wood' character (木) also means 'tree,' which is the original meaning of the character, and the form of the character is based on a drawing of a tree. With only a little imagination you can see the trunk of a tree and various branches jutting out.[1]

The lines that make up a character are called **strokes**. Each character is written as a sequence of strokes. The 'tree' character is written with four strokes, which you can see one by one in the following diagram (the small arrows show the direction in which the strokes are drawn):

一　十　木　木

A single stroke can also have a bend or turn within it. The following diagram shows the 'water' (水) character. You can see that the first stroke has a small hook at the bottom, and the second stroke has a bend in it:

丨　氵　水　水

---

[1] As we will see in Chapter 2, the lower 'branches' were originally roots of the tree.

In the modern style of writing kanji, the strokes of the characters are generally either straight or slightly curved; there are no circles. And the characters are structured to be nearly square in shape (only slightly taller than they are wide), so that they can nicely fill a square box when written.

A 'correct' way to draw each character has been established. This includes, for each character, both a proper **stroke count**—the total number of strokes that make up a character—and a proper **stroke order**—the sequence in which the strokes are drawn as the character is written. The diagrams on the previous page show the correct stroke count and stroke order for the 'tree' and 'water' characters. In those diagrams, stroke count is indicated by the total number of separate images, and stroke order is indicated by the sequence of those images. When learning the characters, Japanese schoolchildren write them repeatedly, practicing drawing them in the proper way. Proper writing is also very important in Japanese calligraphy.

• Reading

The **reading** of a character is how it is pronounced, or simply the sound that is made when the character is read aloud. Many characters have two or more possible readings, and are pronounced—or *read*—differently depending on the context in which they are used.

Each of our first five characters has multiple readings. For example, the 'fire' character (火) is read differently in each of the following words:

Word	Reading of Word	Meaning of Word	Reading of 火
火	hi (ひ)	fire	hi (ひ)
花火	hanabi (はなび)	fireworks	bi (び)
火山	kazan (かざん)	volcano	ka (か)

For characters with more than one possible reading, knowing which reading to use requires recognizing the word (or other context) in which the character is being used. The reasons for characters having different possible readings, such as in the table above, will be explained later in the book, beginning in Section 1.8 of this chapter. Once you understand these reasons, it will become possible to guess readings of unfamiliar words.

• Meaning

Each character has a **meaning** associated with it. In fact, many characters have more than one meaning associated with them. Originally, each character had only one meaning, but over time some picked up additional meanings, just as words in English sometimes do. For some characters, one or more of the meanings have been phased out of usage; for others, several different meanings still apply.

Each time a character is used in a particular word, though, it only has one meaning. Just as with the reading, it is necessary to identify the context in which the character is being used to know which meaning applies.

All of our first five characters have multiple meanings. As explained already, the first character originally meant 'tree,' but later also acquired the meaning 'wood.' Similarly, the third character can mean both 'the ground' (in the sense of what you stand on) and 'earth' (in the sense of the soil in the ground). The fourth character means 'metal' in general, but also is commonly used with the meaning 'gold.' And it has yet another meaning, as well: 'money.'

It is easy to see the relationships between these sets of meanings. For example, gold is a type of metal, and is used as a form of currency. But sometimes the different meanings of a character are not obviously related to each other. For example, from their important role in representing the 'five phases' of Chinese philosophy, each of the first five characters was long ago borrowed and assigned to represent one of the five planets visible with the naked eye: Mercury, Venus, Mars, Jupiter, and Saturn. Later, when a seven-day week was implemented in Japan, the different weekdays were named after the sun, moon, and five visible planets (patterned after what was done in western culture). Thus, these same five characters inherited yet another meaning: each was used to represent a different day of the week. As a result, our fifth character, for example, can mean not only 'water,' but also 'Mercury' and 'Wednesday.'

The following table summarizes all the different meanings of our first five characters that have been mentioned up to this point:

木	火	土	金	水
wood; tree	fire	earth; ground	metal; gold; money	water
Jupiter	Mars	Saturn	Venus	Mercury
Thursday	Tuesday	Saturday	Friday	Wednesday

But remember that each character only has one meaning with each usage, and that meaning is determined by the context of that usage.

1.6 Elements

The 'tree' character (木) is an example of a character that consists of just one single object, in this case a depiction of a tree.

But most characters consist of multiple, discrete objects assembled together. For example, the following characters all contain the 'tree' object, but also include one or more additional objects:

相 査 楽 困

In these characters, the tree is an 'element,' or one part of the character. An **element** is any one of the simplest parts a character can be separated into that still has meaning associated with it.[2]

---

[2] Elements are also sometimes referred to as 'components' or 'graphemes.' In this book, the term 'component' has a different meaning, defined in Chapter 2.

Each of our first five characters consists of only a single element, but these five characters all appear as elements within many other characters.

Below are five more characters, each of which contains one of our first five characters as an element within it. Look at each of these characters and make sure you can spot one of the first five characters within it.

箱　畑　型　銀　泉

Did you find them?

You can see them more clearly in the following images, where the other parts of the characters have been grayed out:

箱　畑　型　銀　泉

Note that when included within a more complex character, elements are sometimes stretched or compressed to fit in a given space, and the strokes of elements are sometimes modified from the original form. When compared to the original, full-character forms on the previous page, some differences in the above forms include: the lower right stroke of the 'tree' element and the upper right stroke of the 'metal' element are both slightly shorter, the bottom stroke of the 'metal' element is drawn at an angle instead of horizontally, and the upper right-hand stroke of the 'water' element touches the neighboring stroke at a different point.

The elements that make up a character often give a clue as to the meaning (or meanings) of the character; you can often use them to assist with remembering character meanings.

1.7 Compound Words

Each of our first five characters when used by itself forms a complete word in Japanese. In modern Japanese, there are many words that can be written with just a single character by itself. But it is much more common to find two or more kanji put together to form a word. Such a word is called a 'compound word,' or simply a 'compound.'

A **compound** is a fixed word (or, alternately, a fixed expression or set phrase) that is made up of two or more characters put together.

Compounds can consist of two, three, or even four or more kanji together. Two character compounds are by far the most common. Compounds of more than four kanji are rare.

Sometimes the meaning of a compound is easily determined by simply combining the meanings of each character that appears in the compound. This can be seen with the word *kanji* itself. *Kanji* is a compound word, written with two characters:

As already mentioned, the first character, read as *kan*, means 'Chinese,'[3] and the second character, read as *ji*, means 'character' (as in writing character). And put together, the compound simply means 'Chinese character.' This is very straightforward.

But in a number of cases, the meaning of a compound is more complicated than just the combination of the meanings of the characters it contains. There are many compound words where it is difficult to guess the meaning of the compound simply by knowing the meanings of the characters that are in it.

Let's look at an example of such a word involving two of our first five characters:

The reading of this compound is *doboku*. In this compound word, the first character is read as *do* and the second as *boku*.

If you tried to guess the meaning, you would probably start by thinking of the meanings of the two characters in the compound: 'ground' (or 'earth') and 'tree' (or 'wood'). Maybe you would guess that the compound means 'tree planting': putting a tree into the ground. Or maybe 'shade,' since the ground below a tree is often in the shade. Or perhaps 'petrified wood,' as wood becomes petrified when it is buried in the ground.

As it turns out, none of these meanings is correct. The word *doboku* means 'public works,' and (together with additional characters) is used to write phrases such as 'civil engineering.' The meaning of this compound derives from the fact that soil and lumber (as well as stone and other natural materials) are used in the construction of bridges, roads, and other public works projects.

The meaning of this compound is not obvious based on the characters in it. After first learning the meaning, it will probably require some practice and repetition to be able to remember it.

Fortunately, though, many compounds are either of the type where the meaning is easily determinable based on the characters in it, or of the type where once you learn the meaning, it makes sense based on the characters in it, and can be relatively easily remembered.

A crucial point to realize, though, is that when studying Japanese, to be able to understand what you are reading, it's not enough to simply learn the characters and their meanings individually; you must also learn the meanings of compound words that are made up of multiple characters.

Of course, it's not necessary to learn all compounds containing a character at the time you first learn that character. For example, a beginning learner of Japanese should be familiar with the characters 土 and 木, but doesn't yet need to know the compound 土木; it can be learned later. Learning some common compounds which include a character can help you to remember the character itself, though, so it is often useful when learning a character to also learn some of the frequently encountered compound words that use it.

---

[3] This first character can also more specifically mean 'Han Chinese,' referring to either the Han Dynasty or the Han ethnicity, but in the word *kanji* refers to China as a whole.

Compounds can represent not only single words, but also what in English would be short phrases or expressions, such as 'bottle opener' or 'bluish-purple.' There are even compounds for concepts not typically found in English, and requiring many words to describe, such as 'reverently welcoming the sunrise from the top of a mountain.'

But whether translated into English as a single word, a fixed phrase, or even a loose concept, compound words in the Japanese language are set phrases with specific, well-defined meanings.

In Japanese, compounds are called *jukugo*. The term *jukugo* can be roughly translated as 'matured word' (or, alternately, 'matured phrase'). This implies that the meaning of the compound has 'matured,' or been synthesized into something more complex than just the combination of the meanings of the characters it is written with.

We'll look at compounds in more detail in Chapter 9.

1.8 The Two Major Ways to Read Characters

One of the most important and fundamental features of kanji as used in the Japanese language is that there are two major different ways of reading the characters. They are called the '*on* reading' (in Japanese: *on yomi*) and the '*kun* reading' (*kun yomi*). To clearly understand the distinction between these two types of readings, it's useful to look back at how the characters were first incorporated into Japanese.

At the time of the first extensive contact between people from Japan and people from other nearby Asian countries, Japanese was only a spoken language and had no native writing system. When kanji were first introduced to Japan, they were brought not as individual characters, but as part of various documents written in Chinese, notably texts concerning philosophy and religion (Confucianism and Buddhism).

With the spread of Buddhism into Japan, and the strong influence of Chinese culture and thinking, which was seen by many Japanese as more advanced than their own, new concepts and ideas flooded into Japan. Chinese texts were carefully studied by educated Japanese, but without a written Japanese language could not be translated, and so were studied in their original form. The texts were read by imitating the Chinese pronunciations of the characters. Many words of Chinese origin entered the Japanese language, pronounced in this way. In some cases, native Japanese words were even replaced with Chinese counterparts, as was done with the number system. This is the origin of the *on* readings.

Simply put, the **on reading** of a character is a rough approximation of the way the character was pronounced in the Chinese language at the time the character was introduced into Japan. Because Chinese spoken sounds were quite different from Japanese spoken sounds, the *on* reading was not an exact match with the original Chinese pronunciation, but rather the closest match obtainable using the Japanese sound system. You can think of an *on* character reading as 'the sound Japanese people made when trying to imitate the sound spoken by Chinese people.' The term *on yomi* means 'sound reading,' or reading based on sound, reflecting this origin.

Soon, the Japanese began using the characters to write their native Japanese language as well. At first several ways of doing this were attempted, but the principal method settled on was one where characters were used based solely on their meaning, and applied to Japanese words with identical or similar meaning. This is the origin of the *kun* readings.

The **kun reading** of a character is the way the character is read when it is used in the writing of a native Japanese word. The term *kun yomi*, roughly translated, means 'explanatory reading.' This refers to the fact that when first adopted, *kun* readings helped the Japanese people to understand the meanings of the characters. Note that when referring to these terms even in English, the words *on* and *kun* are commonly used, instead of translating these words into English.

Because the *on* reading is based on a pronunciation originating in China, and the *kun* reading is based on a pronunciation native to Japanese, it might be helpful to think of the *on* reading as the Chinese reading (or Chinese-based reading), and the *kun* reading as the Japanese reading.

To illustrate the difference between the two readings, let's look at one of our original characters, the one meaning 'water':

水

When this character was brought to Japan, its pronunciation by Chinese speakers was approximated by the Japanese as *sui*. Today, this reading of the character can be found in many Japanese compound words, such as the word 海水, which is read as *kaisui* and means 'seawater.'

In the native Japanese language, there already was a word for water: *mizu*, and this same character came to be used to write that word as well.[4]

Thus, the character 水 has an *on* reading of *sui*, and a *kun* reading of *mizu*.

As a general rule, *on* readings are mostly found in compound words, especially words borrowed from the Chinese language and words for high-level and abstract concepts. *Kun* readings tend to be found in more basic words. The majority of compound words are read using *on* readings. However, some are also read using *kun* readings; one such example using the 'water' character is 水着 (*mizugi*), which combines words for 'water' and 'clothing,' and means 'swimsuit.'

All characters imported from China have an *on* reading, although for a few of those characters the *on* reading is rarely or not at all used in Japan. However, only those characters which were at some point borrowed to write native Japanese words (roughly 60% of the characters in common usage) have a *kun* reading. Of the small number of characters that were created in Japan, most have a *kun* reading, but a few also have been given an *on* reading.

There are cases where a character was used to write more than one different native Japanese word, resulting in some characters having more than one *kun* reading. There are also many characters with more than one *on* reading. We will study multiple *on* readings in detail in Chapter 7, and multiple *kun* readings in detail in Chapter 8.

---

[4] More specifically, the word *mizu* usually describes cold water, and a separate word is used to indicate hot water.

INTRODUCTION TO KANJI 13

As we will see in more detail later, an *on* reading is always a short sound. In Chinese, the readings of the characters are almost all only one syllable in length. Due to the inexact conversion into the Japanese sound system, though, an *on* reading can be either one or two syllables in length. In contrast, a *kun* reading can theoretically contain an unlimited number of syllables, although five is the most in practice.

Being able to tell apart the *on* reading from the *kun* reading for each character is a very useful skill for mastering the reading of Japanese text. For example, the majority of two-character compound words are read using either the *on* readings of both characters or the *kun* readings of both characters, not as a mix of *on* and *kun* readings. Thus, knowing which reading is which comes in handy toward guessing the readings of newly encountered words, which in turn helps with finding them in a dictionary. Tips for distinguishing *on* and *kun* readings are given in both Chapter 7 and Chapter 8.

1.9 Using Kanji to Write Native Japanese Words

The Japanese word *mizugi* (水着), mentioned in the last section, is written with exactly two kanji, both read with *kun* readings: the first (水) read as *mizu* and the second (着) as *gi*.

However, applying the characters to native Japanese words is not always as simple as this, due to the fact that the native Japanese language makes heavy use of grammatical inflection: the changing of the ending parts of words to express variation in meaning. In Japanese, inflection is used much more than in English, and for a variety of purposes, including expressing tense (past tense, future tense, etc.) and making the negative forms of verbs and adjectives. It also was used, in many cases, to create noun, adjective, and verb forms of words which are closely related to each other; in Japanese there are many sets of words with related meanings which share the same beginning part (called a 'stem') but have a different word ending.

The following three words, all of which are native Japanese words, illustrate this last type of inflection:

Word	Meaning	Part of Speech
まる (*maru*)	circle	noun
まるい (*marui*)	circular; round	adjective
まるめる (*marumeru*)	to curl, roll	verb

To make the following explanation simpler, each of these words is shown above written in hiragana (with the equivalent Latin alphabet form in parentheses). Note that all of these words share the same stem: まる (*maru*). In this particular case, the stem used by itself is a noun, and by inflecting—or modifying—the ending (in this case by adding sounds to the stem), other words related in meaning have been formed.

When each of these words is written using kanji, the same single character is used:

Despite its non-circular form, the character's meanings include 'circular' and 'to make round.'

When this character is used to write the three words on the previous page, it is substituted for the part in common (the stem), and the remaining hiragana (if there are any) are left in place:

$$
\begin{array}{ccc}
まる & \rightarrow & 丸 \\
まるい & \rightarrow & 丸い \\
まるめる & \rightarrow & 丸める
\end{array}
$$

The last two words are written with both kanji and hiragana together. The hiragana characters that still remain when words are written using kanji are called **okurigana**. For example, the characters め and る in 丸める are *okurigana*.

Although the noun form in this case is written without any *okurigana*, some nouns, when written with kanji, do contain *okurigana*. Examples of this will be seen later.

In Japanese, both verbs and adjectives have a tense (for example, past tense) associated with them. The verb and adjective forms shown on the previous page are both in plain form, non-past (i.e., present or future) tense. ('Plain form' refers to everyday, casual speech, as opposed to 'polite form' used in more formal situations.)

No matter which tense is used, the part of the word indicating tense is always written with okurigana. For example, to note that something *was* round, you would use the word 丸かった (まるかった, *marukatta*), the past tense form of 丸い. The kanji again takes the place of the stem, while the inflected part, in hiragana, indicates the tense.

We have now seen three different ways to write words using kanji: a single character by itself (for example, 水), multiple characters together in a compound word (for example, 土木), and a single character with trailing okurigana (for example, 丸かった). These are the most common ways that words are written in Japanese. Other word forms, such as multiple kanji together with okurigana, are more complicated; examples will be given in later chapters.

1.10 The Structure of Japanese Sentences

Now that we know what words look like, let's take a look at a sentence:

火曜日にテレビで丸いボールを見た。
(かようび / まる / み)

In English, this sentence translates to:

'On Tuesday, I saw a round ball on television.'

The sentence is written using a mixture of kanji, hiragana, and katakana. You should be able to spot in this sentence two kanji we have already studied. (Don't worry about the unfamiliar kanji at this time.)

And what about those small hiragana characters above all the kanji?

They are put there to assist in reading kanji, and are called *furigana*. **Furigana** are small, usually hiragana, characters that can be placed next to kanji to indicate the reading of the kanji. The use of furigana is optional. They are most commonly added to assist readers less familiar with Japanese, but can even be found in reading material aimed at Japanese adults, placed next to characters and compounds with non-standard or difficult readings. For horizontally-running text, *furigana* are often placed above the kanji they mark, and for traditional vertical Japanese writing, *furigana* are normally placed to the right of the kanji.[5]

One frustration of new learners of Japanese is that Japanese sentences do not have spaces. Because many words consist of two or more characters together, when reading text you do not always process the characters in a sentence one by one, but instead break up what you are reading into recognizable words, so without spaces to help it's necessary to figure out where the word breaks are. Fortunately, the structure of modern Japanese, being written using a combination of kanji, hiragana and katakana, helps the reader to find those word breaks.

When writing Japanese sentences, there is some flexibility as to when to use kanji, hiragana, and katakana, but generally the usage follows these guidelines:

1. Kanji are used to write the stem portion of nouns, verbs, and adjectives. This is only the case, though, when these words are of native Japanese origin, or were borrowed from other East Asian countries and incorporated into Japanese long ago (i.e., words that *feel* native).

2. Katakana are used to write words of foreign origin (other than words borrowed long ago from other East Asian countries).

   Katakana is generally thought of by the Japanese as a kind of 'phonetic alphabet,' used to express sounds. So, in addition to foreign words, onomatopoeic words which represent noises (such as the sound effect words 'bam!' or 'whap!' found in English-language comic books) are also written in katakana. Japanese has a very large number of onomatopoeic words. Because the characters are simple in appearance, katakana is also sometimes used to write words that would normally be written with kanji or hiragana, to place emphasis on them and help make them stand out from the surrounding text.

3. Hiragana are used to write the equivalent of English prepositions and other small grammatical helper words, such as the two uses of the word 'on' in the English translation of the sentence we just learned. Instead of prepositions, which come before the word they refer to, Japanese primarily uses words which come after, most commonly referred to as 'particles.' Hiragana are also used to write okurigana and furigana, as we saw earlier.

Note that hiragana is the first writing system learned by Japanese children, and so books written for the youngest children are written entirely in hiragana, with katakana and then more and more kanji being gradually added as the target age increases.

---

[5] *Furigana* are also sometimes referred to as 'ruby' characters (based on the name of a typeface in which they were once often written) or as 'gloss.' The act of placing *furigana* characters next to kanji is sometimes called 'glossing.'

Keeping these guidelines in mind, the sentence we learned can be broken down into separate words as follows:

- 火曜日 (*kayōbi*), a three-character compound word, is a noun meaning 'Tuesday.' It is written entirely with kanji. We have already seen the first character.

- テレビ (*terebi*) and ボール (*bōru*) are nouns borrowed from English, and so are written in katakana. ボール is a transliteration (conversion of a word directly into the sound system of another language) of the word 'ball,' and テレビ is an abbreviated transliteration of the word 'television.'

- 丸い (*marui*), which we have already seen, is an adjective meaning 'round' and is written with a mix of kanji and hiragana.

- 見た (*mita*) is a verb meaning 'see,' and is written here in plain form past tense, with kanji for the stem part, and the tense of the verb expressed with hiragana.

- Finally, に, で, and を (*ni*, *de*, and *wo*) are grammatical particles, and are written in hiragana.

Written with spaces included to show word breaks, the sentence looks like this:

火曜日　に　テレビ　で　丸い　ボール　を　見た。

For new Japanese learners, sentences with spaces in them are certainly easier to read than those without, but Japanese written with spaces is uncommon. It's necessary even for beginning learners to learn to read sentences that don't have spaces. Keeping the guidelines of this section in mind will assist in doing that.

The Japanese language can also be written using the Latin alphabet. In Japanese, the Latin characters are called ***rōmaji*** (literally: 'Roman letters'). Written in *rōmaji*, the sentence looks like this:

Kayōbi ni terebi de marui bōru wo mita.

Fortunately, Japanese written in *rōmaji* always uses spaces. It would be too difficult to read without them. Also, note the mark (called a macron) that appears over the 'o' in the first and sixth words of the sentence (as well as in the word *rōmaji* itself). This is one way to indicate a long vowel sound using *rōmaji*.[6]

1.11 Character Etymology

Let's take another look at one of our first five characters:

---

[6] The writing of Japanese in *rōmaji* is briefly described in Appendix B.

Again, this character means 'metal' / 'gold' / 'money.' But why does it have that form?

All characters have the form that they do for a reason. This reason is commonly referred to as the 'etymology' of the character. The **etymology** of a character is the explanation of the origin of the form of the character: the reason why it looks the way it does.

The simple truth is that most characters were created so long ago that we cannot know the true etymology with certainty. Looking at the characters in the earliest forms we now have available to us, scholars can often make educated guesses about the origin, but nothing is certain. And there are many characters for which scholars disagree as to the origin.

Even for a common character like the 'metal' / 'gold' / 'money' one, there is not a clear consensus of the origin. One theory is that the character depicts an image of a mine containing gold or some other metal. Specifically, per that theory, the lower part of the character consists of dirt (the 'earth' element: 土) combined with nuggets of metal (the two short diagonal lines), and the top of the character is the roof of the mine. From this depiction, we get a meaning of 'metal' or 'gold.' Another theory is that the character is based on an image of a bell cast in metal, indirectly conveying the idea 'metal.' And there are even other theories. Maybe all of the theories are wrong and the true etymology is no longer known. But it really doesn't matter; as long as when you see that character you can remember what it is and what it represents, that is the most important thing.

Most kanji learning materials describe character etymologies as if they are known facts. But they are not. Keep in mind that they are only theories, no matter how widely accepted they are. Certainly, though, learning an etymology which nicely relates the form and meaning of a character—whether it is known to be true or not—can be a useful method for remembering that character. For that reason this book does include some character etymology information. But only etymologies that have strong support among scholars of the characters are used.

Despite the uncertainty with character etymology, there is a lot that we do know about how characters were created. We will study this in Chapter 2.

1.12 The Characters are Primarily Phonetic

In Chapter 2, when character creation is discussed, we will see one design feature that was used frequently: many characters contain a *phonetic* (that is, sound-indicating) component within them. Except for the earliest created characters, such as our first five characters, built into the vast majority of characters are elements (or groupings of elements) which help indicate the pronunciation of the character. These phonetic components are described further in the next chapter.

As you study more and more characters, if you learn to recognize the phonetic components, you can much more quickly remember how to pronounce each character. This greatly speeds up the learning process. Unfortunately, this phonetic system was designed for the Chinese language, not for Japanese, so one can only take advantage of it when working with *on* readings, as it is not applicable at all to *kun* readings. Learning *kun* readings requires additional memorization.

1.13 The Common Use Characters

Having separate *on* and *kun* readings is unique to Japanese; in the Chinese languages (dialects), many characters have only one reading, and for those with multiple readings, the readings are only slightly different.

In the past, the large number of diverse, multiple readings for many characters in the Japanese language made using kanji particularly difficult. The Japanese writing system was long in need of reform, and starting in 1923, proposals for limiting the number of characters in use were made. The climate for reform changed following World War II. Just after the war, the Japanese Ministry of Education formally established a set of what they considered to be the most important characters needed for daily life, now referred to as the **jōyō kanji**, meaning 'common use kanji.'

The idea was that only a small set of essential characters would be used in any kind of writing that the general public needed to be able to read, and the use of any other characters would be limited. For example, publications aimed at the general public, such as newspapers, would be expected either to avoid using characters not on the *jōyō kanji* list, such as by using hiragana or katakana in their place, or, when using such characters, to assist readers by attaching *furigana* to them to indicate their readings. Furthermore, the list would be used as a basis for the teaching of the characters to Japanese schoolchildren.

This list of *jōyō kanji* continues to be used to this day, but has been revised on several occasions to reflect changes in common character usage in the Japanese language. Although some characters have been dropped from the list, with each of these revisions the total number of characters included has continually increased. After the changes made in the year 2010, there are 2136 characters on the list.

All of the *jōyō kanji* are taught to Japanese schoolchildren during the period of compulsory education: from elementary school through junior high school. The first 1006 of these characters are taught during the years of elementary school, and are referred to as the **kyōiku kanji** (educational kanji). Thus, the *kyōiku kanji* are a subset of the *jōyō kanji*.

The *jōyō kanji* list is certainly not perfect. Some characters not on the list are more commonly encountered than some on the list. Also, there are some characters not on the list which an educated Japanese adult should certainly be expected to recognize and be able to read. Furthermore, many common place names and family names use characters not on the list. But this list generally reflects the most common characters used in Japanese, and so is a good place to start for those learning the characters.

1.14 Chapter Summary

Chinese characters, called **kanji** in Japan, were invented in China more than 3200 years ago, and are now used primarily to write only the Chinese and Japanese languages. There are more than 90,000 characters in existence, although most of those are never encountered in daily life. Japanese writing is made up of kanji together with two syllabaries: **hiragana** and **katakana**.

Each individual kanji has a **form**, and one or more **readings** (pronunciations) and **meanings** associated with it. For characters with more than one reading or meaning, the correct one which applies in any given instance depends on the context in which the character is being used. The reader needs to determine this context.

Every character is written as a series of **strokes**. For each character, a proper **stroke count** and **stroke order** has been established. Most characters are composed of separate piece parts, called **elements**.

In writing words, kanji can be used alone, combined with additional kanji into a **compound** word, or used together with trailing hiragana characters, called **okurigana**. The meaning of a compound word is sometimes more complex than just the combined meanings of the kanji in the word; when learning to read, Japanese compound words must be learned in addition to individual characters. Kanji have two major different ways of being pronounced: the **on reading** and the **kun reading**. The *on* reading is an approximation of the way the character was pronounced in China. The *kun* reading is the reading of the character when it is used to write a word of native Japanese origin.

In Japanese writing, small hiragana characters called **furigana** can be placed next to kanji to indicate the character reading.

Japanese sentences are normally written without spaces. Japanese can also be written using the Latin alphabet, called **rōmaji**. When written in *rōmaji*, spaces are inserted between words.

The characters were created so long ago that we cannot know the **etymology**, or origin of character forms, with certainty. There are some commonly accepted theories, though. The characters are generally phonetic in nature, with many characters containing an element (or group of elements) which indicates the *on* reading of the character. These elements do not indicate the character *kun* readings, however.

The Japanese government has established a list of frequently used characters, called the **jōyō kanji**. Kanji from this list are taught to Japanese schoolchildren. The first 1006 of these characters, called the **kyōiku kanji**, are taught during elementary school. The set of characters actually used in Japan exceeds that of the *jōyō kanji* list.

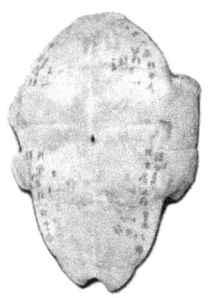

Chapter 2

Character Design and History

The origin of the Latin alphabet that the English language uses, and the major changes it went through before reaching its modern state, is an interesting subject to learn. But, of course, it is not necessary to know any of that history to use the alphabet today.

The Chinese characters also have an interesting history and also have undergone extensive changes throughout their history. Unlike with the Latin alphabet, though, understanding some aspects of the origin and development of the Chinese characters helps you to understand why the characters appear the way they do today, and can actually be very helpful for learning and remembering the characters.

In this chapter we will look at the origin and development of the Chinese characters, and learn about the major different methods by which the characters were created.

2.1 The Legendary Origin

With anything created before recorded history, myths often arise to explain the origin. In China, the creation of the Chinese writing characters has sometimes been attributed to a single man, named Cangjie. It is said that Cangjie got the idea of creating characters by observing that the tracks left by birds and other creatures have distinctive markings by which the animal leaving them can be identified. Cangjie then used that principle to create distinctive characters to represent objects such as these animals, by which they could uniquely be identified. Of this invention, in the ancient Chinese text *Huai-nan-zi*, it is written: 昔者倉頡作書、而天雨粟、鬼夜哭, which can be translated as:

> When our ancestor Cangjie invented writing,
>
> grain rained down from the heavens
>
> and spirits cried out in the night.

The truth, of course, is likely much more mundane than this.

2.2 The Spoken Language Came First

Before taking a close look at the creation of the characters, one point needs to be emphasized: the creation of a character did not usually correspond to the creation of a word. Instead, words already existed in the spoken form and the characters were created to be able to represent in writing those already-existing spoken words. The fact that the characters were designed based on spoken sounds figures heavily into their structure, as we will see.

2.3 The First Stage: Pictographs

Just as with other early writing systems around the world, some of the earliest Chinese characters were **pictographs**: characters that stand for specific objects and have forms which resemble those objects. In other words, they are characters that look like the thing they represent. Early pictographs were sometimes crude and simple, but sometimes showed extensive detail. These characters represented all kinds of things found in the daily lives of the early Chinese who created them: animals, people, things found in nature, food containers, tools, clothing, ceremonial objects, musical instruments, jewelry, and even weapons.

Early forms of the characters for 'tree,' 'fruit,' 'person,' 'eye,' and 'rain,' respectively, looked like this:

The character on the left depicts a tree, with high, raised branches and roots at the bottom. It's similar to the modern form, which we already studied: 木. The second character depicts ripened fruit on a tree. Note that the bottom part is the same 'tree,' but is somewhat compressed to fit into the bottom half of the character. The third character appears to depict a person standing sideways and slightly stooped over with arms outstretched. It is unknown why the person is depicted in this position, but the character meaning is simply 'person.' The fourth character shows a human eye. Finally, the fifth character shows drops of rain falling. The horizontal line may represent part of a raincloud, or simply the sky.

As each of these characters directly stands for the object depicted, they are all pictographs. Almost all pictographs consist of only a single element. The 'fruit' character, however, is an exception. Technically, it contains two elements: a tree and the fruit itself. If this were a pictographic character in the strictest sense, the meaning would be 'fruit tree.' But the inclusion of the tree just helps to identify what is depicted, and the meaning of the character is simply 'fruit.'

In the early forms of these characters shown on the previous page, it is possible to recognize the objects depicted. As we will see in more detail later, the forms of most of the characters gradually changed over time, sometimes with only small changes, but sometimes with significant changes. With later forms, it is often no longer possible to recognize pictographic objects.

Here are the modern forms of these five characters:

You can see that the first three characters have undergone mostly minor changes (the third has been flipped left-to-right and had the lower part removed), while the other two, especially 'rain,' have more noticeable changes. Interestingly, the 'eye' character has been rotated nearly 90 degrees. In their modern forms, none of the five objects depicted are as recognizable as they were in their earlier forms.

Many of the earliest-created characters were pictographs like these. It is a relatively simple matter to design pictographic characters to represent concrete, simple objects such as 'mountain' or 'fish' or 'spear.' But in order to develop a comprehensive writing system, capable of representing anything in the spoken language using characters, there were two major challenges. One was to find a way to represent more abstract concepts and words such as 'underneath' or 'dream' or even 'when.' The other was to find a way to represent many similar but slightly different objects, such as 'pine tree' and 'maple tree.' It was not feasible to create characters using only pictographs. Other methods were needed.

2.4 The Next Stage: Ideographs

For representing more abstract concepts, another type of character: an ideograph, was sometimes created. **Ideographs** are characters which use concrete objects not in the literal sense, but to suggest an idea or notion, and thereby express the meaning of the character in an indirect way. An ideograph can involve just a single object (i.e., a single element), but it is much more common for it to include multiple objects, with all the objects working together to convey the meaning of the character. Below are early forms of ideographic characters representing the meanings 'see' and 'rest':

The first character consists of two basic elements: an eye and a person, with the eye placed on top of the person. The eye is proportionally much larger than the person, and thereby emphasizes the activity that the person is engaged in: seeing. If this character were a pictograph, it would represent something like 'person with a giant eye': the literal object it depicts. But because it represents something other than what it literally depicts, it functions as an ideograph.

The second character also is made up of two basic elements: a person and a tree. Again, if it were pictographic, the character meaning would be something like 'a person and a tree,' or maybe 'standing next to a tree.' Instead, it is an ideograph, and represents 'rest' or a 'break.' With this character, it is easy to see how ideographs indirectly express their meaning: a person leaning against a tree is resting.

Here are these characters in their modern forms:

見　　　休

Note that in the modern forms, the 'eye' and 'tree' elements appear the same as they do as standalone characters (目 and 木), but the two 'person' elements do not. In these characters, the 'person' elements have been transformed, each in a different way. In the character on the left, the 'person' element has changed into two disconnected strokes, and has only a very slight resemblance to the modern form of the standalone 'person' character (人). In the character on the right, the 'person' element more closely resembles the standalone 'person' character, but the second stroke, instead of moving down and to the right, drops straight down, and is longer than the first stroke.

Among the modern character forms, elements have sometimes undergone this kind of transformation when they are compressed into limited spaces within a character. These altered forms of elements are sometimes given their own special names. The 'person' element in the character on the left above is called *hitoashi* in Japanese, referring to both the meaning of the element itself (*hito* = 'person') and the location of the element at the bottom of the character (*ashi* = 'foot'). Because *ashi* also means 'legs,' it may be helpful to think of this element as a pair of human legs, which it does loosely resemble with some imagination. (But keep in mind that this element represents an entire person, not just the legs.)

The 'person' element in the character on the right is called *ninben*, again referring to the meaning of the element (*nin*, another way to say 'person') and the location of the element on the left-hand side of the character (*hen*, altered here to *ben*). We will see more examples of this kind of element form change in Chapter 6 (in the 'Element Variations' section), and learn the names of the various regions of characters, such as *ashi* and *hen*, in Chapter 4 (in the 'Character Regions' section).

Single Object Ideographs

Although it is uncommon, an ideographic character can also consist of just a single object. This is true of the following two characters, both shown in early forms:

Like the 'person' character, the character on the left also depicts a human figure, but this one is facing forward with arms and legs spread out. The modern meaning of this character is 'large.' It is believed that the character depicts an adult man; the earliest meaning of the character might have been 'adult man.' There are several theories as to how the character came to mean 'large,' including simply from the notion that an adult man is large (larger than women and children), or that the spreading of the arms and legs suggests the idea 'large.' With either of these interpretations, the character functions as an ideograph, because its meaning does not correspond directly to the object depicted, but is instead indirectly suggested. If this character were a pictograph, its meaning would be something such as 'adult man' or 'person' or 'person with spread arms and legs': the literal object it depicts.

The character on the right depicts a human figure much like the one on the left. In this image, though, the figure's legs are crossed, one over the other, which suggests the character meaning: 'mix' / 'exchange.' It is an ideograph because the meaning is indirectly implied by the depiction. If the character were purely pictographic, the meaning would be something like 'person with legs crossed' or 'crossing the legs.'

Here are the modern forms of these characters:

In its modern form, the character on the left looks a lot like the modern form of the 'person' character we saw earlier (人), but with an extra horizontal line through the middle. To remember the modern meaning ('large'), perhaps it's helpful to think of that horizontal stroke as the arms of a man being stretched out wide to indicate the size of something large. With the character on the right, you can see how the curved lines of the earlier form have been replaced with mostly straight lines in the modern form, and each leg has been broken into two disconnected segments.

These last two characters may seem like pictographs because the original forms are simple picture images. They are classified here as ideographs only because of the way they function: suggesting a meaning other than what is literally depicted. But don't worry about memorizing things such as whether a character is classified as a pictograph or ideograph. It is only important to understand that both of these principles were used in the construction of characters.

Repeated Elements

Ideographic characters can also contain more than one of the same element. Here are two more ideographic characters, shown in their modern forms:

Each of these characters contains only the 'tree' element, but that element appears multiple times. In general, the repeated use of an element suggests a large number of the object represented. The character on the left means 'grove,' a place with many trees, and the character on the right means 'forest,' a place with an even larger number of trees. Note how the lower right stroke of a tree element gets shortened when another element appears to the right of it.

Indicative Characters

Another kind of ideographic character is what is sometimes referred to as an 'indicative' character. An **indicative character** is one in which, in addition to the use of recognizable pictographic objects, simple line segments are used to help indicate the character meaning.

Here are two examples of indicative characters (the first is shown in the modern form, and the second in an early form):

The character on the left above is of the type where a single additional stroke is added directly onto or near one part of an element to indicate or emphasize the part of an object that the character represents. This character consists of our familiar tree, but with an extra line added through the bottom stroke. That extra line acts as an indicator, emphasizing that the part of the tree marked (that is, the main root) is what is being referred to. The meaning of this character is 'origin' or 'source,' a meaning suggested by indicating the part of the tree from which the tree originates. (In Japanese, this character also represents additional meanings, including 'book,' but the original character meaning is 'origin' / 'source.')

The early form of the character on the right above consists of a short line above a longer line. In this case, the shorter line is the indicator, with the longer line perhaps representing the ground or the horizon. The character means 'above,' as the short indicator line is located above the main lower line.

This simple indicative relationship is harder to see in the modern form of this character, which now includes an additional vertical line, and has the top short line offset slightly to the right:[1]

Indicative characters are sometimes classified as separate from ideographs, but in this book are grouped together with ideographs for simplicity.

Revisiting the 'Metal' / 'Gold' / 'Money' Character

In Section 1.11 of the last chapter, we studied the etymology of the 'metal' / 'gold' / 'money' character: 金. Note that if either of the two theories presented in that section were true, the character would be ideographic. That is, whether the character depicts a mine with metal deposits, or a cast metal bell, neither of those depictions literally show the character meanings of 'gold' or 'metal.' Rather, they both suggest the character meaning indirectly. (The literal meanings would be 'mine with metal deposits' and 'bell,' respectively.)

Many characters have been created using both pictographic and ideographic methods. The majority of characters in existence are of neither of these types, though. Before looking at the most common type of character, it is helpful to first take a closer look at ways that character meanings have been extended and have changed over time.

---

[1] The early form of this character is very similar to the modern character meaning 'two': 二. The form of the 'above' character may have been changed to avoid confusion with the 'two' character.

2.5 Meaning Extension and Change

Today, it is very common for characters to have **extended meanings**: additional meanings that have been acquired in addition to the original meaning. We have already seen several examples of this, such as how the 'tree' character (木) also means 'wood,' and how the 'metal' / 'gold' character (金) also means 'money.' Yet another example is the character we have already seen which means 'fruit' (果); this character also means 'result.' As you study kanji, you will see that a large number of the characters have multiple, sometimes very diverse meanings.

Why did this happen?

There were numerous causes. The simplest is that the words represented by characters naturally took on new meanings over time. This is common in all languages. Clearly, the word 'tree' is closely related to the word 'wood,' as wood is the main substance of trees, so it is not surprising that the same word was used to represent both meanings. Even in traditional Japanese (the Japanese spoken language which existed prior to the adoption of Chinese characters), the word for 'tree' also means 'wood.'

There are countless examples in English, too, of words that gradually acquired additional meanings. Take the word 'wood' as an example. It not only refers to the hard substance of trees, but can also be used to refer to a group of trees (often in the plural form 'woods'), and even a type of golf club (a meaning which derived from the fact that the club head was originally made of wood). The relationship between 'fruit' and 'result' exists in English, too, in expressions such as 'the fruits of one's labor.'

As Chinese words acquired new meanings, the characters used to write them also acquired those additional meanings. In this way, characters adopted additional meanings closely related to the original.

Character Borrowing

Some characters gained meanings by being borrowed. As the character set was being developed in China, in addition to the formation of new characters to represent words, such as by pictographic and ideographic methods, another practice was also regularly taking place: the borrowing of characters already in use to represent additional spoken words. In some cases, instead of making a new character to represent a given word, a character already being used to represent some other word was borrowed to do that. This resulted in a single character acquiring the meanings of multiple, different words.

In some cases, the borrowing was done when there was a meaning link between the word already represented by the character and the additional word in need of a character.

Take, as an example, the character:

Originally, this character meant 'nose,' and was a pictographic representation of a person's nose. (This is difficult to see in the modern form, but can be seen more clearly in earlier forms.) Later, this character acquired the additional meaning 'self.' The spoken words were clearly different, though: 'nose' with the reading *bi*, and 'self' with the reading *ji*.[2] But there was a meaning connection: in China (and Japan) people point to their nose to refer to themselves. And that may have been the basis for this character acquiring the meaning 'self.'

Eventually, a new, different character was created to represent 'nose,'[3] and then 'self' became the principal meaning of the character shown on the previous page. But remnants of the old meaning 'nose' can still be seen in a few characters which use 自 as an element within them. For example, the characters

息 and 臭

mean 'breath' and 'smell' (as in odor), respectively.

Phonetic Borrowing

With the previously explained methods of meaning extension, there is a relatively clear connection between the different meanings represented by a character. But what about characters that have two or more very different meanings with no clear relationship between them?

In Chapter 1, we saw one explanation for this. Our first five characters were integral to Chinese philosophy, and from that role were borrowed for other uses, such as the naming of the five 'naked-eye planets.' Then, from that usage, they were later borrowed again to represent weekdays. This kind of re-purposing has taken place with a number of characters.

But there is another major process by which characters acquired multiple, very diverse meanings, and its use dates back to an early stage of character development: the borrowing of characters for their sound.

In old Chinese, most basic words consisted of a single syllable. That, combined with the limited amount of different possible sound combinations in the language, meant that there were many homophones (words with different meaning that sound identical), and near-homophones (words with different meaning that sound nearly identical). In many cases, an existing character was borrowed to write an additional word primarily or exclusively because of the similarity between the sounds of the two words (that is, the word already represented by the character and the word in need of a character). This practice of borrowing a character for its sound is called **phonetic borrowing**.

Many characters have been phonetically borrowed to represent additional, unrelated words. Notably, many pronouns (including, in English, words such as 'he,' 'everyone,' 'who,' 'this,' and 'which'), which are difficult to represent using pictographs or ideographs, were assigned characters via phonetic borrowing. But plenty of other words were assigned characters in this way, too.

Let's look at a specific example: the borrowing of a character to write the word 'that.' The character that was borrowed was originally a pictograph, and depicted what is called a winnowing basket, which was a simple agricultural tool that was held in the hands and shaken in order to separate grain from chaff.

---

[2] These are Japanese *on* readings. The Chinese readings are similar.
[3] We will see the modern character for 'nose' in Section 2.7.

Over time, the character progressed through several forms:

originally depicting only the basket itself (the leftmost character), and then with an added pair of hands to help identify the object (middle),[4] and finally arriving at the modern form (on the right), where the hand elements have been modified and merged into the basket element.

But not only did the character form go through changes, the meaning did as well. The 'winnowing basket' character was borrowed to write a word meaning 'that,' a word which would be hard to design a character for using a pictograph or ideograph. It was chosen because the spoken word for 'that' was identical to (or at least quite similar to) the sound of the word already represented by the 其 character: 'winnowing basket.'[5] In other words, because the spoken word for 'that' sounded similar to the spoken word for 'winnowing basket,' the 其 character was phonetically borrowed to also represent the word 'that.'

In modern times, this character no longer means 'winnowing basket'; now it only means 'that.' The original meaning of 'winnowing basket' is now represented by a different character, which we will see in the next section. Note that in Japanese, 其 is not one of the *jōyō kanji* (common use characters), but it is still encountered somewhat frequently, such as in the writing of the native Japanese words その (*sono*) and それ (*sore*), where it replaces the first hiragana character (i.e., 其の and 其れ). These words, however, are more frequently written entirely in hiragana. Although this character itself is not a *jōyō kanji*, it is nonetheless useful to know, as it appears as an element in a number of other characters which are.

Character Replacement

Characters were also sometimes phonetically borrowed to replace other characters. This happened with a character now used to write the number four. Originally, 'four' was written as a set of four horizontal strokes, such as on the left below. The characters for one, two, and three are still written in this fashion (一, 二, 三). Later, perhaps because it could be easily confused with these other characters in vertical writing, 'four' came to be written with a borrowed character which was pronounced the same way (shown on the right below in its modern form).

$$三 \rightarrow 四$$

The original meaning of the character on the right is not known with certainty. It may have represented an open mouth exhaling breath or possibly a runny nose. Regardless, the character now only means 'four.' Eventually, the original character with the four horizontal strokes was phased out of usage, and now only the character on the right is used to write 'four.' The modern way of writing 'four,' therefore, is based entirely on phonetic borrowing.

The practice of phonetic borrowing has even continued in modern times. For example, in Japan, a character meaning 'talent' (才) is sometimes informally written in place of a character

---

[4] This is similar to how a 'tree' element was included to help identify the 'fruit' character, as explained in Section 2.3.
[5] We can't know for certain if the sounds were identical, or merely similar, at the time of borrowing due to sound changes that have taken place in Chinese since that time.

meaning 'years of age' (歳) because it has the same reading, but only three strokes, as opposed to the thirteen strokes of the proper character. Thus, the simpler character has, in effect, acquired the meaning of the more complex one. Also, from the once-common practice of writing words from foreign languages using the characters borrowed phonetically, some characters have acquired meanings of foreign words and concepts. For example, characters originally meaning 'rice,' 'to stand,' and 'roof tile' (米, 立, and 瓦) now also stand for the metric system words 'meter,' 'liter,' and 'gram,' respectively, simply because of their sounds. This way of using the characters, called *ateji*, is explained in Chapter 5.

Meaning Shift

As we have just seen, the characters 自, 其, and 四 were each borrowed to represent other words, but at some point the newer meaning became the main meaning, and the original meaning of the character was either phased out of usage or transferred to a different character. This process is called **meaning shift**: the change in meaning of a character, such that an extended meaning becomes the new principal meaning, and the original meaning is no longer represented by the character. Simply put, the main meaning of the character is shifted from one thing to another.

One more example of a character that underwent meaning shift is:

The original meaning was 'cloud.' The character was probably pictographic in origin, depicting an image of a cloud, but this is especially difficult to see in the modern form, as what was once a single curvy line in the lower portion has been converted to straightened strokes in the modern form, similar in appearance to the katakana *mu* (ム) character.

Although not closely related to the meaning 'cloud,' the character long ago was borrowed to represent a word with the meaning 'say,' probably via phonetic borrowing. Today, the newer, extended meaning ('say') is the only meaning of this character encountered in Japanese, since, from an early time, the 'cloud' meaning came to be written with an alternate, modified form of this character, which we will see in the next section.[6]

As a result of this meaning shift, the modern meaning of this character (and of 自, 其, and 四, as well) is not directly related to the form of the character. The same thing is true of quite a few other characters, as well. This leads to an important point to keep in mind about the characters: although the forms of many characters are directly tied to their meanings, this is not always the case; there is not always a clear connection between a character's form and its meaning.

In Japanese, the 云 character is infrequently encountered. It is only used in certain specific contexts (mostly in older writing). Most instances of the verb 'say' are written with a different character. Like the 其 character, it is not among the *jōyō kanji* (common use characters), but it is nonetheless useful to know as it appears as an element within a number of characters which are.

---

[6] Interestingly, as a result of character simplifications in mainland China, this character has reverted back to the 'cloud' meaning, making this an example of a character which now has different meanings in simplified Chinese and Japanese.

Retained Multiple Meanings

While some characters have undergone meaning shift, others have retained multiple meanings. One such example is the character:

The principal, and original, meaning of this character is 'foot' / 'leg.' From the modern form above, it is nearly impossible to recognize that part of the human body, but from an earlier form:

the character can be seen to be a pictograph, depicting a person's foot (facing left at the bottom) together with either a full leg, or the lower leg from the knee downward. In the modern form, the foot portion has been rotated to face upward with the strokes significantly altered, while the leg portion has been simplified into a box shape.

In addition to the original meaning, this character has also taken on the meanings 'to be sufficient' and 'to add.' In words that use this character, it can have any of those meanings, but 'foot' is the most common.

Another character that has multiple, different meanings is:

This character combines two elements we have already seen: 'tree' / 'wood' on the left, and 'mix' / 'exchange' on the right. The original meaning of this character was, over time, phased out of usage, and is no longer known with certainty. The character may have represented wooden shackles used to bind the legs in a crossed position, depicted by combining an element representing wood with an element representing the crossing of legs. Alternately, it may have originally represented a kind of fencing made by the interlocking of wooden slats, again combining the meanings of the character elements.

Now, the principal meaning of this character is 'school': a place where students are taught. This character also has a secondary meaning: 'proofread': to review and make corrections, and yet another meaning: 'military officer.'

When learning a character such as 校, it is not always necessary to learn all of its possible meanings at once, especially the lesser-used ones. Instead, it is sometimes best to just learn the principal one or two meanings, until you have achieved a comfortable level of familiarity. Rarer meanings can be learned later.

In the case of this character, it is not clear how the modern meanings were acquired. The 'school' meaning may have actually derived from sound similarities with another character pertaining to education (a kind of phonetic borrowing). When the true derivation of a character meaning is unknown or excessively complicated, if you find it helpful it's certainly acceptable to make up a new one, such as: a school building is made of wood (represented by the 'tree' element), and inside ideas are exchanged (represented by the 'exchange' element).

Just as we cannot know the original etymologies of character forms with certainty (as explained in Chapter 1, Section 1.11), we also often cannot know precisely how a character came to represent each of its extended meanings. It is often a matter of speculation. But that is not so important. The most important thing is to be able to know the modern meanings when you see a character. But being familiar with the various processes that characters underwent, such as taking on extended meanings, phonetic borrowing, and meaning shift, helps us to understand that characters may no longer represent their original meaning, that characters with multiple meanings are commonplace, and that the various meanings of a character can be quite different from each other.

2.6 The Determinative

In the previous section we saw how some characters came to have two (or sometimes more) seemingly unrelated meanings connected to them. This, of course, could be a source of confusion. As the character set evolved over time, this potential for confusion was in some cases cleared up by splitting the meanings apart and representing each with a different character. This was usually accomplished by restricting the character already in use to represent only one or two of the meanings, and creating a new, different character to represent the others.

To accomplish this, a new method of character creation was devised: taking an existing character and adding to it one additional, basic element whose purpose was to identify the general category of meaning of the word represented by that new character. Let's look at a specific example to see how this was done.

In the previous section, we saw that the character 云 originally meant 'cloud,' but then took on an extended meaning of 'say.' Later, to distinguish between these two meanings, a new character was created to represent 'cloud.' That new character was formed by starting with the original character (云) and adding to it the 'rain' element (雨):

Within this character, the rain element does not specifically signify rain. Rather, it is used in a more general sense, signifying any kind of weather condition or phenomenon. In other words, the 'rain' element is used in this character to tell us: 'this character has to do with weather'—as is true of clouds.

An element used in this fashion is referred to as a 'determinative' (because it helps you to *determine* the character meaning). A **determinative** is an element (or, rarely, a group of elements) used within a character for the purpose of indicating the general category of the character meaning.

Rather than create new elements to use as determinatives, existing elements were used for this role, such as the 'rain' element above. A number of other basic elements were also used as determinatives to indicate a wide variety of other general categories as well, including: 'parts of the head or face,' 'emotions / feelings,' 'things associated with illness,' and 'things made of wood.' A list of the most commonly used determinatives is provided in Part 2 of the book.

To better understand this concept, it's helpful to look at some more characters which use the 'rain' element as a determinative:

Character	Meaning	Character	Meaning
雪	snow	露	dew
霧	mist	雷	thunder
霜	frost	電	(flash of) lightning †

† Today, the principal meaning of this character is 'electricity.'

As you can see, although these characters all contain the 'rain' element, none of them refer specifically to rain itself. Rather, they all refer to various types of weather phenomena, whether found on the ground or in the sky. In these characters, the 'rain' element serves a special role: it signifies that the characters which contain it have meanings which are 'having to do with weather.'

In the previous section, we examined a character which originally meant 'winnowing basket.' The meaning 'winnowing basket' is now represented with a character which was created by adding a determinative meaning 'object made of bamboo' (竹)⁷ to the top of the original character (其), reflecting the fact that a winnowing basket is made of bamboo. The character now appears this way:

The way to think of a determinative is as a single part (usually just one element) of a character that stands apart from the remainder of the character and identifies the general category of meaning that the character as a whole can be grouped into. This is an important concept to understand, as we will see that the vast majority of characters, primarily ones created later, contain a determinative component. But don't worry if this concept is not clear yet. After seeing in the next few sections more examples of how determinatives are typically used, things will become clearer.

Broad Meaning

As we just saw with the 'rain' element, when an element is used as a determinative it generally covers a broader range of meaning than when it is used as a simple meaning-indicating element or a standalone character. Let's look at two more characters that further demonstrate this concept:

The character on the left, when used by itself, means 'mountain.' (This character is pictographic, and what are now vertical lines were closer in resemblance to mountain peaks in an early form.) But when used as a determinative, the 'mountain' element can indicate a larger range of meanings, including things that are associated with a mountain, such as 'peak' or 'ridge,' but also any kind of large land formation, such as 'hill' and 'cliff,' and even 'island.'

---

⁷ The 'bamboo' character was originally created as a pictograph, depicting an image of a bamboo plant. When placed as an element at the top of a character, the form is slightly simplified.

This element is used as a determinative in characters representing each of the previous words, as well as in characters meaning 'crag,' 'cape,' 'valley,' 'gorge,' and 'coast.'

The character on the right on the previous page, when used by itself, means 'meat' or 'flesh.' It is probably pictographic, depicting a cross-section of meat, with the lines in the middle likely depicting ribs or perhaps the marbled fat of the meat. When used as a determinative, though, it indicates the category 'parts of the body.' This element is used as a determinative in characters representing all kinds of body parts, including 'leg,' 'elbow,' 'back,' and 'chest.' Note that this element is not used as a determinative to denote parts of the head and face; that role is handled by a different component.

The following table demonstrates the differences in meaning between a character when used by itself and the same character when used as a determinative. For each character in the table, examples of characters which use it as a determinative are also given. With these characters, one advantage of using determinatives can be seen: if you have already studied a character but can't recall its exact meaning, the determinative can help to narrow down the category of meaning, which can make recalling the specific character meaning easier.

Character	Meaning(s) when used as a standalone character	Meaning(s) when used as a determinative
雨	rain	weather-related conditions, objects, or phenomena (examples: snow 雪, thunder 雷)
山	mountain	things associated with a mountain; large land formations (examples: crag 岩, coast 岸)
肉	meat; flesh	body parts (examples: knee 膝, arm 腕) †
木	tree; wood	objects made of wood; types of trees; parts of a tree (examples: maple tree 楓, branch 枝)
水	water	bodies of water; types of liquids; things associated with liquids (examples: sea 海, oil 油) †
火	fire	things pertaining to burning, or the giving off of heat or light (examples: smoke 煙, lamp / light 灯)

† The forms of the determinative elements within these example characters are different from the standalone-character forms on the left. The reason for this is explained later (in Sections 2.11 and 6.6).

In characters which contain them, the determinative is the principal meaning-indicating component of the character. But you can't assume that because a character contains a particular element used as a determinative (or any element used in any way, for that matter) that the meaning of that character has anything to do with the meanings indicated by the determinative. This is because the meanings of quite a few characters have changed over time, as discussed in the previous section.

For example, there are some characters which use the 'tree' element as a determinative but have nothing to do with trees or wood. We already saw this with the 校 character. Its modern meanings 'school,' 'proofread,' and 'military officer' all have little or nothing to do with trees or wood. But despite such meaning changes, many characters containing a determinative still have a meaning that falls within the category identified by that determinative, so learning to recognize determinatives is still worthwhile and will still help to speed up character learning.

Similarly, note that it is not the case that all the characters for words in a given category contain the determinative that represents that category. For example, there are characters for parts of the body that do not include the 'meat' / 'flesh' character (肉) as an element. In fact, we already saw one: the character for 'foot' (足). One reason such characters might not contain a given determinative is that they were created before the practice of using determinatives had become common.

Determinative Forms

Most determinatives, including all six in the previous table, consist of only a single, basic element. A few, though, come from characters that are (or were originally) made up of more than one element. For example, the commonly-used determinative:

which denotes the general category 'movement' (especially of a person on foot), was derived from a character which contained two elements: one meaning 'road' and one meaning 'foot.' These elements can no longer be individually recognized in the above modern form of the determinative, though; they have been merged together.

Although most determinatives also exist as standalone characters, not all do. For example, the 'movement' determinative shown above does not appear by itself as a full character. Rather, it is used only in combination with other elements.

Because determinatives were often added to already existing characters, they are frequently found located along an outside edge (or edges) of characters, such as on the left-hand side, or at the top, or the left and bottom sides together, which is where the above 'movement' determinative is commonly located. But they can also be found anywhere within a character, including the interior. To help describe the locations of determinatives within characters, the major different regions of a character have been assigned names, such as the regions *ashi* and *hen* that we already saw in Section 2.4. The full set of region names are listed and described in Chapter 4.

This book places a great emphasis on identifying determinatives within characters that have one. There is another component within characters, called the 'radical,' which will be explained in Chapter 4. The radical is different from the determinative (although for many characters they both refer to the same part), and this book makes a clear distinction between these two different concepts. (In Chapter 4, the differences are explained in detail.) Most other kanji learning materials, though, confuse the two concepts, using only the term 'radical' to describe both. As a result, be aware that the term 'determinative' may not be encountered in other learning materials.

2.7 The Phonetic

As the number of different characters in existence grew, making them more difficult to remember and easier to confuse with each other, methods were devised to make characters easier to recognize. One such method was shown in the previous section: adding a component which acts as a determinative, identifying the general category of meaning of the character. Another method was devised, which, rather than helping to indicate the character meaning, helped to indicate the sound of the character, i.e., its reading. Specifically, a component was added to indicate, or at least hint at, the spoken sound of the character. Having a sound hint included within a character could help a reader to quickly identify the character reading, and from that identify the character, recognizing the word it stood for.

This goal was accomplished by taking another character with the same or similar reading and inserting it, as a single component, into the target character. (This is similar to phonetic borrowing, discussed in Section 2.5.) Initially, sound-indicating components were added to some existing characters. Later, new characters were created from the start including sound-indicating components.

Let's look at a specific example of how this was done. In the last section, we saw how two different meanings represented by the same character could be differentiated by making a new character to represent one of the meanings. This is precisely what was done with the 自 character, first mentioned in Section 2.5. To distinguish this character's separate meanings, a new character was created, not by the addition of a determinative, but by the addition of a sound-indicating component.

The 自 character originally meant 'nose' (read as *bi*), and later the character also acquired the meaning 'self' (read as *ji*). At some point, these two meanings were differentiated by the creation of a new character to represent the original meaning of 'nose.' The new character was created by taking another, different character which had the same reading as the word for 'nose' (*bi*), and adding it to the 自 character.

The character built in that fashion is now the modern way of writing 'nose,' and looks like this:

You can see that the original 'nose' character is the topmost part of this new character. The other part of this character (畀) is read as *bi* when appearing as a standalone character, and is used here only as a sound-indicating component.[8] The meaning of that lower part is not important in this case (it means 'to confer on' or 'to give to'). Here, it only serves a sound-indicating role: providing a hint as to the reading of the full character, which is also *bi*.

Within a character, a component whose primary role is to indicate the reading of the character is referred to as a **phonetic component**, or simply as a **phonetic**.[9] The term 'phonetic element' is also sometimes used to refer to this kind of component. It is best to

---

[8] As a standalone character, the character form is slightly different: 畀. Furthermore, the character is read as *bi* in China, but has a slightly different reading in Japan. We will learn the reason for this kind of difference later in this section.

[9] Another term used for this part of a character is 'phonophoric.'

avoid this term, though, because it can be a little misleading: many phonetics are—or at least were originally—actually made up of more than one basic element. For that reason, the term 'phonetic component' is used here instead, and in this book the term 'component' will be defined differently from 'element.' Specifically, a **component**, as used in this book, is any portion of a character, whether it be a single element, a group of elements taken together, or even just part of a single element. A phonetic component, thus, could be just a single element, but also could consist of a set of elements together as a group.

Most phonetics began as standalone characters, but some no longer exist that way, having long ago been phased out of usage, and are now only seen as components of other characters. Because they were originally full characters, these phonetics have meaning associated with them, but as we will see it is often the case that a phonetic is used primarily for its sound—its meaning does not always factor into the meaning of the character that uses it. And when the meaning does play a role, it is often only a secondary, supplemental role.

Phonetics are useful when learning characters. If you can recognize a phonetic component within a character, and you already know the reading of that phonetic component, you can more quickly learn and remember the reading of the whole character. And, as you will see, many characters contain phonetic components, and a number of these phonetic components appear repeatedly, within many different characters, so learning to recognize them can help speed up the learning of the *on* readings of many characters. (As mentioned in Chapter 1, in Japanese the phonetics are only tied to character *on* readings; *kun* readings must be learned separately.) A list of the most commonly used phonetic components is provided in Part 2 of the book.

Dividing a Character

The particular phonetic in the 'nose' character is not a commonly used component; it does not appear within many different characters. In fact, among the *jōyō kanji*, this phonetic appears only once: in the 'nose' character. But it still serves a very useful role: simply knowing that it is the phonetic of the character helps you to be able to mentally divide the character into two parts: the top part, which by itself now has the meaning 'self,' and the remainder of the character, which is the phonetic.

If you treat a character such as 'nose' (鼻)—consisting of a total of fourteen strokes—as one single object, it can be rather complicated to learn and remember it. But if you can break it up into parts, it is easier to learn. And in this case mentally breaking up the character into those particular two parts (the original character at the top, and the phonetic below it) has the added benefit of making memorization of the character meaning easier, due to the meaning correlation between the top part and the 'self' character (i.e., pointing to your nose to refer to yourself).

As you will understand more clearly after reading the next section, mentally breaking characters into parts will often be a useful tool for learning and remembering them.

Component Replacement

Another way that phonetics were backfit onto characters was as a replacement for certain other parts of the character. Let's look at an example of a character that was modified by the addition of a phonetic.

The following character, in the old form shown here, depicted a kneeling person (facing to the left), with a giant ear on top:

This character was an ideograph, with the enlarged ear indicating the character meaning: 'listen.' (This is equivalent to the character back in Section 2.4 which depicts the meaning 'see' as a large eye placed onto a person's body.) Over time, as the forms of many characters underwent change, this particular character was modified by the addition of a phonetic component. Specifically, the character for a word meaning 'gate' / 'door,' which had the same reading as the word 'listen,' was added as a phonetic to help indicate the character reading. At the same time, the body component was dropped out, leaving only the elements 'ear' and 'gate' remaining.

These elements, in their modern forms, appear as full characters like this:

The character on the left is the modern form of 'ear.' It is based on a pictograph of a person's ear. You can see that it has changed considerably from the earlier form appearing at the top of the 'listen' character above, and is no longer recognizable as a human ear. As with most pictographic characters, the image is easier to see in older forms of the character.

The character on the right means 'gate' or 'door.' It is a pictograph of a set of doors, such as those used as a gate. To remember the meaning of this character, it may be helpful to note the resemblance to swinging half-height doors (together with the door frame on the sides) stereotypical of saloons in the American Old West.

After the addition of the 'gate' character as a phonetic, and the removal of the body component, the character for 'listen' now appears this way (shown in the modern form):

聞

Like the modern 'nose' character, this character now consists of two parts: a meaning indicator (ear) and a sound indicator (gate). Note how this character is assembled by placing the 'ear' element into the empty space of the 'gate' element. Optimal use of space like this is common in character composition. We will see more examples of this in Chapter 6.

When choosing a component to act as a phonetic, it was desirable to have a phonetic that matched the character sound as much as possible, and also ideally that had a meaning that fit with or could at least somehow be related to the meaning of the character that contained it. Thus, many phonetics also help to suggest the meaning of the character, even if only slightly. Matching the sound was given priority, though, and as a result there are many characters with phonetics that mostly just help indicate the reading of the character, and have little or nothing to do with the character meaning. With the meaning extensions and meaning shifts that occurred with many characters over time, this is especially true today: there are many phonetics which have no discernible connection to the modern character meaning. It is best to just treat these phonetics as a sound indicator, and ignore their intrinsic meaning.

The principal reason for the selection of the 'gate' element as a phonetic for the 'listen' character was for its sound; there's not a clear meaning relationship. For some students learning kanji, though, when trying to remember character meanings it is helpful to concoct a story that utilizes the meanings of all the elements within the character. With the 'listen' character, such a story could be: 'a person puts his/her ear to the door in order to listen (to what is happening on the other side).' Stories such as this can be useful for remembering character meanings. But in addition to learning character meanings, it's also necessary to learn character readings, and because the use of phonetics is so widespread among kanji, recognizing phonetic components within characters is helpful for remembering character *on* readings, and will be emphasized in this book.

Reading Inconsistencies

Unfortunately, the reading of a phonetic by itself, as a standalone character, is not always exactly identical to the reading of characters that use it as a phonetic. That is true of the previous example: in modern Japanese, the 'listen' character has a principal *on* reading of *bun*, while the 'gate' element as a standalone character has a principal *on* reading of *mon*. At first glance, these two readings seem completely unrelated. But, in fact, there is a correspondence between them. This same pair of readings can be found in other characters as well. For example, the character[10]

which has numerous meanings, including 'writing,' has two major *on* readings: *bun* and *mon* —the exact same two readings as just mentioned. In some common compound words that use this character it is read as *bun*, and in some others it is read as *mon*. (This character also has a separate *kun* reading, as well.)

So not only can phonetic components have multiple, different readings, but, as first mentioned in Chapter 1, many individual characters themselves also have multiple *on* readings. In this book, these multiple, similar *on* readings associated with an individual character or phonetic component are called **related readings**. In addition to the *bun* and *mon* pair of related readings, there are many other pairs or groups of related readings found among characters and phonetics. In fact, these related readings will often be encountered when studying kanji; they are a challenge that all kanji learners must face.

As more characters (and phonetics) are learned, the patterns of correspondences of related readings, such as *bun* and *mon*, become easier to see, and the readings become easier to remember. In Chapter 7, we will look at examples of the most commonly occurring sets of related readings, and study the patterns shared by them. We will also take an in-depth look at multiple *on* readings and their causes.

Of course, this kind of inconsistency certainly complicates the use of phonetics for learning character readings, and because of it, some kanji learning materials avoid utilizing phonetic components for learning character readings, except in cases where the phonetic and the reading of the character containing it are identical. But that isn't necessary. Even when phonetics are not read identically among different characters, the phonetic can still be used to assist in the learning of character readings.

---

[10] This character is quite similar in appearance to the 'mix / exchange' character we already studied (交), but is unrelated.

Not Always a Phonetic Role

Note that sometimes a component acts as a phonetic in some characters, but only as a meaning element in other characters. For example, the 'gate' element is used as a phonetic in at least one other common use character (問, with the *on* reading *mon*), but in other common use characters, such as ones meaning 'open' and 'close' (開 and 閉), it is used only for its meaning ('door' / 'gate') and not for its sound. When you first study a new character, it's necessary to learn how the various components in it are used.

Determinative Paired with Phonetic

Taking one more look at the 'listen' character in its modern form (聞), you can see that the 'ear' element plays the role of a determinative: indicating that the full character has to do with sound and hearing. Thus, as a result of the form changes it underwent, this character has been transformed from an ideograph into a character which consists of two parts put together: a determinative and a phonetic. And this is precisely the method that was used for the creation of the majority of characters: combining a determinative with a phonetic component. Among all kanji ever created, this type is by far the most prevalent.

2.8 Determinative-Phonetic Characters

Eventually, as new characters continued to be created, the earlier methods of creation, such as the construction of pictographs and ideographs, were mostly abandoned, and the vast majority of new characters were made by combining a phonetic component with a determinative. It became the standard way of forming characters. In fact, there are even cases where characters which were originally pictographs or ideographs were redesigned and replaced with a determinative and phonetic pair. As described in the previous section, the 'listen' character is one such example of that.

In this book, this type of character will be called a determinative-phonetic character, and because this term is used frequently, we will use the abbreviation 'D-P character.' Note that this is not a standard term for this type of character. In some other kanji learning materials, for example, these characters are called either 'semanto-phonetic' or 'phono-semantic' characters, terms which combine words meaning 'sound' and 'meaning.'

A **determinative-phonetic character** is a character that is composed of one component which indicates the general category of meaning of the character (i.e., the determinative) and another component which identifies, or at least strongly hints at, the (original) reading of the character (i.e., the phonetic). The phonetic component may also help to identify the character meaning.

Note that there exist characters that have a determinative but no phonetic, and characters that have a phonetic but no determinative. However, these types are rare.

Remarkably, more than 90% of all characters ever created are of the D-P type. If you consider the fact that many non D-P characters, such as pictographic and ideographic characters, are used as determinatives and/or phonetics within D-P characters, you can see that this type of character is truly fundamental to kanji.

The method of creating characters by combining a determinative with a phonetic wasn't developed until after quite a few kanji had already been created. As a result, characters for the simplest, most common objects are often not D-P characters, whereas characters representing more advanced or complicated objects or concepts are usually D-P characters.

To better understand exactly what a D-P character is, it's helpful to look at some more examples. The following table shows three D-P characters, each of which has as a determinative the element 辶 ('movement' - mentioned in Section 2.6). All are *jōyō kanji*.

Character	Character Meaning	Character *On* Reading	Phonetic (phonetic meaning)	Phonetic *On* Reading
近	near	キン (KIN)	斤 (an axe)	キン (KIN)
遠	distant; far	エン (EN)	袁 † (a long, flowing robe)	エン (EN)
速	fast; quick	ソク (SOKU)	束 (a bundle)	ソク (SOKU)

† As a standalone character, the strokes at the bottom of this phonetic component are slightly different from those in the 'far' character on the left. Most notably, the straight downward stroke ends in a hook in the standalone form, which is absent from the 'far' character. This is due to a slightly abbreviated form of the component being used in the 'far' character. Despite the differences, these should be treated as the same component.

In each of these three characters, the determinative is located along the left and bottom sides, and the phonetic fills the remainder of the character. The meaning of the determinative, 'movement,' is closely related to the meanings of each of the three characters in the table: 'near,' 'far,' and 'fast.'

As you can see from the table, the phonetic component in each character gives a strong indication of the character *on* reading. In fact, for all three of these characters, the principal *on* reading of each phonetic component exactly matches the principal *on* reading of the character itself. However, the meaning of the phonetic component has little or no connection with the character meaning. It is difficult to see how an axe has anything to do with being 'near,' how a flowing robe has anything to do with being 'far,' and how a bundle has anything to do with being 'fast.'

For each of these characters, the determinative has a much stronger connection to the character meaning than does the phonetic. When these characters were created, the phonetic components were most likely chosen not primarily for their meaning, but rather primarily because their sound matched the sound of the spoken word for which the character was being created.

To continue to develop a feel for D-P characters, let's look at some more examples. In the following table are another set of D-P characters. These characters all have different determinatives, but share the same phonetic component: the 'winnowing basket' character (其). All are *jōyō kanji* (common use characters).

In the table, principal *on* character readings are written in katakana. The *rōmaji* equivalents are also provided for each of these readings, in uppercase text. Principal *kun* readings are written in hiragana, with the *rōmaji* equivalents in lowercase. This is a standard way of expressing these different readings, and helps to distinguish them from each other. This practice will be followed throughout the remainder of the book for individual character *on* and *kun* readings.

Character	Determinative (meaning) †	Principal Character Reading(s)	Character Meaning
期	月 (unit of time)	キ (KI)	1. a period of time; 2. wait for (in expectation)
旗	𠂉 (flag-related)	キ (KI) はた (hata)	a flag
基	土 (ground-related)	キ (KI) もと (moto)	foundation; origin
棋	木 (made of wood)	キ (KI)	a board game (especially Japanese chess)
碁	石 (made of stone)	ゴ (GO)	*go* (Japanese checkers)

† The meanings given here (in parentheses) are the meanings of these components when used as a determinative in the corresponding character in the left-hand column. The meanings of these components when used as standalone characters are different. As discussed in Section 2.6, a component used as a determinative can represent a broader range of meaning than when used as a simple standalone character.

Three new elements we haven't already studied appear in this table. The determinative for the first character comes from a standalone character meaning 'moon' or 'month': 月. It was originally a pictograph of a crescent moon. (The 'month' meaning is based on the fact that a full revolution of the moon around the earth takes approximately one month. In English, the words 'moon' and 'month' are similarly related.) As a determinative, it is applied to characters having to do with either the moon itself or a period of time (deriving from its 'month' meaning).

The determinative for the second character in the table is based on a pictograph of a flag mounted on a pole and waving in the wind. It no longer occurs as a standalone character. When used as a determinative, it indicates characters having to do with flags or banners (e.g., specific types of flags or banners).

The determinative for the fifth character comes from a standalone character meaning 'stone': 石. When used as a determinative, it identifies characters representing either objects made of stone or processes involving stones, such as grinding or polishing.

From this group of D-P characters, we can make the following observations:

• The principal *on* readings of these characters are not all exactly identical; there is a small degree of variation. The first four exactly match the reading of the phonetic component (the phonetic by itself is read as *KI*), but the fifth (*GO*) has a voiced, rather than non-voiced consonant sound (indicated by the *dakuten* mark [゛] placed on the katakana character), and also a different vowel sound. This is often the case with phonetics: they are not always an exact match, but are usually closely related.

Even when its reading is not an exact match, the phonetic is, without question, useful for remembering character *on* readings. Taking the five characters in the table as an example, it is certainly efficient to learn *KI* as the principal *on* reading of this phonetic, and then memorize each character *on* reading based on that, taking into account the variations from that principal reading. To demonstrate the value of this approach, imagine if the *on* readings of these five characters were all unrelated and randomly different from each other. Memorizing the readings in that case would clearly be a greater task.

As you study more and more characters, you will find that even when the phonetic is not an exact match, it is often quite close, and is a good starting point to remembering the character reading or for guessing the reading of a newly encountered character. Rather than an absolute indicator of the character reading, think of the phonetic as a strong hint.

• As with the three D-P characters in the earlier table, each character meaning is much more closely tied to the determinative than to the phonetic. For each of these characters, the determinative can be relatively easily related to the character meaning. In the first character, the 'moon' determinative is used to indicate a character meaning related to a period of time. (The second meaning of this character—'wait for'—is an extended meaning.) In the second character, the 'flag' determinative meaning is identical to the full character meaning. (Previously, this character probably meant a specific kind of banner, but now means 'flag' in general.) In the third character, the 'ground' determinative is used because a foundation (both literally and figuratively) is built at the ground level. In the fourth character, the 'tree' determinative identifies that the game pieces are made of wood. In the fifth character, the 'stone' determinative refers to the fact that the game pieces of Japanese *go* (painted either black or white) are made of stone (or resemble stones).

However, none of the meanings of these characters are related to the meaning of the phonetic component. Even if you have taken the time to learn the etymological origin of this phonetic component (namely, that it depicts a winnowing basket held in two hands), or the modern meaning of the component as a full character ('that'), it is of limited help in learning and remembering the meanings of these five characters. With some creative thinking, it might be possible to relate the phonetic to the meanings of these characters, but in truth the component was chosen primarily for its sound, not for its meaning, when the characters were originally created—just as it was chosen for its sound when borrowed to write the word 'that'—and any meaning connection was secondary.

While it is true that the meanings of some phonetic components contribute to the meanings of the characters that contain them, many phonetics are used primarily for their sound. When learning characters that were built using the D-P principle, if you always try to learn each character meaning by creating a story involving the meanings of all of its components, including the phonetic, you will likely find that learning and remembering character meanings will become a cumbersome task. Instead, it is easier to think of a D-P character as a character whose category of meaning is conveyed by the determinative, and whose sound (that is, the *on* reading) is conveyed by the phonetic. For example, when you are learning the 棋 character, think of it as a character having to do with wood which has a sound (*on* reading) based on the component 其.

• Finally, note that only two characters in the table have commonly-used *kun* readings. And these two *kun* readings are not at all similar to each other in sound. This is typical among *kun* readings of characters which share a phonetic. Kanji were applied to native Japanese words based only on meaning; their phonetic aspect was ignored.

The Characters Are Phonetic by Design

Because the majority of Chinese characters are of the D-P type, this means that kanji, viewed as a whole, are essentially phonetic characters—a fact which is often overlooked, especially in Japan. Why is that?

One reason is that many of the earliest characters learned by students are not D-P characters and do not contain phonetic components. When most students first learn kanji, they generally learn the most commonly used characters first. Many of the most commonly used characters were also among the earliest created, when pictographic and ideographic creation methods were more frequently employed. As a result, the percentage of D-P characters among the earliest characters studied is not as high as it is among more advanced characters. In fact, of the first 80 characters taught to Japanese schoolchildren (the characters taught during the first grade of elementary school), less than ten are D-P.

Thus, many of the earliest characters studied must be remembered one at a time as unique, individual characters, without finding commonalities, such as phonetics, among them. It isn't until a few hundred characters have been studied that students can take full advantage of recognizing phonetics within characters to make learning *on* readings more efficient.

Secondly, in Japan the *kun* readings are not at all phonetic in nature. Instead, those readings are all meaning-based: a result of applying the characters to native Japanese words closest in meaning. There is no phonetic shortcut to learning the *kun* readings.

Finally, as demonstrated in this and the previous section, phonetic components are not always read consistently from character to character; they are not always an exact match. Although there are correspondences between the different readings, they can be hard to recognize.

For these reasons, especially the last one, many kanji learning materials do not place much emphasis on identifying phonetic components within characters and using them as an aid to learning character *on* readings. Remarkably, many students of Japanese kanji never fully appreciate that the characters they are learning are primarily phonetic in design. Some students continue to learn hundreds and hundreds of characters under the illusion that the components appearing within a character were originally chosen primarily to best convey the meaning of the character—a clear fallacy. For a student of kanji striving to learn thousands of characters, not paying attention to phonetics is wasteful.

2.9 Character Nesting

Most D-P characters were originally formed simply by taking an already existing character, used in its entirety, and combining it with a determinative component identifying the class of meaning of the new character being created. The existing character was used as a phonetic component (that is, its *on* reading was similar to or the same as that of the new character being made), and possibly additionally for its meaning contribution to the new character, as well. This is precisely what was done, for example, to create all five characters in the previous table: each character was built by combining the 'winnowing basket' character, using it primarily for its sound, with a determinative that indicated the category of meaning of the new character being made.

This process for building characters was utilized often. As a result, among all kanji in existence today are many characters that were built from other, already existing characters.

In some cases, a character built this way was then subsequently used again in the same process, combining it with yet another determinative to create yet another character. This resulted in a kind of character 'nesting.'

In such cases, it might seem that the new character has more than one determinative: the one from the original character, and the one that was added to make the new character. But this is not the case: only the final added determinative should be thought of as the determinative for the new character.

This nesting process could theoretically continue indefinitely, with successive determinatives added to make new characters, but in practice it is rare that more than two levels of determinatives were added in this way. The characters in the following table demonstrate one such rare case where a sequence of four determinatives have been added, one at a time, to build new characters. Note that the characters become increasingly more cluttered and harder to read as additional determinatives are added.

Character (*on* reading)	Determinative (meaning)	Phonetic Component	Character Meaning
戕 (SHŌ)	戈 (weapon)	爿	a cut (on the body) made with a blade
臧 (SŌ)	臣 (underling)	戕	a subject; follower (especially one who is armed)
藏 (ZŌ)	艹 (vegetation)	臧	storehouse (for storing grains, etc.)
臟 (ZŌ)	月 (body part)	藏	viscera; internal organs

Don't worry about unfamiliar determinatives and other components in these characters. But do note the following:

• The *on* readings of the four characters in the table (see the left column) are not all exactly identical, but are very similar. This is common with phonetics, as we have been seeing.

• The first character consists of only two elements: the determinative on the right and the phonetic on the left. In this particular character, the phonetic (which means 'bed') plays no role in the character meaning; it only provides an indication of the character reading.

• Starting with the second character, the two elements of the first character have become connected together and slightly altered in form.

• The second through fourth characters were each made by adding a determinative to the previous character. The previous character, as a whole, in essence plays the role of the phonetic. Furthermore, among all of these characters the phonetic component has a minimal role, or no role at all, in the character meaning.

• Although in the 'phonetic component' column of the table the entire character from the previous row is shown, it is also acceptable to think of the original phonetic (爿) as the phonetic component for all of these characters. Either way of thinking of this is fine. With D-P characters, you can treat everything that is not the determinative as the phonetic, although possibly only one part of that is the part that truly provides the indicator of the character reading.

• Of these four characters, only the bottom two are commonly encountered today. The others are very uncommon, and are shown here only to demonstrate this method of character construction. In modern writing, each of the bottom two characters has been simplified in Japan by means of the elimination of the left-hand portion of the original phonetic, and they now appear this way:

蔵   臓

Interestingly, in the case of these two characters, the only part of the character that was removed during simplification was part of the element originally used to help indicate the character reading. So the *on* readings of the modern forms of these characters must be learned without the assistance of a phonetic. But because these two characters have the same *on* reading as each other (ZŌ), and one contains the other, the burden of learning the *on* readings is minimal if the two characters are learned together.

• The determinative is often, but not always, added to the outside of the character. In the case of the second character in the table, the determinative is added to the interior.

• For each character, the determinative is the component which gives the strongest indicator of the character meaning. For most D-P characters, when trying to learn and remember the character meaning, it is best to focus mainly on the determinative, rather than try to, for example, incorporate each of the individual elements of the character into a kind of story. Take the final character in the table as an example. Trying to create a story involving all of its elements (a bed, a weapon, an underling, vegetation, and a body part) would be very complicated and not especially helpful for remembering the character meaning. But the meaning of the determinative alone ('body part') is closely related to the character meaning ('internal organs').

• Finally, note that the 'body part' determinative appearing in the final row is an altered form of the 'meat' / 'flesh' character we first saw in Section 2.6 (肉). When compressed to the left-hand side or bottom of a character, the form is usually modified in this way. This altered form happens to be identical to the 'moon' character we saw in the previous section. This similarity is discussed in Section 2.11.

2.10 The Traditional Six Principles of Character Creation

In this chapter, we have learned three major methods that were used to create characters: pictographic, ideographic, and determinative-phonetic, as well as ways in which character meanings were extended and shifted, such as by phonetic borrowing. A few other lesser-used methods have also been used to create characters, but these will not be discussed in this book.

Many modern kanji books and dictionaries identify exactly six separate principles of character creation. The reason for the number six is traditional, going back to a very influential character dictionary created in China in the second century AD, called the *Shuowen Jiezi*. In reality, there are not exactly six methods that were used to create all the characters, but this number has persisted for a long time and is widely taught.

In that ancient dictionary, the six principles it identified were not all clearly explained, and so among modern texts that cite six principles, the particular six methods described vary somewhat from source to source.

This book will not categorize the characters based on a set of six principles. For those wishing to learn more about the traditional six principles, they are discussed further in Appendix D.

2.11 Transformation of Character Forms

In this chapter, we have already seen a few examples of early forms of characters, and could observe how in some cases they are very different from their modern forms. These changes in character form were largely the result of changes over time in the style in which the characters were drawn.

As the characters continued to be used generation after generation, the style in which they were drawn gradually changed, transitioning through several distinct stages. These style changes affected the way that individual strokes were drawn, and thus changed the appearance of the characters as a whole. Gradually, the character forms moved further and further away from their origins.

Every single character has undergone at least some degree of change to the way it is written. In some cases, the change is dramatic, to the point that the early version and modern version of the character do not resemble each other at all.

This deviation in form was able to occur because over time previous examples of writing were lost. Those who wrote with the characters in each successive generation primarily only had access to recent writing to use as a model, and so were not aware of the original shapes of the characters. In the modern era, from writing samples discovered in archaeological digs we are able to see early forms of characters, but writers in the past could not. And so shapes that were once pictographic gradually turned into seemingly random collections of strokes.

Looking back on all the samples of writing that have been discovered to date, the way the characters were written can be traced back through at least five distinct stages.[11] The style of writing the characters in each of these stages is formally referred to as a **script**. The following table shows the transitions of several characters through these five principal styles.

	Script				
	Oracle bone	Bronze	Seal	Clerical	Regular
fire	🜂	🜂	火	火	火
water	水	水	水	水	水
mountain	山	山	山	山	山
ear	耳	耳	耳	耳	耳
elephant	象	象	象	象	象
woman	女	女	女	女	女
red	赤	赤	赤	赤	赤

The first column of characters in the table are examples of the earliest forms of the characters that have been discovered to date. The surviving samples were found engraved onto animal bones (and other hard objects such as the underside shells of tortoises) which were used in fortune-telling rituals. This style is thus commonly referred to as **oracle bone script**.

The second column shows examples of characters found molded or carved onto bronze artifacts. During the era in which these **bronze script** characters appeared, many different forms of the characters existed, as people in different regions of China wrote the characters differently. The ones shown here are representative of the typical appearance of that time.

The way of writing the characters became reunified in China around 200 BC, with the official style consisting of uniformly thin, long, curved strokes. This style, exemplified by the characters in the third column, is now called **seal script**, based on the fact that after it fell out

---

[11] Other historical styles of writing the characters were also developed, some of which have influenced the modern forms of the characters, but to a comparatively limited extent. The two most notable of these styles (semi-cursive and cursive scripts) are described briefly in Appendix N.

of favor its use was limited primarily to personal name seals (a kind of ink stamp). This style can still be seen today on some such seals, both in China and in Japan.

The change in writing style leading to the fourth stage was driven by a practical need. Until then, the writing of the characters had been somewhat limited, both in terms of the number of people who wrote with them and the frequency with which they were written. As the need developed for more people to write more frequently, such as due to the increased output of government documents, a simpler, faster means of writing was needed. In the style that resulted, the curved strokes of the seal style were replaced with mostly straight lines, many of which ran horizontally or vertically. In English, this style is called **clerical script**, stemming from its association with government clerks who wrote in the style. One notable characteristic of this style was that strokes moving down to the lower right tended to 'flare out,' becoming quite wide at the end. You can see this in some of the characters in the fourth column of the table.

Finally, the fifth column of the table shows the most recent of these styles, still in use today—sometimes referred to as **regular script** or standard script. As with the clerical style, this style's appearance is based on the drawing of the characters calligraphically: with a brush and ink. For most characters, this style is similar to clerical, although the characters are somewhat taller than they are wide, and some of the strokes have more of a flourish to them. Some characters in this style (not appearing in the table) are even more noticeably different from their clerical style forms; this reflects the influence of other writing styles not described here.

Now let's take a look at the specific characters in the table.

The first six characters in the table each consist of only a single element. These six elements were all originally pictographic, but as you can see, each element became less recognizable as the writing style changed. By no later than the 'seal' stage, the pictographic images once visible in the characters had become mostly unrecognizable.

The 'fire' character originally was a simple depiction of flames from a fire. To remember it, the modern version can be thought of as a single flame in the middle with sparks on the sides.

The 'water' character is believed to have originally depicted flowing water, possibly in a stream. The shorter strokes in the early forms could be water outside of the main flow. (The early character for 'river' was similar, except the shorter strokes were in the middle and long strokes were on the outsides.) The modern form of the 'water' character resulted from the turning inward and connecting of the four short strokes. If it is helpful, you can visualize it as a stream of falling water in the center, with spray shooting out to the sides.

With the 'mountain' character, you can see how the individual peaks of the early form became simple vertical lines in the modern form.

We already saw the fourth character ('ear') in both the 'oracle bone' form and the modern form. In the table, you can see the rough sequence of transitions between these styles.

Complicated characters with many strokes often had the most dramatic form transformations. The fifth character in the table ('elephant') demonstrates this especially well. In the earliest form it is easy to see an elephant (turned 90 degrees clockwise) with its long trunk. But as the strokes were redrawn in each new style, it became completely unrecognizable. Note that many characters representing animals were originally oriented sideways. This may have been to facilitate writing them onto thin, vertical bamboo slats, which were a commonly used medium of early writing.

The sixth character in the table ('woman') originally depicted a kneeling figure facing left, with arms crossed. Over time, it became rotated 90 degrees counterclockwise. (A few other characters were also rotated like this, such as the 'eye' character, as we already saw earlier in the chapter.) Also, what was the lower body in the original pictograph was at some point removed, and does not appear in the modern character.

The last character in the table (the color 'red') combines the basic elements 'man' and 'fire.' (The element for 'man' used here is the one with arms and legs spread wide, that as a standalone character now means 'large.') The character is an ideograph, but it is not clear how it suggests its meaning. Perhaps the implication is the color of a man's skin after he has been burned by fire. You can see that with the change in writing style the two separate elements became mixed together. In the modern form, the two elements that make up this character cannot be individually distinguished; they no longer resemble the same elements appearing as standalone characters: 大 and 火. Such merging of once separate elements has occurred with other characters as well.

Characteristics of Form Transformation

Character form transformations resulted in several characteristic features in the modern appearance of the characters. The following two characters, shown in both 'seal' and modern forms, demonstrate two of these features.

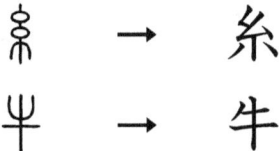

The first character demonstrates the change from rounded lines to straightened ones. The character means 'thread' or 'string' and is a pictograph, possibly of either thread wound on a spool or perhaps even of a silk cocoon. Loose threads dangle below. In the modern form, you can see that all of the rounded lines have been transformed into straightened strokes which approximate the original curvature. (This characteristic is also observable with the 'mix' / 'exchange' character, shown in both an early form and the modern form back in Section 2.4.)

The second character demonstrates a loss of symmetry. The character means 'cattle' and depicts the head of a cow or bull, with curved horns. In the modern form, you can see that the part which was once the horns has been straightened, but the left and right sides are no longer a mirror image of each other. With the lack of symmetry, it's harder to visualize the original object in this case.

In addition to the shapes of the character elements changing, in some cases the actual elements comprising the characters also changed. One character this happened to is shown here in both an early form and the modern form:

The character originally meant 'to take apart,' and now still has this meaning as well as a number of similar meanings including 'to separate' and 'to solve' (such as a puzzle). Originally, the character was an ideograph depicting two hands removing a horn from a cow or bull. At a later point, the two 'hand' elements were removed and replaced with a 'knife' element.

The modern form still contains these three elements: a horn (on the left), a knife (upper right), and the cow or bull itself (lower right). Unlike the character for 'red,' in the modern version the forms of each of these three elements appear the same as they do when used as standalone characters (角, 刀, and 牛).

Deviation of Forms

Form changes were not without side effects. Sometimes what were once identical or nearly identical forms shared by two different characters diverged when the characters were transformed, and now no longer appear as similar as they once did.

The following two characters, shown in both early and modern forms, mean 'woman' (upper character) and 'mother' (lower character):

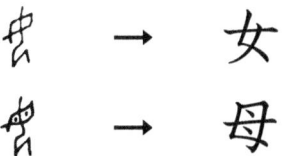

You can see that the early forms are almost identical, except for the addition of two dots to the 'mother' character, which probably represent either breasts or nipples, suggesting a mother capable of nursing a child. Like the 'woman' character, the 'mother' character also was rotated and lost the lower body portion, but the two characters still diverged from each other. Specifically, the modern 'mother' character has a horizontal stroke at the top, which is absent from the modern 'woman' character, and the downward stroke on the right-hand side has only a slight curve with a hook at the end, rather than a greater curve.

The following two characters demonstrate a more dramatic divergence of forms. Although one was originally constructed using the other as a component, they do not appear similar in their modern forms (the rightmost characters below).

Bronze	Seal	Regular
𠂇 →	肙 →	及
	㤕 →	急

The upper character means 'reach' or 'extend to,' and originally consisted of a hand reaching out to grab a person, as can be seen in the 'bronze' form. The two elements are merged together in the modern form.

The lower character has meanings such as 'to hurry' and 'urgent.' It is a D-P character, with the phonetic located above the determinative. The determinative at the bottom is an element that was originally a pictograph of a heart, and now means 'heart,' 'mind,' or 'spirit.' Used as a determinative, it identifies characters having to do with feelings or emotions (such as the feeling of being rushed or hurried, expressed by the lower character).

The phonetic of the lower character is the 'reach' character. You can confirm this by comparing the 'seal' forms of the two characters (the versions in the middle column). The components are essentially the same, with only slight differences due to the component being vertically compressed in the lower character. And these two characters are still read the same today: both have an *on* reading of *KYŪ*, as do most other characters containing this same phonetic component.

But what were only slight differences in the 'seal' forms became more pronounced as the characters were transformed further; the modern forms appear rather different from each other. As a result, the phonetic relationship between these characters has been obscured. (Note that only the 'hurry' character diverged. In all other common use characters which contain the 'reach' component, the component form is similar to that of the 'reach' character.)

Merging of Forms

Not only did once-similar forms sometimes diverge, the opposite effect also occurred: in some cases different components that once had a different appearance from each other were transformed into the same shape. The most well-known example of this change is one we already saw: in the modern form, when the 'meat' / 'flesh' character (肉) is compressed, it usually takes on an altered form which happens to be identical to that of the character meaning 'moon' / 'month' (月). Two characters which we have already seen:

期　　　臓

contain these respective elements. The left character contains the 'moon' element, while the right character contains the 'meat' / 'flesh' element—here signifying 'body part.'

But these are not even the only two possible meanings of elements with this shape. Each of the following four characters contains a component with this identical shape:

勝　朋　青　龍

However, the common component has a different origin and different meaning in each of these characters, none of which are 'moon' or 'meat.' (Of course, as you learn each of these four characters, to help remember them you may choose to come up with a story involving either 'moon' or 'meat,' but the truth is that the origin of each of these characters had nothing to do with either.)

Another element which has numerous different meanings among different characters is:

田

---

[12] Note that the left side downward stroke of the component is drawn in two slightly different ways (curved and straight) among these characters. This is only a minor variation in the form. The stroke is usually straight when the component is located underneath another component, and curved otherwise. The two variations (curved and straight) should be thought of and treated as the same component.

Used as a standalone character, as shown here, the element means 'cultivated field,' such as where crops are grown. We already saw another character with the element in which the meaning is different, though—the 'fruit' character:

果

This kind of transformation in form happened not only with individual elements, but also with components consisting of groups of elements. Note the modern forms of the following two characters (meaning 'hill' and 'soldier,' respectively):

丘   兵

These two characters seem as if they must be related, because their forms appear identical except for the additional two strokes at the bottom of the second character. But that similarity is coincidental. The derivations of these two characters are completely different, as you can see by looking at the transformations of the characters over time:

The character on the left was originally a pictograph of hills. The character on the right was an ideograph, conveying the idea 'soldier' by combining a weapon (a kind of axe) with hands holding it. In the modern style, the forms of these characters became nearly identical.

The same thing happened with characters meaning 'to sell' and 'to read,' shown here in their modern forms:

売   読

In their modern forms, the 'sell' character is identical in form to the component on the right-hand side of the 'read' character. By comparing their 'seal' forms (the leftmost versions below), though, you can see that there once were a number of differences between the two characters. Even in their original modern forms (i.e., prior to character form simplification), there were slight differences (see the middle versions below), but in their simplified modern forms the characters now share an identical component.

賣 → 賣 → 売   讀 → 讀 → 読

There are numerous other examples, as well. The important point here is that when you see a given element or component within a character, you cannot always assume that it has one particular meaning.

One Object, Multiple Representations

One of the complications resulting from character form transformation is that there are now cases in which what is essentially the same object appears in the modern characters in many different forms. A notable example of this is the 'hand' element.

When written as a standalone character, 'hand' appears this way, shown in both an early form and the modern form:

It's difficult to recognize a hand in the modern form, but from the earlier form you can somewhat see that the shorter lines depict the fingers of a hand, all pointing upward. This character is often used as a determinative, indicating actions involving the hands. When used as a determinative, the element is most often placed on the left-hand side of a character. In that location, the form is altered and simplified. An example character using 'hand' as a determinative on the left-hand side is:

which means 'to hit.' You can see that the topmost stroke of the 'hand' element has been eliminated, and the other strokes have been somewhat altered, as well.

But these are not the only ways that a hand is represented in characters. In a number of early characters, when a hand was only one of several elements in the character, a simpler representation was used. It originally looked like this:

This element could be oriented in any direction (facing up, facing down, turned sideways, etc.), and the orientation in early characters affected how the element was transformed into the modern form, resulting in many different appearances of 'hand' among the modern characters.

Furthermore, another separate element also sometimes took on the meaning 'hand':

As a full character, this element probably was an indicative character, with the small stroke at the bottom indicating a particular part of the hand or arm, such as the wrist or perhaps the point on the forearm near the wrist where the pulse can be measured. As a full character, the meaning is 'a small amount' or 'a unit of measurement of approximately three centimeters.' Among some characters which contain this element, though, the meaning is simply 'hand.' In fact, as the characters were transformed through the various writing styles, this element was sometimes freely interchanged with the simpler version of 'hand' shown above.

The various different forms of the 'hand' element within early versions of the characters were transformed in numerous different ways, resulting in a variety of different appearances of the hand element (or multiple hand elements placed together) within modern characters. The table on the next page shows some of the most common forms seen today.

The first column shows various forms of 'hand' elements in an earlier style (the 'seal' style is chosen, as it is easiest to see how the modern style derived from it). The second column shows how each of these elements appears in its modern form. In the third column are example characters in the modern form containing the corresponding elements.

Early Form of Component	Modern Form	Example Character	Description
ψ	手	拳	main form
ψ	扌	打	left side determinative
⇒	又	取	left-facing hand
⇒	⇒	雪	left-facing hand, variation
⇒	⇒	書	left-facing hand, holding object †
⇒	ナ	左	right-facing hand
⇒	龷	卑	previous element, smaller
爫	爪	爬	downward-facing hand
爫	爫	妥	previous element, smaller
ヒ	ヒ	印	previous element, rotated
𠬞	廾	戒	two hands merged together
𦥑	𦥑	興	four hands, bottom two merged
⇒	寸	村	separate element (not 'hand')

† This component is only used in modern forms when a stroke from another element is passing vertically through it, such as in the example character.

These examples demonstrate how the same object can take many forms among the modern characters. However, you should be careful not to assume that any time you encounter any of these elements they will always represent a hand. There are some characters which, in their modern forms, contain elements identical in form to some of those in the table, but which originally meant something other than 'hand.'

Transformation into Commonplace Elements

Sometimes a complicated character was transformed in such a way that it now resembles a combination of common elements, even though the original form had nothing to do with any of those common elements.

A character meaning 'young' originally appeared to depict a kneeling woman reaching up to touch her flowing hair. Transforming through various stages, it changed form in this way:

Now, in the modern form, it appears to consist of two components: an element meaning 'vegetation' on top of an element meaning 'right.' Neither of these elements has anything to do with the reading or meaning of this character, however.

Corruption of Meaning-Indicating Components

In some cases, the part of the character with the largest contribution to the character meaning was altered in a way such that it can no longer be used to provide a hint to the character meaning.

Originally, the key part of a character meaning 'follow' was two 'people' elements side by side, conveying the meaning 'follow' in an ideographic way (one person following another). Supporting elements 'foot' and 'road' were added (probably as a determinative) to assist with conveying the meaning. Each of these elements is still recognizable in the character even in its original (pre-simplification) modern form (the third version below).

從 → 訓 → 從 → 従

As the modern form of the character was simplified, though (the fourth version above), the two 'person' elements were corrupted. As a result, the most important elements in this character are no longer recognizable.

In mainland China, this character has been simplified, reverting back to its simplest form:

从

This simplified form of the character is not used in Japan, though.

Abbreviations and Mistakes

Sometimes, as characters were transformed, parts of them were deliberately or accidentally removed. The following character, shown in an earlier form and the modern form, means 'write.'

This character originally consisted of an upper part depicting a hand holding a writing brush (聿), and a lower part which was a phonetic component. At some point, most of the strokes of the phonetic component were eliminated from the character, and what remains is no longer recognizable or usable as a phonetic.

There were even cases where, due to copying mistakes, what was once a particular element mistakenly was changed into a similar-looking but different element. These mistakes often have persisted all the way to the modern form. For example, the bottom component of the character:

契

was originally a 'tree' element, but was at some point inadvertently changed to the 'large' element, and still exists that way to this day.

In cases like this, only when samples of older writing were rediscovered centuries later would the original forms be verified, and the mistake be realized.

Modern Character Form Simplifications

Although the standard way of writing the characters became settled on the current 'regular' style more than a thousand years ago, the forms of individual characters continued to be modified even into modern times.

The most recent modifications were driven primarily by a desire to simplify the reading and writing of the characters. Writing the characters by hand can take time, especially with complicated characters of many strokes. And complex, visually cluttered characters can be troublesome even just when reading. Over time, abbreviated, informal ways of writing some of the characters were developed, and the use of many of those became widespread. The simplifications were at first considered non-standard forms, but in Japan as the list of *jōyō kanji* (common use characters) was officially adopted, some of the informal, abbreviated character forms became designated as the new standard versions.

Some of these simplifications were similar to what was done long ago to the 'write' character (shown on the previous page): a number of strokes were removed to eliminate clutter, making the character simpler to read and faster to write, while still retaining the same overall shape. We already saw several examples of this kind of simplification, including with the character meaning 'storehouse':

where a few strokes were removed from the lower left-hand side.

While some simplifications were applied to specific characters, others were applied to specific components, affecting multiple characters containing those components. A notable example of this is the 'movement' determinative:

This component had been written with a total of four strokes, including two 'dots' in the upper left. Following simplification, one of the dots was removed.

Other characters were altered by replacing a complicated portion of the character with a simpler, common element that was similar in appearance. This was done to the character meaning 'to count':

The modern form of this character, prior to simplification, is on the left. The entire left-hand side of this character is used as a component in this and several other characters, but its original meaning is not clear. The bottommost portion of that left-hand side is clearly a 'woman' element, but there are various theories as to what the component as a whole depicts, including: a woman with her hair decorated and piled high on her head, a woman who is isolated from others, or even a string of beads. Regardless of the original meaning, the parts located above the 'woman' element have been completely replaced by the element 米 in the modern simplified form (on the right). As a standalone character, this replacement element means 'rice' (in particular, grains of rice). It wasn't placed into this character for its meaning, though; it was used only because it (somewhat) visually resembled the parts it replaced, but was simpler to write.

Another way that some characters were simplified was by replacing all or part of them with strokes derived from their 'cursive' form. **Cursive script** is another old way of writing the characters, in which the writing brush is moved rapidly as a character is drawn, and only a few simple strokes are made to very roughly approximate the overall form of the character. Characters written in the cursive style only vaguely resemble their standard form and are very difficult to read without special training.

The following character was completely replaced by its 'cursive' version:

Oracle Bone	Regular Traditional	Cursive	Regular Simplified
𦥑 →	盡 →	𠱃 →	尽

The character now has meanings such as 'to exhaust,' 'to use up,' and 'to accomplish completely.' From earlier forms of the character, it's clear that it originally depicted a hand holding a brush, inserted into a bowl. The character may have been designed as an ideograph, perhaps depicting the cleaning of an empty bowl following a meal, to suggest the meaning 'used up' or 'completed.'

The regular script form of the character before simplification (the second character above) depicted the same three elements as the earliest form: a hand (top) holding a brush (middle plus top vertical stroke) held above a bowl (bottom). The regular script simplified form (on the far right) was derived from the 'cursive' style of writing the character (the third character). With that form, none of the individual elements can be recognized; only the very rough overall appearance of the character remains.

Yet another kind of simplification involved replacing the phonetic component of a character with a different phonetic component that was simpler to write, but still had the same (or a similar) reading. The character meaning 'transmit' / 'communicate' was simplified this way:

傳 → 伝

The right-hand side of each version of the character above is the phonetic component. The two phonetics are read similarly. The one on the right, which is much simpler to write, was used as a replacement for the one on the left. This particular simplification was also very practical, as the new phonetic (which, as we have seen, as a standalone character now means 'say') helps with remembering the character meaning; with the simplified form above, the two elements ('person' and 'say') give a strong hint of the character meaning ('transmit' / 'communicate').

Sometimes, rather than just a few strokes, an entire portion was removed, noticeably changing the look of the character.

In the case of the following character, meaning 'group':

團 → 団

the upper part of the component inside the outer enclosure was removed, leaving only the 寸 element. That entire inner component had been the character's phonetic, so this simplification resulted in a loss of the phonetic hint of the character reading.

Finally, some characters were simplified by replacing them in their entirety with a completely different character, simpler in form. This was done with the character meaning 'body':

體 → 体

On the left is the original form of the 'body' character. Because it is especially complicated, even hundreds of years ago alternate, simpler informal ways of writing it were used, one of the most popular of which was the character on the right above, consisting of the elements 'person' and 'root.' It was favored because it had few strokes and elegantly represented the meaning 'body' in an ideographic way: 'the root of a person is the body.' When the common use characters were established in Japan, this shorthand form became the official form.[13]

Another character simplified in the same way is one meaning 'beach.' The original character and its replacement are shown below. The original character (on the left) was rather complicated in form. It was replaced with a simpler substitute (on the right), a previously rarely-used character originally meaning 'creek':

濱 → 浜

Now, the word 'beach' is always written with the simpler character on the right. However, some people and place names still use the older version on the left (or another slightly different character). As was done with the 'body' character, the *on* reading of the simpler character was changed to fit the new role: in this case from *HYŌ* to *HIN*, resulting in its phonetic component (on the right-hand side) no longer having a phonetic role.

In Japan, the kinds of character simplifications described over the last few pages were officially applied to characters at the time of their inclusion on the *jōyō kanji* list. However, characters not on the *jōyō* list were left unchanged. (This was done because the intention was that characters not on the common use list would become limited in usage.) So, for example, characters not on the *jōyō* list that contain the 'movement' determinative (辶) will still have two short strokes in the upper left, instead of one, in their official standard forms. This has resulted in inconsistencies between characters on and characters not on the *jōyō* list.

---

[13] The character on the right was already in existence before the replacement, having a different meaning and reading. (The original meaning is no longer known with certainty.) The right-hand component (本) had been the character's phonetic, but when the character was borrowed to be the substitute character for 'body,' its reading was replaced with the reading of the 'body' character, thus ending the phonetic role.

Roughly 25% of characters underwent some kind of modification upon being incorporated into the common use list. In Appendix G, these modifications are described in detail.

Because these simplified characters only became the official forms relatively recently, the previous forms of some of these characters (in use just prior to simplification) are still sometimes encountered. For example, some of them are still in use in people and place names, where the simplified characters were not always adopted.

Because they are much less commonly encountered, though, it is not necessary to memorize these older forms at the time you first learn the characters. Educated readers are expected to be able to recognize and read some of those older versions, but this can come later in your studying once you've already achieved familiarity with the more common standard forms. Note that learning the older forms is not as difficult as it may seem. If you have already learned the standard, simplified form, you do not have to memorize new readings and meanings; you only have to recognize that the older form is an equivalent character to the standard form version, and therefore shares its readings and meanings.

These older forms can now be thought of as variant versions of the standard characters. A **variant character** is an alternate way to write a character which has the exact same meaning(s), reading(s) and usage as the standard version. So two characters that are variants of each other can be treated as the exact same character that just happen to be written differently. Variant characters are discussed further in Chapter 6, and examples of various types are shown in Appendix G.

2.12 Character Substitution

Earlier in the chapter, we learned several ways in which character meanings have changed and expanded. Yet another way, which has taken place both long ago and in comparatively recent times, as well, is through **character substitution**, in which one character takes over one, several, or all of the roles of another character, replacing it in those contexts. We already saw one type of character substitution in the previous section, in the case of characters meaning 'body' (體 and 体) and 'beach' (濱 and 浜). In both of these cases, the character with the simpler form completely took over the roles of the character with the complex form. Essentially, the simpler character was substituted for the complex one. This section looks at two other kinds of character substitution which have occurred with the characters.

Replacement of Taboo Characters

In ancient times in China, certain characters were sometimes designated as taboo—forbidden to be used in writing. This most commonly happened when a given character made up part of the name of the current ruler. Some rulers did not want the characters in their name to be written—no matter the context. And so it became necessary to find alternate ways to write words that used the taboo characters, generally by choosing a different character to act as a substitute.

Usually, after a ruler was no longer in power, the characters that had been declared taboo could then be used again. In some cases, though, the alternate ways of writing to avoid a taboo character had already become popular, and some substitutions became permanent.

CHARACTER DESIGN AND HISTORY

Such a permanent substitution occurred with a character meaning 'crime.' In this case, the character didn't appear in the ruler's name, but merely resembled a character that did.

The original form of the character meaning 'crime' was:

Emperor Qin Shi Huangdi (who ruled in China circa 200 BC) felt the character, with such a negative meaning, too closely resembled one of the characters in the title he gave himself (皇), and so ordered it replaced. It was replaced with:

This substitute character originally identified a type of container for catching fish, and was a D-P character. The upper part was the determinative: a net, indicating that the character had to do with nets or catching things. The lower component of this character was the phonetic.

It is not known why this particular character was chosen as the substitute, but it is known that when the character was reassigned to mean 'crime,' it was given a completely new reading, to match the reading of the character it replaced. As a result, the phonetic component in this character no longer served a phonetic role.

Even after the emperor was no longer in power, the substitute character continued to be used with the meaning 'crime,' and its old meaning was abandoned. Even to this day, the character meaning is 'crime.'

Consolidation: Reduction of Total Number of Characters

One goal of designating a set of common use characters in Japan was to keep to a minimum the number of characters used in writing aimed at the general public. Once the *jōyō kanji* were established, words using characters outside of that set were intended to be written using hiragana. But reading Japanese can sometimes be easier when kanji are used, and so shortly after the establishment of the *jōyō kanji*, a method was devised to allow more words to be written using kanji without adding additional characters to the *jōyō* list. Specifically, the ways of writing some words with kanji were revised, replacing non-*jōyō* characters with *jōyō* characters.

This change resulted in a kind of character consolidation, as some characters were phased out of use after their roles were taken over by other characters. One example of this consolidation was the replacement of the character on the left below by the character on the right:

諳 → 暗

The character on the left means 'to memorize' / 'to remember off the top of one's head.' The original meaning of the character on the right is 'dark' / 'dim.' Both characters have the same phonetic component (located on the right-hand side), and both are read with the *on* reading AN. However, only the character on the right was chosen as a *jōyō kanji*.

The two characters were consolidated by using the character on the right as a replacement for the one on the left in compound words which contained it. For example, the word *anki* ('memorization') was formerly written as 諳記, but is now written as 暗記.

This resulted in an extension of meaning of the character on the right: in addition to 'dark' / 'dim,' it now also means 'to memorize.' It has taken over the role once served by the character on the left. And the character on the left has been phased out of usage in Japan.

Numerous other characters were purged in this same way, with other more common characters chosen as substitutes. The character chosen as the substitute always had the same *on* reading as the character it was replacing. It often, but not always, had the same phonetic component, as well, as is true of the characters 暗 and 諳. This type of character substitution is known in Japanese as **kakikae**, meaning 'changed writing.'

In a limited number of cases, both versions of a compound word (the original version and the version using a substitute character) are still in use today. For example, the word *shōgai* ('obstacle; impediment; disability') can be seen written today in two different ways:

障碍   障害

The version on the left was the way the compound word was written prior to character consolidation, with a non-*jōyō* character in the second position. The version on the right was the way the compound appeared after consolidation, with a *jōyō* character substituted.

At some point, the newer form of the compound became controversial among advocates for disabled people, as its second character (meaning 'injury' / 'harm' / 'damage') is seen as having a negative connotation, and therefore not appropriate for describing people with disabilities. The second character of the first compound (meaning 'interfere' / 'obstruct') is less objectionable, and therefore this way of writing the compound, even though it involves a non-*jōyō* character, is preferred by some people.[14]

Another word which can be seen today written in two different ways is *kirei* ('pretty; clean'):

綺麗   奇麗

The version on the left is the original form. The character in the first position was not selected as a *jōyō* kanji, though, and so the word was rewritten as shown on the right, with a *jōyō* character substituted in the first position. The *jōyō* character chosen for replacement is identical to the phonetic component (on the right-hand side) of the character which was replaced. Because the meaning of the substitute *jōyō* character ('strange; uncommon; peculiar') is not a good match with the word *kirei*, the version on the left has retained popularity, and is actually encountered more often than the version on the right, despite the fact that it uses a non-*jōyō* character.

Compounds such as the previous ones, which can be written in two different ways, are the exception. Most characters that have been replaced via consolidation are very rarely encountered anymore.

---

[14] Some people instead choose to write the compound as 障がい, avoiding both the use of an objectionable character and the use of a character not on the *jōyō* list.

The Effects of Character Transformation and Substitution

We have already learned that character forms do not always have a direct relationship with the character meaning, due to processes such as meaning shift and phonetic borrowing. Transformation of character forms and character substitution have further compounded this disparity. As a result of character substitution and some methods of character transformation, the modern forms of characters (including the individual elements that they consist of) are often no longer the same as they were when the characters were originally designed. Those changes, combined with character meaning changes that have also taken place, have resulted in many characters for which the specific elements which appear in them no longer have a connection to the character meaning.

This may make learning the characters seem very difficult. But it is actually not as difficult as it may seem. When you learn a character, it is not necessary to learn all of its earlier forms, only the modern standard form. For some pictographic and ideographic characters, the relationships between form and meaning still hold. Furthermore, many characters are of the D-P type, and contain a determinative that can still be related to the character meaning, and a phonetic component that can still be used to learn the character *on* reading. And characters that have changed too much from their original form and meaning can still be learned with repetition, associating the character, with whatever form it may take today, with the meanings it represents and the readings it goes by. In the next chapter, we will study techniques for learning the characters.

2.13 *Kokuji* – 'Made in Japan' Characters

In addition to adopting the Chinese characters, the Japanese also created some original characters of their own. These characters are known as **kokuji**, which can be roughly translated as 'Japan's own characters.'

As previously explained, kanji from China were applied to words of Japanese origin based on similarity of meaning. *Kokuji* can be thought of basically as having been created to represent already-existing Japanese words for which no suitable equivalent Chinese kanji could be found. Accordingly, most of these characters have very specific meanings, such as a specific kind of fish found in Japanese waters, or a specific man-made object with no equivalent in China. A few of the *kokuji* do have more general meanings, though. A number of the characters continue to be used in people and place names, as well.

Kokuji were created using the same principles that were used to create the characters in China, including both ideographic and determinative-phonetic principles. With kokuji, though, ideographic principles tended to be favored. As they were created to write Japanese words, most of these characters have only a *kun* reading, although some were also given an *on* reading. Interestingly, a few of these characters were subsequently introduced back into China.

In excess of a thousand kokuji have been made, but only a limited number of them are regularly used today; most are unknown to the average Japanese person today. In fact, only a small percentage of them have been assigned codes such that they can be readily represented in computer-based information processing. Ten of the characters are included on the *jōyō kanji* list, and two of those are also among the *kyōiku kanji* (characters taught during the six years of elementary school). Appendix H lists some of the most commonly encountered kokuji, including all of the ones that are on the *jōyō and kyōiku kanji* lists.

2.14 Side Note: Comparison with the Latin Alphabet

At the beginning of the chapter, it was mentioned that the Latin alphabet had gone through numerous changes in reaching its modern state. Interestingly, the origins of both the Chinese characters and the modern Latin alphabet are very similar.

The Latin alphabet grew out of earlier alphabets that can be traced back to the Middle East. The earliest of these, in turn, was heavily influenced by Egyptian hieroglyphs. Hieroglyphs are much like kanji in that there are thousands of characters, many of which were originally symbols designed to look like recognizable objects—in other words: pictographs. But a subset of hieroglyphs were used only for their sound (i.e., the sound of the word represented by the pictured image), and the meaning of the pictured image was ignored. In other words, they were used purely as phonetics. This 'phonetic only' usage was adopted by the earliest ancestor to the Latin alphabet. That early alphabet consisted of pictographic characters (including, apparently, borrowed hieroglyphs), but the images in the pictographs were only used as a prompt to produce a given sound, and the meaning was ignored. The entire alphabet consisted essentially of one pictograph for each different sound that could be produced in the language that used it.

Later alphabets that evolved from this ancestor then simplified the pictographic images into a few lines, losing the connection with the original images. But you can still see some of these images today. For example, the character now used as a capital 'A' was originally a graphical representation of the head of an ox, which can be recognized if the letter is looked at upside-down.

The point here is that the Latin alphabet can trace its origins to a writing system similar to kanji, but evolved in a different way to end up where it is today.

2.15 Chapter Summary

Kanji were originally constructed using several different design principles. The simplest of these is **pictographic**, wherein the object depicted is identical to the character meaning. With **ideographic** characters, the object or objects depicted do not literally display the character meaning, but instead indirectly suggest it. One type of ideographic character, an **indicative** character, uses line segments to help indicate the character meaning, such as by marking one particular part of an object.

Characters designed with the **determinative-phonetic (D-P)** principle consist of two parts: a **determinative**, usually a simple element, that identifies the broad category of meaning that the character can be grouped in, and a **phonetic**, which provides an indicator of the *on* reading of the character. Different characters containing the same phonetic component are not always read the same way, but the readings are usually similar, having a correspondence between them. Such readings are called **related readings** in this book. The reading of the phonetic of a character has no bearing on the character's *kun* reading.

Over 90% of all characters ever made are of the D-P type. This means that the characters as a whole are primarily phonetic in design. Generally, in D-P characters the determinative is a much more reliable indicator of character meaning than is the phonetic. Often the phonetic component was chosen primarily as a sound aid, although some phonetics also contribute to the character meaning.

Many characters have taken on **extended meanings** in addition to their original meanings. One way this was done was by **phonetic borrowing**: the borrowing of characters for their sound to represent additional words having the same or similar sound. Today, many characters still represent multiple meanings, and sometimes the various meanings of a character do not have a clear relationship to each other. Some characters have undergone a **meaning shift**, whereby the original meaning is no longer represented by the character, and an extended meaning has become the new principal meaning.

The way of writing the characters transitioned through several distinct styles: **oracle bone script**, **bronze script**, **seal script**, **clerical script**, and **regular script**, with the look of the characters changing each step of the way. As a result of these transformations, many character elements that were originally pictographic are no longer recognizable. Some characters also have been simplified, such as by removal of strokes or substitution of simpler components, in order to reduce writing complexity, and other characters have been replaced via **character substitution**, with their roles being taken over by another similar character. Because of meaning extension and shifting, as well as form transformation and character substitution, it is not unusual for the form of a character to no longer directly relate to its meaning.

Sometimes two different forms of the same character can still be encountered. In most such cases, one form is considered the official form, and the other is considered to be a **variant character**.

In addition to importing the characters from China, the Japanese also created some characters of their own, referred to as *kokuji*. Only a limited number of these characters are still commonly used.

Chapter 3

Learning the Characters

Learning the characters is inevitably a long, time-consuming process. Before embarking on such an endeavor, it is useful to have an idea of what the learning process involves. Thus, in this chapter, we'll take a look at the issues pertaining to learning the characters, including what to expect and the challenges of learning such a large number of characters. We'll also look at some learning strategies, including this book's recommended approach.

3.1 Myths and Misconceptions

There are a number of common myths or misconceptions some people have regarding kanji. In this section, we'll examine a few of these myths, and learn the truth about them. Some of these myths should have already been dispelled after reading the first two chapters of this book, but are still included here to emphasize key points you should understand well.

Myth #1: Kanji are pictographs: each character is a picture of the thing it represents.

Reality: Only a very small fraction of the characters in use today can be said to be pictographic. The majority were developed by other methods, as described in Chapter 2. Furthermore, because the forms, or way of writing the characters, have evolved over thousands of years, even among the relatively few truly pictographic characters it is often difficult or impossible when looking at the modern form to see the object originally depicted.

And precisely what was intended by many of the pictographic objects found in characters has been lost to time, and is now unknown.

Myth #2: The meaning of each character is based on combining the meanings of each piece part that makes up the character.

Reality: There are a few characters that were designed in this way, but as discussed in the last chapter, most characters are actually determinative-phonetic: one part of the character is used to indicate the general category of meaning of the character, and the remaining part of the character is used primarily to indicate the pronunciation of the character.

The characters were created to represent spoken words, and the vast majority of these characters were designed with that in mind, with some piece parts included not so much for meaning, but to indicate pronunciation. Many characters take the form they do because of the spoken sounds of the Chinese language at the time of character creation.

Because the phonetic aspects of the characters were ignored when they were applied to the writing of Japanese words, the fact that the characters are overwhelmingly phonetic in design is sometimes overlooked by speakers of Japanese, which helps to perpetuate this myth.

Myth #3: Kanji are a carefully designed, elegant set of characters, with each character specifically chosen to represent a concept. There is a deep philosophy embedded in the characters.

Reality: One facet of kanji that makes them attractive to many people is the sense that they are not just a tool for writing, but that the characters have profound philosophical underpinnings. Although that aspect of the characters can be found, it was not a significant factor in character construction.

Furthermore, the characters were designed gradually, over upwards of one thousand years by different groups of people using varying design methodologies. The modern character set evolved haphazardly, and some characters look the way they do today because of reasons such as transcription mistakes that occurred long ago, or the shifting of a character's meaning as the original meaning became obsolete. There are many inconsistencies among the characters, not by design, but rather because of the use, and modification, of the character set by many different people over a long period of time.

Myth #4: Each character has one unique meaning.

Reality: The characters have been in use over an extremely long period of time, and during that time many of them have come to represent more than one meaning. Such characters may have one meaning when appearing within one word, but a completely different meaning when appearing in another word. And often the different possible meanings of a single character are not that similar to each other.

Myth #5: Native users of kanji know the etymology (derivation / origin) of each character.

Reality: This is completely untrue. Although every character was designed with a specific reason in mind, for many characters those origins are no longer known with certainty—that information has been lost to time. But even if the true etymology could be known, it would not always be relevant, as the meanings of many characters have changed since they were first created, and even the elements that they are made of have often been either changed or distorted beyond recognition.

Japanese people sometimes use stories of character origins (either stories that are generally accepted as credible, or popularly spread yet clearly false stories) to remember some characters, but they learn most characters using rote memorization.

While it is true that, unlike the letters of the English alphabet, kanji do include elements that can be used to help remember character meanings, when Japanese people learn characters, they treat them largely as symbols, albeit very complicated symbols. They associate meanings and sounds with these symbols to assist in decoding the words they read.

Myth #6: Chinese and Japanese use the same character set. If I can read Japanese, I can also read Chinese.

Reality: Although the characters used to write the Japanese language have their origin in China, the character set used in Japan has diverged from the set used in China. For instance, the forms of many Japanese characters were altered or simplified following the end of World War II, and many of these modified characters no longer resemble those used in China. The characters used in mainland China also underwent a separate, even larger-scale reform shortly after the Japanese reform, creating even more differences. There are also many cases where different characters are used for the same words. For example, 'I,' 'you,' and 'mother' are each written with different characters in Japan and China.

Furthermore, the Japanese and Chinese do not use the same characters with the same frequency. There are numerous characters that are frequently used in one language, but hardly at all in the other. And there are many compound words (words containing two or more characters) that are common in one language but not used at all in the other. And finally, when comparing modern Chinese and modern Japanese, many characters have different meanings. Sometimes the difference is only slight, but sometimes it is significant. A Japanese person who has not studied Chinese might be able to look at Chinese text and, at best, understand the gist of what is written, but cannot read Chinese.

Myth #7: I have to know two or three thousand kanji to be able to read Japanese.

Reality: Different characters vary in terms of frequency of usage. Some are seen every day, some very infrequently or not at all, and others somewhere in between. Knowing infrequently encountered characters is not essential to beginning literacy in Japanese.

Consider this: if you are a beginning or intermediate English language learner, do you need to know words such as 'antediluvian' or 'ersatz'? Words such as this are encountered infrequently when reading, and beginning and intermediate English learners are unlikely to encounter them at all. For such students, it's not practical to study these words until other basic aspects of English have been mastered. And if they do happen to encounter those words, they can simply look them up in a dictionary at that time.

Analogous to this, when you are a beginning or intermediate Japanese language learner, there are many characters that are unlikely to be encountered at all. Such characters are only used in higher-level words, words that are rarely encountered, or words that are most commonly written in hiragana or katakana rather than kanji.

Trying to study and memorize 2000 or 3000 characters while your Japanese ability is only at a beginning or intermediate level is not practical, because you are not likely to encounter many of those characters in typical writing, and so it will be difficult to accurately remember the rarer ones; they will need to be studied again later. Mastering kanji requires repetition, and it is difficult to get a sufficient amount of repetition from rarely-encountered characters.

Learning just the *kyōiku kanji* (the first 1006 characters taught to Japanese elementary school children) and common words using these characters will take you a long way toward Japanese literacy. You won't be able to read everything, but you will be able to read some of what you encounter. After that, learning the rest of the *jōyō kanji* then gets you even further, enabling you to read most (but not all) of what you encounter.

Myth #8: If I learn all the kanji, I have learned much of the Japanese language.

Reality: First of all, 'learning all the kanji' is not a practical possibility. There are many very infrequently encountered characters, and even Japanese people encounter unfamiliar characters from time to time. Even for someone with a good memory, it is difficult to remember characters that are rarely encountered. Learning requires reinforcement, which, as already mentioned, is difficult to get with rarely-encountered characters.

But even so, kanji are just one piece of the Japanese language. There are also many words, phrases, and expressions that are not even customarily written using kanji. Plus, there are many compound words (words containing two or more kanji) whose meanings cannot be simply deduced by just being familiar with the individual characters in them.

Certainly, learning kanji gets you further toward learning Japanese than learning the alphabet gets you toward learning English, but much more than just the characters must be learned to gain proficiency in the Japanese language.

3.2 What to Expect

It is helpful when starting to learn the characters to have some idea of what to expect as you learn. This section describes expectations you should be aware of and keep in mind as you learn the characters.

A. As described in the last section, characters are used with very differing frequencies. Some are encountered often as part of many different words, while others are seen only occasionally, and even others are seen very infrequently. (And, as mentioned in Chapter 1, there are tens of thousands of characters that will never be encountered in a lifetime.) Frequently seen characters are easier to learn because they are reinforced through repetition. Because learning is dependent upon repetition—and this is especially true when it comes to kanji—it is advantageous to study the most frequently seen characters first, and save the study of rarer characters for later when you have become more experienced at learning characters, and have developed kanji study methods that work for you.

B. In addition to varying frequencies of usage, there are also different patterns of usage among the different characters. For example, some characters are used in the writing of many different frequently encountered compound words. Others, when encountered, are almost always part of the same one or two compound words, and rarely encountered in any other context. Others are almost exclusively used by themselves or with trailing okurigana, but rarely as part of any compound word.

C. All readers of Japanese, including Japanese adults, will from time to time encounter characters that are unfamiliar. This is normal. It is similar to encountering unfamiliar English words. And, just like with unfamiliar English words, these characters can be looked up in a dictionary at the time they are encountered.

D. Even when you have been familiar with a particular character for a long time, you will still probably encounter words using it that you have not seen before. As you first learn a character, it is not necessary (nor practical) at that time to learn every compound word that uses that character. Learning just a few of the most common ones is sufficient. You can learn less commonly encountered compounds at a later time, after you've already achieved a strong familiarity with the character.

E. It's quite common to recognize and confidently know a character that you have become used to seeing in certain common contexts, but then when seeing it in a different context (perhaps even with a different meaning or different reading) not even realize that it is the same character, or even feel as if it is an unfamiliar character you have not seen before. This can be discouraging, but with experience won't happen so often, as you learn to recognize characters and distinguish them from each other.

F. Many characters closely resemble other characters, sometimes with only one or two slight differences between them. To be able to master kanji, you will have to become skilled at noticing small differences so that you can tell similar characters apart from each other. Part of the process of learning kanji—in addition to learning readings and meanings—is to learn how to confidently recognize characters and distinguish similar characters from each other. To be able to do this well requires a large amount of practice and repetition. Comparing similar characters side-by-side is helpful.

G. Most characters consist of a number of distinct elements. Some of these elements are very common and you will see them again and again in many different characters. For such elements, it is useful to give them a name or some kind of identifier. It's easier to remember something when it has a name. Any kind of name is fine, even if it's not etymologically accurate, if it helps you to remember.

H. Character elements with the same form do not always have the same meaning. In other words, when you see a particular element within a character, there is no guarantee that it will have the same meaning as that same element does in other characters. One reason for this is that as the forms of the characters were altered and simplified over hundreds of years, sometimes different but similar-looking elements merged in shape and now appear identical.

I. The first time you see a new character, you will typically try to take it in as a whole: to view the character as one whole object. Over time, you will learn to break it into components as you look at it and decipher it. Interestingly, as you completely master the character, you will once again be able to see it as a whole. This takes lots of repetition and practice, though. When trying to gain familiarity with a particular character, it is often useful to mentally break it apart into the elements that make it up.

J. Being able to write the characters is significantly harder than being able to read them. It is not unusual to be able to instantly recognize a character upon seeing it, but not be able to write it from memory just a few minutes later. For most Japanese people, the number of characters that they can read, in context, is considerably greater than the number of characters they can write from memory without a mistake.

It's not necessary to learn how to write the characters to be able to read them, but an advantage of learning to write is it helps build recognition skills: the ability to look at a character, confidently know what it is, and be able to tell it apart from other similar characters. For people who only read but never write the characters, it is harder to do this.

K. To be able to read, it is not enough just to learn individual characters. As mentioned in Chapter 1, you must also learn compounds: words that contain more than one character. Just as with the characters themselves, learning compounds requires practice and repetition, and frequently seen compounds are easier to learn than those rarely encountered.

L. Determining the correct way to read a character, by itself or in a compound word, can be complicated, and there are numerous exceptions and inconsistencies. This can be frustrating. The best approach to doing this is to focus on learning the most common readings first, and treat others as exceptions. The exceptions can be learned gradually over time as needed.

M. Furigana—small characters sometimes placed near kanji to indicate the proper reading—can hinder the development of reading ability. Although furigana is certainly helpful because it provides the correct readings, you should avoid relying on it too much. Being forced to figure out readings, without having furigana to rely on, is important for learning.

N. There are many words that *can* be written with kanji, but customarily are not, usually being written instead with either hiragana or katakana. There are not fixed rules for how such words are written, though, so they may be seen written in multiple, different ways. (This topic is discussed in detail in Chapter 5, Section 5.1.)

3.3 Why Learning the Characters is Challenging

Without question, mastering kanji is a significant challenge. In this section, we look at the main factors that make it so challenging. This section is not meant to discourage those learning kanji, but instead to make sure they appreciate the challenges associated with mastering the characters, and are aware of strategies for overcoming them.

A. Character Form Similarities

Many characters closely resemble others, and can easily be confused with others. This is probably the single hardest aspect of learning the characters. There are only so many different ways to draw characters using a set of lines; when a writing system includes thousands of characters, there are inevitably going to be ones that resemble each other.

LEARNING THE CHARACTERS

For example, there is a character that looks very similar to one of our first five characters—the one meaning 'ground' / 'earth.' The only difference is that in the 'ground' character the bottom horizontal stroke is longer than the middle horizontal stroke. In the other character, meaning 'gentleman' (or 'samurai'), it is the opposite: the upper stroke is the longer of the two. Both characters are shown here, with the 'ground' character on the left:

土　　士

Following are some more pairs or groups of characters which bear a strong resemblance to each other. Look at each set and make sure you can identify the differences. Being able to differentiate characters such as these is a necessary skill when reading Japanese.[1]

未末　　人入　　矢失　　午牛　　各名
圧庄†　西酉†　鳥烏†　巨臣　　文交
受愛　　拾捨　　追迫　　廷延　　村材
輸輪　　統銃　　熱熟　　九丸　　減滅
力刀刃　学字宇　了子予矛　日目白自

To someone looking at these sets of characters for the first time, it must seem like it would be very difficult to distinguish between similar characters when reading. One key to doing so is repetition; after seeing a character many times, you learn how to recognize it confidently. It is also very helpful to compare similar characters side-by-side. That way, you know which parts to pay attention to in order to distinguish the characters. Even simply being aware that two similar-looking characters both exist helps you to remember them and distinguish them from each other.[2]

One factor that helps in distinguishing similar characters from each other is knowing in which contexts they are usually seen. For any two characters which resemble each other, the compounds that each character is most often seen in—i.e., the other characters they are most commonly paired with to form words—are often different from each other. Knowing which compounds are common for each character helps in distinguishing the characters from each other.

Similar characters are harder to distinguish when they are encountered in the same kinds of circumstances. For example, the following two similar characters are both often seen by themselves as single-character words:

緑　　縁

---

[1] All characters shown here are among the *jōyō kanji*, except for those marked with the † symbol, which, although not *jōyō kanji*, are nonetheless encountered fairly frequently. These characters are included on the *jinmeiyō kanji* list: a list of characters acceptable for personal name use, described in Chapter 4.

[2] In the phonetic listings in Part 2, similar-looking phonetics are placed close together to assist with distinguishing them, and the characters which contain them, from each other.

The first character by itself is read as *midori* and means 'green.' The second character by itself can be read as *EN* or *yukari*, meaning 'link' / 'tie,' but can also be read as *fuchi* or *heri*, meaning 'edge' / 'rim.' The correct reading and meaning must be determined from the context.

Because both characters frequently appear as single-character words, they can be especially hard to differentiate. But by knowing that both exist, you learn to pay attention to the only part that differs between them—the lower right—and use that to tell them apart.

Similarly, the following two similar characters are both often seen with the hiragana characters *e-ru* attached as okurigana, as shown here:

教える　　　数える

The first word above is read as *oshieru*, and means 'to teach.' The second is read as *kazoeru*, and means 'to count.' Just as with the characters 緑 and 縁, simply being aware that each of these similar words exists helps you to be able to distinguish them.

Each kanji learner is different. You will probably find that the characters you often confuse with each other are different than those of others. It's useful to try to recognize which pairs of characters cause you the most confusion, and then study them together so that the differences are clear.

B. Multiple Character Meanings

As described in detail in Chapter 2, many characters have acquired multiple meanings. For some such characters, the different meanings are similar to each other, and so it is not too difficult to remember them together, and even possibly to come up with a single, broad meaning for the character that covers all of its different meanings. For other characters, though, the various meanings are so dissimilar that it is simply not possible to come up with one single universal meaning that accurately defines the character in all contexts in which it is used. Each meaning must be memorized separately.

In Chapter 2, for example, we learned that the character 足 can mean any of 'foot' / 'leg' or 'to be sufficient' or 'to add'—all very different meanings. In the following two compounds, which both use this character, the character reading is the same in each word (*SOKU*), but the meaning is different:

Compound	Compound Reading	足 Meaning	Meaning of Other Character	Compound Meaning
土足	ドソク (*dosoku*)	foot / leg	dirt (or mud, etc.)	feet with shoes on; muddy or dirty feet
不足	フソク (*fusoku*)	to be sufficient	not	shortage

When learning a character such as this, it is necessary to learn each of the character's meanings separately, and be aware that in newly-encountered words containing the character, any one of those meanings could apply.[3] This adds an extra challenge to learning the characters. To help in remembering each of the meanings, it is often best when first learning a character to learn at least one common word for each meaning of the character.

C. Multiple Character Readings

Just as character meanings vary, character readings do as well.

In Chapter 1, we saw the following table, showing three different readings of the 'fire' character (火):

Word	Reading of Word	Meaning of Word	Reading of 火
火	hi (ひ)	fire	hi (ひ)
花火	hanabi (はなび)	fireworks	bi (び)
火山	kazan (かざん)	volcano	ka (か)

The first two of these readings are both *kun* readings, and the third is an *on* reading. The two *kun* readings are different from each other because of a phenomenon called *rendaku*, in which the starting sound of a word sometimes changes when it is used as the second or later part of a compound word. In the case of *hanabi*, the *hi* sound changes to *bi* because of *rendaku*. *Rendaku* is described in detail in Chapter 9.

There are even some words in which the characters are read in special ways, not even using any of the character *on* or *kun* readings. For example, the 'fire' character can be seen in the compound word *yakedo*, meaning 'burn' (as in a burn injury to the body). This word is usually written using hiragana (やけど), but can be written in kanji as 火傷. Although the 'fire' character appears in this compound, none of its *on* or *kun* readings contribute to the reading of the compound word. That's because the characters in this word are used only for their meanings. This type of word reading, referred to as *jukujikun*, is discussed in Chapter 5.

Another complicating factor is that there are many characters with multiple *on* readings or multiple *kun* readings. Having to deal with all of these various possible character readings certainly complicates the reading of Japanese. Again, practice and repetition are important. Also helpful is being familiar with the typical formats of words read with *on* and *kun* readings. Many aspects of *on* readings are discussed in Chapter 7, and *kun* readings in Chapter 8.

D. Homophones

The native spoken Japanese language is made up of a relatively limited number of different basic sounds. As a result, there are a large number of **homophones**: words which have the same pronunciation as each other but differ in meaning. A couple of well-known examples of native Japanese homophones are *ame*, which means both 'rain' and 'candy,' and *hashi*, which can mean any of 'bridge,' 'edge,' or 'chopsticks.'[4]

---

[3] Of course, if one of a character's meanings is rare and only used in uncommon words, it can be learned and memorized later, after the character itself and its common meanings have already been mastered.

[4] Some of the sets of words presented in this section are not true homophones because there are slight pitch accent differences between them. Pitch accent can differ by region within Japan. It is not discussed in this book. Because they are written identically in hiragana, the sets of words presented here could also be considered to be *homonyms* (words both pronounced and written the same, but differing in meaning). Because they are written differently in kanji, though, it is most accurate to call these words *homophones*.

Some pairs or groups of homophones originated from the same, single word. In these cases, the original word had a broad range of meanings, and when kanji were assigned to it, different kanji were applied to the major different meanings of the word. This caused what was once a single word to be split into multiple, different words.

Tsutomeru is one such word. Its general, broad meaning is 'to work at,' but it is divided into three different words, each written with a different kanji and each having a different specific meaning:

Word	Reading	Meaning
努める	つとめる	try; endeavor to do
務める	つとめる	serve; act as
勤める	つとめる	work (in an occupation)

There are many such *kun*-based homophone word groups.

There are also a very large number of homophones among compound words read with *on* readings. One such word is *kanji* itself, which, in addition to 'Chinese character,' can also mean 'event organizer' and at least ten other words, each written with a different pair of characters.

Not all of these different *kanji* are common, everyday words. Nonetheless, there are many pairs or groups of *on* compound homophones which are common words. For example, there are four different commonplace words which are each read as *kōen*:

Word	Reading	Meaning
公園	コウエン	a park, public garden
講演	コウエン	a lecture, speech
公演	コウエン	a public performance (such as of music)
後援	コウエン	support, sponsorship, patronage

Such *on*-based homophones result from the limited number of different character *on* readings in the Japanese language. *On*-based homophones are discussed in more detail in Chapter 7 (Section 7.13).

Homophones, especially ones similar in meaning to each other such as the various forms of *tsutomeru* above, can be challenging to learn how to read and write. Learning such pairs or groups of words together helps you to be able to distinguish them from each other.

E. Different Ways of Writing Words

In Chapter 5, we will see that any given word is not always written in one particular way. A word that can be written with kanji may be more frequently written with hiragana instead. The word *yakedo*, mentioned on the previous page, is an example of this. Also, the common word *koko* ('here') can be written in kanji like this: 此処, but it is far more common to see this word written in hiragana: ここ.

Repetition is critical for learning the characters. For words most commonly written without kanji, the kanji versions of the words are sometimes hard to recognize because of the lack of experience seeing them written that way.

3.4 Considering Character Etymology

As explained in Chapter 1, all characters have an *etymology*: an explanation of why they have the form that they have. Learning these etymologies (or, more accurately, generally accepted theories of these etymologies) is sometimes useful for remembering characters, but sometimes is of little use due to the fact that many of the characters have changed so much—both in form and in meaning—since they were first created, making the character origin no longer relevant. Even if you were somehow able to know the true etymologies of all the characters, you would still not know the modern meanings of many of them, making some of that knowledge of character etymology not particularly useful.

Let's look at a specific example. The following two characters, each shown in both an early form and the modern form, originally included the same component.

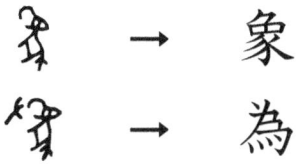

The top character means 'elephant' and was originally a pictograph of an elephant. The image of an elephant is no longer recognizable in the modern form. This character now also has a second meaning: 'shape' / 'figure,' which has nothing to do with elephants. (The different meanings must be learned individually.)

The bottom character above originally consisted of two elements: a hand and an elephant. It may have originally been an ideograph, indicating a person training or controlling an elephant. The precise original meaning is no longer known, but the modern meanings of this character include 'to do; to make,' 'to become; to attain,' and 'sake; benefit.' It can be used to write any of the native Japanese words *suru*, *naru*, and *tame*, but these words are all most commonly written using only hiragana. The character is more commonly seen in compound words, such as *kōi* (行為), meaning 'action' / 'conduct.'

As the forms of the two characters evolved (and the lower character became simplified), they diverged from each other to the point where there is no longer any resemblance between them.

Furthermore, there isn't even a reading similarity between the two characters; the *on* readings (*ZŌ* / *SHŌ* for the upper character, *I* for the lower one) are not at all related to each other.

In short, nothing about the modern form, meaning, or reading of the second character can be learned by knowing the character origin. Even if you go to the trouble of learning the original components that made up this character (i.e., a hand and an elephant), it is of virtually no help in recognizing the character from its modern form, or in remembering the character meaning if you do recognize it. This character has changed to the point where it has become only a symbol, and bears no relationship whatsoever to the character origin. When learning this character, it is best just to treat it as a symbol.

Unclear Origins

Looking back at their ancient forms, the images that were depicted in these previous two characters (象 and 為) can be identified by people today. But for many other characters, what was originally depicted is no longer certain. For example, the character:

要

originally meant 'waist.' Clearly, the element occupying the lower part of the modern form of the character is 'woman.' But what the upper part originally represented is unclear.

In ancient writing, this character appeared in several different forms. Each of these forms seemed to show two hands, one on each side of a person, but the specific action being depicted is no longer clear. One theory is that the hands were tying a sash around a woman's waist; another is that the hands were helping to deliver a child. The character was likely an ideograph, somehow indicating or suggesting a woman's waist, but even this is not certain.

But it doesn't matter. This character no longer means 'waist,' anyway.

Due to phonetic borrowing, the above character now means 'necessary.' And the original meaning of 'waist' is represented by a different character:

腰

which consists of the original character on the right-hand side together with a determinative indicating the meaning 'body part' added to the left-hand side.

With the character 要, even if we did know with certainty what was originally depicted, it is no longer relevant anyway, as the character meaning has completely changed. Like 為, this character has become nothing more than a symbol.

Fortunately, the above two characters (要 and 腰) share the same *on* reading (*YŌ*). Because of that, when learning these characters, the first character can be treated as the phonetic component of the second, which will assist with the memorization of both readings.

False Etymologies

For some characters, **false etymologies** have become widely known. These are explanations of character origins that are not grounded in serious research by character scholars, but rather have been created informally because they seem plausible, even though they are not actually true. Some false etymologies have become well known because they are simple explanations which make character meanings easy to remember.

When learning character meanings, if a particular etymology (whether based on serious character scholarship, or just a false etymology) is helpful for remembering the character meaning, then using it is certainly fine. But learning or attempting to learn the etymology of each character you study can add unnecessary complication to the learning of the characters. In this book, some character etymologies are provided, but only when they are particularly helpful for remembering characters, and not too complicated. This book avoids false etymologies.

3.5 Considering Character Meaning

To remember character meaning, some kanji learning materials recommend associating a single English word with each character. For characters that truly have only one precise meaning, this can certainly be useful. For characters with multiple, diverse meanings, though, this is usually not a good idea. To condense the various meanings of a character down to one single word is too much of a simplification and is likely to produce awkward interpretations of compounds that use the character.

With some characters, even ones that usually have the same single meaning in most compounds that use them, it is difficult to express the meaning with only a single English word. For characters such as this, rather than associate a rigid, single-word English definition with the character, it is better to develop a 'sense' of the character meaning.

As an example, consider the character:

The principal *on* reading of this character is *ZEN*. The modern meaning of this character is somewhat hard to define. Primarily, this character is used as the second character in two-character compound words, and provides the meaning 'having the nature of' or 'having the quality of' or 'in that fashion' in relation to the meaning of the first character of the compound. Basically, it reinforces the meaning of the first character, and also in some cases produces the adverb or adjective form of that character's meaning.[5]

For example, when combined with the character 全, meaning 'all,' it forms a word meaning 'entirely' (全然, *zenzen*). (This word is commonly used together with a negating word, to express 'not at all.') When combined with the character 突, meaning 'protruding,' it forms a word meaning 'suddenly' (突然, *totsuzen*). And when combined with the character 同, meaning 'the same,' it forms a word meaning 'equivalent to' (同然, *dōzen*).

Defining this character meaning in English is not a simple matter. Expressing it with only one English word, such as 'nature' or 'quality,' is too ambiguous. For a character like this, it is better to explain the meaning using a phrase, such as 'having the nature of,' together with a brief description of how the character is used, such as that just given.

As much as possible, it is recommended that character meanings are remembered using phrases or multiple words that give a sense of the meaning, rather than one single, rigid English word.

---

[5] The original meaning of this character was 'to burn,' but that meaning is now expressed with the character 燃 (the original character, with the fire element [火] added as a determinative to the left-hand side).

3.6 Breaking Down a Character

Often, when learning how to recognize and remember a character, it is helpful to mentally break the character into its constituent parts. Doing this makes it easier to remember how to read and write the character.

For example, the *jōyō* character:

$$想$$

which means 'thought' / 'idea,' can be separated into three distinct elements, having the meanings 'tree' (木), 'eye' (目), and 'heart' (心). Remembering this character as consisting of those three elements is easier than trying to memorize it as a single character of thirteen strokes.

Sometimes, though, characters should not be broken all the way down into their most basic individual elements. This is because in many characters there are groupings of several elements which function together as a unit. Most commonly, such element groups serve as the character phonetic. And often, those phonetics appear in not just one, but a number of different characters. For that kind of element group, it is best to treat it as a single component.

The above character contains one such element group. Specifically, the top two elements ('tree' and 'eye') together are the character phonetic. The character 想 was originally created not as a combination of three separate elements, but rather as a combination of the 'heart' element at the bottom and the phonetic element group at the top of the character.

This particular element group is also a standalone *jōyō* character:

$$相$$

This standalone character has several different meanings, including 'mutual,' 'appearance,' and 'government minister.' The character etymology is unclear. The two principal *on* readings of this character are *SŌ* and *SHŌ*. These readings are not connected with the readings of either element in the character, but rather are an original reading formed when the two elements are combined. (Interestingly, as full characters, the elements 'tree' and 'eye' each have the same pair of *on* readings: *BOKU* and *MOKU*.)

This character is also used as a phonetic component in two other *jōyō kanji*, meaning 'box' (as in a container) and 'frost,' respectively:

$$箱 \qquad 霜$$

These two characters, as well as 想, are all determinative-phonetic characters, with 相 as the phonetic, and the other element as the determinative. All three of these D-P characters have the same *on* reading: *SŌ*. For each of these characters, the determinative is the strongest indicator of character meaning, as is clear from the following table.

Character	Determinative (meaning)	Principal Character Readings	Character Meaning
想	心 (emotions; thoughts)	ソウ (SŌ) おも・う (omou)	idea; thought; conceive
箱	竹 (made of bamboo)	ソウ (SŌ) † はこ (hako)	box
霜	雨 (weather-related)	ソウ (SŌ) しも (shimo)	frost

† The *on* reading of this character is rarely encountered.

When learning how to recognize (and, perhaps, write) any of these three characters, it is best to mentally keep the 'tree' and 'eye' element pair together, treating them as a single component, and to think of the characters as consisting of two parts: that two-element phonetic component and a determinative, rather than as a group of three elements.

By mentally keeping together the 'tree' and 'eye' elements, you can quickly remember each character's *on* reading, and then focus on the component that most directly relates to the character meaning (the determinative) as you learn and remember the character meaning.

If you were instead to try to compose a story involving each of the three elements in each of these characters to explain how they all come together to form the character meaning, it would be difficult to come up with stories involving both a 'tree' and an 'eye' that could be used to explain all the various character meanings ('idea,' 'box,' and 'frost').

By repeatedly studying the list of commonly-used character phonetics provided in Part 2, you can develop a sense of which multi-element groups are used as phonetics, and from that, learn when and when not to mentally break down the elements of the characters you learn.

3.7 Character Quantity and Frequency of Occurrence

In Chapter 1, we first discussed the number of different characters a Japanese learner should be expected to know to be proficient in Japanese. In this section, we will take a deeper look at that topic, paying special attention to the frequency with which different characters are encountered in typical writing.

What It Means to 'Know' a Character

Certainly, knowing enough kanji to be considered literate is substantially more challenging than knowing the 26 letters of the Latin alphabet (52, actually, if you consider both the uppercase and lowercase forms).

But what exactly does it mean to 'know' a character? Does it mean that you know every compound word that the character appears in? That you know every possible reading and meaning that it can have? That you can write it without making a mistake?

A more practical definition, and the one we will use in this section, is that 'knowing,' or being familiar with, a character means:

- being able to clearly recognize the character when encountering it, distinguishing it from any similar looking characters

- knowing the major senses of meaning of the character

- knowing the major readings of the character

- being able to read and determine the meanings of common words using the character when encountered in typical contexts, without the assistance of furigana or any other aid

Using this definition of 'knowing' a character, how many characters should a person be expected to know in order to be proficient at Japanese? First, let's get a clear idea of how many characters there are.

Measuring Character Quantity

The total number of different kanji ever created is quite large. The largest character dictionaries ever compiled list more than 90,000 separate characters. But such dictionaries are filled with extremely rare characters; the majority of these characters will never be used, or even seen, by most people. A typical Japanese character dictionary, designed for more practical use, lists far fewer characters than this: roughly somewhere between 10,000 and 14,000 different characters, depending on the dictionary.

But these dictionaries treat variant forms as separate characters. Variant forms, described in Section 2.11, are alternate ways of writing characters that are otherwise identical in reading, meaning, and usage to the standard form of the character. If you ignore these variant forms and instead count only the number of distinct, unique characters in these Japanese dictionaries, you will find that there are less than 10,000.

If you then take into consideration how many characters can readily be displayed in computers, cell phones, and other information processing systems, this total drops even further. To be able to represent characters in a computer system—so that they may be used within software programs, such as word processors—a set of characters must be chosen and then *encoded*: each assigned a unique identifying number. But not all characters ever created have been encoded in the common character sets used for information processing today. Characters that were not included in these sets are clearly not essential, so by counting the number of different characters in one of these character sets, we can have an idea of the upper limit of the number of characters actually needed to read and write Japanese.

One of the most common character sets used in information processing systems (established by a standard called JIS X 0208) includes exactly 6355 different kanji. These characters are split into two levels. Level 1 consists of 2965 characters, and includes all the common use (*jōyō*) characters, plus all kinds of other relatively commonly-encountered characters, including those used in people and place names (such as the names of cities, towns, and villages). The characters in Level 2, a total of 3390, were chosen to include all other characters not on the Level 1 list that might need to be represented in information processing systems for any reason whatsoever, including variant forms of characters and characters needed to be able to write technical terms, names found in literature, names of antiquated objects, and names of historical figures or places. Characters outside of these 6355, then, are simply not at all necessary for writing the Japanese language.[6]

The Level 2 set of 3390 characters consists mostly of rarely encountered characters. In fact, most Japanese people are unfamiliar with most of these characters. If any of these characters are encountered in writing, they will likely be annotated with the reading (such as with furigana). The 2965 characters of Level 1 are sufficient for most people to be able to read anything they encounter.

And even among the Level 1 characters are quite a few characters which *can* be used to write common words, but for various reasons customarily are not (usually because the characters are considered to be difficult to read and write). Instead, words using these characters are often written using only hiragana. So some of these Level 1 characters, if encountered in writing, will also be annotated with the reading.

To fully appreciate the rarity of less commonly-encountered characters such as those just described, it is helpful to have a clear understanding of the frequency with which characters appear in typical writing.

Character Frequency

Character frequency refers to how often a character is encountered in writing. It can be measured by collecting a large sample of writing and counting the number of occurrences of each different character that appears within the sample.

In the late 1990s, a group of researchers analyzed a year's worth of articles from a major Japanese newspaper: the Asahi Shinbun. All articles from every morning and evening edition were included in their study.

A total of 23,408,236 kanji appeared within these articles.[7] Among these, there were 4476 unique characters.[8] The researchers counted the occurrences of each of these characters, and then ranked them based on frequency of occurrence, with number one being the most frequently encountered character.

The table on the next page shows a small portion of the results. From the table, you can see that over the course of the entire year, the single-most common character (which was 日, meaning 'day' or 'sun') appeared a total of 336,465 times within that newspaper. Taking into account the total number of kanji that appeared in the paper during the whole year, approximately 1 out of every 70 characters in the paper was this top-ranked character. And the second-most common character (which was 一, meaning 'one') appeared in the paper 285,089 times during the year, approximately once in every 82 characters, and so on.

---

[6] There are also two additional levels of kanji: Levels 3 and 4, specified in another character set standard (JIS X 0213). These characters are all either obscure characters or outdated variant versions, and thus are not at all needed in daily life in Japan. Many of these characters are not even supported in common computer typefaces.
[7] The results of this study are presented in: Chikamatsu N., Yokoyama S., Nozaki H., Long E., & Fukuda S. (2000). A Japanese logographic character frequency list for cognitive science research. *Behavior Research Methods, Instruments, & Computers*, 32 (3), 482–500.
[8] Following the establishment of the *jōyō kanji*, the use in newspapers of characters not on the *jōyō* list was significantly reduced. Nonetheless, characters not on the list still do appear in newspapers, often annotated with the character reading.

Character Ranking	Total Number of Occurrences of the Character	Character Occurrence Frequency
1	336465	1 in 70
2	285089	1 in 82
50	79738	1 in 294
100	50768	1 in 461
200	30219	1 in 775
500	11273	1 in 2076
1000	3387	1 in 6911
1500	948	1 in 24692
2000	206	1 in 113632
2500	40	1 in 585205
3000	13	1 in 1800634

As you can see from this small excerpt of the data, character frequency drops off rapidly. Outside of the 2000 most common characters, for example, no other character appeared within the newspaper more than 206 times among all the articles during the entire year. And no character beyond the 3000 most common characters appeared more than 13 times during the entire year. The 3000th most common character, in particular, was only encountered in the paper once in every 1.8 million characters.

Most remarkably, the data from the study revealed that nearly forty percent of all the different characters which appeared in the newspaper (1725 out of 4476) occurred with a frequency of no more than one out of every one million characters.

If this study had sampled a different kind of writing, such as novels or magazines, the total number of unique kanji would probably have been a little larger, but the same frequency profile would be observable: namely, that a sizable portion of the characters found in the sample appear with a frequency of less than one out of every one million characters.

Character Study Strategy

It's important to be aware of this frequency profile when choosing what order in which to study characters. Mastering kanji requires repetition, and for characters encountered infrequently it is harder to get the necessary amount of repetition to be able to remember them well. On top of that, many less common characters are used to write less common words, which are also harder to learn and remember both because of lack of repetition and because many of them have complex meanings. Thus, rarer characters require more effort to learn—both because they are encountered infrequently, and because the words they are used to write tend to be harder to learn as well.

Because of this, it is advantageous for a kanji learner to start by learning the most common characters, saving the study of rarer characters for a time when he or she has become more experienced at learning kanji and more skilled at recognizing, distinguishing, and remembering characters.

Also, it's best to first get basic proficiency in Japanese itself before tackling rarer characters. For words written with rarer characters, it is usually easier to learn the word itself first before memorizing the character used to write the word. Simply put, a beginning Japanese learner should not devote a large amount of effort to learning characters that appeared in a newspaper less than once out of every one million characters. The study of these characters should be deferred for later.

How Many Characters You Really Need to Know

Clearly, in the case of the newspaper study, if you 'knew' all 4476 of the characters appearing in those editions of the paper in advance of reading the articles, you would not encounter an unfamiliar character when reading that newspaper that year. But no one is expected to have memorized that amount of characters. Doing so would be a considerable burden. In those newspapers, many of the rarest characters were likely annotated with the character reading (such as with hiragana placed in parentheses after the character) to assist the reader in reading the character and identifying the word meaning.

This is true in general of writing aimed at the general public: many of the rarer characters have additional supplementary information included with them to help in determining the character reading or meaning, making it less important to have fully memorized these characters. Knowing the proper reading can help you to infer the word meaning, or at least quickly locate the character in a character dictionary to determine the meaning.

Disregarding the rarest characters that, when used, almost always have the character reading appended to them, the true number of unique characters that a literate Japanese adult should be expected to know is only about 3000, corresponding to the majority of the Level 1 characters and just a few of the Level 2 characters mentioned earlier in this section.

Beyond this quantity, characters do not need to be studied in advance, and instead can be dealt with at the time they are encountered in writing. These very rare characters can be thought of as analogous to the most uncommon English words. It does not make sense to study in advance every English word you might possibly encounter anywhere in any reading material. Instead, it is simpler to learn the rarest words as you encounter them.

Just as a person whose native language is English will sometimes encounter words he or she does not know, and need to look them up in a dictionary to understand them, an adult native Japanese reader will also sometimes encounter words using unknown characters. Even well-educated Japanese people sometimes need to use a character dictionary to check or confirm a character meaning. It would be an arduous task to memorize in advance all characters you might possibly encounter anywhere when reading Japanese.

Of course, literate Japanese adults are expected to know more than just the *jōyō kanji*. And this was even more true in the past. For example, up until the year 2010, thirteen Japanese prefectures (similar to provinces or states) had characters in their names that were outside of the *jōyō kanji* list. Clearly, these are characters an educated Japanese adult would be expected to know. (Those characters, along with nearly 200 others, were added to the *jōyō kanji* list with the 2010 revisions.)

3.8 Recommended Approach to Learning Characters

This section presents this book's recommended methodology for learning the characters.

1. Study Order

Based on the character frequency considerations discussed in the last section, it is recommended that the *jōyō kanji* be learned first—and in roughly the same order in which they are taught to Japanese schoolchildren. This order is a close enough approximation to the frequency with which characters are encountered in typical reading material, and will therefore make it easier to retain what you have learned through repetition. Plus, learning in this order allows you to use the wealth of kanji study materials designed for Japanese children. As of the year 2010 changes to the list, there are a total of 2136 *jōyō* characters. Familiarity with these 2136 characters will take you a long way toward literacy in Japanese.

2. Character Form

As mentioned in Chapter 1, for each character, there are three things to learn: the form, the reading(s), and the meaning(s). As you learn each new character, start by carefully paying attention to its form. If the character is made up of multiple elements, take note of each of those elements.

Also, note the type of character. If the character is of the determinative-phonetic (D-P) type, mentally divide it into two parts: the determinative (usually a single element) and the phonetic (usually all other components taken together as a unit). For most D-P characters, you can use the phonetic as a key to remembering the *on* reading(s) of the character, and use the determinative, with the support of the phonetic, as a key to remembering the character meaning(s).

If the character is not of the D-P type, try to develop a way to associate its form with its meaning, either using the true derivation (etymology), as best as it is known today, or whatever other method works for you.

For characters that have other similar 'look-alike' characters, compare the characters side-by-side to help you learn how to distinguish the differences, which can sometimes be subtle. (The most comprehensive kanji learning materials will, for each character, identify the character type and include look-alike characters.)

3. Character Reading

If the character contains a phonetic component, focus on using it to assist with memorizing the character's *on* reading. In Part 2, Section 2 of this book, all commonly-used character phonetics are listed, together with the common readings they indicate, and a list of all *jōyō* characters which contain them.

Although a very large percentage of characters include a phonetic component, unfortunately many of the most commonly used characters (i.e., the characters which are studied earliest) do not. This is because these characters tend to have been created before use of phonetic components had become standard. Once the most common characters have been learned, though, being able to take advantage of the presence of phonetic components greatly helps with memorizing character *on* readings. For students wishing to master thousands of characters, utilizing these phonetic components will result in a large time savings.

Be aware, though, that the phonetic reading and the character reading may not be exactly the same, but rather related readings. Over time and with experience, you will become familiar with the correspondences between related readings. In Chapter 7, a chart showing the most common correspondences among related readings is provided.

Most characters are not used by themselves as single-character words read with an *on* reading. Instead, when the *on* reading is used, the character is more likely to be part of a compound word. Nonetheless, it is useful to remember the most common *on* readings of individual characters. That way, you can have an idea of how to read them when you encounter an unfamiliar compound word which contains them.

For learning a character's *kun* readings, it is best to do so by studying actual Japanese words containing the character and having those readings.

4. Character Meaning

For characters with complex meanings, develop a 'sense' of the meaning of the character, rather than memorize a rigid one- or two-word English translation of the meaning. Memorizing an English keyword forces you to translate the character into English, whereas learning a sense of the character allows you to understand the character without the need for translation.

Of course, associating just a single English word with each character is simple, but can lead to problems with inflexibility as the meanings of compound words are learned, since character meaning can vary among different compounds. And it ties your learning to English, which is a poor approach to learning a foreign language.

In addition to the sense of meaning, also become familiar with any special types of character usage, such as characters that are commonly used as a prefix or suffix (see Chapter 5 for a discussion of prefixes and suffixes).

Using character etymologies to remember meanings can be helpful, but be aware that many etymologies seem memorable when first learning them, but are easily forgotten. When learning thousands of characters, trying to remember an etymology for each one is very cumbersome. Furthermore, because character meanings have drifted over time, even if a particular etymology is very memorable, it may have nothing to do with the modern meaning(s) of the character, making it not useful at all.

Only when the etymology of a character helps make remembering the modern meaning easier is it really useful. Unfortunately, many character etymologies do not do that; instead, if anything, they fill your head with extraneous information irrelevant to the character as it exists today. There is already so much to learn and memorize when studying kanji that learning extra information not directly helpful to remembering the modern meanings and usages of the characters should be avoided as much as possible.

You may wish to use or create a story involving all the character elements which relates them to the character meaning, even if it differs from the actual etymology. This approach is useful, but can also cause problems: there are many groups of characters which share the same complex phonetic component. When you associate this complex phonetic with a story, you now have to fit that same story to all characters that contain that phonetic, and the stories get more and more complicated the more characters there are (as discussed in Section 3.6 with respect to the 相 phonetic). Another weakness with this method is that the stories often reduce the character meaning to a single English word, which, as discussed earlier, is often not the optimal way to remember character meanings.

5. Vocabulary

When you learn a character, it is helpful to also learn some words that use the character, including compound words which pair the character with other characters, and words which use the character together with trailing okurigana (which usually, but not always, are words in which the character is read with a *kun* reading). This helps you to get a sense of how the character is used, and also helps to reinforce the character meaning.

But realize that learning kanji is separate from learning vocabulary, and avoid mixing the two together too much. As in any language, learning infrequently used vocabulary words takes time and effort. If you tie that to your kanji learning, it will slow it down. So it is recommended that you learn only very common vocabulary words as part of kanji study. Then, after characters have already been mastered and you are comfortable recognizing and reading them, you can learn more challenging vocabulary words that use them.

For characters with more than one distinct meaning or usage, it is best to study a variety of compounds—at least one for each meaning or usage.

6. Repetition

Repetition is critical for learning and remembering the characters. Most students will wish to repeatedly drill the characters, relating the character form with its meaning(s) and reading(s). Note that when drilling *on* readings by themselves, you may want to focus on principal *on* readings first, and deal with less common *on* readings later.

Paper flash cards are useful for drilling, as they can be looked at anywhere and at any time. With modern computer software, though, the process can be made much faster and more efficient. Some software products include features such as recording past performance and using that to target future drills on areas of weakness. This can be done with paper flash cards, too, but is much simpler with software.

3.9 From This Point Forward

At this point, you have learned enough background information that you are ready to start learning the characters one by one. There is still much useful information in the remaining chapters of Part 1 which will help you as you learn the characters, though, so please be sure to read those chapters at some point in your studies.

And be sure to take advantage of the reference lists in Part 2 to assist you with your studies.

Happy studying!

Chapter 4

Character Organization

In this chapter we will learn about ways that the characters are organized, including the method used to arrange characters in most character dictionaries. We will also learn about the regions of a character, and take a closer look at the list of common use characters and other related lists.

4.1 The Radical

Long ago, as the number of different characters in existence grew to a considerable level, Chinese scholars began to compile **character dictionaries**: dictionaries which have an entry for each character and provide information about the character, such as its meaning(s) and reading(s). Due to the large number of characters, it was necessary to find some way to organize them so that they could be looked up in an orderly fashion.

Arranging characters based solely on *stroke count* (the total number of strokes that make up a character) was not a good option, as there were too many characters which shared the same stroke count, and so it would be too cumbersome to locate a particular character. An ingenious method was conceived to solve this problem: designating for each character one 'key' component within it, and then grouping together characters which share the same key component. In English, this key component is most commonly referred to as a **radical**.

For some simple characters, such as 'tree' (木), the entire character as a whole has been designated as the radical, but for most characters the radical is only one part of the character—usually a single element. Regardless, every character has exactly one designated radical.[1]

In most modern character dictionaries, characters are arranged using both the radical and stroke count. This is done by first designating a radical for each character, then separating the characters into groups that share the same radical, then ordering the characters within those groups based on stroke count, and finally arranging the different groups within the dictionary based on the stroke count of the group's radical. This results in a relatively fast way to look up characters based on their form.

In Japanese, the radical is called *bushu* (written 部首), which literally means 'chief part.' The two kanji in this word can also be interpreted as 'section header,' which is how the term is sometimes translated. This is fitting, as in the typical kanji dictionary, as just explained, the characters are divided into sections, with each section 'headed' by—or based on—one radical, and containing all the characters assigned to that radical.

Character radicals were first designated long after the characters were originally created. As such, the radical is not an intrinsic part of a character, but rather something that was specified in retrospect.

The English word 'radical' has several different meanings. In this case, it is used for its meaning of 'root' or 'origin,' suggesting that the radical is the root of the character. This notion can be misleading, though, since, as we know, the characters were not created with one root part in mind.

In Japanese kanji education, the knowledge of character radicals is deemed important, primarily because the radical is the principal means by which to look up characters in a dictionary. Japanese students are expected to learn and memorize the radical of every character they study.

In this book, however, special study or memorization of character radicals is not recommended, for reasons explained at the end of this section. For students who nonetheless wish to learn character radicals, the remainder of this section explains them in detail.

A Brief History of Radicals

The first dictionary to identify a radical for each character and then to arrange the characters based on those radicals was the *Shuowen Jiezi*, a highly influential work written by Xu Shen in China in the second century AD. In his dictionary, Xu identified more than 9000 different characters, and separated them into exactly 540 different sections, each section headed by a different radical. But Xu's choice of radicals was not particularly streamlined, and over time various other dictionaries revised radical designations, with the goal of reducing the total number of different radicals. Eventually, a set of 214 radicals became standard. This set, or one quite similar to it, is still used by most modern character dictionaries. The radicals in this set are sometimes referred to as the 'Kangxi radicals,' named after the 18th century Chinese *Kangxi Zidian* dictionary, which popularized them.

---

[1] Some people use the word 'radical' when referring to *any* element within a character. This is an incorrect usage of the term.

Choice of Component for Radical

Of course, to look up a character in a dictionary using its radical, it's first necessary to know which part of the character is the radical. Thus, it is a useful skill to be able to look at a character and determine, or at least accurately guess, which part of it is the radical.

In many cases, radicals were chosen to be the component that most clearly relates to the character meaning. Accordingly, for D-P characters—which can be separated into a part which indicates the general meaning (the determinative) and a part which indicates the sound (the phonetic)—it is the determinative which is almost always designated as the radical.

For non D-P characters that consist of multiple elements, though, the radical is often not as easy to determine, because there is not always a component that clearly stands out as being most closely related to the overall character meaning. In those cases, the radical is often either the most basic, commonly-occurring element in the character, or an element located in a prominent position within the character, such as along the left-hand side of the character.

The following two non D-P multiple-element characters, each of which we have already seen, demonstrate this:

果　　　解

The radical of the 'fruit' character, on the left above, is the 'tree' element (木). The tree element is basic, and appears in many different characters. It is much more common than the component located above it.

The character on the right above, meaning 'to take apart,' consists of three elements: an animal's horn (on the left), a knife (upper right), and a cow or bull (lower right). The character is an ideograph, with all elements contributing to the meaning, so the choice of radical is somewhat arbitrary. The 'horn' element (角), which fills the left-hand side of the character, has been designated as the radical.

For characters that consist of only a single element (including characters that have, in essence, become a single element in the modern form due to transformation), obviously only one element was available to choose as the radical. However, making that choice for all one-element characters would result in a dictionary with many radicals that only have one (or a few) characters listed under them.

To avoid this situation, and keep the total number of different radicals to a minimum, sometimes only a portion of one element, rather than an entire element, was chosen to be the radical. This is the case for each of the following characters:

交　　　其

Even though the 'mix' / 'exchange' character on the left originally depicted only a single object (a man crossing his legs), just the top two strokes (亠) were selected as the radical.

Similarly, for the character on the right, which originally meant 'winnowing basket' and now means 'that,' only the bottom two strokes (八) were selected as the radical.

Each of these radicals (亠 and 八) is only part of an element in the corresponding character, and so doesn't have meaning on its own.[2] These two piece parts were chosen as radicals not because of any meaning inherent in them, but only because of their shape. A number of other characters, especially single element characters, also contain one of those same pairs of strokes (亠 or 八) somewhere within them, so designating those parts as radicals, and grouping a number of characters under them, enabled keeping the total number of different radicals to a minimum. If the 'mix' / 'exchange' and 'that' characters in their entirety were made radicals, they would each likely be the only character assigned to the radical, as these two characters are almost exclusively used as phonetics, not as determinatives, within D-P characters—and determinatives, not phonetics, were usually chosen as radicals.

There are plenty of other non-obvious radical choices as well. In some cases, the radical is an element that is not actually part of the character, but was chosen because it bears a resemblance to, or shares some of the same strokes as, part or all of the character. Take, as an example, a character meaning 'offering' / 'tribute':

It originally depicted two hands holding up an object, perhaps some kind of bouquet, as an offering. The modern form, a result of character transformation, consists of only uncommon elements. When it came to designating a radical, even though it is not technically an element of this character, the 'large' element (大) was chosen, simply because it is a common element and the strokes used to write it can be seen (albeit hidden) in the upper part of the character.

For some characters that underwent major simplification in modern times, a new radical had to be chosen, as the previous radical no longer appeared in the character. The simplified version of the character meaning 'to exhaust':

has no elements in common with the version of the character prior to simplification (盡), whose radical was the bottom element (皿). The component 尸 was chosen as the radical of the simplified version simply because it is a commonly occurring element whose strokes can be found within the character.

As these examples show, rather than being a component closely tied to the character meaning, the radicals of non D-P characters, whether those characters consist of one or multiple elements, are often based on an arbitrary choice. Furthermore, the same radical can have a different meaning (or no meaning at all) when appearing in different characters.

Disagreement among Dictionaries

For most characters, the designated radical is consistent from dictionary to dictionary. However, for a few characters there is disagreement among character dictionaries as to which component is the radical. Take, for example, the character meaning 'circular':

---

[2] The 八 pair of strokes is similar in appearance to the character meaning 'eight' (八), and, in fact, both are grouped under the same radical in most modern character dictionaries, but there is no meaning relationship between the two.

which we first saw in Chapter 1. The etymology of this character is unclear, even when looking at the earliest forms that have been uncovered. Modern dictionaries typically classify it simply based on one of the three strokes that comprise it. Some dictionaries classify it under the *ten* radical: 丶 (the short stroke in the lower left of the character), while others classify it under the *otsu* radical: 乙 (similar in appearance to the longest stroke in the character, which starts in the upper left and ends in the lower right). For most characters, however, there is widespread agreement among dictionaries as to which part is the radical.

Error Catching and Computer-based Assistance

To assist in looking up characters whose radical is not easy to guess, many modern dictionaries include 'error catching' references to characters in the dictionary: providing a brief listing of a character in a section where readers are likely to come mistakenly, and directing them to the correct section.

Additionally, modern electronic and software-based kanji dictionaries allow characters to be looked up by any element appearing within the character, and some even have a handwriting recognition feature, with which you can locate a character simply by drawing it in the interface provided. With such dictionaries, knowledge of radicals is unnecessary.

Radicals Not Emphasized in This Book

While it is true that knowledge of character radicals is useful for looking up characters in a paper dictionary (and for answering questions about radicals on kanji tests!), beyond that, radicals are of little importance. For characters that are of the D-P type, this book emphasizes learning and remembering which part is the determinative. As that part is almost always the radical as well, there is no need to specifically learn radicals for D-P characters. The majority of characters are D-P characters, and for those that are not, the radical is often either the most obvious element, or arbitrarily chosen.

The amount of memorization required when learning kanji is significant. Adding to this the memorization of arbitrary radicals which do not further the ability to read and use kanji, and are made mostly obsolete by things such as error-catching references in paper dictionaries and advanced features of electronic and software-based dictionaries, is ill-advised. For these reasons, the author discourages memorization of character radicals. Students, of course, are free to learn them if they wish.

4.2 Determinative and Radical: The Differences

Because they so frequently refer to the same component, the concepts of 'determinative' and 'radical' can be easily confused with each other. This book makes a clear distinction between the two concepts, but most other kanji learning materials do not. To make sure the differences between the concepts are clearly understood, those differences are carefully explained in this section.

A determinative is an element or other component that exists within some characters and has a special role: to identify the general category of meaning into which the whole character can be classified. It stands apart from all other components within a character in that it is the principal meaning-indicating component of the character. Not all characters have a determinative. Apart from D-P characters, most characters do not.

In contrast, the radical of a character is simply the designated component (which may be an element, a group of elements, or one part of an element) by which that character is grouped and ordered within a character dictionary. It is nothing more than that.

Determinatives are fundamental to character composition and were deliberately chosen at the time of character creation. In contrast, radicals were designated long after the characters were first created, and do not necessarily relate at all to the character meaning. As we saw in the last section, for non D-P characters the choice of radical is often quite arbitrary.

Among most D-P characters, the radical and the determinative are the same component. There are a few exceptions, though, examples of which are shown in the following table and discussed in the following paragraphs. All four characters discussed here are *jōyō kanji*.

Character	Determinative	Radical †
旗	㫃	方
書	聿	日
寒	冫 ‡	宀
輝	光	車

† This is the radical according to most character dictionaries. Some dictionaries may differ.

‡ This component appears within the character in an altered form: 冫.

The 'flag' element is used as a determinative in a small number of characters, all having to do with flags, including the first character in the table. The left-hand part of this element is identical in form to another, unrelated element (方), and because of that, characters with the 'flag' determinative are usually grouped under the 方 radical, to help consolidate and minimize the total number of different radicals.

The second character in the table, meaning 'write' / 'writing,' was originally composed of a component consisting of a hand holding a brush (written in the modern form as 聿) together with a phonetic, which, in its modern form, looks like this: 者. But long ago, that phonetic was abbreviated within the 'write' character, and now only its bottommost part (曰) appears in the character. The determinative of the character (聿) obviously has the strongest link to the character meaning, but nonetheless most dictionaries identify the abbreviated phonetic as the radical, as it is a simple, commonly-occurring component.[3]

---

[3] Note that the center stroke of this radical (in the right column of the table) does not quite extend all the way to the right-hand edge. Despite that, some characters assigned to this radical (such as 書) are drawn with this stroke fully extended. This kind of variation in the writing of characters is discussed further in Chapter 6.

The third character in the table, meaning 'cold' (as in temperature), was originally a multi-element ideograph, conveying the meaning 'cold' by showing a man inside a house using some kind of insulating material to keep himself warm. The man and insulation elements have been merged together in the modern form, but the house itself is still recognizable as the 宀 element at the top of the character. The two strokes at the bottom (which appear as 冫 when on the left-hand side of a character) represent blocks of ice, and are used in a number of characters, including this one, as a determinative indicating things having to do with coldness. Clearly, this element best indicates the meaning of the character, yet the 'house' element, which is far more common, is designated as the radical in most dictionaries.

Finally, the fourth character in the table, meaning 'shine; sparkle,' is a D-P character, with a determinative (meaning 'light') on the left and a phonetic (meaning 'military forces') on the right. The determinative by itself is also a *jōyō kanji*. Obviously, the left-hand component most closely relates to the character meaning. However, fewer than five characters use this component as a determinative. In virtually all modern character dictionaries, the few characters having this component as the determinative were all assigned to other radicals based on the other components within the characters. In the case of 輝, the lower part of the phonetic, by itself meaning 'vehicle,' is usually designated as the radical.

It can be confusing when the determinative and radical of a character differ from each other, but the number of such characters is small. For most D-P characters, the determinative and the radical are the same component.

Radical and Determinative Quantities

Most modern character dictionaries group the characters under exactly (or approximately) 214 different radicals. The number of characters or components that have been used as determinatives in the construction of D-P characters is somewhat smaller than this: roughly 140. And only about half of these were used in the creation of more than just a few characters. Most of these determinatives are also designated as radicals.

In Part 2, lists of both the 80 most common determinatives (Section 1) and the 214 radicals, as specified in this book, (Section 4) are provided. In Section 1, the meanings of the determinatives are described, but in Section 4, only the names of the radicals are given, as many of them include more than one unrelated meaning.

Summary of Differences

The differences between determinatives and radicals can be summarized as follows:

- Every character has exactly one radical. (Some dictionaries may differ with others as to which component is the radical.)

- Not all characters have a determinative. For characters that do, there is only one.

- All D-P characters have a determinative.

- Among D-P characters, the radical and the determinative are usually, but not always, the same component.

4.3 Character Regions

To help describe the location of a component within a character, the different regions of a character in which components are most commonly located have been given names. The following table shows all of these regions. For each one, an example of a component occupying that region is also given.

Character Regions

Region Name	Location	Description	Example
へん *hen*	(left)	left side	山 in 峠
つくり *tsukuri*	(right)	right side	見 in 規
かんむり *kanmuri* †	(top)	top	雨 in 雲
あし *ashi*	(bottom)	bottom	皿 in 益
にょう *nyō* ‡	(left-bottom)	left and bottom sides	辶 in 近
たれ *tare*	(top-left)	top and left sides	广 in 病
かまえ *kamae*	(all sides)	surrounding on all sides	囗 in 困
	(top-right)	top and right sides	弋 in 式
	(both sides)	element is split apart and located on both sides of character	行 in 術
	(top-bottom)	element is split apart and located at top and bottom of character	衣 in 衰
	(top-left-bottom)	top, left, and bottom sides	匚 in 医
	(left-top-right)	left, top, and right sides	門 in 閉
	(left-bottom-right)	left, bottom, and right sides	凵 in 凶

† An alternate term for this region is *kashira* (かしら).

‡ This region is also sometimes called *nyū* (にゅう). Technically, this is a mistake, but the usage is widespread, particularly with the 辶 component, often called しんにゅう.

In the table, the region names are written in both hiragana and *rōmaji*. Each of them can also be written with a single kanji character, but writing them in hiragana is more common. In fact, several of these kanji aren't even among the common use characters. (The kanji versions of these region names can all be found in Appendix A.)

Six of the seven regions listed in the table refer to one specific part of a character. The seventh region, called *kamae*, is a generic term for any outer, surrounding part of a character comprising two or more sides, with the exception of two such regions which, because they are so commonly referenced, have been given their own names: *nyō* and *tare*.

Use of Region Names

Primarily, the way the region names are used is by appending them to the names of specific components which are located in those regions, as if to say, 'This is the version of component X as it appears in region Y.' Let's look at some specific examples.

In Chapter 2, we saw two special forms of the 'person' element (人), and learned that each of these forms has been given its own unique name. Those two special forms are shown again below (with the rest of the character grayed out), with the name of each shown below it:

hitoashi   *ninben*

In fact, each of these components is a radical, and the names shown are the names of these specific radicals. In Japan, all character radicals have been given names. As with the two above, some of these radical names include within them the region in which that radical is commonly or always found.

The radical on the left above, when appearing within a character, is always found at the bottom of the character. For that reason, the region name *ashi* is included in the radical name. Specifically, the radical *hitoashi* is named by combining a word for 'person' (*hito*) with the region name *ashi*. The radical name is essentially telling us, 'This is the version of the *hito* component when it is located at the bottom of a character.'

When appearing within a character, the second radical above, *ninben*, is always located on the left-hand side of the character. The radical name combines another word for 'person' (*nin*) with the left-side region name (*hen*). In this case, though, the radical name is modified by a sound phenomenon called *rendaku*, and becomes *ninben*.

Rendaku in Radical Names

The *rendaku* sound phenomenon sometimes occurs in Japanese when attaching words together to form a compound word. With this phenomenon, the initial consonant sound of a word placed in the second or later part of a compound is changed from a non-voiced to a voiced sound. So, for example, instead of *hen*, the left-side region name is modified to *ben* in some radical names, such as *ninben* above.

But the region names do not always change in this way. For example, the version of the 'mountain' (*yama*) element located on the left-hand side of a character, as in the example character in the first row of the table on the previous page, is called *yamahen*, not *yamaben*.

The region names which *can* be altered by the *rendaku* process are:

$$hen \rightarrow ben \qquad tsukuri \rightarrow zukuri \qquad tare \rightarrow dare$$

$$kamae \rightarrow gamae \qquad kashira \rightarrow gashira$$

The *rendaku* phenomenon is described in more detail in Chapter 9. Radicals are listed in Part 2, Section 4, and the naming of radicals is discussed in detail in Appendix F.

4.4 The *Jōyō Kanji*

As described in Chapter 1, the *jōyō kanji*, or common use kanji, are a set of characters that have been designated by the Japanese government as being necessary for daily life. From the time of its implementation just after World War II until 1981, the characters were called the *tōyō kanji*, which meant 'temporary use characters' (because the list was not considered final; changes were planned).

Following the changes to the list in 2010, there are a total of 2136 *jōyō kanji*. Generally speaking, the characters on the list are the ones most commonly encountered. But there are certainly exceptions, both with characters on the list that are not actually all that common, and with relatively common characters that were not chosen for the list. Without question, there are many characters not on the list that an educated Japanese adult is expected to recognize and be able to read, at least in some contexts. Despite the original intent with the creation of the list, the reality today is that learning just the *jōyō kanji* is not enough to be able to recognize all characters appearing in materials written for the general public.

The *jōyō* specification is not just a list of characters; it also specifies character readings. Many characters can be read in multiple ways, but some of the readings are rare. The *jōyō* list defines which of a character's readings are in common use. If a *jōyō* character is to be used, but with an uncommon reading not on the list, an alternate means of writing the character is recommended (such as adding furigana, or replacing the character with hiragana).

In addition to the characters themselves and their readings, the *jōyō* specification also establishes an official form for each character. In cases where a simplified form of a character was being popularly used at the time the list was first created, the simplified form was often adopted as the official *jōyō* form. For characters added later, though, this is not always true. This is because the non-simplified forms of some of these characters had, to some extent, become standard by that point, and so were left unchanged upon addition to the list.

4.5 The *Kyōiku Kanji*

A subset of the *jōyō kanji* are taught to Japanese children during the six years of elementary school. This subset of *jōyō* characters are referred to as the *kyōiku kanji* ('education characters'). Presently, there are 1006 of these characters.

These characters are divided into six groups, each group taught during a different school year. The breakdown by school year is shown below.

Kyōiku Kanji – Breakdown by Grade

1st grade	80 characters
2nd grade	160 characters
3rd grade	200 characters
4th grade	200 characters
5th grade	185 characters
6th grade	181 characters
total	1006 characters

Generally, the more common characters are taught earlier, but there are some notable exceptions. For example, the character used when writing 'I' / 'me' (私) isn't taught until the sixth grade. Exceptions this glaring are rare, though.

4.6 The *Jinmeiyō Kanji*

When the *jōyō kanji* were initially established, they were also considered to be the only kanji that were allowed to be used in the naming of newborn children from that point forward. Prior to this, families could choose any character when naming their children.

The Japanese public felt the *jōyō* list was far too restrictive and wanted additional options, so a second set of special kanji was soon established: the ***jinmeiyō kanji*** ('personal name use kanji'). These are characters in addition to those on the *jōyō* list that may be legally used in naming children.[4]

Similar to the *jōyō kanji*, this list has also been expanded over time, including a large addition in 2004 that more than tripled its size. There are currently 862 characters as of the year 2015. 212 of these, though, are simply variant forms of *jōyō* characters.

Note that when naming a child, although the choice of characters is limited, the choice of reading to assign to them is not; there is much flexibility in choosing the reading of a name to go with its characters.

Prior to the large expansion of the list in 2004, most *jinmeiyō kanji* were used primarily in writing proper names (i.e., people or place names), and rarely seen in any other context. After the 2004 additions, though, many characters also encountered in contexts other than in proper names were added to the *jinmeiyō* list, and so it can no longer be said that the *jinmeiyō* characters are encountered primarily only in people and place names. (Some of those new characters were further promoted to *jōyō kanji* in 2010.)

---

[4] Hiragana and katakana can also be used in the naming of children.

4.7 *Hyōgaiji*

The term ***hyōgaiji*** (literally: 'character not on the list') is sometimes used to refer to characters not on these lists. Depending on the context in which the term is used, it may refer specifically to characters not on the *jōyō* list, or it may refer to characters not on either of the *jōyō* or *jinmeiyō* lists.

4.8 Chapter Summary

Character dictionaries are special dictionaries in which each entry is a specific kanji, and information about that kanji, such as meanings and readings, is provided. Each character has one part of it designated as its **radical**. The radical is the component of a character by which that character is grouped within a character dictionary. The radical can be the entire character, a single element, or even just a part of one element. In most character dictionaries, characters are arranged based first on the radical, and then on stroke count.

For D-P characters, the radical and the determinative are almost always the same component. For multi-element characters which are not D-P, the radical is often either the most commonly-occurring element or an element in a prominent position within the character. For many single-element characters, the radical is only one part of the character—not the complete element. Radicals are designated in this way to keep the total number of different radicals to a minimum.

The most common set of radicals used in character dictionaries consists of exactly 214 different radicals. For a small number of characters, there is disagreement among the major character dictionaries as to which component is the radical.

Seven different regions where components are commonly located within characters have been assigned specific names. These region names are sometimes used as part of radical names.

The ***jōyō kanji*** are a list of 'common use' characters that are considered necessary for daily life. In general, the most commonly used characters appear on this list, although there are certainly exceptions. Some characters not among the *jōyō kanji* appear in writing aimed at the general public. Literate Japanese adults are expected to have familiarity with a number of characters not on the list.

1006 characters on the *jōyō kanji* list are further designated as the ***kyōiku kanji***: 'educational characters.' Japanese schoolchildren are taught these characters during the first through sixth grades of elementary school. Generally, the more commonly used characters are taught earlier.

Separate from the *jōyō kanji* is another list of characters called the ***jinmeiyō kanji***. The characters on this list, together with the *jōyō kanji*, may be used for naming children. Characters not on the *jōyō* list (and, perhaps, the *jinmeiyō* list) are referred to as ***hyōgaiji***.

Chapter 5

Character Usage in Depth

In this chapter, we will learn about various ways in which the characters are used, with a focus specifically on special ways they are used in the writing of the Japanese language. We'll start by looking at situations in which the characters are *not* used.

5.1 When Kanji Are Not Used

It was once possible for the Japanese language to be written in its entirety using kanji exclusively. In fact, that was the only way the Japanese language *could* be written prior to the creation of the hiragana and katakana syllabaries. In modern times, though, this is never done. Kanji are virtually never used in certain cases, such as writing most words borrowed from western languages, writing grammatical particles, and writing word inflections. (Refer to Chapter 1, Section 1.10 to see how each of these are written.)

As you become familiar with Japanese writing, you will encounter numerous other circumstances, in addition to these, where kanji could be used but typically are not.

For example, many plant and animal names, in particular less common ones, are written using katakana. Although many of these words can also be written in kanji, the kanji versions are often two- or three-character compound words, sometimes with characters used in nonstandard ways. It's difficult to memorize such words, especially when not seen that often.

For infrequently encountered plant and animal names, reading and writing them in katakana is much simpler.[1]

Also, many words which can be written, at least in part, using kanji are often seen written entirely in hiragana. For example, the common phrase *arigatō gozaimasu* ('thank you') is most commonly written only in hiragana: ありがとうございます. But this expression can be, and sometimes is, written using a mixture of kanji (for word stems) and hiragana (for word inflections): 有り難う御座います. The kanji used do not closely relate to the meaning of the expression, though, because the meanings of the words in it have changed over time.[2] This, combined with the fact that writing this often-used phrase by hand takes much longer when using kanji, has resulted in the phrase usually being written entirely in hiragana.

It's even possible to replace with hiragana only some of the kanji in a multi-character word, leaving the others unchanged. For example, the word *tomodachi* ('friend') can be written entirely in kanji as 友達. However, this word is often seen written as 友だち, with the equivalent hiragana characters replacing the second kanji. The hiragana substitution is made primarily because, for reasons explained later in the chapter, the meaning of the second character bears little relation to the meaning 'friend.' On top of that, the second character is somewhat cumbersome to write by hand.

There are no absolute rules governing whether a word is written using kanji or not. There are common conventions that are often followed in modern Japanese writing, though. Following are descriptions of some common situations where kanji *can* be used but customarily are not.

A. A Character Is Not on the *Jōyō Kanji* List

The idea behind the establishment of the *jōyō kanji* was that only the roughly two thousand characters determined to be the most important for daily usage would be used in writing aimed at the general public (such as in newspapers), and any others would not. As a result, many words that had up to that point been typically written using kanji, but included characters outside of the *jōyō* set, came to be commonly written without kanji (most often using hiragana).

The use of characters not on the *jōyō kanji* list is not prohibited, though, and in fact a fair number of words written using characters not among the *jōyō kanji* will be regularly encountered in some kinds of writing. The average Japanese reader is expected to be able to read such words. For example, many Japanese adults can read the word 嚙む (*kamu*, 'to bite'), especially when it is seen in an appropriate context, even though the character used is not among the *jōyō kanji*. But in typical newspaper articles, a word such as this is usually written entirely in hiragana: かむ.

There are, though, a number of words that are rarely written in kanji in any situation. For example, the common word *matomeru* ('to wrap up in conclusion') when written with kanji uses a very complicated non-*jōyō* character: 纏める. This character is infrequently used; the hiragana form of the word is more commonly encountered: まとめる. Because many readers

---

[1] Such words could also be written in hiragana, but writing them in katakana helps make them stand out in a sentence, rather than blend in with grammatical constructs.

[2] *Arigatō* derived from a word meaning 'difficult to exist.' *Gozaimasu* derived from a respectful way to refer to a person of high status.

today are not so familiar with the character, if the kanji version of this word were to appear in writing, it might interfere with smooth reading.

B. A Character Is Complicated in Form or Rare in Usage

Even when a character is included in the *jōyō* list, that doesn't guarantee that it will be used.

For example, the word *hifuka* ('dermatology') can be written entirely in kanji as 皮膚科. However, this word is often seen written as 皮ふ科, with a hiragana character (*fu*) replacing the second kanji. This is done because the second character, even though it is one of the *jōyō kanji*, is complicated in form and is not part of many words in common usage, and therefore may be challenging for some people to read.

This style of writing a word (replacing some, but not all, kanji with hiragana) is referred to as **mazegaki**, meaning 'mixed writing.' *Mazegaki* is described further in Chapter 9.

C. A Word Is Used in a Special Way

In the Japanese language, the verb *miru* ('to see') is typically written 見る, with one kanji and one hiragana character indicating the word inflection. This word can also be used as an auxiliary verb, attached to another verb to convey the meaning 'try and see what happens,' such as in 食べてみる (たべてみる): 'taste something to see what it is like.' When used in this special way, it is uncommon for the character 見 to be used; instead, the word is most often written in hiragana only: みる.

Other common verbs can also be used as auxiliary verbs with special meanings, including *iku*, *kuru*, and *oku*. When used in this way, these words are also usually written only in hiragana.

D. There Are Multiple Ways to Write a Word; Confusion Exists

As we saw in Chapter 3 (Section 3.3), in the Japanese language there are many homophones: words with different meanings that are pronounced the same way as each other. Some of these homophones were created when kanji were assigned to native Japanese words which had a broad range of similar meanings. Because kanji were very specific in meaning, but some Japanese words were broad in meaning, sometimes different characters were assigned to the different meanings of the same basic word, resulting in the creation of homophones.

Some of these homophones are commonly written using kanji. The character that is used depends on the specific meaning of the word intended. For other homophones, though, the distinction between the words when written with different kanji is not very clear, and writers are unsure of which kanji is the most appropriate to use in a specific case. As a result, such words are often written entirely in hiragana.

One ambiguous homophone is *wakaru*, which means 'comprehend' / 'understand' / 'appreciate' / 'recognize.'[3] There are three ways to write this word using kanji: 分かる, 判る, and 解る.[4] These three words have quite similar meanings, but there are subtle meaning differences among them. As a result of the confusion due to similar meanings, many people commonly choose to write this word using only hiragana.

---

[3] In addition to these meanings, the word also means 'to divide up.'
[4] Only the first of these three words is an official, common use reading of its character. (See Section 4.4 for a discussion of common use readings of characters.)

E. Usage of a Character Complicates the Word Reading

The use of kanji often helps make reading easier. However, with some words, using kanji can actually make for a more complicated reading. Thus, such words are often written in hiragana.

For example, the word *mazu* (まず), meaning 'first of all' / 'to start with,' can be written using a character meaning 'before' / 'ahead' / 'previous' (先) in place of the first sound of the word, with the remainder in hiragana: 先ず. Written this way, the reading of the 先 character itself is *ma*, a *kun* reading.[5] But among all the various words that use this character, it is much more commonly read in two other ways: *SEN* (an *on* reading), and *saki* (the principal *kun* reading). In the case of *mazu*, writing it entirely in hiragana is simpler, as it avoids confusion with the other more common readings of the character.

F. The Character Meaning Is Not Relevant to the Word Meaning

As we already know, many characters have multiple meanings, and sometimes the meanings are very different from each other. But in addition to this, sometimes characters are used without consideration of their meaning at all—only the sound is what matters. This practice is called *ateji*, and is explained in more detail in the next section.

When a word uses a kanji only for its sound, or for an uncommon meaning, in some cases it is simpler not to use the character when writing the word. We already saw this with the word *tomodachi* ('friend'), which is sometimes written 友だち. The same is true of *kodomo* ('child'). In kanji, the word is written 子供. But the second character, which means 'to accompany as an attendant' and is also used to write a word meaning 'offering,' is not directly relevant to the meaning 'child,' and was chosen primarily for its sound. The use of this character to write 'child' is also viewed by some Japanese as inappropriate, due to its connotation of 'offering.' This word is therefore sometimes seen written as 子ども.

Another word commonly written in hiragana is *takusan* ('many in number'). Written in kanji (沢山), the word uses characters meaning 'swamp' and 'mountain.' The origin of this word is unclear, but the two characters used to write it, if taken literally, bear little relation to the word meaning. This word is more commonly written in hiragana than in kanji.

Finally, some words bear absolutely no relation to *any* of the characters they are written with, as all of the characters used to write the word were chosen exclusively for their sound, without regard for their meaning. In other words, all of the characters in the word are *ateji*.

An example of a word written entirely in this way is *kega*, which means 'injury.' Using kanji, the word is written 怪我, consisting of characters whose meanings are 'suspicious' / 'mysterious' and 'oneself,' respectively. As the characters bear little or no relation to the word meaning, this word is usually written entirely in hiragana: けが.

Summary

There are numerous kinds of situations where kanji can be used, but typically are not. There are even many everyday words in the Japanese language for which kanji have been assigned, and could be used, but commonly are not.

---

[5] This is a *kun* reading because the character is being used to write a word of native Japanese origin (*mazu*).

There are not strict rules as to whether a word is written with kanji or not, and so some words will be seen written with kanji in some kinds of writing, and in hiragana or katakana in other kinds of writing. A reader of Japanese needs to become accustomed to sometimes seeing certain words written with kanji, and sometimes without.

How a word is written depends on several factors, including the expected target audience of the writing. Writers can choose to write a word using kanji when they expect that their readers will be able to read the word—used in an appropriate context—with minimal difficulty.

There are quite a few words that are most frequently written in hiragana, but experienced readers of Japanese are still expected to be able to read them when written with kanji. Some of the words mentioned in this section, including *mazu* and *takusan*, are examples of such words.

For someone learning Japanese as a foreign language, reading words such as these can be challenging, because they are not always seen written in kanji, and so it is difficult to get reinforcement through repetition. If these words were always seen written with kanji, they could be much more quickly learned.

5.2 *Ateji* – Using Characters Only for Their Sound

As we know, individual kanji have meaning associated with them. It's natural to assume, then, that in words written with kanji, the meanings of the characters in the word contribute to the meaning of the word itself. And that is usually the case.

But not always.

There are some words in which the characters are used primarily or exclusively for their sound, and the character meaning is irrelevant. Characters were chosen to write these words simply because their pronunciation (reading) matched the reading of part (or all) of the word. That is, the characters were only used phonetically.

This kind of usage of kanji is called **ateji**. The term *ateji* can be loosely translated as 'applied character.' You can remember this by imagining characters being applied to words strictly for their sound, with no regard for the character meaning. The term *ateji* can refer to the characters themselves, or to this method of assigning characters.

Assigning characters to words using *ateji* is common in the Chinese language. Because kanji are the only component of the writing system,[6] when words of foreign origin are brought into the language they need to be written using kanji. For words where it is desirable to have the Chinese pronunciation of the word resemble the original pronunciation, such as people or place names, the words are represented in Chinese by choosing a set of characters whose readings, when put together, most closely match the spoken sounds of the words. The meanings of these characters are not important—only their sound. For example, in Chinese the country name 'Italy' is written 意大利, which has a modern pronunciation of 'Yi da li' in

---

[6] In the principal Chinese dialect, the characters are called *hanzi*, not kanji. For simplicity of the discussion, though, they will be referred to here as kanji.

the Mandarin dialect. These characters were chosen to approximate the sound of this place name. The meanings of the three characters in the word ('thought,' 'large,' and 'benefit,' respectively) have nothing to do with the name of the country.

This same method of importing foreign words was once commonly used in Japanese, too, but the practice was eventually discontinued. In modern Japanese, these types of words are primarily written using the katakana syllabary, viewed as the 'phonetic alphabet' of Japanese.

But in Japanese, foreign words weren't the only words written using *ateji*. Words of native Japanese origin were, too.

As we know, most kanji used in the writing of native Japanese words were assigned to those words based on the similarity in meaning between the character and the word (this was the origin of *kun* readings). But some native Japanese words are written using *ateji* instead.

We saw several of these words in the last section, including *tomodachi* ('friend'), which is written in part using *ateji*. As a spoken word of native Japanese origin, *tomodachi* originally meant a multiple number of friends. Specifically, *tomo* meant 'friend,' and *dachi* was a suffix indicating a multiple number of people (equivalent to the suffix *tachi* used today in words like *watashitachi* and *hitotachi*). The meaning of this word has been broadened, though; today, *tomodachi* can refer to just a single friend as well as a multiple number of friends. When this word was first written using kanji, the first part of the word (*tomo*) was assigned a character based on its meaning (specifically, the character 友, meaning 'friend,' with the *on* reading of *YŪ* was assigned to the native Japanese word *tomo*, also meaning 'friend'). But the second part of the word (*dachi*) was assigned a character (達) based only on sound (specifically, one of its *on* readings matched the sound *dachi*). The meaning of this character ('to attain, accomplish') has nothing to do with a multiple number of people. In other words, this second character was assigned using *ateji*.[7]

In some words, more than one kanji was assigned using *ateji*. For example, the word *sewa* is written entirely using *ateji*. This word means 'care,' as used in the expression 'to take care of.' It is commonly seen in the expression of gratitude '*o-sewa ni narimashita*,' meaning 'you have taken good care of me.' Although the word origin is unclear, it likely has the same root as the native Japanese word *sewashii*, meaning 'busy' / 'hurried,' suggesting that the person who has taken care of you must have been kept very busy to do so. To write *sewa* using kanji, two characters with the *on* readings *SE* (世) and *WA* (話), respectively, were chosen. Individually, these characters mean 'society; generation' and 'conversation,' respectively—each clearly unrelated to the meaning 'care.' Both characters are *ateji*, chosen only for their sound.[8]

Alternate Ways of Writing

Some words that can be written with *ateji* can also be written in other ways. One such example is the native Japanese word *sushi*. This word is most commonly written using *ateji*: 寿司. Here, the two characters have the meanings 'longevity' and 'government official,' respectively. But *sushi* can also be written using either of the following single characters: 鮨 or 鮓. These ways of writing the word use the character for its meaning, and are not *ateji*. Both are less common than 寿司, though.

---

[7] Words such as *watashitachi* and *hitotachi* can also be written using the character 達 in place of *tachi*, but this is relatively uncommon.
[8] Note that, unlike *sewa*, the word *sewashii* is not written using *ateji*.

Ateji Can Have a Meaning Role

Although not common, there are some cases where character meaning did play a role in the choice of character to use as *ateji*. One such example can be seen within the word *go-zonji*, a polite way of saying 'know.' This word can be written entirely with kanji as 御存知. When written this way, the third character (知) is *ateji*. The word *go-zonji* derives from adding the polite prefix *go* (御) to *zonji*, the noun form of the verb *zonjiru*. *Zonjiru* itself was created by combining a Chinese loan word (存, meaning 'to exist; to survive,' and having an *on* reading of *ZON*) with the Japanese verb ending *jiru* (originally *zuru*). Today, *zonjiru* has the meanings 'know' and 'think.' The character 知, which means 'knowledge,' has an *on* reading of *CHI*—a sound similar enough to *ji* that it is sometimes used (as *ateji*) to write the *ji* portion of *go-zonji*. In this case, the *ateji* character (知) not only provides a sound, but also helps give an indication of the word meaning.

Typical Characteristics of *Ateji* in Japanese Writing

Many Japanese words which were originally assigned characters using *ateji* are now rarely seen written with kanji. Instead, they are most often seen written in hiragana or katakana. This is especially true of non-Chinese words of foreign origin, which are almost always written using katakana. Of the words still seen today written using *ateji*, most are words of native Japanese origin. Examples of this include both *sewa* and *sushi* (the 寿司 variation), each of which is still commonly seen written using kanji.

Almost all *ateji* characters are used for their *on* reading, including all the examples we have seen in this section. There are a few exceptions to this, though, where the *kun* reading is used instead. Because it is so rare, examples of *ateji* using the *kun* reading will not be given.

5.3 *Jukujikun* – Multi-Character Special Readings

Just as characters can be used only for their sound without regard for their meaning (i.e., *ateji*), characters can also be used in the opposite way: only for their meaning without regard for their sound. In fact, this is precisely what *kun* readings are: using the characters to write words based only on similarity of meaning between the target word and the character, ignoring the character's original, intrinsic spoken sound (the *on* reading).

In addition to basic *kun* readings, though, there is another way in which characters are used only for their meaning. In some words, two or more characters grouped together are read with a special reading that cannot be obtained by combining any of the *on* or *kun* readings of the individual characters in them; that is, the characters as a group are read in a way entirely different from how they can be read individually.

A notable example of this kind of special reading can be seen in the name of the annual Japanese festival of *tanabata*. In kanji, the festival name is written with two characters meaning, respectively, 'seven' and 'evening':

七夕

Taken individually, the first character can be read as *nana* (a *kun* reading) or *SHICHI* (an *on* reading); the second can be read as *yū* (*kun*) or *SEKI* (*on*). These individual *on* and *kun* readings can't be combined in any way to produce the word *tanabata*. Instead, it's necessary in the case of this compound word to simply memorize the fact that when these two characters appear together this way they form the special reading *tanabata*. This type of reading is known as **jukujikun**, which loosely translates as 'compound *kun*.'[9]

How did such special readings come about? In the case of *tanabata*, the word came from a Japanese legendary tale, involving a maiden who was chosen to weave a special cloth. The *tanabata* was the loom on which the cloth was woven, and eventually lent its name to a Japanese festival based on the tale. The characters used to write this *tanabata* were:

棚機

This compound is read using the readings of its individual characters: the first is read as *tana*, and the second as *bata* (from *hata*, modified by the *rendaku* process). Later, the original Japanese *tanabata* festival became merged in Japan with a Chinese star festival which took place at the same time of year. Because the Chinese festival always took place on the evening of the seventh day of the seventh month (originally the seventh month of the lunar calendar), its name was written 七夕, with characters meaning 'seven' and 'evening.'

After the merger, the festival was still called *tanabata*, but came to be written using the characters taken from the Chinese festival. In other words, the festival retained its Japanese spoken name, but in writing used the characters of the Chinese festival.

Many other instances of *jukujikun* were created in this same way. Namely, a multi-character (i.e., compound) word was borrowed from Chinese and applied to a native Japanese word of similar meaning, but the original Japanese reading was retained. So the word is spoken in the Japanese way, but written in the Chinese way. As a result, the characters in the word are only used for their meaning; the sounds of the individual characters (both *on* and *kun*) are ignored.

Multiple Readings

Some kanji compound words can be read with both a *jukujikun* reading and a more conventional reading, using the sounds of the individual characters in them. This is true of compound words meaning 'yesterday,' 'today,' and 'tomorrow,' most commonly pronounced *kinō*, *kyō*, and *asu / ashita*, each of which is a *jukujikun* reading. These compound words can also be read using *on* readings of the individual characters in them: *sakujitsu*, *konnichi*, and *myōnichi*, as shown in the following table:

Kanji Compound	昨日	今日	明日
Jukujikun Reading	kinō	kyō	asu / ashita
On-based Reading	sakujitsu	konnichi	myōnichi

---

[9] In this word, '*jukuji*,' similar to *jukugo*, indicates a compound word of multiple characters, and '*kun*' indicates that the word reading as a whole is a *kun* reading. The meaning of the term, therefore, is 'multiple character *kun* reading.'

Each of the *on*-based versions are less common than their counterpart *jukujikun* readings. *Sakujitsu* and *myōnichi* are more formal ways to say 'yesterday' and 'tomorrow.' *Konnichi* is well known from the Japanese greeting *konnichi wa*, but otherwise infrequently used.

An interesting example of *jukujikun* occurs with the Japanese word for the common cold: *kaze*. Written with kanji, the word appears like this:

風邪

The first character, meaning 'wind,' can also be read by itself as *kaze*. But the second character cannot be read as *ka* or *ze* or *kaze*. Thus, when written in kanji, this word is read as if the second character were silent. This unusual case came about because the above kanji compound was borrowed from Chinese only for its meaning ('head cold'), ignoring its reading, and applied to the native Japanese word for 'head cold': *kaze*, a word which just happened to have the same pronunciation (and, incidentally, the same word origin) as the native Japanese word for 'wind,' the first character of the compound. To avoid confusion, the word *kaze*, when meaning 'common cold,' is usually written in hiragana.

Combining with Hiragana

Some words when written as *jukujikun* contain trailing hiragana characters (i.e., okurigana). For example, the adjective *oishii* ('delicious'), when written using kanji, uses characters meaning 'beautiful' and 'taste,' as *jukujikun*, in place of all but the last two hiragana characters: 美味しい. (When written using kanji, only the stem parts of adjectives are replaced with kanji; the rest is always in hiragana.)

Notes

Jukujikun readings, by definition, are only found in multi-character words. They are relatively uncommon, although there are a number of very common words written with *jukujikun*, such as *otona* ('adult'), written with characters meaning 'large' and 'person': 大人.

Appendix K lists some common compound words with special readings that cannot be wholly derived from the individual characters in them. Many of the words listed in group B are examples of *jukujikun*.

While the term *ateji* is very well known among Japanese people, most are unfamiliar with the term *jukujikun*. As a result, some people simply use the word *ateji* as a blanket term to refer to any kind of special character reading, including *jukujikun*. Technically, though, this is incorrect; *ateji* only has the narrow meaning described in the previous section.

5.4 Counter Words

When counting most types of objects in English, one simply puts the quantity, as a number, in front of the word for the object itself, such as in 'three books' or 'seven lightbulbs.' Some objects, though, require an additional word that expresses the form of the object, such as: 'five sheets of paper,' or 'two bars of soap.' Although it's rare in English, some nouns also have a special word used when counting, such as the word 'head' in 'one hundred head of cattle.' Here, 'head' is a special counting word used for indicating a quantity of livestock.

When indicating a quantity of objects in Japanese, the use of a special counting word, such as 'head' above, is standard. Such a word is commonly referred to as a **counter**. Counters are generally written with kanji, and are most commonly a single character read with an *on* reading. There are some exceptions, though, as will be seen in the following examples.

Within a sentence, the counter is used by placing it just after the quantity of the object being described. The object itself, though, can come either before or after the quantity and counter words, depending on the sentence structure. The following example phrases demonstrate the object coming before the counter and after the counter, respectively:

sara wo san mai
皿を三枚
'three plates'

go hon no bōrupen
五本のボールペン
'five ball-point pens'

In the first example, *mai* is a counter word for flat objects. It immediately follows the word expressing the quantity: *san* (three). In the second example, *hon* is a counter word for long, narrow objects. It also immediately follows the word expressing the quantity: *go* (five). The grammatical particle to use (e.g., *wo* or *no* above) depends on the sentence structure; such grammatical rules will not be discussed in this book.

In excess of one hundred different counter words exist in Japanese, but far less than that are in common usage. Some are not well known by the average Japanese person, and in their place other more common generic counters are usually substituted. A complete list of counter words will not be provided in this book.

The list below shows a few of the more frequently used counter words in Japanese, including the kanji used to write them and the types of objects they are used to count.

Character	Reading	Used to Count:
枚	マイ	flat, broad objects (example: sheet of paper)
本	ホン	long and narrow objects (example: pencil)
個	コ	small objects that don't fit the above categories (example: apple)
冊	サツ	books and magazines
杯	ハイ	liquid in a container (example: glass of water)
台	ダイ	appliances; machines (including cars)
頭	トウ	large animals (example: horse)
匹	ひき †	small animals (example: dog)
羽	わ †	birds (and, traditionally, rabbits)

† This counter word uses a *kun* reading of the character.

Some of these counter words, when paired with certain numbers, are modified by the *rendaku* process (the changing of the initial consonant sound from unvoiced to voiced). For example, 3 本 is read as *sanbon*, instead of *sanhon*. Furthermore, some numbers preceding counters are modified by the *sokuon* process (where the final sound of the number is removed and replaced with consonant elongation). For example, 1 個 is read as *ikko*, not *ichiko*, and 6 杯 is read as *roppai* instead of *rokuhai* (here the initial sound of the counter word changes, as well). The *rendaku* and *sokuon* sound phenomena are both discussed in Chapter 9.

Note that characters which are used as counters, such as those listed on the previous page, are not only used as counters, but also have other meanings and roles, as well. The reading can differ, too, when used as a counter. For example, the character 羽 in the list is typically read as *U* (*on* reading) or *ha* or *hane* (*kun* readings), but is read as *wa* when used as a counter.[10]

5.5 Prefixes and Suffixes

In the English language, many words have been formed by combining a root word with either a **prefix** (attached to the beginning) or a **suffix** (attached to the end). That prefix or suffix modifies the meaning of the root word. The prefix 'un,' for example, is attached to the beginning of words to form a new word with the opposite meaning, such as 'unkind,' which is the opposite of 'kind.' And the suffix 'ment' turns a verb into a noun, such as the verb 'entertain' becoming the noun 'entertainment.'

Some kanji can also be used in a prefix or suffix role, being attached to the beginning or end of other, existing words to form new words with modified meanings, just as prefixes and suffixes do in English.

An example of a character used as a prefix is 無, which means 'to not have' or 'to be lacking.' Its use as a prefix is similar to that of the English 'un' prefix. For example, adding the 無 prefix to the word *sekinin* (責任, せきにん), meaning 'responsibility,' produces the word *musekinin* (無責任, むせきにん), meaning 'irresponsibility.'

An example of a character used as a suffix is 人 ('person'). This character is attached to the end of various nouns to form a word meaning a person associated with that noun. For example, 人 can be attached to a place name to form a word meaning a person from that place, as in 日本人 (*nihonjin*, 'Japanese person'): a person from 日本 (*nihon*, 'Japan').

Characters when used as prefixes and suffixes are most often read with the *on* reading. Furthermore, for prefix or suffix characters with two common *on* readings, it is often the case that one of the readings is much more likely to be used than the other when the character is used in the prefix or suffix role. For example, the character 無 has two common *on* readings: *MU* and *BU*. But when used as a prefix, it is more often read as *MU*. Similarly, the character 人, with common *on* readings *JIN* and *NIN*, is more likely to be read as *JIN* when used as a suffix, especially when attached to a place name.

There are certainly exceptions to this, such as the commonly-encountered words *buji* (無事, 'without incident') and *hannin* (犯人, 'criminal'), where 無 and 人 are read as *BU* and *NIN*,

---

[10] When paired with certain numbers, the reading *ba* or *pa* (sounds derived from *ha*, not *wa*) is used instead. For example, '1000 birds' is expressed as *senba*, not *senwa*.

respectively. But knowing which reading is more common in the prefix or suffix role makes it easier to guess the readings of newly encountered words.

Following are a few examples of characters commonly used as prefixes or suffixes, with an example usage for each one.

Prefix Examples

Character	Prefix Meaning / Role	Root Word / Reading / Meaning	Word with Prefix / Reading / Meaning
大	big	規模 きぼ scale; scope	大規模 だいきぼ large-scale
新	new	幹線 かんせん main line; trunk line	新幹線 しんかんせん new main line (high speed rail)
反	anti	体制 たいせい system; structure	反体制 はんたいせい anti-establishment
未	not yet	完成 かんせい complete	未完成 みかんせい incomplete

Suffix Examples

Character	Suffix Meaning / Role	Root Word / Reading / Meaning	Word with Suffix / Reading / Meaning
化	change into; become	国際 こくさい international	国際化 こくさいか internationalization
物	thing	爆発 ばくはつ explosion	爆発物 ばくはつぶつ explosives
感	feeling	無力 むりょく powerlessness	無力感 むりょくかん sense of helplessness
状	shape; form	円錐 えんすい cone	円錐状 えんすいじょう cone-shaped; conic

Even a two-character compound can be used as a prefix or suffix. For example, the word *shugi* (主義) by itself means 'principle.' Used as a suffix, it functions similar to the English word ending 'ism,' meaning 'doctrine.' This suffix appears in words such as 資本主義 (*shihonshugi*, 'capitalism') and 帝国主義 (*teikokushugi*, 'imperialism').

Whereas in English most prefixes and suffixes (such as 'un' or 'ment') do not form standalone words, most kanji that can be used as a prefix or a suffix can also be used outside of that role, perhaps as a standalone character (such as 人), or in other compound words where the character does not have a prefix or suffix role (such as 有無, *umu*, meaning 'existence or non-existence').

Although most prefixes and suffixes are read with the *on* readings of the characters, there are also a few that are read with *kun* readings. Generally, such prefixes and suffixes originated in the native Japanese language. An example of this is the prefix *ma* (ま, but sometimes altered to まん or まっ depending on the starting sound of the root word it is attached to), which conveys the notion 'completely.' It is written in kanji using the character 真. An example word using this prefix is *mannaka* ('dead center'), written 真ん中. (For words in which the prefix takes the form まん or まっ, only the ま portion is written with kanji; the other part is written in hiragana.) One more example is the suffix *saki*, which indicates a destination, such as a place that is visited or a place where something is sent. It is written in kanji using the character 先. An example word using this suffix is *tsutomesaki* ('place of employment'), written 勤め先.

As this particular prefix and suffix are native to Japanese, they are most commonly encountered attached to words read with a *kun* reading, as in the previous examples *mannaka* and *tsutomesaki*. That is not always the case, though. For example, in the word 旅行先 (*ryokōsaki*, 'travel destination'), the suffix *saki* is attached to a word in which the characters are read with *on* readings. The word *ryokōsaki*, thus, is read with a mix of *on* and *kun* readings.

5.6 Single Character Inheriting Compound Meaning

In Chapter 2, we saw some ways in which individual characters have acquired additional meanings beyond their original meanings. One more way that this can occur is when a single character is used as an abbreviation for a compound word that it appears in. In circumstances where this has occurred, the single character, in effect, has inherited the full meaning of the compound word. This process is best demonstrated with some examples.

The principal meaning of the character 誌 is 'to write down; to record.' It is used within compound words having meanings such as 'journal' and 'epitaph' (an inscription on a grave). It is also used in the compound word *zasshi* (雑誌), which means 'magazine' (as in a published periodical). The meaning of this compound comes from the two characters in it: 雑, meaning 'assorted,' and the aforementioned 誌, meaning 'to write down.'

But the single character 誌 can also be used as an abbreviation for the entire compound word *zasshi*, indicating—by itself—the meaning 'magazine.' It is used this way in words such as 週刊誌 (*shūkanshi*), meaning 'weekly published magazine' (consisting of characters meaning 'week' and 'publish,' together with the character 誌, here meaning 'magazine'), and タイム誌 (*taimu-shi*), meaning '*Time* magazine.'

What has happened here is that the character 誌 has acquired the meaning of the entire compound 雑誌, of which it is only one part. In other words, by itself it has become an abbreviation for the whole compound word.

Another character that is used in this way is 社. Consisting of elements meaning 'religious ceremony' and 'ground,' the original meaning of the character is a place where people worship the fertility of the land. It is commonly used in words having to do with religious shrines.

It also appears in the word *kaisha* (会社), whose original meaning was 'association,' as in a group of people working together toward a common goal. (The character 会 contributes the meaning 'gathering of people.') In Japan, the word *kaisha* now also means 'company; corporation.' Furthermore, the character 社 has become an abbreviation of this meaning. It is used with that meaning in other compound words such as 社長 (*shachō*, 'company president') and 新聞社 (*shinbunsha*, 'newspaper company').

Ateji-derived Abbreviations

Some characters have acquired additional meanings in this same way stemming from their use as *ateji*. In Chapter 2, it was mentioned that characters originally meaning 'rice,' 'to stand,' and 'roof tile' now also stand for the metric system words 'meter,' 'liter,' and 'gram,' respectively.

These three metric system words came into Japanese borrowed from the French language. At first, each was written with a set of kanji used as *ateji*. For example, the word 'gram' was originally expressed in Japanese as 瓦蘭姆, with characters meaning 'roof tile,' 'orchid,' and 'wet nurse,' respectively, used only for their sounds to imitate the French pronunciation of the word.[11] Later, the first of these three characters (瓦) by itself became an abbreviation for the entire word 'gram.' In fact, at one point the Japanese created new characters to represent common multiples and divisions of a gram, using this single character as the basis, combining it with other elements. For example, 'milligram' was written as 瓱, and 'kilogram' as 瓩. These terms, as well as the word 'gram' itself, are now more commonly expressed using katakana.

This same phenomenon is also seen with country names. Although most country names are now written in katakana, many country names were originally written using kanji, with the characters chosen based on *ateji*. For some of these country names, one of the characters (typically the first) came to be an abbreviation for the full country name.

For example, 'America' (which can refer to either the United States of America or the continents of the western hemisphere) can be written using *ateji* as 亜米利加, read the same way as the now more common katakana version: アメリカ (*amerika*). The second character alone (米) has become an abbreviation for the full name.[12] It is used in other compounds such as 南米 (*nanbei*, 'South America') and 米国 (*beikoku*, another way to refer to the United States, combining the 米 character with a character meaning 'country'). Note that *beikoku* is used in formal situations; in everyday conversation, *amerika* is more common.

---

[11] There is a slight disparity between the *on* readings of the characters in 瓦蘭姆 (*ga*, *ran*, and *mo*), and the Japanese pronunciation of the word: グラム. This is because the characters were chosen based on Chinese readings, rather than Japanese *on* readings.

[12] The character 米 was chosen as the abbreviation either because it is the first character of an older way of referring to the United States: 米利堅 (メリケン - a corruption of 'American'), or because the first character of 亜米利加 was already being used to represent Asia.

Chapter 6

Character Form in Depth

In this chapter we will take a closer look at some of the features of the forms of characters, including the strokes that make them up, variations in the way they are written, and how they are assembled.

6.1 Strokes, Stroke Count, and Stroke Order

As described in Chapter 1, each character is written as a series of strokes. When writing, one *stroke* is simply a single, continuous line that is created from the time the writing instrument (such as a pen or brush) contacts the writing surface to when it leaves the writing surface.

The total number of strokes that make up a character is called the *stroke count*. Characters can consist of anywhere from one to a theoretically unlimited number of strokes, but characters with more than 30 strokes are rather uncommon. Among the common use characters, the largest stroke count of any character is 29 strokes.

The order in which the strokes are drawn as a character is written is called the *stroke order*. In Japan, an official, proper stroke count and stroke order has been established for every character. Not only is the proper *order* of each stroke specified, but the *direction* of each stroke (i.e., which end is the starting point) is specified as well. Japanese schoolchildren learn to draw the characters with the proper stroke order, reinforced through extensive repetition.

A **stroke order diagram** is a diagram which demonstrates the proper order in which the strokes are drawn. This can be done in numerous different ways. We already saw one kind of diagram in Chapter 1. Here's another similar one:

ノ　ク　夕　夕　名　名

This type of diagram is made up of successive frames each showing the character after the next sequential stroke has been drawn. Note that the second and fifth strokes in this diagram include a bend in them.

In the above type of diagram, the directions of the strokes are not indicated. To show the direction, an additional indicator, such as the small arrows in the Chapter 1 diagrams, must be added. Stroke direction can also be determined in the following type of stroke order diagram:

In this kind of diagram, the small numbers indicate the order in which the strokes are drawn. Furthermore, each number is placed at the starting point of the corresponding stroke, and from that information the stroke direction is also known. This is the style of stroke order diagram that is used in Appendix C, in which a set of principles of stroke order are described.

So is it really necessary to learn the correct stroke order for every character? For kanji learners who want to be able to write the characters, it is very important to learn to write them correctly, using the proper stroke order. Also, for students learning the art of calligraphy, learning proper stroke order is essential; the characters will not look correct if drawn in an improper order.

For students who aren't interested in learning to write the characters, but only want to be able to read them, though, stroke order is not as important. But there is still a benefit to learning it. Learning stroke order helps with being able to determine stroke count, and being able to look at a character and determine (or at least closely estimate) its stroke count is a very helpful skill for being able to locate that character in a dictionary. In most character dictionaries, characters are ordered based on stroke count (among other factors).

Fortunately, the stroke orders of most characters follow a small set of general principles. Once you become familiar with these principles and begin to learn the stroke orders of some characters, learning stroke order for additional characters is not very difficult. These basic principles of stroke order are described in Appendix C.

6.2 Side Note: Handwritten Characters

Although Japanese schoolchildren are rigorously trained to draw characters using the proper stroke order while imitating the forms of model characters, as adults they don't always

CHARACTER FORM IN DEPTH 117

continue to write characters this way. There are some common shortcuts and simplifications used when writing characters by hand. As a result, the forms of handwritten characters often differ from the printed forms, sometimes greatly. Learning to read handwritten characters is a greater challenge than learning to read printed characters, and will not be discussed in this book.

6.3 The *Kaisho* Calligraphic Script

As explained in Chapter 2, Section 2.11, the forms of the characters underwent transformations over centuries, passing through several distinct styles. Eventually, sometime between the fifth and seventh centuries AD, writing became settled on a style which is still commonly used today. This style—called 'regular script' or 'standard script'—is based on a calligraphic representation of the characters, i.e., the drawing of the characters with ink using a brush. In Japanese, this style is called **kaisho**.

In the *kaisho* style, the individual strokes of characters vary in thickness. Today, some computer **typefaces** (sets of characters sharing a consistent design style, used for printing and display) imitate the calligraphic style, with characters whose strokes vary in thickness, just as brush strokes do. Most of the characters shown in this book are printed in such typefaces.

When kanji are written with a pencil or other thin-tipped writing instrument such as a ball-point pen, the same degree of varying stroke thickness can't be achieved. But it is still possible to have a subtle variation in line thickness by applying varying amounts of pressure when writing. When learning to write the characters, regardless of writing instrument, students are trained to write the characters using a calligraphic style as the model.

Although teaching the art of calligraphy is beyond the scope of this book, in this section we will take a look at the characteristics of strokes when depicted in the *kaisho* calligraphic style.

The Various Types of Strokes

When writing the characters using a brush and ink, the angle at which the brush is held and the way the brush is moved creates unique characteristics in the strokes. Among the following characters, all of the most common types of strokes can be seen:

An explanation of the characteristics of these strokes follows. The letters and numbers in parentheses refer to the character letters and stroke numbers in the above diagram. As in the earlier stroke order diagram, the stroke numbers are located at the beginnings of strokes.

- Strokes moving downward to the right tend to get thicker along the length (see A-3), while strokes moving upward to the right get thinner (B-3). Strokes moving downward to the left get thinner along the length, and often slightly curve outward to the left (B-4, C-1, C-4, D-1). Some of these strokes have a pronounced curve in them (A-2).

- Horizontal lines are not truly horizontal, but instead slightly climb to the right (A-1, C-2, C-5, D-3). Strokes moving straight downward can come to an end by simply stopping in place (B-2, C-3), or hooking off to the left (C-6), or angling up to the right (D-2). The angle up to the right is most commonly seen when the downward stroke is on the left side of the character, as in character D.

- Some strokes which move from the upper left to the lower right have a downward curve in them. The downward curve can be slight (D-4), or pronounced (B-5). This kind of curving stroke often ends with an upward hook. Very short strokes not connected to any other (A-4) are usually pointed at the top and rounded at the bottom, or vice-versa.

- Strokes can continue on after a sharp bend, but only if the bend is downward while moving to the right, or to the right while moving downward. Stroke E-3 features both of these kinds of bends: it moves downward, then bends to the right, and then bends downward again, before finally ending in a hook.

- Finally, box shapes, such as that of character F, tend to be wider at the top than at the bottom.

The major different types of strokes, such as those just discussed, have been given names. Those names are used in the study of the art of character calligraphy, but will not be mentioned in this book.

6.4 Character Printing Styles

After *kaisho* became established as the standard script, all character writing styles previously in use eventually either became obsolete, or were relegated to special applications, such as personal name seals.

But *kaisho* is not the only writing style in regular use today. Other styles which were developed based on *kaisho* are also frequently used. For example, as new ways were invented to produce the characters, such as various types of printing, slightly modified character styles were developed, suited to those methods.

The most well known of these is the *minchō* script.

With **minchō script**, nearly vertical and horizontal strokes are made truly vertical and horizontal, and the horizontal strokes are thinner than the vertical ones. Also, there are little triangle-shaped marks (called *uroko*) placed at the ends of the horizontal strokes, similar to serifs in Latin characters.

This style was originally developed in China for use in woodblock printing, and the thickness of the strokes was dictated by the horizontally-running grain of the wood in which the characters were carved. The name *minchō* is the Japanese word for 'Ming Dynasty,' which is the Chinese dynasty during which this style became popular.

More recently, the use of sans-serif typefaces (plain typefaces in which the characters do not have any kind of decorative marks) became widespread, including with kanji. The term used in Japan for this kind of typeface comes from an early term for sans-serif typefaces: **gothic**.

Since modern kanji scripts such as *minchō* and gothic were developed based on the structure of characters in the *kaisho* style, they bear a close resemblance to that style. But there are still some differences, as you can see with the following examples:

Kaisho　　　*Minchō*　　　Gothic

We already took a close look at the features of *kaisho* strokes in the previous section. With the *minchō* style, you can see that the vertical and horizontal strokes are truly vertical and horizontal, and that the horizontal strokes are thinner. Plus, you can see the triangle-shaped serifs at the ends of horizontal lines. The gothic script on the right, like *minchō*, has truly horizontal and vertical strokes, but is an even simpler design, with no serifs and all strokes of equal thickness throughout.

Among these different scripts there are additional small differences, such as the angles of some of the smaller strokes. Nonetheless, characters represented in these different styles are all similar enough in appearance that they can easily be recognized as being the same character.

Another commonly encountered character style is 'textbook.' **Textbook script** is a slightly modified version of kaisho in which the strokes are simplified to assist students who are learning to write the characters. With the two pairs of characters shown below, the main differences between the kaisho and textbook styles can easily be seen:

Kaisho　　　　Textbook

In the top character ('cultivated field'), you can see that the horizontal strokes are much closer to true horizontal in the textbook style. Furthermore, the center horizontal stroke extends all the way across, touching the downward strokes on each side, whereas in the kaisho style interior horizontal strokes often do not fully extend to the nearest downward stroke.[1]

Another difference between the styles is the elimination of optional stroke flourishes. In the bottom character ('thread' / 'string'), the straight downward stroke in the middle bottom can optionally end with a hook to the left. The textbook style removes that hook. Note, though,

---

[1] There are a few characters where, by design, the interior stroke does not extend all the way to the downward stroke on the right—most notably 臼, previously discussed in Section 4.2. With characters like 臼, no matter which script is used, the stroke does not (quite) touch. Fortunately, the number of such characters is small, and none are in common usage. (Note that the aforementioned 臼 character is different from the common use character meaning 'day' / 'sun' [日], in which the interior stroke *does* extend fully across.)

that in some other characters a hook is standard, not optional, and is therefore included even in the textbook style.

Also, in textbook script the characters are always depicted in a way that is consistent with the official stroke count. In contrast, with the kaisho style sometimes what would be a single stroke according to the proper stroke count is represented in a way that could not be duplicated with a single movement of a brush. In other words, the kaisho forms do not always obey the official stroke count.

For example, when the 'thread' character shown on the previous page is drawn with the proper stroke count, each of the first two strokes has a bend in it, first moving down to the left and then turning to the right. But in the kaisho representation, what would be the second stroke using the official stroke count, shown in close-up here:

appears to be two separate strokes, rather than one. In the textbook style representation, though, this same part can be drawn with a single stroke, consistent with the character's official stroke count.

Because the textbook script is the simplest representation for students learning the characters, this script is used as the standard script for displaying characters throughout this book.

With computer-based printing today, any script style can easily be used. Kaisho, textbook, minchō, and gothic are all commonly seen in printed material. There are other scripts in use, as well, but most of these were designed based on the kaisho style, and the characters of those scripts closely resemble the kaisho forms. For writing intended to be easily read, rather than used for decorative purposes, the styles used are inevitably ones closely related to kaisho.

6.5 Stroke Variations

We've just seen how the individual strokes of a character can look a little different when written with different scripts. But even when the same script type is used, there can still be slight differences among versions of the same character represented in different typefaces. Some commonly encountered examples of such stroke differences are shown in the following table. Each difference is demonstrated by the same character, above and below, shown in two different typefaces.[2]

A	B	C	D	E	F	G	H	I	J
戶	均	才	外	北	父	八	家	備	令
戸	均	才	外	北	父	八	家	備	令

---

[2] The characters in the table above are shown in various scripts, including kaisho, textbook, and minchō. Don't worry about which is which, though; the stroke differences shown here sometimes can be found within several different script types. The particular script types used here are not important to this discussion.

Even though some of the characters in the top row look noticeably different from their counterparts below them, they are in fact the same character, and should be treated that way. These variations are equivalent to the typeface differences that can be observed with the Latin lowercase 'a' character, or the numeral four, such as in the following representations:

$$\text{a} \longleftrightarrow \textit{a} \qquad 4 \longleftrightarrow 4$$

The versions of the characters in the top row of the table are somewhat more common, but some of the bottom row variations are also commonly encountered, including the characters labeled 'A,' 'C,' and 'E.' The bottom row variations of characters 'F,' 'G,' and 'H' were more common in the past; they are more likely to be encountered in older printed material or in certain typefaces in which the characters have an older appearance.

Of course, the ten characters in the table are not the only characters with different ways of being written; they are just representative of the types of stroke variation you are likely to encounter among characters. A detailed description of each of these variations follows.

- With the first character ('A'), the uppermost stroke is long and horizontal in the version on the top, but shorter and angled in the version on the bottom. This is one of the most common differences seen among various typefaces.

- The angles of the two short strokes are different in the two versions of character 'B.' A few other characters also exhibit similar variation in their short strokes, sometimes at different angles, though.

- The diagonal stroke of the 'C' character most commonly begins at a point directly on top of or very near to the downward stroke, before moving down to the left. In some typefaces, though, that diagonal stroke begins noticeably to the right of the downward stroke, and then crosses over it, moving down to the left.[3]

- The rightmost stroke of the 'D' character most commonly begins directly on top of the downward stroke. In some typefaces, though, it begins at a point to the left of the downward stroke.

- The lower left stroke of the 'E' character has two principal forms: one in which it touches the bottommost point of the downward stroke and extends a little further beyond it, and another in which it contacts that downward stroke slightly above its bottommost point, coming to an end. Both versions are common.

- With the 'F' character, the lower version has an extra segment at the top of the long stroke going downward to the right. This is still one single stroke, and is drawn starting at the leftmost point, going up, and then going down, similar to the way the hiragana へ (*he*) character is drawn.

- The 'G' character shows the same kind of variation as the 'F' character, but instead of initially going up, the extra segment first goes straight across to the right.

---

[3] The Japan Kanji Aptitude Testing Foundation, which administers the Kanji Kentei test, considers the version shown in the top row, in which the diagonal stroke begins very slightly to the right of the downward stroke, to be the optimal, most proper form of the character.

- In the older variation of the 'H' character (in the bottom row), the final stroke drawn (in the lower right) begins all the way up at a point on the horizontal stroke. In the more common version in the top row, this stroke begins further down, at a point on the main downward curved stroke.

- Characters 'I' and 'J' show the most dramatic kinds of stroke variation. Several different versions of character 'I' can be found, the two main types of which are shown in the table. In the lower version, the part of the character that looks like an uppercase L turned sideways does not come into contact with any other part of the character. In the upper version, this part no longer has an L shape, as the downward segment touches the horizontal segment not at its left end, but further inward. Additionally, both of these segments touch other parts of the character.

- The bottom two strokes of the two versions of the 'J' character differ greatly. In the upper version, they resemble the katakana マ (*ma*) character, but in the lower version, the final stroke is drawn straight downward, starting at a point along the horizontal part of the second-to-last stroke.

The two versions of the 'J' character shown in the table appear so different from each other that they could easily be assumed to be separate, unrelated characters. But they are not. Fortunately, most other stroke variations you will encounter are not as pronounced as this.

6.6 Element Variations

Even within a single typeface, there are many individual elements which can be found written in different ways among different characters. We already saw numerous examples of this in Chapter 2, such as how the 'movement' determinative can have either of two different forms:

The version on the right is the older style of this component, now seen only in characters not on the common use list. Although the appearance is different, these two variations should be thought of and treated as the same element. The following three characters also share a common element:

羽　　曜　　翅

The character on the left originated as a pictograph of the feathers of a bird. The meaning of the character is 'feathers' or 'wings.' That character appears as an element in each of the characters to its right, but with a different form in each one. Specifically, the small strokes that are arranged similar to the katakana ン (*n*) character in the first character above are all horizontal in the second character, and all point down and to the left in the third character. Yet the element is the same among all three characters; only the appearance has changed. (The version of this element in the rightmost character is in an older style, now seen only in characters not on the common use list.)

CHARACTER FORM IN DEPTH

Elements also sometimes change form, sometimes significantly, when compressed to fit in a small space within a character. We already saw a few examples of this in Chapter 2, such as the altered forms of the 'person' and 'meat' / 'flesh' elements, shown again here:

人: 休   肉: 臓

Each element is shown above first as a full character, and then in an alternate form as a single element within another character (with the other elements of the character grayed out to make the component easier to see).

Other elements which also exhibit this kind of form change include those meaning 'fire,' 'water,' and 'heart,' as shown below:

火: 黒   水: 海   心: 忙

When compressed to the bottom, the 'fire' element is reduced to four small strokes. When compressed to the left-hand side, the 'water' element is reduced to three strokes. And when compressed to the left-hand side, the 'heart' element becomes one long vertical stroke with two smaller strokes on its sides. These elements do not always change form when compressed, though. For example, the 'heart' element when placed at the bottom of a character usually retains its full character form.

The following two different characters share a very similar abbreviated form. The abbreviated forms differ by only one stroke:

示: 礻   衣: 衤

The character on the left is frequently used as a determinative to identify characters having to do with religious rites. The character on the right is also frequently used as a determinative, marking characters having to do with clothing. When looking at a character that contains one of these two abbreviated forms, it is necessary to pay attention to whether or not the extra stroke is present in order to identify which of the two elements it is.

The following two characters both take on the same abbreviated form, but they can be distinguished because one of the two is always found on the left side of a character, and the other always on the right:

阜: 院   邑: 郡

The character on the left identifies a hill or other tall place, especially one with steps built into it. As an element, it appears on the left side of a character, where it takes on the altered shape shown above. The character on the right identifies a large region where people live (from the size of a town up to a full province). As an element, it appears on the right side of a character, where it takes on the altered shape shown. Note that the full forms of these elements (阜 and 邑) are infrequently encountered.[4] The abbreviated forms of both are much more common.

---

[4] Although otherwise rare, the 阜 variation appears in the name of Japan's Gifu (岐阜) Prefecture.

Sometimes, the abbreviated form is only different by a few strokes, as with the following two elements:

$$長：髟 \qquad 食：飠$$

The abbreviated forms of many of the elements shown in this section were derived from simplified ways of writing the characters, such as the cursive style.

6.7 Variant Characters

In Chapter 2, it was noted that the official forms of some characters underwent simplification just after World War II, and that the earlier forms of those characters (just prior to simplification) can now be thought of as *variant characters*: alternate forms of characters which have the same meaning(s), reading(s) and usage as the principal forms.

Characters with minor stroke variations, such as those shown in the table in Section 6.5, are generally not considered variant characters. Typically, only one version of such characters appears within any given typeface. The maker of each typeface chooses which of the styles to adopt.

With characters that are considered to be variants, though, more than one form can exist even within a single typeface. In cases such as this, each variation is given a separate computer 'encoding' so that both can be represented within the same typeface. In this sense, they are treated as if they were two different characters. For such characters, one form is considered the standard, and any other form is considered a variant.

The majority of variant characters still encountered today are the versions of characters in use just prior to the post-war simplifications. In other words, they are the pre-simplification versions of characters which have been simplified.

Some other types of variant characters are still encountered, as well. For example, as kanji matured over time, alternate ways of writing a given character sometimes developed in parallel with each other. In many of these cases, one version became the standard long ago, and the others were phased out of usage and are no longer seen. But in some cases, multiple versions continue to exist to this day.

Today, such surviving variations are most commonly found in people and place names. Because some family names or place names continue to use a less common variant of a character, it is necessary within computer typefaces to represent the variant form in addition to the version which has become standard, if these names are to be printed correctly.

The most well-known example of this is the character meaning 'high' / 'tall,' shown below in the more common, standard form (on the left below), and a variant form sometimes seen in people and place names (on the right):

$$高 \qquad 髙$$

Each of these versions has existed for a long time. When the *jōyō kanji* were established, the version on the left was chosen as the standard form, and the version on the right became a variant character. Some people and place names containing this character use the version on the left, and some use the version on the right. But when used to write the word 'tall,' the standard version on the left is always used.

For characters like this with common, well-known variant forms, shorthand terms are sometimes created to enable quick identification of which version is being referred to, such as when someone is explaining how to write his or her name. With the characters on the previous page, the part of each character which is different from the other is used in the terms that were created to distinguish the two versions. The character on the left is called *kuchidaka*, which combines the Japanese word *kuchi*, meaning 'mouth,' with the word *daka*, which is a way of describing the character as a whole.[5] *Kuchi* is used in this term because the unique part of this character resembles the character for 'mouth': 口. The variant version on the right is called *hashigodaka*, combining the Japanese word for 'ladder' (*hashigo*) with *daka*, since the part of the character different from the standard form resembles a ladder.

Another type of variant character contains the same set of elements as the main form, but in a different arrangement. A common example of this is the character meaning 'island.'

The standard form (on the left), and two variant forms are shown below:

Each version consists of the same two elements: 'mountain' and 'bird,' but in a different arrangement in each case. Note that in the standard version, part of the bird element (the four short strokes) has been removed to make room for the 'mountain' element. This method of composing characters is discussed in the next section.

One more example of a character and its variant which contain the same elements is the character meaning 'reverse side' / 'back side':

At first glance, these two characters do not seem to share the same elements. If you refer back to Section 6.6, though, you can see that the element meaning 'clothing' can be written in two very different ways:

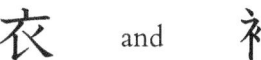

The two versions of the 'reverse side' character shown above each use a different form of the 'clothing' element, together with a phonetic component: 里. Furthermore, the 'clothing' element in the standard version of the 'reverse side' character (the one on the left above) is split into two parts, with the phonetic inserted between the parts.

---

[5] This character is used to write the Japanese word *takai*, 高い. Excluding the okurigana (い), the kanji portion of this word is read as *taka*. Attached as the second part of a compound word, it becomes *daka* via the *rendaku* process, described in Chapter 9.

To someone not familiar with kanji, most variant characters (especially ones such as the last pair) probably appear to be completely different characters, and may seem difficult to learn. But, as explained in Chapter 2, the amount of effort required to learn them is minimal. Once you have learned or mastered a character, it is a simple matter to learn a variant of that character. With the original character, you need to learn how it is written, its reading(s), and its meaning(s), but with a variant character, you only need to learn that it is another way to write a character you have already learned.

Appendix G shows a large variety of variant characters, most of which resulted from character simplification. A few examples of variant characters that came about through other means are also shown.

6.8 Character Composition

Most characters which consist of multiple elements are formed simply by bringing together the various elements, placing them adjacent to one another. When there are only two elements, they are usually placed side-by-side or one on top of the other.

Utilizing Empty Space

But as we have already seen, including in numerous examples in the table in Section 4.3 (Character Regions), one element may also be placed into the empty space of another. We also saw this in Chapter 2 with the 'listen' character, where the 'ear' element is inserted into the empty space of the 'gate' element:

耳 is placed into 門 to create 聞

Sometimes the empty space needs to be created first, either by breaking apart an element or removing some strokes from the element. In the last section, we saw characters constructed in each of those ways:

里 is placed into 衣 to create 裏

山 is placed into 鳥 to create 島

In the case of the first character (meaning 'reverse side' / 'back side'), the top two strokes of the 'clothing' element are split apart from the rest, and the other element is inserted in between the two parts. Besides the 'clothing' character, only one other character is commonly separated in this way: 行, meaning (among other things) 'go' / 'carry out,' which is sometimes separated into left and right parts, with another component placed in between them.

For example,

圭 is placed into 行 to create 街

CHARACTER FORM IN DEPTH

In the case of the 'island' character on the previous page (島), four strokes are removed from the 'bird' element and then the 'mountain' element is inserted into the newly created empty space. Another element frequently modified in this way is: 虎, meaning 'tiger.' The two strokes in the lower right (identical in shape to the *hitoashi* element first mentioned in Chapter 2), are often removed, and other elements put in their place.

For example,

呉   is placed into   虎   to create   虞

More than Two Elements

When there are three or more elements in a character, a decision about arranging them must be made. When the three elements contribute equally to the character meaning, as with the character we have already seen meaning 'to take apart':

解

usually one is made larger and the other two smaller so that they can all fit nicely into a mostly square overall character shape.

But when two of the elements already form a character on their own, they are usually kept together as if they were a single element, with additional elements added on one of the sides or the top or bottom. We saw this in Chapter 3 with the character having the meanings 'mutual,' 'minister,' and 'appearance':

相

When this character is used as a phonetic and combined with an additional determinative component, the two elements that comprise it ('tree' and 'eye') are kept together in the same configuration, and treated as if they were a single element. In characters using this character as a phonetic, such as:

想   and   箱

you can see how the original two elements are kept together as a unit, and the determinative ('heart' in the first character, 'bamboo' in the second) is added above or below, occupying one entire side of the character. Because many characters are composed in this way, determinatives (which are often added to already existing characters) often fill an entire side of a character.

Other Assembly Techniques

In addition to the methods already described in this section, other kinds of alterations can take place, too, as elements are assembled into characters. Following are examples of a few other types of form alteration.

Note that some of these types of form alteration are relatively uncommon in character construction.

1. Extending a Stroke to the Far Edge

A stroke can be extended all the way to a far edge of the full character. Examples:

the last stroke of 免 is extended to the right edge in 勉

the first stroke of 歹 is extended to the right edge in 死

In the first example, the final stroke of the left element of the character is extended to the right edge. In the second example, the top stroke of the left element is extended to the right edge.

2. Shortening the End of a Downward Stroke

When a downward stroke of an element extends below the lowest horizontal stroke of the element, that downward stroke is sometimes shortened to end right at that lowest horizontal stroke when another element is placed below it. Examples:

the bottom of 牛 is cut off in 告

the bottom of 聿 is cut off in 書

Note that in characters where these elements do not have another element located below them, the downward stroke is not shortened. Examples:

牟 and 筆

3. Bending or Moving Parts of Elements to Create Space

Sometimes individual strokes or entire elements are moved or bent to create space within a character. Examples:

the elements 月 and 又 are modified in 祭

the top two strokes of 食 are spread apart in 養

In the first example, the 月 ('meat') element is curved outward to the left, and the bottommost part of the first stroke in the 又 ('hand') element is shortened, in order to create a larger space for placing the lower element (示).

In the second example, the top two strokes of 食 are pushed apart from each other to help minimize the overall height of the character. In this character, the vertical stroke of the upper element (羊) is shortened, as well.

CHARACTER FORM IN DEPTH

4. Eliminating a Redundancy

When the neighboring strokes of two adjacent elements are very similar in appearance, one set is sometimes removed. Examples:

parts of 父 and 金 are merged in 釜

parts of 竹 and 弟 are merged in 第

parts of 斉 and 示 are merged in 斎

In the first example, the combination of 父 and 金 results in the elimination of the top two strokes of the bottom element, which are similar to the lower part of the bottom two strokes of the top element. In the second example, the lowest two strokes of the upper element are quite similar to the topmost two short strokes of the lower element, and so one set of these strokes is eliminated in the character which combines these elements. In the third example, when the 示 element is added to the interior of the 斉 character, its top two strokes are merged with the two lowest horizontal strokes of the 斉 character.

Chapter 7

The *On* Reading in Depth

The *on* readings of the characters are those based on the way the characters were originally pronounced in China before being brought to Japan. In this chapter, many aspects of *on* readings are looked at in depth.

7.1 *Kango*

On readings were originally the only way that the characters were read when first used in Japan. The Japanese simply pronounced the characters by imitating the way the characters were spoken by the Chinese. A little later, a method of assigning characters to native Japanese words based on their meaning became established, creating the *kun* readings. At that point, *on* readings were primarily used in the reading of words that were borrowed from the Chinese language, and *kun* readings were primarily used in the reading of words that were Japanese in origin.

The term **kango** is used to describe a word that is read using the *on* readings of its characters. The *kan* part of this term is written with the same character as the first part of the word *kanji*, and means 'Chinese.' The term *kango* essentially means 'Chinese word(s).'

But just because a word is classified as *kango* does not necessarily mean that it came from China. Some words exist only in Japanese but have been created (or modified) in imitation of the Chinese style. These words are also considered *kango*.

For example, the modern Japanese word *henji* (返事), meaning 'response' / 'reply,' was formed by restructuring the native Japanese word *kaerigoto* (返り事), omitting the okurigana (り) and using the *on* readings of the constituent kanji. The modern form is treated as *kango*.

So *kango*, then, are words that either came from China or have been formed in the same style as words from China. They are read exclusively using the *on* reading of each character in them. Note that words written using *ateji* (discussed in Chapter 5) are special cases. Even if all the characters in them are read using *on* readings, they are not considered *kango*. This is because most words written using *ateji* are actually native Japanese words, and the characters in them are primarily used for their sound, not for their meaning.

Most of the words borrowed from China were compound words, consisting of two or more characters together. There are also quite a few compound words in the native Japanese language, but many of these include inflections (described in Chapter 1), and so are typically written in part using hiragana. As a result, the majority of compound words which consist only of kanji (i.e., do not include any hiragana characters in them) are *kango*, read using the *on* reading of each character in the word.

A few *kango* do consist of only a single character. One such example is *ai* (愛), meaning 'love' (the noun form, as in 'affection'). But there are relatively few such words. Most *kango* consist of more than one character, and most single-character words are originally native Japanese words and are read using the *kun* reading.

In contrast to *kango*, words of native Japanese origin are referred to as either **wago** ('Wa words') or *yamato kotoba* ('Yamato words'). *Wa* and *Yamato* are both former names for Japan, in use long ago.

7.2 Parts of Speech

By themselves, the vast majority of *kango* are nouns. But many *kango* can also be converted into verb, adjective, or adverb forms. To do this, it is usually necessary to place a grammatical modifier just after the word. These modifiers are, by custom, always written using hiragana.

Note, though, that you cannot just add any modifier of your choosing to any word. The allowable modifiers that any given *kango* can be used with (and, therefore, which parts of speech it can be used as) are already established in the language. You can consult a dictionary to learn allowable usages for any particular word.

What follows is a brief summary of the most common modifiers used with *kango*. This summary includes some discussion of Japanese grammar. As a comprehensive explanation of Japanese grammar is beyond the scope of this book, those interested in a more in-depth explanation of this topic should consult a Japanese grammar textbook.

Verbs

For *kango* which can be made into verbs, this is usually done by appending *suru*, or less commonly *wo suru*. For example, the word *ai* (the noun form of 'love,' as in 'affection') can be made into the verb form of 'love' (as in 'to cherish') by appending *suru*: *ai suru*. Of course, for words that can be modified by adding *suru*, other standard grammatical inflections of *suru* such as *shita* (past tense), *shinai* (negation), and *saseru* (causative form) can also be made.

For just a few words, the modifiers *jiru* or *zuru* are appended to make a verb. These endings are mostly applied only to *kango* which consist of a single character, rather than to compound words. An example of a word which can be modified with *jiru* is 信 (*shin*). By itself, the word means 'honesty' / 'trust.' Made into a verb: 信じる (*shinjiru*), it means 'believe.'

Adjectives

Some *kango* can be made into adjectives. Most of these words are in a special class called 'adjectival nouns' (often called *na*-adjectives in Japanese grammar textbooks, and called *keiyōdōshi* in Japanese). With adjectival nouns, the modifier added depends on the usage. If the adjectival noun comes just before the noun it modifies, *na* is appended to it. If the adjectival noun is the sentence predicate,[1] *da* is appended (or an equivalent variation of *da*, such as *desu* in more formal contexts, or *de* when the predicate is not the final part of the sentence).

As an example, the adjectival noun *shinsetsu* by itself means 'kindness.' It can also be made into the adjective 'kind' or the sentence predicate 'is kind':

chiisana shinsetsu 小さな親切	'a small act of kindness'
shinsetsu na kotoba 親切な言葉	'kind words'
Ano hito wa shinsetsu da. あの人は親切だ。	'That person is kind.'

In the first phrase, *shinsetsu* by itself is the noun 'kindness.' In the second phrase, *shinsetsu* is used as an adjective ('kind') to describe the noun that follows it (*kotoba*, 'words'), so *na* is appended to it. In the final example, *shinsetsu* is the sentence predicate ('is kind'), so *da* (or *desu*, etc.) is added.

Some adjectival nouns require the addition of *teki* (的) before the modifier. For example, to make the word 印象 (*inshō*), meaning 'impression,' into the adjective 'impressive,' first *teki* must be added: 印象的 (*inshōteki*). Then, the appropriate modifier, such as *na* or *da*, is added.

A limited number of *kango* are not adjectival nouns but can still be made into an adjective form by appending one of the following grammatical modifiers: *no*, *aru*, *no aru*, or *ga aru*. Of these, the *ga aru* form is used when the word is being used as a sentence predicate, and the others are used when the word precedes the noun it modifies.

An example of this is *naibu*, a word which, used by itself, is a noun meaning 'the inside part' / 'interior.' This word can also be used together with *no* as an adjective meaning 'inner' / 'internal,' placed before the noun it describes. Another example is *ninki*, which can be used by itself as a noun meaning 'popularity,' but can also be used in the adjectival form ('popular') by adding either *no aru*, or *ga aru*. Following are some usage examples for these words.

---

[1] In grammar, a predicate is the part of the sentence that says something about the subject. For example, in the sentence [The chair is brown.], the subject is 'the chair' and the predicate is 'is brown.' In Japanese, predicates are usually located at the ends of sentences.

naibu e mukatte
内部へ向かって   'toward the interior'

naibu no kankaku
内部の感覚   'inner feelings'

ninki no aru hon
人気のある本   'a popular book'

A few *kango* can be used as adjectives by placing them directly in front of the nouns they describe, without additional modifiers placed in between. For example, the word *kokuritsu*, meaning 'national,' is placed directly before *byōin* ('hospital') in the phrase *kokuritsu byōin* ('national hospital').[2]

Adverbs

Some nouns can be made into adverbs by appending *ni* or, less commonly, *de* or *to*. For example, *shinsetsu ni* means 'kindly.'

Summary

The following table summarizes some of the various modifiers that can be added to some *kango*, as discussed in this section, and shows how those modifiers affect the part of speech of the respective *kango*.

Word	Reading †	Part of Speech	Meaning
愛	あい	noun	love ('affection')
愛する	あいする	verb	love ('cherish')
信	しん	noun	faith; trust
信じる	しんじる	verb	believe
親切	しんせつ	noun	kindness
親切な [thing]	しんせつな [thing]	adjective	kind
親切だ	しんせつだ	predicate	is kind
親切に	しんせつに	adverb	kindly
印象	いんしょう	noun	impression
印象的な [thing]	いんしょうてきな [thing]	adjective	impressive
内部	ないぶ	noun	inner part; interior
内部の [thing]	ないぶの [thing]	adjective	inner; internal
人気	にんき	noun	popularity
人気のある [thing]	にんきのある [thing]	adjective	popular
人気がある	にんきがある	predicate	is popular

† For simplicity, all readings, whether *on* or *kun*, are written entirely in hiragana.

---

[2] *Kokuritsu* is an example of one of the few *kango* words which by itself (with no modifiers) has a form other than a noun. It is used almost exclusively as an adjective.

7.3 Polite Modifiers

Some *kango* can be made into more polite words by adding a special prefix. For most of these words, this prefix is *go*, written in kanji as 御. For example, adding the prefix *go* to the word *annai* ('guidance' / 'information') turns it into the more polite form: *goannai* (written 御案内 or ご案内).

The polite forms of words are used in circumstances where politeness is required, such as when speaking with customers or superiors.

A limited number of *kango* instead use *o* as the special prefix. Examples include *otenki* ('the weather') and *odenwa* ('telephone' / 'phone call'). But this is relatively uncommon; as a general rule of thumb, for words that have a polite form, *go* is added to *kango*, and *o* to *wago* (native Japanese words).

Regardless of whether *go* or *o* is added to a word, when this polite prefix is written in kanji, the same character is used: 御.

7.4 Valid *On* Readings

As mentioned in Chapter 1, developing the ability to distinguish *on* and *kun* readings for characters which have both is a very useful skill for mastering the reading of Japanese. One aid to being able to do this is to learn how to recognize a 'valid,' or legitimately possible, *on* reading.

Although a *kun* reading can consist of just about any combination of basic sounds in the Japanese language,[3] all *on* readings are limited in length and adhere to a particular pattern. Readings that fall outside of this pattern, then, cannot be the *on* reading of any character.

To be a valid *on* reading, two basic rules must be met. Before explaining these rules, it is first necessary to understand the concept of a *mora*. In spoken language, a **mora** is the shortest unit of spoken sound. A mora is similar to a syllable, but slightly different in that syllables can vary in duration, some longer than others, whereas a single mora always has the same short duration. A syllable can consist of more than one mora (such as when its vowel sound is long in duration).

This distinction doesn't matter much in English. When speaking, even if individual sounds are spoken more quickly or more slowly, word meaning is unchanged and the speaker can still be readily understood. In Japanese, though, the length of spoken sounds is very important in the language. Long vowel sounds are treated differently than short vowel sounds (and even written differently when using either hiragana or katakana). Changing the vowel length (from short to long, or long to short) actually changes the word.

For example, the Japanese words

                トリ (*to-ri*)   and   トオリ (*to-o-ri*)

---

[3] In the next chapter, the form of a typical *kun* reading will be explained.

meaning 'bird' and 'avenue,' respectively, differ in the length of the first vowel sound: the *o* vowel sound is short in the first word, and long in the second. To the Japanese ear, these words are clearly different.

In Japanese, short vowel sounds consist of one mora, and long vowel sounds consist of two. So トリ has a total of two morae, and トオリ has a total of three morae. ('Morae' is the plural form of mora.)

Counting morae is fairly easy in Japanese. When a Japanese word is written in hiragana or katakana, the number of characters used corresponds to the number of morae in the word, with one exception: the small versions of the *ya*, *yu*, and *yo* characters (ゃ/ャ, ゅ/ュ, and ょ/ョ) do not add to the total mora count. That is because these characters are always paired with the preceding character to indicate a short sound that begins with a consonant cluster.[4]

Take, as an example, 'Tokyo,' which is written in hiragana and katakana as:

とうきょう　　　　トウキョウ

In both written forms above, there are five characters but only four morae, as the third and fourth characters together (*ki* and small *yo*) indicate the single-mora *kyo* sound, and so together are counted as only one mora. When spoken correctly, 'Tokyo' consists of two syllables (*tō* and *kyō*), each with a long vowel sound, consistent with the total mora count of four.

The syllabic *n* character (ん/ン) and the small *tsu* character (っ/ッ), formally called a *sokuon*, each are counted as one mora. When speaking Japanese, the sounds represented by these characters are considered to be the equivalent of one short vowel sound in duration.

Incidentally, morae, rather than syllables, are used in Japanese poetry as the basic counting unit. So, for example, a standard 5-7-5 *haiku* poem consists of 5 morae, followed by 7 morae, followed by 5 morae.

Now that the concept of mora is clear, let's look at the two rules for a valid *on* reading.

Rules for a Valid *On* Reading

Rule 1: Valid *on* readings may consist of only one or two morae.

Rule 2: If there is a second mora, it may only be one of the following sounds:

い、う、き、く、ち、つ、ん

This list of sounds is easier to remember when it is transliterated into the Latin alphabet using Japanese-style romanization:

i,　u,　ki,　ku,　ti,　tu,　n

When expressed this way, you can see that the only vowel sounds contained in the list are /i/ and /u/, and the only starting consonant sounds are /k/ and /t/.

---

[4] A 'consonant cluster' refers to multiple consonant sounds placed together with no intervening vowel sound between them. In written Japanese, the small versions of the *ya*, *yu*, and *yo* characters are used to mark a consonant cluster in which the initial consonant sound is 'palatalized' (i.e., altered to sound as if it is immediately followed by a /y/ sound). Palatalized consonants are discussed further in Chapter 8.

THE *ON* READING IN DEPTH

Per these rules, **all** of the following could be valid *on* readings:

さ	(*sa*)	(only one mora)
ざ	(*za*)	(only one mora)
きょ	(*kyo*)	(only one mora: a consonant cluster with a single vowel sound)
はく	(*haku*)	(two morae, the second is く)
いち	(*ichi*)	(two morae, the second is ち)
たん	(*tan*)	(two morae, the second is ん)
すい	(*sui*)	(two morae, the second is い)
みょう	(*myō*)	(two morae: みょ, and う)

But **none** of these could be valid *on* readings:

からだ	(*karada*)	(there are three morae, violates Rule 1)
ささ	(*sasa*)	(the second mora is さ, violates Rule 2)
きょろ	(*kyoro*)	(the second mora is ろ, violates Rule 2)
かお	(*kao*)	(the second mora is お, violates Rule 2)

When you become familiar with these rules, as you quickly will with practice, it will be a simple matter to determine if a reading *could* be a valid *on* reading. This will help you to distinguish between an *on* reading and a *kun* reading of a character. For example, if there is a character with two main readings, and you know that one is an *on* reading and one is a *kun* reading, if only one of those two readings satisfies these rules, then that one must be the *on* reading, and the other is the *kun* reading.

For example, in Chapter 1 we saw that the character meaning 'water' (水) has readings of *sui* and *mizu*, one of which is the *on* reading, and the other the *kun*. As *mizu* can not be a valid *on* reading (the second mora is *zu*, which does not satisfy Rule 2), *mizu* must be the *kun* reading, which leaves *sui* as the *on* reading.

Another helpful hint in distinguishing *on* and *kun* readings is that when written in hiragana or katakana, all of the following characters: *n* and small *ya*, *yu*, *yo*, and *tsu*, are more commonly found in *on* readings than in *kun* readings. When encountered, these characters are more likely to be part of an *on* reading. This is explained further in the next chapter.

Of course, some characters have a *kun* reading that could also happen to fit the format of a valid *on* reading. These can be difficult to remember, and easy to confuse as *on* readings. Appendix I contains a list of common *kun* readings that fall into this category.

You may wonder why *on* readings are limited in the way described here. Character readings in China (which were the basis for the Japanese *on* readings) were only one syllable in length, but they could optionally end with one of several consonant sounds. Native spoken Japanese was not capable of expressing ending consonant sounds, and so instead a second mora was added to the *on* readings to reflect these ending sounds. Only the sounds い, う, き, く, ち, つ, and ん were used in this role.

Finally, note that there are a very small number of minor exceptions to these rules. For example, the most commonly used *on* readings of the character 直 ('straight') are *CHOKU* and *JIKI*, both valid *on* readings per the rules of this section. However, the character can also be read as *JIKA*, such as in the expression *jika ni* (meaning 'directly; personally'). This reading derived from *JIKI*, and thus should also be considered an *on* reading. Nonetheless, it violates the second rule of a valid *on* reading. Such exceptions are extremely rare.

7.5 Multiple *On* Readings – Character and Phonetic

In the book thus far, we have seen several examples of characters that have more than one possible *on* reading, including the character just mentioned (直) which can be read as *CHOKU*, *JIKI*, or (in a few limited cases) *JIKA*. Also, in Chapter 2, we saw that the character meaning 'writing' (文) has multiple possible *on* readings: it is read as *BUN* in some words that use it, and as *MON* in others. With characters such as these, it's necessary not only to remember several different *on* readings, but also to learn for each word that contains the character which of those readings it uses.

These are far from the only examples. A large number of characters can be read with more than one different *on* reading. And, as we first saw in Chapter 2, the same situation is true of phonetic components, as well; most of them can be read in several ways. For example, we learned that although many characters with the 其 phonetic component have an *on* reading of *KI*, there is also a character with this phonetic component in which the reading is *GO*.

With a few phonetic components, the *on* reading is the same for every character using that component as a phonetic. For example, every *jōyō* character containing the component 扁 uses it as a phonetic and has the *on* reading *HEN*.[5] This makes things very simple: whenever you learn a new *jōyō* character with that component, you immediately know what the *on* reading is, and memorization (of the *on* reading, at least) is simple.

However, this component is the exception rather than the rule: such phonetics with only a single reading are few in number. Most phonetic components can be read with one of several similar readings.

But even though there is variation in their readings, phonetics are still useful for remembering character *on* readings. Recognizing the existence of a phonetic component in a character can still give a clue to and help the learner to more quickly home in on—and commit to memory—the correct reading of that character. When dealing with phonetics, it's useful to think of them as components which give an approximation, or hint, of the character reading, rather than components which indicate one single, precise reading. This approach is still more efficient than just disregarding phonetics and memorizing the *on* reading(s) of each character individually.

---

[5] While this is true of all *jōyō kanji*, there exist a few rare non-*jōyō* characters with this phonetic that have a slightly different reading. These characters are unlikely to be encountered in typical reading materials.

In most cases of multiple *on* readings, whether it be those of an individual character such as 文 or of a phonetic component such as 其, the various readings are not randomly different from each other, but in fact share similarities and correspondences. Such readings are called *related readings* in this book.

The same correspondences among related readings can be found both with individual characters and with phonetics. Becoming familiar with the most frequently encountered of these correspondences will speed up the learning of character *on* readings. We will study related readings in detail in Section 7.10.

7.6 The Principal *On* Reading

Among characters with more than one *on* reading, it is often the case that one of the readings is much more common than any other.

For example, the character for 'body' that we first saw in Chapter 2 (体) is read as *TAI* in almost all common *kango* compounds that use it. However, it is read as *TEI* in one common word: *teisai* (体裁, 'appearance'). (As we will see later, *TAI* and *TEI* are related readings.)

For such characters, the recommendation of this book is to treat the most common reading as the **principal reading** of the character, and to consider any other reading of the character a secondary reading. Thus, the principal *on* reading of 体 is *TAI*, and a secondary *on* reading is *TEI*.

With a character such as this, when first learning and memorizing it, it is best to focus on the principal reading, as that is by far the most common reading. Being familiar with related readings then helps with remembering the secondary reading(s) of the character.

In the phonetics section of Part 2 of the book, primarily only principal *on* readings are provided for the example characters listed. In a few cases secondary *on* readings are also provided, but are placed in parentheses. Some characters have two different readings that are both used fairly often. In those cases, both readings are treated as principal readings.

7.7 Different Readings for Different Meanings

For a small number of characters with multiple *on* readings, the different readings each have a different meaning associated with them. A notable example of this is the character:

This character has two major meanings: 'music' and 'enjoyment.' The character etymology is unclear. It may have originally depicted an early stringed instrument made of wood, with the bottom of the character (our familiar 'tree' element) indicating that it is made of wood, and the top of the character, in its earliest form, showing the strings and other parts of the instrument. Another theory is that the character originally depicted a type of oak tree in which silkworms made cocoons. Regardless of the true origin, at some point—perhaps as an extended meaning or perhaps from phonetic borrowing—the character meaning became 'music,' and then was extended further to 'enjoyment.' The connection between these latter two meanings is easy to see: music is a source of enjoyment.

With this character, the *on* reading is different for each of the two meanings. Among words that use this character read with an *on* reading, when the character represents 'music,' the reading is *GAKU*, and when it represents 'enjoyment,' the reading is *RAKU*. These are actually a pair of related readings, as we will see in Section 7.10. For most characters with multiple *on* readings and multiple meanings, however, the meanings and readings are mixed, rather than clearly separated as in this case.

7.8 Causes of Multiple *On* Readings

Why do many characters (and phonetic components) have multiple *on* readings?

The full answer to this question is rather complicated, and involves numerous different factors. This section briefly summarizes the major reasons multiple *on* readings came about. The causes are divided into those which took place in China, prior to the characters being brought to Japan, and those occurring as or after the characters came to Japan.

A. Causes Occurring in China

1. New Readings for Additional Meanings

In China, many of the characters only have a single reading. But there are also a number of characters with more than one reading. For characters with multiple readings, the readings are usually quite similar, sometimes only differing by nothing more than pitch accent.

In some cases, the branching into multiple readings occurred when characters took on additional meanings. The different readings served to distinguish the separate meanings, such as in the case of the 楽 character mentioned in the previous section. This character has different readings for its different meanings both in Japanese and in Chinese.[6]

2. Inexact Application of Phonetics

Linguists who attempt to recreate ancient Chinese character pronunciations theorize that even from the beginning, the readings of phonetic components used by themselves did not always exactly match the readings of characters that use them.

In other words, just as there is sometimes disparity today between the reading of a phonetic component and the reading of a character which uses that component as its phonetic, these same differences, in some cases, existed even back when the phonetic was first chosen. If true, it means that phonetics have always been considered to be an approximate indicator of the character reading, rather than an absolute indicator.

---

[6] Note, though, that characters with multiple readings in Chinese do not always have multiple readings in Japanese, and vice versa.

B. Causes Occurring in Japan

1. Importation at Different Times from Different Locations

One of the biggest causes of multiple *on* readings was due to the way the characters and their readings were brought to Japan. The characters did not all arrive at one point in time, but rather came to Japan during several distinct waves, with each wave originating from a different region within China and having its own unique character pronunciations.

The differences in character pronunciation were due to changes in the Chinese language over time and distance. Even among a population of people who remain in one region, over centuries of time the spoken sounds of their language will undergo change. And as people who speak a given language spread apart from each other, the sounds of the spoken language in each separated group will gradually diverge from each other.[7]

Both of these effects can be seen in the Chinese language. During China's extensive history, as different dynasties rose and fell, the spoken Chinese language continually changed. And, as the language spread over a large area, it splintered into different dialects. Although they can be traced back to a common language, some modern dialects (such as Mandarin and Cantonese) have drifted so far apart from each other that they are mutually unintelligible and are considered by some linguists to be separate languages, comparable with the difference between, say, two of the Romance languages. Although these different dialects, if written using kanji, share many of the same characters, the pronunciations of the characters are noticeably different.

Because different compound words came to Japan at different times (i.e., part of different waves), many characters developed more than one *on* reading, with the 'proper' reading dependent upon which compound word the character was being used in.

Note that the spoken Chinese and Japanese languages have continued to change since the time the characters were imported. As a result, for many characters none of the modern Japanese *on* readings closely match the modern reading in any Chinese dialect.

2. Custom Readings

Over time, some characters in Japan acquired an additional *on* reading beyond any of those based on spoken Chinese sounds. This often happened due to some kind of mistake, such as Japanese speakers assuming that a character should be read the same way as its phonetic, even when that was not actually the case for a given character (a phenomenon referred to somewhat derogatorily in Japanese as *hyakushō yomi*). Some of these 'custom' readings eventually spread widely and became established as acceptable alternate character readings.

7.9 Classification of *On* Readings

In the previous section we saw that the characters and their corresponding *on* readings were brought to Japan in several waves. In most Japanese-made character dictionaries, each character's different *on* readings are labeled based on which particular wave they were part of.

---

[7] Of course, mass communication of the modern age affects how these changes occur.

By this system of classification there are four main types of *on* reading:

呉音	漢音	唐音	慣用音
go on	*kan on*	*tō on*	*kanyō on*

The first three of these categories each refer to a different period of time in which the characters, together with associated readings and words using them, were imported from China. The first (*go*) takes its name from a region within China. The second and third (*kan* and *tō*) each take their name from a ruling dynasty of China. However, rather than referring to the dynasty itself, these two actually refer to a name by which China as a whole was known at one time. For that reason, the period during which the characters were imported and the period the corresponding dynasty ruled China are not the same.[8]

The fourth category (*kanyō*) refers to the 'custom' readings mentioned in the previous section. *Kanyō* means 'colloquial expression.'

It's very rare for one character to have all four of these types of *on* reading. Most have at least two, though.

An example of a character that can be commonly read with more than two of these types of *on* reading is 行. The character means, among other things, 'go' and 'carry out.' It can be found in relatively common words using each of the first three types of *on* reading, as shown in the following table:

Word	Word Reading	Meaning	Reading of 行	Type of Reading
行事	*gyōji*	event	GYŌ	*go on*
旅行	*ryokō*	trip	KŌ	*kan on*
行脚	*angya*	walking tour; pilgrimage	AN	*tō on*

This character has multiple meanings, but unlike the 'music' / 'enjoyment' character (楽) mentioned in section 7.7, the *on* reading of this character in any given compound word does not identify which meaning is intended. Rather, the reading is primarily dependent on when that compound word was incorporated into Japanese (i.e., which wave it was a part of).

Note how the *go on* and *kan on* readings for this character, while different, have some similarities. This is often the case with *go on* and *kan on* readings. GYŌ and KŌ are, in fact, related readings, as will become clearer in the next section.

This Classification Scheme Not Used in the Book

The system introduced in this section of classifying *on* readings into four types will not be used in this book. So, for example, in the Part 2 phonetic listings, as various *on* readings are given, there is no distinguishing between the different types, such as *go on* and *kan on*. This is because the author feels that learning this information adds unnecessary complexity to the learning of the characters, while providing minimal benefit.

---

[8] The modern Mandarin Chinese pronunciations of these first three names are: 'Wu' (呉), a region of southern China, 'Han' (漢), the dynasty which ruled China from 206 BC-220 AD, and 'Tang' (唐), the dynasty which ruled China from 618-907 AD.

Instead, the author recommends becoming familiar with pairs or groups of common related readings, which are explained and listed in the next section: 7.10. Those who do not wish to learn further about the four types of *on* reading may skip ahead to that section.

A Brief History of Each Type of Reading

Although not much is known about the first major wave of characters coming to Japan, it is believed to have taken place during the fifth and sixth centuries AD, possibly via the Korean peninsula. The readings from this first wave, now called *go on*, may have been consistent with spoken Chinese from a region of China south of the Yangtze River; this type of reading gets its name from that region. The transmission of Buddhist and Confucian texts was a major part of this wave, and even today many words related to Buddhism are still read with *go on* readings. The transmission of characters at this time was thorough, such that virtually all characters from China have a *go on* reading associated with them.

The second major wave of characters coming to Japan took place during the seventh and eighth centuries. These *kan on* readings were brought back by Japanese partaking in missions to China: both diplomatic envoys and those participating in cultural exchange, such as the studying of Buddhism, medicine, and art. The Chinese capital during this time, whose standard dialect was the source of these readings, was the city now known as Xian. As with the *go on* readings, virtually all characters used in Japan have a *kan on* reading.

The *tō on* character readings came to Japan sporadically during the 10th to 19th centuries. The readings were used with words introduced to Japan by merchants, Zen Buddhist monks, and others participating in exchanges between China and Japan. Unlike the *kan on* and *go on* readings, the *tō on* readings are not a comprehensive set, covering most characters, but rather apply only to a small number of characters, and only when these characters are used in certain words. This is because these readings entered Japan only together with certain words that used them—words for objects and concepts that were new to the Japanese at that time. As a result, only a small percentage of characters have *tō on* readings.

Rather than coming from a particular region or time period in China, the fourth category (*kanyō on*) refers to readings that do not correspond to any of those coming from China, but rather are custom readings developed in Japan, as described in the previous section. This category also includes other less common cases, such as readings which may have come from China, but from a different time or place than any of the three major waves. One such example is the character 茶 ('tea'). Its most common *on* reading, CHA, is different from all of the *go on*, *kan on*, and *tō on* readings, and therefore it is classified as a *kanyō on* reading. As with the *tō on* readings, not all characters have *kanyō on* readings.

Frequencies of the Various Reading Types

As just explained, most characters have both a *go on* and a *kan on* reading, but only some characters have *tō on* or *kanyō on* readings. For some characters, only one of the reading types is commonly seen, and the others are rare. For characters with two common *on* readings, most often the readings are a *go on* reading and a *kan on* reading. For many characters, the *go on* and *kan on* readings are similar to each other, and sometimes even identical.

In Japan's history, there were attempts to standardize all *on* readings in all words to the *kan on* type, but they were not successful, as words with non *kan on* readings were already too well established in the language. Nonetheless, in part due to this effort, the *kan on* reading is the most dominant reading found within words today.

Modern Word Importation

In modern times, a few Chinese words continue to enter the Japanese language. However, even though in Chinese these words are written using characters which already exist in Japan, they are typically imported to Japanese only in katakana. This is done so that the modern Chinese pronunciations of the words (or at least a close approximation to them) can be used. Because the modern readings of most characters in Chinese (in particular, the official Mandarin dialect) no longer closely match any of the Japanese *on* readings, if these newly imported words were to be written with the same kanji in Japan as they are in China, it would be necessary either to establish new *on* readings for these characters (in order to imitate the modern Chinese sounds), or to use existing *on* readings, which would result in a word pronunciation noticeably different from that of modern Chinese.

7.10 Related Readings

In this section, the most commonly occurring types of related readings are shown, demonstrated by sets of reading pairs. At first glance, the reading pairs may seem randomly different from each other, but with repeated exposure to character *on* readings, you will slowly become familiar with the underlying correspondences among related readings.

It is not necessary to memorize any of the readings shown here. And certainly, all character *on* readings must ultimately be learned one character at a time. But without question, developing a feel for even *some* of the correspondences shown in this section will assist you both in the learning and memorization of the multiple *on* readings of characters which have them, and in the learning and memorization of the *on* readings of various different characters which contain the same phonetic component. When considering all of the memorization that is required to learn character readings, regardless of the method used, developing a feel for these correspondences will surely assist not only with initially learning the *on* readings of newly encountered characters, but also with remembering those readings over time.

Each pair of readings shown are those of either a single character which can be commonly read in either way shown, or two different characters which share a phonetic component (or in which one is the phonetic component of the other), each having the associated reading shown as their principal reading. For most of the correspondences shown here, more than one pair of characters demonstrating the pattern are shown. In all cases, the readings associated with each character are readings found among common words containing that character. In other words, none of the character readings shown here are obscure.

The various correspondences are divided into different categories, starting with readings that differ only in the initial consonant sound. The different types of reading are each described by means of a pattern. The '//' mark separates the two related patterns, and the '~' symbol denotes the part of the patterns that the different readings have in common.

The readings themselves are all expressed in *rōmaji* using uppercase letters, to make it easier to see the correspondences shown. As in the rest of the book, macrons (lines above characters)

THE ON READING IN DEPTH

are used to indicate long vowel sounds. Vowels without macrons are short vowel sounds. The pairs of readings given are not exhaustive, but merely representative examples of each correspondence type.

Some, but not all, of the pairs of related readings listed here are a *go on* reading paired with a *kan on* reading, but those labels are not used here. Readers of this book are advised to become familiar with the related readings presented here, but not be concerned with the type of *on* reading, such as *go on* or *kan on*, under which each is categorized.

A. Initial Consonant Differences

1. Voiceless Initial Consonant // Voiced Initial Consonant

The initial consonant sound is voiceless in one reading and voiced in the other. (When written in katakana, voiced sounds are indicated with the *dakuten* mark [゛], as shown in the examples below.)

Examples:
干 KAN (カン)　　岸 GAN (ガン)
古 KO (コ)　　胡 GO (ゴ)
次 SHI (シ)　　次 JI (ジ)
煎 SEN (セン)　　前 ZEN (ゼン)
大 TAI (タイ)　　大 DAI (ダイ)
波 HA (ハ)　　婆 BA (バ)
地 CHI (チ)　　地 JI (ジ - previously written ヂ)

2. M~ // B~

Examples:
馬 MA　　馬 BA
万 MAN　　万 BAN
美 MI　　美 BI
無 MU　　無 BU
盲 MŌ　　亡 BŌ

3. K~ // R~

Examples:
課 KA　　裸 RA
監 KAN　　覧 RAN
格 KAKU　　絡 RAKU
兼 KEN　　廉 REN
京 KYŌ　　涼 RYŌ

4. N~ // J~ or Z~ (voiced 'S' sounds), or D~ (voiced 'T' sound)

    Examples:

人	NIN	人	JIN
児	NI	児	JI
燃	NEN	然	ZEN
男	NAN	男	DAN
内	NAI	内	DAI

5. ~ (no initial consonant) // K~

    Examples:

影	EI	景	KEI
遺	I	貴	KI
黄, 押	Ō	黄, 甲	KŌ

B. Non-Palatalized Initial Consonant vs. Palatalized Initial Consonant

6. ~~ // ~Y~

    Examples:

格	KAKU	客	KYAKU
興	KŌ	興	KYŌ
相	SŌ	相	SHŌ (also written SYŌ)
島	TŌ	鳥	CHŌ (also written TYŌ)

C. Initial Vowel Differences

7. ~A // ~I

    Example:

波, 把	HA	皮, 肥	HI

8. ~A~ // ~E~

    Examples:

家	KA	家	KE
元	GAN	元	GEN
月	GATSU	月	GETSU
反	HAN	返	HEN
西	SAI	西	SEI

9. ~I~ // ~O~

    Examples:

記	KI	己	KO
金	KIN	金	KON
音, 因	IN	音, 恩	ON

THE ON READING IN DEPTH

10. ~E~ // ~I~			
Examples:	気 KE	気 KI	
	施 SE	施 SHI (also written SI)	
	便 BEN	便 BIN	
	賢 KEN	緊 KIN	

11. ~O // ~U			
Examples:	素 SO	素 SU	
	都 TO	都 TSU (also written TU)	

12. ~AKU // ~OKU		
Examples:	握 AKU	屋 OKU
	殻 KAKU	穀 KOKU

13. ~ATSU // ~OTSU		
Examples:	滑 KATSU	骨 KOTSU
	発 HATSU	発 HOTSU

14. ~EN // ~ON		
Examples:	建 KEN	建 KON
	言 GEN	言 GON

D. Short Vowel vs. Long Vowel Differences

15. ~U // ~Ū		
Examples:	風 FU	風 FŪ
	愚 GU	遇 GŪ
	由 YU	由 YŪ

E. Word Ending (Second Mora) Differences

16. ~ (no second mora) // ~KU		
Examples:	亜 A	悪 AKU
	作 SA	作 SAKU
	富 FU	福 FUKU

17. ~ (no second mora) // ~TSU		
Example:	奈 NA	捺 NATSU

18. ~CHI // ~TSU			
Examples:	一 ICHI	一 ITSU	
	節 SECHI	節 SETSU	

19. ~I // ~TSU			
Examples:	祭, 最 SAI	察, 撮 SATSU	
	例 REI	列 RETSU	

F. More Complex Differences

20. ~YŌ // ~EI			
Examples:	京 KYŌ	京 KEI	
	青 SHŌ (SYŌ)	青 SEI	
	丁 CHŌ (TYŌ)	訂 TEI	
	明 MYŌ	明 MEI	
	領 RYŌ	令 REI	

21. ~YAKU // ~EKI			
Examples:	借, 石 SHAKU (SYAKU)	昔, 石 SEKI	
	役 YAKU	疫 EKI	
	嫡 CHAKU (TYAKU)	敵 TEKI	

22. ~YOKU // ~IKI			
Examples:	力 RYOKU	力 RIKI	
	色, 職 SHOKU (SYOKU)	色, 識 SHIKI (SIKI)	

23. ~AKU // ~Ō			
Examples:	爆 BAKU	暴 BŌ	
	拡 KAKU	広 KŌ	

24. ~Ō // ~U			
Example:	工, 拘 KŌ	工, 句 KU	

25. ~I // ~AI			
Examples:	味 MI	妹 MAI	
	鬼 KI	塊 KAI	
	否, 悲 HI	杯, 排 HAI	

THE ON READING IN DEPTH

26. ~E // ~AI

Example: 外 GE   外 GAI

27. Initial *T* consonant sound paired with *O* vowel sound // Initial *S* consonant sound paired with *U* vowel sound

Note that the vowel sound may be long (e.g., *TŌ* instead of *TO*), the initial consonant may be palatalized (e.g., *CHO [TYO]* instead of *TO*; *SHU [SYU]* instead of *SU*), and the initial consonant may be voiced instead of unvoiced (e.g., *DŌ* instead of *TŌ*; *ZU* instead of *SU*).

Examples:
図 TO   図 ZU
頭 TŌ   頭 ZU
統 TŌ   充 JŪ (also written ZYŪ)
冬, 透 TŌ   終, 秀 SHŪ (also written SYŪ)
調, 彫 CHŌ   周, 週 SHŪ
重 CHŌ, 動 DŌ   重 JŪ, 種 SHU

G. Two of the Previous Differences Combined

Sometimes more than one of the above differences can be seen combined in a pair of related readings. The following pairs of readings contain two of the above differences. The numbers in parentheses on the right-hand side below correspond to the item numbers listed earlier.

Examples:
楽 GAKU	楽 RAKU	(1, 3)
強 GŌ	強 KYŌ	(1, 6)
額 GAKU	客 KYAKU	(1, 6)
弟 DAI	弟 TEI	(1, 8)
間, 感 KAN	間, 減 GEN	(1, 8)
画 GA	画 KAKU	(1, 16)
税 ZEI	説 SETSU	(1, 19)
形 GYŌ	形 KEI	(1, 20)
米 BEI	米 MAI	(2, 8)
文, 聞 BUN	文, 問 MON	(2, 11)
日 JITSU	日 NICHI	(4, 18)
会, 絵 E	会, 絵 KAI	(5, 26)
留 RYŪ	留 RU	(6, 15)

7.11 Unrelated Readings – Special Role Borrowing

As we have seen, the various *on* readings of a character are typically very closely related to each other in sound. There are a very small number of characters, though, which have a secondary *on* reading which is noticeably different from any other *on* reading of the character. This discrepancy usually occurred due to a special kind of character role borrowing, in which one character took over the role of another character with a dissimilar reading, but continued to use that other character's reading when performing the role. Following are a few examples of this kind of role borrowing.

For people who read about Japanese history, the term *koku* is commonly encountered. It was the standard measure of capacity used to identify the amount of rice production in a region, and was used as an indicator of the region's wealth and power. The character originally used to write this word was 斛. However, this usage became confused with another, separate measure of weight, which was written with the character:

The original meaning of 石 is 'rock' / 'stone.' Its two principal *on* readings are *SEKI* and *SHAKU*, which are related readings, as shown in Section 7.10 (item 21). But as a result of being borrowed to take over the role of 斛, this character now also has the reading *KOKU*, but only when referring to the measure of rice.

Another character similarly borrowed was:

This character has a principal *on* reading of *HAN*, and means 'anti' or 'against.' It also has a secondary *on* reading: *TAN*. With that reading, it is used to indicate a unit of measure, in particular for the area of a field or for a length of fabric. The reading *TAN* was borrowed from the characters 段 and 端, respectively, for these two roles. It can be seen in words such as 反物 (*tanmono*), which means textiles (especially raw materials to be processed and made into clothing).

Finally, the character meaning 'fishing' which is usually read as *GYO*:

漁

is also sometimes read as *RYŌ*. The latter reading is seen in words such as *ryōshi* (漁師, 'fisherman') and *tairyō* (大漁, 'large catch'). It was borrowed from the character 猟, which pertains to the hunting of animals. The reading is said to have been borrowed by whale hunters, who saw their profession as more similar to the hunting of animals on land than to traditional fishing. In this case, the reading *RYŌ* is not restricted to a particular role.

The borrowed readings shown in this section are too different from their principal character readings to be considered related readings (especially *KOKU* and *TAN*). Instead, they can be thought of as 'unrelated readings.'

7.12 False Phonetics

There are cases where what strongly appears to be a phonetic component within a character in fact is not. In such cases, you may be tempted to assume that the component gives a hint to the character reading, although it does not. Such a component is a **false phonetic**.

One way that this can happen is when a component that is used frequently as a phonetic in many different characters appears in some other character where it is not used that way. For instance, it may be used in a character only for its meaning and not for its reading. We already saw this in Chapter 2 with the character meaning 'gate' / 'door':

門

This character is used as a phonetic in several common use characters (including 聞 and 問), indicating the *on* readings *BUN* and *MON*. However, it also appears as an element in several common use characters only in a meaning role, including 開 ('open'), and 閉 ('close'). The fact that the component is sometimes used as a phonetic and sometimes not could result in confusion.

Some other false phonetics came about due to a change in the form of a character, whether deliberate or due to an error. Take, for example, the character:

仮

The right-hand side of this character (which we saw in the previous section) is used as a phonetic in many other characters, each having the *on* reading *HAN* or *HEN*. Here, though, the character *on* reading is *KA*. This discrepancy occurred because the above character was simplified in Japan from its earlier form: 假, in which the right side *was* a phonetic, indicating the reading *KA*. This is an example of a character simplification made in Japan which caused a phonetic connection to be lost.

False phonetics have also been created when what were once different character forms were modified and merged into the same form. For example, the following two characters, both commonly used as phonetics, were once clearly distinct from each other:

東   柬

The character on the left means 'east.' Its principal *on* reading is *TŌ*. The character on the right means 'choose.' This character itself is very rare and basically never encountered, but it is used as a phonetic component in a number of common use kanji, all of which have a principal *on* reading of either *RAN* or *REN*—clearly a very different reading from *TŌ*. The forms of these common use characters have been simplified, though, and the 'choose' component within them now appears identical in form to the 'east' character.

The table on the next page shows several common use characters which use one or the other of the above characters as a phonetic component. For each character, the principal *on* reading is shown. Note that these phonetic components now all appear identical in form.

Phonetic Component (with reading)	東 TŌ	柬 KAN / KEN[9]
Common Use Characters Using the Phonetic (with reading)	棟 TŌ 凍 TŌ	練 REN 錬 REN 欄 RAN

Clearly, false phonetics can complicate the memorization of *on* readings, but the number of them is comparatively rather small. To assist with awareness of these false phonetics, they are identified in the phonetic components section of Part 2 wherever they occur.

7.13 *On* Compound Homophones

In Chapter 3, it was mentioned that among *kango* there are many homophones: words that have the same pronunciation (i.e., reading) but are written with different kanji and are different in meaning. Many of these are two-character compound words. The large number of homophones is due to the limited number of different possible *on* readings in Japanese.

Even before being imported into Japanese, spoken Chinese character sounds were already limited in number. They were all one syllable in duration, there were only four different ending consonant sounds, and, as in traditional Japanese, there were no consonant clusters (two consonants spoken together with no vowel sound in between).

In Chinese, these character sounds had one of several tones associated with them (e.g., rising, falling, flat, etc.) that allowed them to be distinguished from each other. But this system of tones was not incorporated into Japanese; when the characters were imported into Japan, these tones were ignored and not included in the resultant *on* readings. This further limited the number of possible different sounds.

Among the thousands of characters in use in writing Japanese, there are only approximately 300 distinct *on* readings. And even among these, some readings are much more commonly used than others. For example, there are 28 different *on* readings which are each the principal *on* reading of 20 or more different *jōyō kanji*. Particularly notable among these are the *on* readings KAN, KŌ, SHI, and SHŌ, each of which is the principal *on* reading of 45 or more different *jōyō kanji*.

Because of this large number of frequently used *on* readings, there are also a large number of pairs or groups of common two-character compound words which share the same reading. (For an example, refer back to the Chapter 3, Section 3.3 table regarding the word *kōen*.)

---

[9] The readings of the various characters in the right-hand column, while not identical, are related readings of each other, following the K ↔ R and A ↔ E relationships listed in Section 7.10 (item numbers 3 and 8).

Chapter 8

The *Kun* Reading in Depth

In this chapter, we will take a detailed look at various aspects of *kun* readings: the way characters are read when they are used to write words of Japanese origin.

8.1 The Sounds of Native Japanese Words

As we learned in the last chapter, an *on* reading of a single kanji contains only one or two syllables—more accurately called 'morae,' as explained in that chapter. The *kun* readings of characters do not have such limitations. This is because they were applied to native Japanese words, which can consist of many morae. Although the *kun* readings of some characters are only one mora in length, many are longer, with some containing as many as five morae.

Kun readings are different from *on* readings in another important way, too. Most native Japanese words, and therefore most *kun* readings, do not contain a certain subset of sounds found in the modern Japanese language. These sounds are commonly found within *on* readings, though. The reason *kun* readings tend to lack these sounds has to do with the way the language developed over time. Having a feel for which sounds are typically found within native Japanese words—and which are not—is one more tool to help you distinguish between *on* and *kun* readings. We'll start this chapter by looking at the sounds of the Japanese language, and learning which of them are usually not found within *kun* readings.

Traditional Japanese Sounds

In many languages in the world, the set of basic spoken sounds that make up the whole of the language (called a 'phonology') gradually changes over time. There are numerous differences between the sounds used in the modern Japanese language spoken today and those used in, for example, the Japanese language that was spoken more than a thousand years ago. In the following discussion, the term **traditional Japanese** is used to refer to the Japanese language as it was spoken prior to the adoption of words from Chinese and other languages.[1]

All words in traditional Japanese can be divided into basic sound units which consist of either just a short vowel sound by itself or a combination of a leading consonant sound and a short vowel sound together. Examples of such sound units include the sounds /ka/, /mo/, /bi/, and /e/, the first three with a leading consonant sound followed by a short vowel sound, and the last just a short vowel sound by itself. These sound units can be expressed as (C)V, where the V indicates a vowel sound and the C indicates an optional leading consonant sound.

Using the definition of *mora*, as explained in the last chapter, each of these sound units is exactly one mora in length. They can also be thought of as being one syllable in length, but as a syllable can have a long or short vowel sound, the term *mora* is more accurate.

There were no ending consonant sounds in traditional Japanese. Thus, a word such as *tak* (with an ending /k/ sound) did not exist in traditional Japanese, although a sound such as *tako* (consisting of two morae: /ta/ and /ko/, each with a starting consonant together with a short vowel sound) could and did exist.

These basic sound units are the basis of both the hiragana and katakana syllabaries. Each of the original characters in these syllabaries represented one of the possible sound units in this traditional Japanese language.

Non-traditional Japanese Sounds

Notably absent from traditional Japanese words are several types of sounds which entered the language later, and can now be found in many modern Japanese words—especially words that are read using *on* readings. It is believed that these sounds were incorporated into Japanese after the language had already matured, and some time after words of Chinese origin first entered the language. Evidence that these sounds came late to the language can be seen in the fact that most of them were not represented in the original hiragana and katakana syllabaries. Instead, the syllabaries were later modified to be able to represent them.

In particular, these sounds are:

- the **syllabic /n/ sound** (called *hatsuon* in Japanese): a highly nasal sound with no associated vowel sound, such as either of the /n/ sounds in *konban wa*. Written with the character ん (hiragana) or ン (katakana).

- the ***sokuon***: an elongation (to one full mora) of the initial spoken sound of a consonant, such as the elongated /s/ sound in *isshūkan* ('one week'). Written with the small version of the *tsu* kana (っ/ッ).

---

[1] In linguistics, this language is called 'old Japanese.' Note that another term used throughout this book: 'native Japanese,' simply refers to words of Japanese origin (i.e., not borrowed from or based on words from another language), regardless of when in history the words were first developed. Also note that this discussion has been simplified; old Japanese phonology was more complex than what is discussed here.

- the **palatalized consonant** (called *yōon* in Japanese): a /y/ sound immediately following another consonant sound, with no vowel sound in between, such as the initial sound of the word *ryokan*. In Japanese, palatalized consonants only occur in morae with the *a*, *u*, or *o* vowel sounds. These morae are written using the small versions of the *ya*, *yu*, and *yo* kana (や / ヤ, ゆ / ュ, and よ / ョ) paired with and placed after a single hiragana character which, in *rōmaji*, ends in *i*. For example, *ryo* is written as り ょ (*ri* with small *yo*).

- the **long vowel sound** (called *chōon* in Japanese): the consecutive occurrence in a word of two identical short vowel sounds, with no consonant in between them. Expressed in terms of morae, a long vowel sound occurs when a bare vowel mora (a vowel without a leading consonant, such as *a* or *e*) is located just after another mora with the same vowel sound. For example, when the word *okāsan* ('mother') is written in hiragana: おかあさん, you can see that the long vowel sound (the *ā* part) occurs because a /ka/ and an /a/ sound appear consecutively in the word.

Because they came later to the language, the various sounds just described are not found in traditional Japanese words. But this does not mean that these sounds are not found in any word of Japanese origin. A small percentage of words of native Japanese origin do, in fact, contain one or more of these sounds. This is generally due to one of the following two reasons:

1. The word is a relatively modern creation, formed after the Japanese sound system had already been changed to incorporate the new sounds.

2. The pronunciation of the word changed over time, and came to include one or more of these newer sounds.

An example of a word of the first type is *okāsan*. In traditional Japanese, bare vowels only appeared at the beginnings of words, not in the middle, and so traditional Japanese words did not have long vowel sounds within them. In older Japanese, a different word for 'mother' was used; *okāsan* is a relatively modern creation.

The following table shows examples of common words of native Japanese origin which are of the second type described above. The original forms of these words did not contain the newer sounds, but over time their pronunciations became modified, such that they now include those sounds. Both the modern and earlier form of each of word is shown, in both hiragana and rōmaji.

Sound	Modern Form of Word Containing the Sound (*rōmaji*, meaning)	Older Form of the Word (*rōmaji*)
syllabic /n/	おんな (*onna*, 'woman')	をみな (*womina*)
sokuon	まっすぐ (*massugu*, 'straight')	ますぐ (*masugu*)
palatalized consonant	きょう (*kyō*, 'today')	けふ (*kefu*)
long vowel	ほのお (*honō*, 'flame')	ほのほ (*honoho*)

Words such as those in the table are relatively uncommon; the majority of modern words of native Japanese origin do not contain any of the non-traditional sounds. Therefore, these sounds are not so commonly found within *kun* readings, as *kun* readings originate from native Japanese words.[2]

The important point to be taken from this discussion is that these non-traditional sounds are found much less frequently in *kun* readings than in *on* readings. Whether or not a word contains these sounds can give you a hint as to whether it is likely to be a word of Chinese origin or a word of Japanese origin, and whether the characters it is written with are being read with the *on* or *kun* reading. Furthermore, a character reading which contains a syllabic /n/ sound (ん), a *sokuon* (っ), a palatalized consonant (identifiable by the presence of や, ゆ, or よ), or a long vowel sound (especially a long *e*, *o*, or *u*)[3] is much more likely to be an *on* reading than a *kun* reading. As you learn more and more words, you can use these tendencies to help you develop a feel for distinguishing between *on* and *kun* readings.

8.2 Word Inflection and *Okurigana*

As first described in Chapter 1 (Section 1.9), the Japanese language makes heavy use of inflection: the changing of word endings to produce different meanings or tenses. Take, as an example, the verb *hiku* ('to pull'). In its standard 'dictionary form,' the word can be broken down into two basic sound units (morae): *hi* and *ku* (ひ and く). But this verb, like all Japanese verbs, can be altered (inflected) to convey variations in meaning. For example, to express the negative sense ('to not pull'), the verb ending *ku* is changed to *ka* and a suffix expressing negation (*nai*) is appended, resulting in *hikanai* (ひかない). And to express volition, or intention, (conveyed in English with expressions like 'I shall pull' or 'let's pull'), the verb ending *ku* is changed to *kō* (*kou*), resulting in *hikō* (ひこう).

In Japanese, not only can verbs be inflected, but adjectives can be as well, as was demonstrated in Chapter 1.

Because word inflections involve the changing of syllables (such as the second mora of *hiku* changing from *ku* to *ka* or *ko*), applying kanji to these kinds of words is not simple. It has become standard for inflecting syllables (those which change) and those that come after them to be written using hiragana, with only the part of the word prior to the inflection being written with kanji. So, for example, when *hiku* or variations of it (such as *hikanai* or *hikō*) are written with kanji, only the part of the word preceding the inflected sounds (that is, just the *hi* part) is written with kanji (the character 引), and the rest is written in hiragana:

ひく	→	引く
ひかない	→	引かない
ひこう	→	引こう

---

[2] One exception to be aware of is the long *i* vowel sound. It appears in many adjectives ending in *shii*, such as *atarashii* (あたらしい)—words of native Japanese origin.

[3] Within *on* readings, the long *e* and *o* sounds are customarily written with the い and う characters, respectively, in the second mora. For example, *on* readings containing a starting /k/ consonant sound paired with a long *e* and a long *o* sound are written, respectively, as けい and こう, not as けえ and こお. The long *u* sound is written with the う character, as in くう.

The hiragana characters used to write inflected word endings (such as く, かない, and こう in the previous examples) are referred to as *okurigana*.

For many words, determining the split between kanji and okurigana when writing the word is as simple as knowing on which syllable the word changes when it is inflected. Then, the part before the inflection is replaced with kanji, and the rest is written with okurigana. Be aware, though, that there are exceptions to this.

One exception occurs with the verb *kuru* ('to come'). In this case, the word inflection goes all the way back into the first mora. When written in hiragana, even the first character changes with inflection; only the initial consonant sound is unchanged. *Kuru* and its inflected forms are written with the same kanji (来), but to be able do this, it is necessary for that character to be read in multiple, different ways. The following table shows how the reading of the character changes with different inflections of the word *kuru*:

Word	Meaning	Written with Hiragana	Written with Kanji	Reading of 来
kuru	come	くる	来る	ku
konai	not come	こない	来ない	ko
kitai	want to come	きたい	来たい	ki

Okurigana with Nouns

Some, but not all, nouns are written using okurigana. Primarily, nouns which are written using okurigana are those for which there are related verb or adjective forms which are inflected variations of the noun form. That is, there are verb or adjective forms which share the same beginning (called a 'stem') as the noun form. The following table shows four nouns of this type, together with a related verb or adjective. For a small number of adjectives, such as *hiroi* in the table below, a noun form can be made by replacing the final *i* sound with *sa*.

Noun	Written with Kanji	Meaning	Related Word (part of speech)	Written with Kanji	Meaning
warai	笑い	a laugh; laughter	warau (verb)	笑う	to laugh
yasumi	休み	a break	yasumu (verb)	休む	to rest
kotae	答え	an answer	kotaeru (verb)	答える	to answer
hirosa	広さ	width; breadth	hiroi (adjective)	広い	wide

Not all nouns of this type are written using okurigana, though. For example, the noun *kemuri* ('smoke') has a related verb form: *kemuru* ('to give off smoke'), written with kanji as 煙る. Although the noun form *could* be written with okurigana (as 煙り), it is standard to write it using only the kanji by itself: 煙. As a result, in this case the reading of the character is slightly different between the verb and noun forms, as shown in the following table.

Word	Part of Speech	Written with Hiragana	Written with Kanji	Reading of 煙
kemuru	verb	けむる	煙る	kemu
kemuri	noun	けむり	煙	kemuri

Simple, common native Japanese nouns that do not have inflected verb or adjective variations are typically written entirely in kanji. Examples of these include *yama* (山, 'mountain') and *mimi* (耳, 'ear').

Note that when looking at a written word, another hint as to whether it should be read with an *on* or *kun* reading is whether or not there are okurigana characters immediately following the kanji. The presence of okurigana often, but not always, indicates a *kun* reading.

8.3 Transitive and Intransitive Verbs

In Japanese, many verbs come in pairs: a transitive form and an intransitive form.

A *transitive verb* is used to describe the action of a subject onto an object different from itself. An *intransitive verb* does not apply to an object, but instead says something about the subject itself.

You can see the difference in the following two sentences:

(1) I plant trees in the forest.

(2) I swim in the ocean.

In the first sentence, the verb 'plant' is a transitive verb. It is used to describe an action performed by a subject (I) upon an object (trees). When using this verb, it is necessary to provide an object (the thing which is planted). In the second sentence, the verb 'swim' is an intransitive verb. The verb applies to the subject of the sentence (I), and cannot apply to an object. You cannot 'swim' a thing.

In English, many words can be used both as a transitive verb and an intransitive verb without a change in the word form. For example, the word 'move' is used in each way in the following sentences:

(3) Please help me move the bookshelf to the third floor.

(4) Glaciers can move as quickly as 30 meters per day.

In the first sentence, 'move' is a transitive verb; the object is 'bookshelf.' In the second sentence, it is the subject itself ('glaciers') which is moving—there is no object, and so 'move' is an intransitive verb. In English, the exact same word ('move') is used in both the transitive and intransitive cases.

In Japanese, the transitive and intransitive forms of the same verb are often expressed with different words. For example, the transitive form of the verb 'move' (as in sentence 3 on the previous page) is expressed with the verb *ugokasu*. The intransitive form (as in sentence 4) is expressed with the verb *ugoku*.

Pairs of Japanese transitive and intransitive verbs usually have the same beginning (stem) but different ending parts. In the previous example, the two forms of the verb 'move' both begin with *ugok*, but end differently.

For most such pairs of words, when written with kanji, kanji is used in place of the morae that are the same in each word, and the first morae which diverge are the beginning of okurigana. In other words, if the words were written entirely in hiragana, kanji would replace, starting from the beginning, all the hiragana characters that are the same between the two words, and the remaining parts would be written with okurigana. For example, the above word pair is written this way:

Word	Hiragana	with Kanji
ugokasu	うごかす	動かす
ugoku	うごく	動く

In Japanese, transitive and intransitive word pairs tend to follow one of a handful of different patterns. It is beyond the scope of this book to show all the different patterns, but a few more examples of word pairs using common patterns are shown in the following table. In the table, the word endings (in the left two columns) are expressed in *rōmaji* to make it easier to see word inflections.

Transitive Ending	Intransitive Ending	Word / Meaning	
		Transitive	Intransitive
~eru	~aru	曲げる (*mageru*, まげる) bend (a thing)	曲がる (*magaru*, まがる) turn; veer; bend
~eru	~u	立てる (*tateru*, たてる) stand up / raise (a thing)	立つ (*tatsu*, たつ) stand; rise
~su	~ru	戻す (*modosu*, もどす) return (a thing)	戻る (*modoru*, もどる) come back; go back

By comparing the hiragana and kanji representations of these words, you can see that the words in each pair in the table are written with kanji using the method just described. That is, kanji replaces only the initial hiragana characters that are the same in both words in a pair.

For a small number of word pairs, the change goes all the way back to the first mora of the word, just as it does with the various forms of the word *kuru* as shown in the previous section. In these cases, as with *kuru*, to be able to write the words with the same kanji it is necessary that the character reading be different between the two forms. Two example pairs of such words, each word in the pair written with the same kanji, are shown in the following table. Just as with the word *kuru* as shown in the previous section, the kanji only replaces the first hiragana character (i.e., the first mora), and is read differently, depending on the word.

Word	Verb Type	Meaning	with Kanji	Character Reading
dasu	transitive	to take out (e.g., from a pocket)	出す	*da*
deru	intransitive	to go out; to leave, depart	出る	*de*
kesu	transitive	to put out (e.g., a fire)	消す	*ke*
kieru	intransitive	to fade, go out	消える	*ki*

8.4 Native Japanese Compound Words

In linguistics, native Japanese is categorized as an *agglutinative language*: a language in which concepts that might usually be expressed with multiple words in another language are often expressed by 'gluing,' or attaching, prefixes and suffixes on to words. For example, as we saw earlier in the chapter, in Japanese the negative forms of verbs, such as *hiku*, are made by attaching a suffix meaning 'not' directly onto the verb, as in *hikanai*. (In contrast, verbs in English are made into the negative form by adding a separate word before the verb—for example, 'not pull.')

Also quite common in agglutinative languages like Japanese are compound words: two full standalone words merged together to form a word that combines their meanings.

Of course, you can find a number of compound words in English, too, such as 'birdhouse' which combines 'bird' and 'house.' But compound words are much more common in Japanese. Even many verbs in Japanese are expressed as compound words.

When forming native Japanese compound words, the words within the compound often change form, in a way similar to what we have already seen. For example, the verbs *hiku* ('to pull') and *dasu* ('to take out'), can be combined into the compound word *hikidasu* meaning 'to pull out.' When these words are combined, the ending sound of the first word (*hiku*) is changed from *ku* to *ki*.

The compound word *hikidasu*, which is a verb, can even be made into a noun, by changing its final sound from *su* to *shi*, forming *hikidashi*, a word meaning 'drawer' (such as in a desk).

These two compound words (*hikidasu* and *hikidashi*) are commonly written in the same way that other inflecting words are written: by using kanji for the parts of the words that don't change (inflect), and hiragana for the parts that do:

ひきだす → 引き出す
ひきだし → 引き出し

This way of writing these words is by far the most common. However, there is some flexibility with the way that native Japanese compound words can be written. In addition to the above representations, these words can also be written with the internal hiragana character removed:

ひきだす　→　引出す
ひきだし　→　引出し

And the word *hikidashi* can even be written by removing all hiragana entirely:

ひきだし　→　引出

A word like *hikidasu* cannot be written with all okurigana removed, though, because all verbs, by convention, must end in a hiragana character.

Only the first way of writing *hikidasu* and *hikidashi* shown here is common; the other forms, with some or all okurigana removed, are uncommon.

Certain other words, though, are most commonly written with okurigana removed. For example, the word *kumiai*, meaning 'association; union' (as in a group of people sharing a common interest) is a compound word made by combining the words *kumu* (組む, 'to join') and *au* (会う, 'to come together'), and altering their forms in a similar way as was done with *hikidashi*. The way you would expect this compound word to be written, using the rules described in the last two sections, is 組み合い. However, this word is most commonly written as 組合, with all of the okurigana removed.

Another compound word usually written without okurigana is *uketsuke*, meaning 'reception' (such as the front desk of a hotel). It is formed from the combination of the words *ukeru* (受ける, 'to receive') and *tsukeru* (付ける, 'to attach'). With all okurigana included, the word would be written 受け付け. However, this word is much more commonly written as 受付.

Note that there are some verbs which, when used in certain grammatical forms, never have okurigana included, simply because there is none to include—that is, there is no inflected part of the word. For example, when the words *miru* (見る, 'to see') and *deru* (出る, 'to go out' / 'to appear') are used in their noun or combining forms, the ending *ru* sound is simply dropped, rather than changed into a different sound such as *ri*.[4]

Thus, when words like these are used as either the first part of any type of compound word or the ending part of compound nouns, they are never written with okurigana (as there is none). Example compound words that include these words in these forms are:

見守る　　(mimamoru, みまもる)　　'to watch over'
思い出　　(<i>omoide</i>, おもいで)　　'a memory'</p>

Compound Word Meanings

Just as with *on*-based compound words, quite a few *kun*-based compound words have meanings which cannot be easily guessed by simply knowing the meanings of the words that comprise them. A good example of this is the word *hikidashi*. Even if you knew that this word was a noun, and that the verb form (*hikidasu*) means 'to pull out,' you might not guess that the word means 'drawer.' Similarly, knowing the meanings of *ukeru* and *tsukeru*, you probably would not guess that the compound word *uketsuke* means 'reception.'

---

[4] These verbs are inflected in this special way because they belong to the 'Group 2' (also called 'Type II') class of verbs. A discussion of the various types of Japanese verbs is beyond the scope of this book.

The word *mikomi* (見込み) is a compound noun consisting of two parts: *miru* (見る, 'to see') and *komu* (込む), a word with numerous meanings, including: 'to go into' and 'to be crowded or congested.' If you were to guess the meaning of *mikomi*, based on the words it is made from, it would probably be difficult to guess the correct meaning. The actual meaning of this word is 'expectation' / 'prospect' / 'likelihood,' a meaning not easily guessed by the words used in the compound.

So just like what must be done with *on*-based compound words, the meanings of *kun*-based compound words must often be learned separately from and in addition to the meanings of the words they are made from.

8.5 Multiple *Kun* Readings

In this chapter, we have already seen several examples of individual kanji which have multiple *kun* readings. For example, the character 煙, when used by itself as a single-character word, is read as *kemuri*; when appearing as part of the verb 煙る, though, the character is read as *kemu*. These two *kun* readings are only slightly different from each other.

Similarly, we saw that the character 出 is read as *da* in the word 出す (*dasu*), and as *de* in the word 出る (*deru*). The words *dasu* and *deru* are very similar in meaning, are related in origin, and, in fact, are a complementary word pair, with one being a transitive verb form and the other an intransitive verb form.

Cases such as these are not uncommon, where a pair or group of closely related words only slightly different from each other have been assigned the same kanji, and the various *kun* readings of that kanji vary slightly from each other.

There are also cases, though, where a single character has been used to write two or more words of native Japanese origin whose spoken forms are completely different from each other, resulting in multiple, completely different *kun* readings assigned to the same character. Such cases generally occurred due to one of the following two reasons:

1. Several different words in the native Japanese language, although different in sound, were quite similar or even identical in meaning to each other. The same character was used to write each of the words.

2. The character, even in China, already had more than one different meaning associated with it, and was used to write native Japanese words corresponding to each of the meanings.

A pair of words which are of the first type above both use the character:

The character means 'fish.' It is used to write both the traditional Japanese word for fish (*uo*), and the modern word (*sakana*), as well.

Two different sets of words which are of the second type are written using the characters:

指 and 上

The character 指 has two principal meanings: the noun 'finger,' and the verb 'to point at' / 'to indicate.' The character already had both of these meanings in China before being imported into Japan. The native Japanese language already had words with each of these meanings (*yubi* and *sasu*, respectively) and this same character was used to write both of these words. Because *yubi* is a simple noun, it is written with just the character itself and no okurigana, whereas *sasu*, a verb, is written with both kanji and okurigana, as shown here:

ゆび → 指
さす → 指す

The original meaning of the character 上 is 'above.' Even in China, it also has a number of other closely related meanings, including 'upper,' as in located toward the top of something, and 'to elevate,' as in to bring oneself or something else to a higher position. When kanji were assigned to write native Japanese words, several different words having these slightly different meanings were each assigned this same character.

The following table shows various native Japanese words with these meanings which can be written using 上. Note that some of these words are written with just the character itself, while others include okurigana.

Meaning	Word	Written with Kanji
above; the top; upper	ue[5]	上
upper part; initial part	kami	上
to raise a thing / to rise	ageru / agaru	上げる / 上がる
to go up to a high place	noboru	上る

Of course, characters having multiple possible *kun* readings can make deciphering writing more challenging. But for many words the attached okurigana can be used to distinguish between different words written with the same character. For example, in the above table, the three words appearing in the bottom two rows are all written using okurigana, and the okurigana is different for each of the words, and so can be used to distinguish those different words from each other.

This can't be done with the topmost two words in the table, though, as they are each written without okurigana. In this case, it is necessary to look at the context in which the character is used to determine the intended reading. The second of these two words (*kami*) is much less common than the first. When guessing the reading of a newly encountered word, it is better to start by guessing a more common reading (in this case, *ue*). Being familiar with the contexts in which particular readings are used also helps you to guess the character reading.

---

[5] Another *kun* reading of this character is *uwa*; this reading is only used in compound words. It is a variation of the *ue* reading, as explained in Section 8.10.

Different Words Written Identically

In the table on the previous page, the words which contain okurigana are each written differently from each other. This is usually the case for characters with multiple *kun* readings. However, there are also a few cases where different words are written identically—with both the same kanji *and* the same okurigana.

Take, for instance, the words *aku* and *hiraku*, which are approximately the same in meaning. Although both mean 'to open,' the words have different nuances and are used in different contexts. The words are both written using the same character: 開. Furthermore, the words have the same word ending (*ku*), and when written using kanji and okurigana, both words appear exactly the same:

$$\text{あく} \quad \rightarrow \quad \text{開く}$$
$$\text{ひらく} \quad \rightarrow \quad \text{開く}$$

Thus, when the word 開く is encountered while reading, it is necessary to determine from context which of the above two words is intended.

There are also cases where words only appear the same when expressed in certain forms, but not in others. For example, the character 行 is used to write both the word *iku* ('to go') and the word *okonau* ('to carry out'). In their normal 'dictionary forms,' the words appear differently:

$$\text{いく} \quad \rightarrow \quad \text{行く}$$
$$\text{おこなう} \quad \rightarrow \quad \text{行う}$$

In the plain (that is, non-polite) past tense, though, the word *iku* has a non-standard form: いった (*itta*). Because of this, both words appear identical in the plain past tense form:

$$\text{いった} \quad \rightarrow \quad \text{行った}$$
$$\text{おこなった} \quad \rightarrow \quad \text{行った}$$

Again, it is necessary to determine from context which of the two words is intended. Such pairs of identical words can be a challenge to read. Fortunately, there are not many of them.

8.6 Applying Kanji to Fixed Expressions

In some cases, kanji have been applied to words only when they are part of a particular phrase or fixed expression, but not when used outside of the context of that expression.

For example, the Japanese word *motto*, used by itself, means 'more.' This word is used together with the grammatical particle *mo* in the phrase *motto mo* (もっとも), a fixed expression having the meaning 'most.' The character 最, also having the meaning 'most,' can be used in the writing of *motto mo*, substituting it for the first part of the expression: 最も. But this character is not used to write the word *motto* when it is used by itself (i.e., without being followed by *mo*). Thus, the character 最 can be read as *motto*, but only when used in the writing of the expression *motto mo*.

8.7 Derived Words Appear to Broaden Character Meaning

Kanji were applied to native Japanese words based on similarity in meaning. So you would expect, then, that if a character is used to write a given native Japanese word, then the meaning of that word is one of the meanings of that character. This is not always the case, though. In fact, kanji can be used to write words whose meanings are significantly different from any of the intrinsic meanings of the character.

This is best explained with an example. The original core meaning of the native Japanese sound *hiya* is 'cold.' This can be seen in words in common use today such as *hiyari* ('a shiver'), *hiya* ('cold water'), and *hiyasu* ('to cool [something]'; 'to chill [something]').

But one word written with this stem (and originally having a meaning similar to those of the words just mentioned), has taken on an extended meaning. Specifically, the word *hiyakasu* originally meant 'to cause something to be cold,' but now has a second, more common meaning: 'to ridicule' (perhaps originating from the cold feeling someone gets when being ridiculed).

When kanji were applied to native Japanese words, all of these words containing *hiya*, including *hiyakasu*, were assigned the same character: 冷, meaning 'cool.'

So now not only is *hiyasu* ('to cool [something]') written 冷やす, but also *hiyakasu* ('to ridicule') is written 冷やかす. This makes it appear that the character 冷, in addition to 'cool,' also means 'ridicule.' But that's not really the case. It's not really correct to say that the character 冷 means 'ridicule.' It's more accurate to say that the character 冷, which means 'cool,' is used to write a word meaning 'ridicule.'

8.8 *Kun*-based Homophones

We first saw in Chapter 3 (Section 3.3) that many *kun* homophones (native Japanese words with the exact same pronunciation, but different in meaning and written with different kanji) are actually closely related in meaning. For example, the word *tsutomeru* can be written using kanji in three different ways, but all three words have a similar (but not identical) meaning.

Such sets of words have the same origin as each other; they all derive from the same common word. When kanji were assigned to the writing of these words, different characters were assigned to different shades of meaning of the same word, so what was actually a single word with a broad range of meanings in essence became split up into multiple, different more specific words, each written with a different kanji.

Some homophones of this type are more or less completely interchangeable with each other: any of the variations can be used in a given context. Others, though, are completely separate words with no overlap in meaning, such that only one of the words in the group can be correctly used in any given context. This is the case with *tsutomeru*.

The number of such groups of homophones is rather large, and so it is not possible to provide in this book a comprehensive list of such words.

8.9 Kanji Can Hide Word Connections

In the Japanese language, many words were derived from other words. Due to the similarity in sound and meaning between such words, it is still sometimes possible to see the relationships between the words.

When kanji were assigned to the writing of native Japanese words, though, many of these related words ended up being assigned different kanji from each other. As explained in the previous section, this happened because kanji were very specific in meaning, so words even only moderately different in meaning were assigned different kanji. Because of this, the connections between native Japanese words are often obscured. Thus, kanji, while precisely indicating meaning, can also in essence hide meaning relationships between words.

Consider the pair of words *kōri* (氷, こおり), 'ice,' and *kōru* (凍る, こおる), 'to freeze.' These words are clearly related to each other. They share the same word stem (*kōr*); only the final sound differs. The first word is in the noun form, and the second in the verb form. The meanings of the words are obviously related. Because there were different kanji to convey the two meanings ('ice' and 'to freeze'), though, these words were written using different kanji.

Another pair of words which share a relationship are *semai* (狭い, せまい, 'narrow') and *semaru* (迫る, せまる, 'to close in on in a threatening way' / 'to pressure, compel'). As with *kōri* and *kōru*, these words have the same word stem (*sema*). Just as with *kōri* and *kōru*, though, the word meanings are not exactly identical, and so a different character was used to write each word. When compared to each other, it is possible to see the meaning connection between the two words, although it is not as clear as it is with *kōri* and *kōru*.

Because different kanji are used to write pairs of words such as *kōri* and *kōru* or *semai* and *semaru*, it is easy to overlook the fact that there is a meaning connection between the words; the use of different kanji to write the words causes the meaning connection between the words to be obscured. This is especially true if the words are not first learned together at the same time.

For sets of words like these, where a meaning and sound connection is shared even though the words are written with different kanji, it's sometimes helpful to be aware of the connection between the words, and use it to help you remember the words. For example, in the case of *kōri* and *kōru*, most Japanese learners are likely to learn the word *kōri* first, as it is the more common of the two; likely, by the time you encounter and learn the word *kōru*, you will already be familiar with *kōri*. When learning *kōru*, then, you can use the connection with *kōri* to help remember either the pronunciation or the meaning (or possibly both). Knowing the relationship between the two—rather than just treating them as two separate, dissimilar words—will help you to more quickly remember *kōru*.

Word Groups

Sometimes its not just a pair of words, but a group which share a sound and meaning relationship. One such group is shown in the following table. These words all share the same stem: *kiwa*, which means 'edge' or 'brink.' The verb form: *kiwameru*, means 'to take to the brink,' but a corollary meaning of this word is 'to research thoroughly.' These two meanings of *kiwameru* are expressed with different kanji, as shown in the table.

THE *KUN* READING IN DEPTH

Word	with Kanji	Meaning
kiwa	際	edge; brink; verge
kiwameru	極める	to take to the extreme
kiwameru	究める	to research thoroughly

It may be helpful to be aware of these meaning connections when trying to learn groups of words like these.

Another group of words shares the stem *tat*, which conveys the idea of verticality, or something being piled vertically on top of something else. You can see this concept in all of the words in the following table.

Word	with Kanji	Meaning
tate	縦	longitude
tate no	縦の	vertical
tateru	建てる	to build (such as a house)
tatsu	立つ	to stand, stand up, rise

In fact, there are quite a few sets of words such as these, which derived from the same source word but are now written with different kanji.

Hidden Compound Words

Word meaning can also be hidden when a single kanji is used to write what was originally a native Japanese compound word.

For example, the word *kemono*, which means 'beast' (usually referring to a four-legged mammal), is written with just a single character by itself: 獣. In actuality, though, *kemono* is a compound word, combining *ke* (毛, 'hair') and *mono* (物, 'thing') to produce 'hairy thing'—another way to say 'beast.'[6]

As another example, the word *hagane*, which means 'steel,' is written with the single character 鋼. The word meaning, though, comes from the combination of *ha* (刃, 'blade') and *kane* (金, 'metal'; changed to *gane* by the *rendaku* process), a compound word originally referring to the metal used in sword blades.

Written with just the 獣 or 鋼 character, the origins of these words are concealed. Knowing these word origins, though, may make these words easier to remember.

At least one word of this type can be written both with just a single character and in a way that reveals the compound meaning. *Tamago* (たまご, 'egg') can be written with a single kanji: 卵, but can also be written as 玉子, a way that shows each part of the original compound meaning: *tama* (玉, 'ball') and *ko* (子, 'child'; changed to *go* by the *rendaku* process). These two different ways of writing the word are sometimes used differently, with 卵 referring to whole, unbroken eggs, and 玉子 referring to eggs such as when served as a meal. This is not an absolute rule, though.

---

[6] An earlier form of this word was *kedamono*, which has the same meaning.

It is not always possible to know the meaning connections between different words. One reason for this is that the origins of many words have been lost, and are now a matter of conjecture. In other cases, the pronunciations of words have drifted apart over time, so it is no longer easy to see the connection between them.

For example, the words *uchiage* (打ち上げ、うちあげ) and *utage* (宴、うたげ) have a common origin. One meaning of *uchiage* is the end of a job or a performance, or the feast that takes place at that time. From this, a slightly abbreviated form of the word: *utage* was developed (merging the *chi* and *a* sounds), taking on the meaning 'feast.' Due to the pronunciation changes between these words, though, it is not as easy to see the relationship as it is with the word groups presented earlier in this section. It is probably simplest to learn the words *uchiage* and *utage* separately.

In some cases, though, being aware of hidden word connections can help with learning and remembering words.

8.10 Mostly Obsolete Word Inflections

As we have already learned, the Japanese language makes heavy use of inflection, where word-ending sounds are changed to express variations in meaning. This inflection is most noticeable today with verbs and adjectives, but even nouns are affected.

Inflection was even more common in the Japanese language in the past. Although it has been mostly phased out of the modern language, traces of one style of inflection—referred to in Japanese as *boinkōtai* (母音交代, literally: 'vowel exchange')—can still be seen in certain words today. With **boinkōtai**, the vowel sound in the final syllable (mora) of a noun changes when it is used as the first part of a compound word. A few examples follow.

In Japanese, the word for 'eye' is *me*. In some compound words, though, where 'eye' is the first part of the compound, the *me* sound is changed to *ma*. One such word is 'eyelid': *mabuta* in Japanese. This compound word is made up of *me* (changed to *ma*) and *futa*, meaning 'lid' (changed to *buta* by the *rendaku* process). The same type of inflection can be found in the words *mayuge* ('eyebrow') and *manako* ('eyeball').

Another example can be seen in the native Japanese word for 'gold': *kogane*. This compound word was formed by combining *ki* ('yellow') and *kane* ('metal'). However, when used as the first part of this compound, the *ki* sound was inflected to *ko*. (The second part of the compound has also been changed, from *kane* to *gane*, by the *rendaku* process.)

Inflections such as the one from *ki* to *ko* are difficult to recognize today, as there are not so many words in modern Japanese which exhibit them. However, the most common type of *boinkōtai* still encountered in Japanese today—the changing of the vowel sound from an /e/ sound to an /a/ sound, such as with the *me* to *ma* change just described—still can be seen in many words. For example, this change can be seen in the word *amagasa* ('umbrella [especially for protection against rain]'). This word is made up of the parts *ame* ('rain') and *kasa* ('umbrella'). In the compound, the first word is inflected from *ame* to *ama* (and the second part is changed by the *rendaku* process).

In some cases, the relationship between the two inflected forms of a word is especially hard to see because of changes that have occurred in the spoken sounds of Japanese. For example, the word *ue* ('above') inflects to *uwa*, as seen in words such as *uwabaki* ('indoor shoes'; a word derived from the fact that the insides of places were usually at a higher elevation than the ground outside). But it is difficult to see the relationship between the second morae of *ue* and *uwa*, because the starting consonants of these sounds are different (one is the bare vowel /e/ and the other begins with a /w/ sound). In the past, these two morae had the same starting consonant sound as each other, but the sounds drifted apart.

The word *kudamono* ('fruit') is one more example of a word whose meaning has been obscured by sound (and grammar) changes in the language. *Kudamono* originated as a compound word--a word which would be expressed in modern Japanese as *ki no mono*: 'the things of a tree.' In the word, *ku* is an alteration of *ki* (tree), and *da* is a possessive which would be expressed today with the grammatical particle *no*. If this compound word were written using the corresponding kanji of each of its piece parts (that is, *ki*, *no*, and *mono*), it would be written 木之物 (or 木乃物). Instead, the compound is written 果物, with the 'fruit' character (果) used only for its meaning, combined with the 'thing' character (物) used for both its sound (もの) and its meaning.

Boinkōtai word inflection has been largely phased out of the language, and is now seen in only a relatively small number of words. Being aware of this type of inflection may make recognizing and remembering such words easier, though. More examples of *boinkōtai* appear in Appendix J.

8.11 *Nanori* Readings

In addition to the various possible readings characters may have when they are applied to everyday Japanese words, many characters also have a few additional special readings which may be found in some Japanese personal names. These readings are called **nanori** readings. The term *nanori* means 'giving one's name' (such as when introducing oneself).

For example, the characters:

一 and 三

(meaning 'one' and 'three,' respectively) can often be seen in men's given names with the readings *kazu* and *sabu*, respectively.[7] These are both *nanori* readings. Generally speaking, *nanori* readings of characters are not found in any words outside of personal names.

In some cases, *nanori* readings were once valid *kun* readings of a character, but were phased out of general usage as part of an effort to reduce the number of readings associated with characters in order to simplify the language.

Because of the large number of possible different readings, learning to read personal names is more complicated than learning to read everyday words, and is beyond the scope of this book. *Nanori* readings will not be discussed further.

---

[7] Note, though, that these characters can be used in people's names using other readings as well; *kazu* and *sabu* are not the only ways to read these characters within people's names.

Chapter 9

Compound Words in Depth

Compound words—that is, words which are written using more than one kanji—are a big part of the Japanese language. In this chapter we will take a closer look at compound words, and various concepts pertaining to them.

Among other things, we will look at ways that compounds are assembled together, how the meaning of a compound can differ from the meanings of its constituent kanji, various sound phenomena that occur within compounds, and compounds that have special readings.

Some of the concepts described in this chapter apply only or primarily to *on*-based compounds (i.e., *kango*), while others apply to both *on*-based compounds and *kun*-based compounds (*wago*) as well. In written Japanese, *on*-based compounds are much more prevalent. We'll start by looking at the composition of *on*-based compounds.

9.1 Two-Character Compounds

The majority of *on*-based compound words are made up of exactly two characters. There are also three- and four-character compound words, but more than that is rare.

In most cases, the meanings of compound words derive from a combination of the meanings of each character in the compound. For many compounds, the way the meaning is derived from the characters is very straightforward. We have already seen some examples of this, such as how the word *kanji* (漢字) is made up of characters meaning 'Chinese' and 'character,' and the meaning of the compound word is simply 'Chinese character.' In this type of compound, the second character specifies an object, and the first character describes that object.

There are also other ways that characters can be combined to form a compound. This section looks at the most common ways that compound words have been composed.

A. Pairing Characters with Nearly Identical Meanings

In this type of compound, two characters having nearly identical meanings as each other are paired together. The meaning of the resulting compound word is the same, or nearly the same, as the meanings of the individual characters, as well. The compound word basically reinforces the meaning of the two characters in it.

Examples:

    変化 (*henka*): 'change; transformation' – both characters mean 'change'

    停止 (*teishi*): 'suspension; stopping' – both characters mean 'stop'

    思考 (*shikō*): 'thought; thinking' – both characters mean 'think'

    樹木 (*jumoku*): 'tree' – both characters mean 'tree'

    絵画 (*kaiga*): 'painting; picture' – both characters mean 'picture'

B. Pairing Characters with Opposite or Complementary Meanings

In this type of compound, two characters either (roughly) opposite or complementary to each other in meaning are paired together.

The meanings of some compound words formed in this way are simply a combination of the meanings of the two characters, in either the form 'A and B,' or 'A or B,' where A and B are the meanings of the individual characters.

Examples:

    売買 (*baibai*, 'sell' + 'buy'): 'buying and selling'

    勝負 (*shōbu*, 'win' + 'lose'): 'victory or defeat'

Such concepts usually cannot be expressed with a single word in English, instead requiring multiple words, such as 'cause and effect.'

Some compounds of this type have a simple 'A and B' meaning, but also a secondary, different meaning as well. For example, the compound *sayū* (左右) is made up of characters meaning 'left' (左) and 'right' (右), and simply means 'left and right.' But this word has a second meaning, as well: 'influence' / 'control.' It can also be made into a verb: *sayū suru* (左右する) with the meaning 'to control' / 'to have influence upon.'

Other compounds of this type have a meaning which is difficult to translate directly into English. For example, pairing characters meaning 'exist' (有) and 'not exist' (無) produces the word 有無 (*umu*), which conveys the notion 'whether or not something exists or is present.'

This word can be used in a phrase such as:

zaiko no umu
在庫の有無

which means 'whether or not something is in stock.' (*Zaiko* means 'stock on hand' / 'inventory.')

Still other compounds of this type can be used to indicate the amount or extent of something. For example, the pairing of characters meaning 'difficult' (難) and 'easy' (易) produces the word 難易 (なんい, *nani*), which conveys the notion '(amount of) difficulty.' Among other uses, this word, when combined with the suffix 度, meaning 'degree,' forms the word 難易度 (なんいど, *nanido*), meaning 'degree of difficulty.'

Note that concepts such as 有無 and 難易 are often expressed in English using only one of the two parts of the compound. For example, you can speak of either the 'presence' or the 'absence' of something, and either the 'ease' or the 'difficulty' of doing something.

Some compounds of this type are made up of characters that, rather than being exact opposites, are counterparts of each other. Examples include 'husband and wife' (夫婦, *fūfu*) and 'hands and feet' (手足, *teashi*).

In some cases, the two characters in a compound are themselves abbreviations of other compound words. For example, the compound 収支 (*shūshi*) which means 'income and expenditures' is made up of the first characters of 収入 (*shūnyū*, 'income') and 支出 (*shishutsu*, 'expenditures'). And the compound 出欠 (*shukketsu*) which means 'presence or absence (of a person, such as at an event)' is made up of the first characters of the compounds 出席 (*shusseki*, 'presence') and 欠席 (*kesseki*, 'absence').

C. Negated Meaning

In this type of compound, the first character negates the meaning of the second, to form a word that is basically the opposite of the second character. This is similar to words using the English prefixes 'un-,' 'dis-,' 'non-,' 'in-,' etc. Several different characters are commonly used as the negating first character, with some slight differences in meaning between some of them. The most common of these characters are shown in the table below, together with an example compound word for each.

Negating Character (Reading)	Meaning	Example Compound (Reading)	Compound Meaning
無 (MU / BU)	absent of; without	無限 (*mugen*)	('without' + 'limit'): 'infinite'
未 (MI)	not yet	未来 (*mirai*)	('not yet' + 'come'): 'future'
不 (FU)	un-, non-	不安 (*fuan*)	('un' + 'ease'): 'anxiety'
非 (HI)	un-, non-	非常 (*hijō*)	('non' + 'ordinary'): 'extraordinary; emergency'

Note that, as already discussed in Chapter 5 (Section 5.5), these negating characters can also be used, with the same meanings as in the table on the previous page, as prefixes attached to compound words of two or more characters. For example, the character 不 can be attached to the two-character compound 都合 (*tsugō*), meaning 'convenience,' to form the word 不都合 (*futsugō*), meaning 'inconvenience.'

D. Descriptor Plus Object

In this type of compound, already mentioned at the beginning of this section, the second character indicates an object, and the first character is a descriptor of that object. The word *kanji* (漢字, 'Chinese character') is an example of this. In grammatical terms, the second character is a noun, and the first character is an adjective, describing that noun.

Other examples:

    洋服   (*yōfuku*, 'western' + 'clothing'): 'western-style clothing'
    悪人   (*akunin*, 'bad' + 'person'): 'wicked person; villain'
    寒風   (*kanpū*, 'cold' + 'wind'): 'cold winds'

E. Action Plus Object

In this type of compound, the first character refers to an action, and the second character is an object that is the recipient of that action. In grammatical terms, the second character is a noun, and the first character is a verb, describing an action done to that noun.

Examples:

    防災   (*bōsai*, 'prevent' + 'disaster'): 'disaster prevention'
    植樹   (*shokuju*, 'plant' + 'tree'): 'tree planting'
    消火   (*shōka*, 'put out' + 'fire'): 'fire fighting'

9.2 Three- and Four-Character Compounds

Among compound words which consist of more than two characters, most have either three or four characters.

An example of a three-character compound word is 自転車 (*jitensha*, 'bicycle'), made up of characters meaning, respectively, 'self' (自), 'move (especially by rolling)' (転), and 'vehicle' (車). This is a very simple type of compound, where the meanings of each of the characters taken together succinctly describe the compound meaning.

Unlike *jitensha*, many three-character compound words actually consist of a two-character compound word with a third character added as a prefix or suffix (see Chapter 5 for a discussion of prefixes and suffixes). For example, the word 社会学 (*shakaigaku*) is made up of a two-character compound meaning 'society' (社会, *shakai*), with a suffix that in this case means 'the study of' (学, *gaku*). The resulting three-character compound word means 'sociology': the study of society.

Some four-character compound words are made up of two two-character compound words placed together. For example, the four-character word 短期大学 (*tankidaigaku*) is composed of the two-character compound words *tanki*, meaning 'short-term,' and *daigaku*, meaning 'university.' Put together, the meaning is 'junior college' (i.e., a short-term institution of higher education).

Four-character compound words are also frequently used to represent proverbs and idioms. This practice originated in China and was carried over to Japan. To do this, four key words from the proverb are chosen and assembled together as a compound word. For example, the idiom that originated in English as 'to kill two birds with one stone' has been adopted into Japanese as the four-character compound word 一石二鳥 (*issekinichō*), with characters meaning 'one,' 'stone,' 'two,' and 'bird(s),' in that order. More examples of four-character compound idioms are presented in Appendix M.

9.3 Mixed *On* and *Kun* Compounds

The majority of two-character compound words are read using the *on* reading of each character in the compound. Among compounds not read this way, most are read using the *kun* reading of each character.

So, as a rule of thumb, when encountering an unfamiliar two-character word, the correct reading most likely uses either the *on* readings of each character in it, or the *kun* readings of each character in it. When guessing the reading of a newly-encountered word, those readings should be guessed first.

Furthermore, if the word appears to have okurigana included in it, then it is most likely read using the *kun* readings of its characters. If there is no okurigana (that is, the compound consists of only kanji with no hiragana mixed in) there is a strong likelihood that the compound is read using the *on* readings of both characters.

Mixed two-character compounds, in which one character is read with an *on* reading, and the other with a *kun* reading, are relatively rare. Of these mixed compounds, ones that are read in the order *on-kun* (that is, with the *on* reading of the first character and the *kun* reading of the second) are said to have a **_jūbako_ reading**, while ones that are read in the order *kun-on* are said to have a **_yutō_ reading**. Some of the more common compound words with these mixed readings are listed in Appendix L.

9.4 Characteristics of Some Compound Words

Same Set of Kanji, Different Word

Some compound words can be read in more than one different way. For most such compounds, regardless of the reading, the compound meaning is the same (or approximately the same). In a few cases, though, the different readings have different meanings. That is, the same written compound represents more than one completely different word.

In Chapter 5, we saw some examples of compounds with different readings but the same meaning. For example, the compound word 昨日 can be read as *kinō* (a special *kun* reading) or *sakujitsu* (an *on* reading of the two characters), but in either case the meaning is 'yesterday.'

In contrast, the different readings of the compound 分別 have different meanings. When read as *bunbetsu*, the compound means 'classification.' When read as *funbetsu*, the meaning is 'discretion.' For words such as this, the intended meaning (and reading) must be determined from the sentence context. Fortunately, there are very few compound words like 分別 which have multiple readings with different meanings.

Character Reversal

For some two-character compounds, another compound word exists which has the same characters, but in the opposite order. These 'reversal' words sometimes have nearly the same meaning as their counterpart, but sometimes the meanings are different.

Two common compound words which contain the same characters but in the opposite order from each other are 会社 (*kaisha*) and 社会 (*shakai*). Each is made up of a character meaning 'a gathering of people' (会) and a character originally meaning 'a place where people worship the fertility of the land' (社). As mentioned in Chapter 5, the word *kaisha* originally meant 'an association,' but now primarily means 'company' or 'corporation.' And *shakai*, as mentioned in Section 9.2, has a different meaning: 'society.'

Another pair of words which are written in the opposite way from each other are 物置 (*monooki*) and 置物 (*okimono*). Each consists of characters meaning 'thing' (物) and 'to put, place' (置). The meanings are different, though. *Monooki* means 'storeroom,' while *okimono* means 'ornament.' The key difference between these words is that a *monooki* is a place where you put things, while an *okimono* is a thing that is put in a place.

This phenomenon is not unique to Japanese. An example in English of compound words which are the reverse of each other are 'farewell' and 'welfare.' Although the spellings are different, the components of the words ('fare' and 'well') have the same origin and meaning in each word. And yet, the meanings of the compound words are different.

9.5 Compound Etymologies and Meaning Change

Just as individual characters have an etymology—the story behind the creation of the character—compound words have etymologies as well. For many compounds, including most of the ones already discussed in this chapter, the etymology is very simple: it merely comes from a combination of the meanings of the characters in it. This is not always the case, though; with some compounds the meaning is not obvious from the characters it contains. For such compounds, there is, of course, a reason why the compound came to have the meaning it does.

The origins of some compound words are very interesting and memorable. One compound with an especially memorable origin is the word 矛盾 (*mujun*), meaning 'contradiction.' It is made up of characters meaning 'pike' (a long, bladed thrusting spear) and 'shield.' The compound and its meaning derive from an ancient Chinese story (told as a parable) of a man who sold both pikes and shields. The man boasted that his pikes could pierce through anything. He also claimed that nothing could penetrate his shields. But then he was asked what would happen if one of his pikes were to strike one of his shields, and was unable to answer. Clearly, his claims about his weapons could not both be true, as that would be a contradiction. From this story came the word 矛盾, with the meaning 'contradiction.'

Not all non-obvious etymologies are based on memorable stories like this one, though. For example, the etymology of the word *chūmon* (注文), which means 'order' (such as an order for food placed in a restaurant), is rather complex. The individual characters in the compound mean 'pour' (注) and 'writing' (文), neither of which have any obvious connection to an order placed in a restaurant.

In fact, the compound was originally written as 註文, with a first character meaning 'explanatory note' / 'comment.' The two characters in this original form of the compound both pertain to writing because the compound itself originally referred specifically to a more formal kind of order that is put in writing, such as when providing specifications for an item to be manufactured. The character 注 actually has nothing to do with the word meaning, but was simply used as a replacement for 註 as part of an effort to consolidate the total number of different characters in use. (This kind of character consolidation is explained in Chapter 2, Section 2.12.)

With this particular compound word, not only the way it is written, but also the word reading itself was changed; originally, it was a native Japanese compound word, read as *shirushibumi*. At some point, the compound reading was shortened by changing it to use the *on* reading of each character: *chūmon*.

Compound Meaning Change

Knowing word origins such as those just explained can sometimes help with remembering a compound's meaning (and sometimes not). Even if you choose to learn word origins, though, it is important to realize that meanings change. There are many compounds whose original meanings did simply follow from the characters in them, but then subsequently the word meaning changed, a natural occurrence in any language.

An example of a compound whose meaning changed is *shimatsu* (始末), consisting of characters meaning 'begin' (始) and 'end' (末). The original compound meaning was, roughly, 'the full course of events of something, from its beginning to its end.' Now, though, the principal meaning of this compound is 'disposal' or 'disposition,' referring to how an issue or an object is wrapped up and resolved—a meaning not at all obvious from the characters in the compound. Furthermore, this word has taken on several other meanings, as well, including 'end result' (usually when the result is undesirable) and 'thrift; economy.'

Another compound whose meaning underwent change is *meyasu* (目安), consisting of characters meaning 'eye' (目) and 'easy' (安). Originally, the word referred to marks which made something easier to read or see. Today, the meanings of this word include 'aim' / 'goal,' 'criterion' / 'standard,' and 'rough idea' / 'rough estimate.'

As these last two examples demonstrate, not only have the meanings of some compounds changed, but some compounds have also acquired multiple, different meanings. For these words, the specific meaning intended in any given sentence must be determined by context.

When trying to learn and memorize such compounds, it is not enough to come up with a story that relates the characters in the compound to the compound meaning, because doing that would only help you remember one of the compound meanings. Instead, it is necessary, with repetition, to be able to associate a compound word with each of its various meanings. Of course, just as with individual characters, not all meanings of a given compound are used with the same frequency. A good strategy is to learn and memorize the most common meanings of a compound first, and then learn rarer ones later.

Learning Word Etymologies Not Always Feasible

For many compounds whose meanings don't obviously follow from the characters in them, it is simply not always possible to learn the compound etymology at the time you first learn the compound. Some origins are complicated (such as *chūmon*), and others are rather obscure.

But even for compounds whose etymologies are well known, this information is often not easily accessible to beginning Japanese learners. For instance, it may not be available in any language other than Japanese.

As a result, it is often necessary for students to learn and memorize compound meanings without fully understanding why the compounds acquired those meanings.

9.6 Compound Reading Sound Changes

Many compound words are read by simply reading each component of the word using one of its standard *on* or *kun* readings. In some compound words, though, the reading of the compound is not a simple combination of the readings of the words that make up the compound. For example, some compounds undergo a slight sound change when parts of the compound fit certain criteria. Other compounds have even greater changes in their readings.

In the next three sections, we will learn in detail about three different kinds of sound change phenomena that occur within some compounds. Then in Section 9.10 we will look at examples of compounds with other kinds of special readings.

9.7 Special Sound Change: *Sokuon*

In some compounds, primarily *on*-based compounds, when the two parts of the compound are brought together, a sound change takes place where the final sound (mora) of the first part is dropped out and replaced with an elongation of the initial consonant sound of the second part. In linguistics, the process of lengthening a consonant sound is called gemination.

In Japanese, this consonant elongation is called *sokuon* (meaning 'rushed sound'). In hiragana and katakana, it is written using a small version of the *tsu* character: っ / ッ . This small character itself is also called a *sokuon*. (More informally, it is called *chīsai tsu* [small *tsu*].)

When preceding consonant sounds /t/, /k/, or /p/, the *sokuon* sounds like an inaudible pause of one beat. Preceding /s/, it sounds like a one-beat hold of the start of the /s/ sound.

Many compound words are affected by this process. One such example is the word *kesseki* (欠席: 'absence [of a person]'). The principal readings of the two components which make up this word are *ketsu* (欠) and *seki* (席). When brought together into a compound word, the final mora of *ketsu* (*tsu*) is dropped, and replaced with a *sokuon* (represented with the small *tsu* character below):

$$けつ\ (ketsu)\ +\ せき\ (seki)\ =\ けっせき\ (kesseki)$$

When writing Japanese using *rōmaji*, the *sokuon* is expressed by the doubling of the consonant which follows the *sokuon* character. For example, in the case of *kesseki* the *s* is doubled. This writing convention is standard for geminated (elongated) consonants.

Among *kango* (compound words read with the *on* reading), this sound only occurs in certain circumstances. Specifically, it is only used as a replacement for one of the following sounds in the final mora of the first part of the compound: *ki*, *ku*, *chi*, or *tsu*. Furthermore, it occurs only when the second part of the compound begins with one of the following consonants: k, t, p, or s. Even so, the sound does not always occur when these conditions are met.

Among compound words that meet these conditions, the *sokuon* occurs most consistently when the final mora of the first part of the compound is *tsu*. This is why the *sokuon* has come to be written in hiragana and katakana using the *tsu* character (more specifically, the small version of that character).

Note that this phenomenon generally does not occur when prefixes or suffixes are attached to compound words, even if the above conditions are met. The following examples, in which the prefix *aku* and the suffix *kan* are added to established two-character compounds words, demonstrate this:

$$あく\ (悪, aku)\ +\ かんじょう\ (感情, kanjō)\ =$$
$$あくかんじょう\ (悪感情, akukanjō),\ \textbf{not}\ あっかんじょう\ (akkanjō)$$
$$たいいく\ (体育, taiiku)\ +\ かん\ (館, kan)\ =$$
$$たいいくかん\ (体育館\ taiikukan),\ \textbf{not}\ たいいっかん\ (taiikkan)$$

The *sokuon* is found primarily within *kango* (words read with *on* readings). However, it also can be found in words of native Japanese origin. Notably, the *sokuon* appears in a number of adverbs, including words such as *yukkuri*, *hakkiri*, and *shikkari*. In some cases, native Japanese words containing a *sokuon* were derived from earlier Japanese words which did not have one. Native Japanese words containing a *sokuon* tend to be comparatively new to the language, as the *sokuon* did not exist in traditional Japanese (as described in Chapter 8).

9.8 Special Sound Change: *Rendaku*

Another kind of sound change phenomenon occurring within compound words affects the beginning sound of one of the latter parts of the compound (usually the second part). Specifically, that beginning sound changes from an unvoiced sound to a voiced sound.

We've already encountered a number of words which exhibit this phenomenon. For example, when the words *hana* ('flower') and *hi* ('fire') are combined to form a compound word meaning 'fireworks,' the resulting word is *hanabi*, not *hanahi*. The starting sound of the second word in the compound changes from an /h/ to a /b/ sound.

The same thing has happened in the compound *mizugi* ('swimsuit'). The component words in this compound are *mizu* ('water') and *ki*, which is the noun form of the verb *kiru* ('to wear') and means 'clothing.' When combined into a compound word, the starting sound of the second part of the compound changes from a /k/ to a /g/ sound.

A well-known word affected by this process is *origami* ('paper folding'). It is a compound word consisting of *ori* (the combining form of the verb *oru*: 'to fold') and *kami*: 'paper.' In the compound, the starting sound of *kami* changes from a /k/ to a /g/ sound.

In each of these cases, the sound that has changed has gone from an unvoiced sound (one in which the vocal cords are not vibrating) to a voiced sound (where the vocal cords are vibrating). In Japanese, this phenomenon is called **rendaku**, which roughly translates to 'sequential voicing' (because the sound which becomes voiced occurs when it is placed within a sequence, in other than the first position).

In Japanese, the sound changes that occur because of this phenomenon can be classified into four types:

$$k \rightarrow g \qquad s \rightarrow z \qquad t \rightarrow d \qquad h \rightarrow b \text{ or } p$$

Note that an /h/ sound can transform into either /b/ or /p/.[1]

Because of the way Japanese sounds are usually expressed in *rōmaji*, the changes to certain of these sounds are expressed differently, including the following:

$$shi \rightarrow ji \qquad chi \rightarrow ji \qquad tsu \rightarrow zu \qquad fu \rightarrow bu \text{ or } pu$$

These sound changes can be much more easily seen when the words are written in hiragana or katakana. Then, the voiced sound is written simply as the character for the unvoiced sound with an extra *dakuten* (゛) mark added to it. For example, the three sound changes

$$ka \rightarrow ga \qquad shi \rightarrow ji \qquad he \rightarrow be$$

appear this way in hiragana:

$$か \rightarrow が \qquad し \rightarrow じ \qquad へ \rightarrow べ$$

Changes from *h* to *p* are expressed with the *handakuten* (゜) mark, as in:

$$は \rightarrow ぱ \quad (ha \rightarrow pa)$$

Occurrences of *rendaku* within words are inconsistent and somewhat unpredictable; this phenomenon does not strictly obey a set of rules. There are some general guidelines that help with predicting when it does and does not occur, but these are somewhat complicated, and will not be discussed in this book.

---

[1] The sound change from *h* to *b* may seem unusual, as technically the *b* sound is not a voiced version of the *h* sound. Long ago in the Japanese language, this change used to be *p* (unvoiced) → *b* (voiced)—a more natural change. The modern '*h* → *b* or *p*' structure resulted from sound changes in the Japanese language.

Rendaku occurs most commonly within native Japanese compound words, such as *hanabi*, *mizugi*, and *origami*, but can also occur within compound words read with *on* readings (i.e., *kango*). For example, the compound word *shunjū*, meaning 'spring and autumn,' is made up of the individual parts *shun* (春, 'spring') and *shū* (秋, 'autumn'). When put together as a compound, the latter part changes from *shū* to *jū*:

しゅん (*shun*) + しゅう (*shū*) = しゅんじゅう (*shunjū*)

Similarly, the word *shinpai* (心配), meaning 'concern; anxiety,' is written with characters read as *shin* (心) and *hai* (配). When combined into a compound, though, the second part changes from *hai* to *pai*:

しん (*shin*) + はい (*hai*) = しんぱい (*shinpai*)

Entire compounds can also be altered by *rendaku* when they are the latter part of an even larger compound word. For example, the *on* compound word *kaisha* (会社, 'company') is commonly read as *gaisha* when it is the latter part of a larger compound word, such as *kabushiki gaisha* (株式会社, 'corporation').

For *on* compound words affected by *rendaku*, it is simpler to think of the full compound word as having a (slightly) special reading, than to think of the latter character as having an additional alternate *on* reading. Using a specific example, don't think of *JŪ* as an alternate *on* reading of the character 秋 ('autumn'). Instead, just think of the compound word 春秋 as having a special reading (*shunjū*).

9.9 Special Sound Change: *Renjō*

The *rendaku* sound change phenomenon described in the previous section affects the starting consonant sound of one of the latter parts of a compound word. There is another similar sound change phenomenon in which, instead of a consonant sound being changed, a bare vowel sound gets a starting consonant sound added to it. The consonant added is similar in sound to the ending sound of the preceding part of the compound. This sound change phenomenon primarily occurs with *on*-based compound words (*kango*).

As an example, a compound word meaning 'reaction' / 'response' is made up of two characters: 反, normally read as *han*, and 応, normally read as *ō*. In this compound, though, the sound of the second part changes to *nō*. A starting /n/ sound has been added to it, matching the ending /n/ sound of the preceding word (*han*). Expressed in hiragana:

はん (*han*) + おう (*ō*) = はんのう (*hannō*)

In Japanese, this sound change phenomenon is called **renjō**. In English, it is called 'liaison.'

Compared to *rendaku*, relatively few words are modified by the *renjō* process. It can only take place when the second part of a compound word begins with a bare vowel sound, and does not always occur even when this condition is met. More common in the past, *renjō* is seen today only among a few established words, such as *tennō* (天皇, てんのう, 'emperor').

In most words modified by *renjō*, an /*n*/ sound is added, but in a few cases other sounds are added instead. For example, in some words, combining *san* (三) and *i* (位), produces *sanmi*, with an /*m*/ sound being added to the second part of the compound. Today, the word is more commonly read as *sani* (さんい), but the reading *sanmi* can still be seen in the expression *sanmi-ittai* (三位一体), meaning 'the doctrine of Trinity.'

Some character dictionaries identify sounds altered by *renjō* as possible *on* readings of characters. For example, such dictionaries would identify both Ō (オウ) and NŌ (ノウ) as possible *on* readings of the characters 応 and 皇. Technically, this is incorrect. It is better, and probably simpler, to consider word readings such as *hannō* and *tennō* to be special compound readings, and not think of NŌ as one of the possible *on* readings of the 応 and 皇 characters.

No Indication of These Phenomena in Kanji

Note that when a compound word is written using kanji there is no way to tell whether or not any of the three sound change phenomena described in the last three sections (*sokuon*, *rendaku*, and *renjō*) occur within the word. For example, it is impossible to tell simply from looking at the characters 天皇 ('emperor') whether or not the correct reading of this compound word is affected by *renjō* (or any other phenomenon). The presence of these phenomena can only be determined when a word is written using hiragana or katakana.

Because occurrences of these phenomena cannot always be predicted, it is necessary to learn compound word readings on a case by case basis. The correct reading of each word must be learned at the time the word is learned, whether or not it has a special reading.

9.10 Other Kinds of Special Readings

Most compound words are read using the individual *on* or *kun* readings of each character in the word, possibly slightly modified by the sound changes described in the previous three sections. But there are also a number of compounds not read in this way. In some of these specially-read compound words, the reading closely approximates the *on* or *kun* readings of the characters in the compound, but in others it is completely dissimilar.

Specially-read compound words were derived in various ways. Some of them are *jukujikun*, discussed in Chapter 5, in which native Japanese words are written using the kanji from a Chinese compound word with the same meaning. That is, the word is spoken as a native Japanese word, but written as if it were a Chinese compound word.

For a number of such words, the characters used to write them today were not the original characters in the compound, but were substituted later, as a replacement for the original characters.

For any compound word read with a special reading, understanding how that reading came about can be helpful for remembering it. It's not always possible to do this, though, as many of these special readings have existed for a long time, and the origins are either complicated or unclear. In this section, the origins of a few words with special readings are looked at in detail to give you an idea of how some such words have come about. Appendix K lists more examples of common compound words with special readings.

otona (大人, おとな)

Otona is a native Japanese word meaning 'adult.' Written in kanji, this word is made up of two characters meaning 'large' (大) and 'person' (人), which together are a way to define 'adult.' The way of writing this word in kanji comes from Chinese. The spoken word, however, is of native Japanese origin, and so this word is a straightforward example of *jukujikun*, as explained in Chapter 5.

musuko (息子, むすこ)

Musuko is a native Japanese word meaning 'son.' Written in kanji, this word is made up of two characters meaning 'breath' (息) and 'child' (子). Although the second of these characters can be read as *ko*, *musu* is not a recognized reading of the first character. The spoken word derives from the verb *musu*, meaning 'to give birth to' (written as 生す or 産す) combined with the noun *ko*, meaning 'child,' although in this case referring specifically to a male child. Why a character meaning 'breath' was chosen to write this word is unclear, but this same character also appears in a similar word: *shisoku* (子息), used to refer to another person's son.

tokei (時計, とけい)

The word *tokei* means 'clock' / 'timepiece.' The modern way of writing this word in kanji is made up of two characters meaning 'time' (時) and 'measure' (計). The compound reading can be obtained from these characters by taking the first half of the *kun* reading of the first character (*toku*) and the *on* reading of the second character (*kei*). But the word origin does not involve these characters; they were backfit onto the word at a later date. The word *tokei* was originally written with the characters 土圭 (whose *on* readings can produce *tokei*), and referred specifically to a type of sundial. With the advent of mechanical timepieces, the way of writing the word was revised, and now it is almost exclusively written as 時計. The use of these characters is a kind of *ateji*: using characters for their sound (see Chapter 5). In this case, the meaning of these characters was also a factor in the choice.

keshiki (景色, けしき)

From the *on* readings of the characters in this word, the expected reading of this compound would be *keishiki*. The slightly different *keshiki* reading originates from a different first character. The word was originally written with the characters 気色, whose *on* readings can produce *keshiki*. The original word meaning was 'the outward appearance of something,' such as a facial expression which reflects a person's mood. When the word was extended to also mean 'landscape' / 'scenery,' a character meaning 'scenery' / 'view' was substituted for the first character. This substitute character had a slightly different *on* reading (*kei* instead of *ke*), but the existing word reading was retained, resulting in the special reading.

9.11 Compounds Built from Abbreviation

Abbreviations are very common in the Japanese language. Unlike in English, where many abbreviations are formed by taking the first letters of each word in a name or phrase, Japanese abbreviations often take the first full character of each word in a name or phrase, forming a new compound word with those characters.

For example, vending machines in Japanese are called *jidōhanbaiki* (自動販売機). This word consists of three parts: *jidō* (自動, 'automatic'), *hanbai* (販売, 'vending'), and *ki* (機, 'machine'). When abbreviated, only the first characters of each of the two-character compound words are used, together with the final character, resulting in the abbreviated form *jihanki* (自販機).

This kind of abbreviation is also commonly seen in the names of routes that connect two locations together, such as train lines. Routes are often named by combining one character each (usually the first) from the names of the locations at each end of the line. For example, the line between Tokyo (東京) and Yokohama (横浜) is called the *tōyokosen* (東横線), a word formed by taking the first characters of Tokyo and Yokohama and combining them with a word meaning 'line' (線, *sen*).

Abbreviations are almost always read using the *on* reading of each character in them, even when the non-abbreviated form uses a *kun* reading. There are a very small number of exceptions to this, though, including the *yoko* part of the above word *tōyokosen*, which is a *kun* reading.

Although usually the first character in a place name is used, there are exceptions to this as well. In the case of Osaka (大阪), it is usually the second character (阪, with the *on* reading *HAN*) which is used, as the first character in the name is very commonplace, but the second character is unique and thus distinctive. This character is used, for example, in the name *hanshin* (阪神), a word describing not only routes between Osaka and Kobe (神戸), but also the general region which includes both of these cities. (Note that the word *hanshin* uses *on* readings of both the 阪 and 神 characters.)

Even when a character is already read with an *on* reading prior to its inclusion in an abbreviation, sometimes a different *on* reading of the character is used in the abbreviated form. For example, Kyoto (京都) is read using *on* readings of both its characters: *KYŌ* and *TO*. When used in the name of the route between Kyoto and Osaka, though, a different *on* reading of the first character (京) is used: *KEI*. This route is called *keihan* (京阪). Usually, changes of this type occur when a word (before abbreviation) uses an *on* reading other than the *kan on* reading (see Section 7.9 for a discussion of the different types of *on* readings, such as *kan on*). In the abbreviated form, the *kan on* reading of a character is often used, as these readings are generally thought of as the most standard of the character *on* readings.

9.12 *Mazegaki*

Some compounds that can be written entirely in kanji are most commonly seen written with a mixture of kanji and hiragana instead. Usually, this is done when one of the characters is uncommon or considered to be difficult to read.

We already saw an example of this in Chapter 5 with the word *hifuka* ('dermatology'). In kanji, the word is written as 皮膚科. All three of the characters in the word are among the *jōyō kanji*, but the second one (read as *fu*) is not used to write many different words, and its reading is not easy to guess based on the components in it. For those reasons, the word *hifuka* is often seen written with hiragana in place of that second character: 皮ふ科.

COMPOUND WORDS IN DEPTH

This type of writing, where hiragana are used to replace only certain kanji in a single word or term, is called *mazegaki*, meaning 'mixed writing.' *Mazegaki* is not all that common, as it can cause confusion when reading, making it difficult to realize where word boundaries are. When it is used, it's almost always in the case of a compound word where one character is especially rare, but writing the entire word in hiragana might be too confusing. So the compromise is to write part of the word in kanji, and part in hiragana.

Another word commonly written using *mazegaki* is *hatan*, meaning 'bankruptcy.' In kanji, the word is written 破綻. However, the second character in this compound is rather uncommon, and its reading is not easy to guess from the components in it.[2] Therefore, this word is commonly written as 破たん, with hiragana replacing the second character. Of course, the word could be written entirely in hiragana, instead, but having one part of the word expressed in kanji helps the reader to recognize which word is intended.

Although the characters 膚 and 綻 in the previous examples are among the *jōyō kanji*, most cases of *mazegaki* occur when a character is outside of the *jōyō kanji*.[3]

9.13 Conversion of Native Japanese Words into *Kango*

Some words in modern Japanese have been reconfigured, converted from an original native Japanese form into a form modeled after words borrowed from China. In other words, these words have been restructured from *wago* (native Japanese) to *kango* (Chinese style, where characters are read using *on* readings).

We already saw one example of this earlier in this chapter (Section 9.5): the native Japanese word *shirushibumi* was revised to *chūmon*, a reading which was derived by combining *on* readings of each of the characters in the word. Also, in Chapter 7 (Section 7.1) we saw this with a word meaning 'response' / 'reply.' The word was originally a native Japanese compound word: *kaerigoto* (made up of parts meaning 'return' and 'thing'), and was written 返り事 (かえりごと). Later, the word was altered to *kango* by using only the two kanji in it, each read with an *on* reading, producing *henji* (返事, へんじ). This is the modern form of the word.

Usually, this type of conversion of words into *kango* was done when the *kango* version was seen as being a simpler, shorter word. This is precisely what happened to the entire Japanese number system.

In the native Japanese way of counting, numbers larger than ten tended to be very long. For example, the number thirty-nine was expressed in native Japanese as:

misoji amari kokonotsu

This phrase consists of three parts, meaning, respectively, 'thirty,' 'extra,' and 'nine' (i.e., thirty plus an extra nine). It is rather lengthy.

---

[2] Although the right-hand side component is the character phonetic, that phonetic usually has a much different reading in other characters which contain it.
[3] The character 綻 in *hatan* was not originally chosen as a *jōyō kanji*, but was added to the list in 2010.

The Chinese way of expressing large numbers was simpler and shorter, and so the Japanese converted their numbering system to a new system modeled after the Chinese way of counting.

With this new system, thirty-nine is expressed as:

san jū kyū

with three parts meaning 'three,' 'ten,' and 'nine' (i.e., three tens plus nine). This is a much shorter way of expressing the same thing. Using the Chinese method, numbers could be spoken much more quickly.

The changeover to a Chinese-based system in counting is the reason why numbers in Japanese are usually read using *on* readings (with a few special exceptions).[4]

---

[4] Within some words, the numbers 4 and 7 are read using words of native Japanese origin. This is done to avoid the spoken sound *shi*, which is considered bad luck because it matches the sound of a word meaning 'death.'

Part 2

Reference Lists

Part 2 Breakdown

Part 2 is divided into four sections:

- Section 1 lists the 80 most common elements used as determinatives within characters. A set of information is provided for each determinative, including a description of the various meanings indicated by the determinative.

- Section 2 lists 500 of the most commonly used phonetic components, together with the most common readings of these phonetics, and a list of all of the common use characters (and others) which use the phonetics.

- Section 3 lists other components that appear within multiple characters, but which are not easily classified as either determinatives or phonetics.

- Section 4 lists the set of 214 character radicals identified in this book. As there is much overlap between radicals and determinatives, this section is recommended only for those students who specifically wish to gain knowledge of character radicals. For other students, Section 1 is sufficient.

Section 1

List of Major Determinatives

1.1 Overview

This section lists the most commonly occurring determinatives used in the composition of characters, as well as the various meanings that these determinatives typically indicate in those characters. Each determinative is designated with the letter 'D' followed by a number (e.g., D-21).

The order in which the determinatives are listed here generally corresponds to the frequency with which they are used in characters, with the more commonly encountered determinatives appearing earlier in the list. A few of these determinatives, though, are grouped together with others similar in meaning, to make learning them easier.

Only those components that were deliberately used as determinatives—serving in the role of identifying the overall category of meaning of a character—are listed here. Some components which have been used as determinatives are not listed here, but these are only rarely-used ones, used in a determinative role in only a few characters, primarily or exclusively outside of the common use character set.

Most determinatives are usually found located in only one or two particular regions within a character. This information is also listed in the table, in graphical form, under the heading 'principal locations.' Only the most common locations are shown.

For some of the determinatives, alternate forms are shown. In most cases, these are simplified forms that are substituted when the component is compressed into a particular location within a character. For that reason, all of the alternate forms are shown within a box, to indicate the region of the character in which these alternate forms are usually found.

Most of the determinatives listed in this section are also commonly classified as radicals (the differences between determinatives and radicals are described in Part 1, Section 4.2).

As mentioned in Part 1, Chapter 2, it is important to note that you cannot assume that the components listed in this section are used as determinatives in every character they appear in, and even when they are used as determinatives, you cannot assume that the modern meanings of the characters containing them still relate to the determinative meaning.

List of Major Determinatives (page 1 of 4)

#	Main Form	Alternate Form(s)	Principal Location(s)	Principal Categories of Meaning (Notes)	Example Characters	
D-1	木	朩	▯▮ ▮▯	objects made of wood; types of trees; parts of a tree; actions involving trees	机 desk	松 pine (tree)
D-2	水	氵	▯▮	types of liquids; things associated with liquids; bodies of water	池 pond	注 to pour
D-3	艹		▮▯	flowers / plants / vegetation (standalone character form: 艸)	花 flower	草 grass
D-4	金	金	▯▮	objects made of metal; types of metal	鎖 chain	銀 silver
D-5	土	士	▯▮ ▮▯	things pertaining to the ground or land; objects made of dirt or clay, or formed by piling dirt	塚 mound	堤 (river) bank
D-6	竹		▮▯	objects made of bamboo; parts of the bamboo plant (standalone character form: 竹)	笛 flute	筒 tube
D-7	火	灬 ⺌	▯▮ ▮▯	things pertaining to burning, or the giving off of heat or light	煙 smoke	煮 boil
D-8	雨	雨	▮▯	weather-related conditions, objects, or phenomena	雲 cloud	霜 frost
D-9	山		▯▮ ▮▯	things associated with mountains; large land formations	峡 gorge	峰 peak
D-10	石		▯▮	objects made of stone; processes involving stones	礎 cornerstone	磨 grind; polish
D-11	人	亻	▯▮	things pertaining to people: types of people, actions or relations between people, etc.	僧 monk	伴 companion
D-12	手	扌	▯▮ ▮▯	actions performed with the hands; things pertaining to the hands	握 grasp	拳 fist
D-13	心	忄 小	▯▮ ▮▯	emotions; feelings; states of mind; things pertaining to the heart	恨 resentment	恐 fear
D-14	口		▯▮	actions performed with the mouth (other than speaking)	吸 inhale; suck	叫 shout
D-15	言		▯▮	things related to verbal or written communication: speaking, words, etc.	読 reading	論 discussion
D-16	頁		▯▮	parts of the head / face	顔 face	額 forehead
D-17	肉	月 月	▯▮ ▮▯	body parts (other than the head / face); things having to do with the body	肺 lungs	腎 kidneys
D-18	目		▯▮	having to do with the eyes or seeing, or involving the watching of something	眼 eyeball	督 supervising
D-19	見		▯▮	things pertaining to vision or sight	観 observe	覗 peek
D-20	足	𧾷	▯▮	having to do with the feet or legs, or actions involving them	踊 dancing	跳 leaping

List of Major Determinatives (page 2 of 4)

#	Main Form	Alternate Form(s)	Principal Location(s)	Principal Categories of Meaning (Notes)	Example Characters	
D-21	虫		▯▯ ▯▭	types of insects / reptiles / shellfish (i.e., smaller creatures)	蛇 snake	蚕 silkworm
D-22	犬	犭	▯▯	types of animals, especially smaller mammals	猫 cat	猿 monkey
D-23	魚		▯▯	types of fish or other similar sea life; things related to fishing	鯨 whale	鮭 salmon
D-24	鳥		▯▯	types of birds (especially larger birds)	鶏 chicken	鶴 crane
D-25	馬		▯▯	having to do with horses, or the use of or characteristics of horses	駅 a station	驚 surprise
D-26	牛	牜	▯▯ ▯▭	things pertaining to cattle; large animals similar in size to cattle	牧 ranch	犀 rhinoceros
D-27	隹		▯▯	types of small birds; things associated with small birds	雀 sparrow	雉 pheasant
D-28	糸		▯▯	1. having to do with thread, or with tying / binding / interconnectedness; 2. colors	緩 loosen	絹 silk
D-29	日		▯▯ ▯▭	1. having to do with the sun or stars, or light or heat; 2. pertaining to a day or other short period of time	昭 shining	暑 hot
D-30	辶		▙▁	things pertaining to movement (standalone character form: 辵)	進 proceed	退 retreat
D-31	彳		▯▯	things pertaining to movement; actions (left half of D-76; similar in meaning to D-30)	従 follow	徐 move slowly
D-32	貝		▯▯ ▯▭	things pertaining to money, wealth, gifts, etc., or other things held in high regard	購 purchase	賃 fee
D-33	玉	王	▯▯	types of precious gems or jewels; round objects	珠 pearl; gem	球 sphere; ball
D-34	衣	衤	▯▯ ▯▯ ▯▭	types of clothing; parts of clothing; things having to do with clothing or fabric	襟 collar	装 attire
D-35	巾		▯▯ ▯▭	objects made of cloth; types of small cloths, towels, etc.	帆 a sail	幕 a curtain
D-36	車		▯▯	types of vehicles; objects which rotate or roll	軸 axis	輪 wheel
D-37	食	飠 𩙿	▯▯	types of food; things pertaining to food or eating	飯 cooked rice	飢 starvation
D-38	疒		▙▁	types of diseases; things pertaining to illness or injury	痛 pain	療 cure
D-39	宀		▔▔	types of buildings; parts of a building	宮 shrine	寮 dormitory
D-40	广		▙▁	types of buildings; parts of a building (similar in meaning to D-39)	店 store; shop	庭 courtyard

List of Major Determinatives (page 3 of 4)

#	Main Form	Alternate Form(s)	Principal Location(s)	Principal Categories of Meaning (Notes)	Example Characters	
D-41	阝		▨	things made of dirt; hills / steep areas; dark places; steps; barriers (standalone character form: 阜)	陶 pottery	険 steep
D-42	阝		▨	populated areas, especially those covering a large area (standalone character form: 邑)	郊 suburb	郡 county
D-43	女		▨ ▤	things pertaining to women, including matters relating to marriage	姉 older sister	嫁 wife; bride
D-44	示	礻	▨ ▤	items used in religious ceremonies; things pertaining to religious worship	祈 pray	神 a god
D-45	田		▨	things pertaining to plowed fields or borders between regions; areas of land	町 town	畔 ridge; bank
D-46	酉		▨	things pertaining to alcoholic beverages or other fermented substances	酔 drunkenness	酢 vinegar
D-47	刀	刂	▨	types of cutting implements; actions involving cutting or severing	剣 sword	刺 pierce; stab
D-48	戈		▨	things having to do with weapons, fighting, or warfare	戦 a battle	賊 bandit
D-49	力		▨ ▤	things pertaining to the performing of work, or the exertion of force	助 assistance	勢 force; inertia
D-50	穴	宀	▤	things pertaining to holes, hollowed-out spaces, or empty space	空 air; sky	窓 window
D-51	囗		▢	types of enclosures; enclosed areas (this element is larger than D-14)	園 park; garden	国 country
D-52	弓		▨	things having to do with archery and archers' bows, or loosening or tightening	弦 bowstring	張 stretch
D-53	皿		▬	types of food containers (bowls, plates, etc.)	盆 serving tray	盤 shallow bowl
D-54	攵		▨	actions involving hitting or coercing; any kind of action in general (pre-simplification form: 攴)	攻 attack	敗 be defeated
D-55	革		▨	objects made of leather	鞄 bag	靴 shoes
D-56	冫		▨	things having to do with ice; cold or frozen things	冷 chill	凍 freeze
D-57	舟		▨	things having to do with boats, or travel over water	航 sailing	艦 warship
D-58	禾	𠂉	▨	types of grain; things having to do with cereal crops	稲 rice plant	穫 harvest
D-59	米	米	▨	things pertaining to rice (post-harvest); finely granulated or powdery substances	糠 bran	粉 flour
D-60	麦	麥	▣	things having to do with cereal crops (especially wheat, barley, and oats)	麺 noodles	麩 wheat bran

List of Major Determinatives (page 4 of 4)

#	Main Form	Alternate Form(s)	Principal Location(s)	Principal Categories of Meaning (Notes)	Example Characters	
D-61	尸			1. things associated with the body's midsection, or bodily excretion; 2. a building roof	尻 buttocks	屁 (bodily) gas
D-62	戸			things associated with doors or entryways; rooms	扉 door	房 room
D-63	門			things pertaining to gates, doorways, or enclosures	関 checkpoint	閣 pavilion
D-64	鬼			things having to do with the spirit of a deceased person, or a god or demon; supernatural things	魂 soul; spirit	魅 enchantment
D-65	歹			things having to do with death, loss, or injury; remains	殉 martyrdom	残 remnant
D-66	欠			actions performed with the mouth (e.g., blowing, yawning, sighing, shouting, coughing); happiness	飲 drink	歌 sing
D-67	耳			things having to do with the ears or hearing	聞 listen	聖 sage; saint †
D-68	子	孑		things pertaining to children	孤 orphan	学 studying
D-69	月			1. things having to do with the moon; 2. short periods of time	期 period of time	朗 bright
D-70	髟			types of body hair	髪 (head) hair	髭 beard
D-71	彡			1. types of designs / patterns / decorations; 2. things pertaining to the emitting of light	彫 engraving	影 shadow
D-72	罒	鬥		nets; things involving the use of nets, such as capturing (pre-simplification form: 网)	置 put; place †	罠 a trap
D-73	耒	耒		things having to do with the plowing of fields, or tools used for plowing	耕 till; plow	耗 decrease †
D-74	羽			things having to do with wings, flight, or the movement of wings	翼 wings	翻 fluttering
D-75	走			things pertaining to running, or moving quickly	起 rouse; awaken †	越 surpass †
D-76	行			things pertaining to roads, or traveling along roads (similar to D-30 and D-31)	街 street; district	衛 protect †
D-77	音			things having to do with sound	韻 rhyme; meter	響 reverberation
D-78	豸			mid-sized mammals (similar in meaning to D-22)	貌 appearance †	豹 leopard
D-79	骨			things having to do with bones; objects made from bone	髄 marrow	骸 corpse
D-80	瓦			ceramics, pottery, and similar objects	瓶 bottle	甕 large pot

† The meanings of these characters have changed, and are no longer as closely related to the determinative meaning as they once were.

Section 2

List of Phonetic Components

2.1 Overview

As explained in Part 1, Chapter 2, a large percentage of kanji were built with a phonetic component—an element or group of elements which fills the role of indicating the *on* reading of the character. More than 90% of all characters ever created contain a phonetic component.

Many hundreds of different components have been used in a phonetic role. Some of these are very simple in form, while others are quite complex. Some are found only in relatively uncommon characters, but quite a few appear within multiple different kanji in the set of common use characters. Having familiarity with commonly-used phonetics, and the readings they indicate, can greatly assist in the learning of the characters, especially with the memorizing of character *on* readings and with distinguishing between characters similar in appearance.

In this section, 500 of the most commonly used phonetic components are listed, together with characters that contain them. As with determinatives in the last section, this section does not include all components that have ever been used as phonetics; rather, the phonetics chosen for the list are primarily those which are used in a phonetic role in at least two different common use characters. Some others, though, are included mainly to assist with distinguishing between phonetics similar in form.

The phonetics in this section are organized into groups which either share a common element or share a visual similarity. As much as possible, phonetics that resemble each other in appearance are located near each other in the list. Each phonetic is labeled with 'P' and a three-digit number (e.g., P-009).

With some phonetics, all characters (or at least all common use characters) which contain them have the exact same *on* reading as each other. If you memorize that one *on* reading for that phonetic, you then know the *on* readings of all common use characters which contain it. (See P-048 for an example.) Unfortunately, this is the exception, rather than the rule; most phonetics can indicate any of several different *on* readings. In most cases, though, these different readings are related readings, as described in Part 1, Section 7.10. A feel for related readings can be developed with practice.

Learning the various readings indicated by a commonly-used phonetic is quite useful, as it helps to greatly narrow down the set of possible *on* readings of a character containing that phonetic. This helps both when learning newly-encountered characters, and when trying to recall readings of characters that have already been studied. Of course, additional memorization is necessary to learn the exact reading (or readings) of each character containing the phonetic.

Some of the phonetics in this list indicate a set of different readings which are not exactly related readings, but nonetheless follow a particular pattern. For example, phonetic P-445 appears in characters read as *KAN* (漢), *NAN* (難), and *TAN* (嘆), all of which end with the /an/ sound, with only the initial consonant differing. If you can remember that the **AN* pattern is associated with this phonetic, you can more quickly memorize the *on* readings of the characters which contain it.

The set of possible readings of a few of the phonetics listed in this section is admittedly rather complex. For characters containing such complicated phonetics, though, simply being able to look at the character and identify which component is the phonetic, and having a vague idea of the possible readings it can indicate, is a useful hint to have when attempting to memorize the character.

Rote memorization of the contents of the list is not necessary, but periodic review should be helpful.

Standalone Characters

Most phonetic components were originally created as standalone characters, and, like all kanji, had meaning associated with them. Once created, they began to be borrowed and used as components in other characters. A large number of phonetics still appear as standalone characters, but for some the standalone character has been completely phased out of usage—or is an obscure character which is essentially never encountered—such that the phonetic is only seen today as a component of other characters, and never by itself as a full character.

Component Meaning

Many phonetic components were added into characters only or primarily for their sound, without regard to their meaning. Even for those that were also used for their meanings, the meanings of the characters which contain them may have shifted, such that the phonetic component meaning is no longer relevant to the character meaning, anyway. For these reasons, the meanings of phonetic components are not especially pertinent to character study, and so are not included in this list.

Identifying Phonetics

There are a number of cases where a component is used in some characters as a phonetic, but the exact same component can be found in other characters *not* used in a phonetic role. In other words, the component is a phonetic in some characters but not in others. Take, as an example, the component P-001 (士, *SHI*), which is used in a phonetic role in all of the following characters, each of which has a principal *on* reading of *SHI*:

仕　志　誌

Each of the following characters also contain this same component, but not in a phonetic role. All have entirely different *on* readings (the readings are shown below each character):

LIST OF PHONETIC COMPONENTS

読　　声　　壮　　吉
DOKU　SEI　SHŌ　KICHI

There are several possible reasons why a character might not be read with the sound of a phonetic component it contains. For each of the four characters above, the reasons are described as follows. The first two characters do not actually contain 士 as a discrete element, but rather contain a more complex component, of which 士 is just one part. In other words, the characters include a piece part which appears identical to the 士 component, but is unrelated and of a different origin. In the case of the third character, the phonetic of the character is on the left-hand side, and the 士 component is used only as a meaning indicator. Finally, in the case of the fourth character, the character origin—although unclear—is possibly ideographic, with the character meaning formed by a combination of the two elements in the character. In ideographic characters, the character *on* reading is usually different from the *on* readings of any of the elements within it.

Exceptions such as those just described are not so rare among phonetic components which are simple in form, such as 士. With more complex phonetic components, though, such inconsistencies are less common; most characters containing a complex phonetic component use it in a phonetic role. Of course, such inconsistencies can complicate remembering *on* readings, but over time as you learn characters you will learn to recognize and remember which parts of the characters are phonetics and which are not. Even with complications such as that just described, recognizing character phonetics still speeds up the learning of *on* readings.

Altered Phonetic Forms

For most characters which contain a phonetic component, that component is clearly identifiable within the character. For a few characters, though, the phonetic component may be obscured and hard to recognize, either because it is hidden within the character or because its form has been somewhat altered from the standard form. Two such examples follow.

The two characters in the table below contain the phonetic components shown directly to the right of them. Each character's principal *on* reading exactly matches that of its phonetic.

Character	Phonetic	Character and Phonetic *On* Reading
裏	里	RI
勲	薫	KUN

In the first character, the phonetic is located in the middle, with the other component in the character split apart and surrounding it, above and below. Not only because it is in the middle of the character, but also because it directly touches the part of the component located below it, the phonetic may be hard to recognize in this character. In the second character, the phonetic can be thought of as consisting of two familiar elements: 重 and 灬. Normally appearing directly above and below each other, these two elements have been altered in this second character, such that the bottom element stretches across the full width of the character, while the top one only occupies the left half of the character. Being distorted in this way makes the phonetic component difficult to recognize in this character.

Fortunately, very few characters contain altered or hidden phonetics such as those in the previous examples. Where they do occur, they are identified in the list in this section.

New and Old Phonetic Forms Both in Use

When the *jōyō* characters were first established, some characters placed on the list had simplified forms already in common usage which then became the official forms of the characters. However, characters outside of the *jōyō* list with the same components were generally not simplified. Then, as some of these non-*jōyō* characters were later added to the *jōyō* list, their non-simplified forms, which had, in effect, become standard, became their official forms, causing inconsistencies among the forms of components appearing in multiple *jōyō* characters. Two such examples are shown below, each showing one *jōyō* character with the traditional component form (on the left), and one with the simplified form (on the right).

Phonetic P-195 appears in: 箋 浅

Phonetic P-283 appears in: 猿 遠

Phonetic P-195 originally consisted of two 戈 components stacked together. In the simplified form, these two components were merged together into a single element consisting of one 戈 component with two horizontal strokes added to it. With Phonetic P-283, the bottom strokes originally were the same as those of the 'clothing' character: 衣. In the simplified form, the strokes are slightly moved, and the hook in the lower left has been removed.

In the list in this section, for most phonetics having both newer (simplified) and older (traditional) component forms, the newer form is listed in the 'Form' column, while the older form is shown in the 'Notes' column. (See P-195 and P-283 for examples.)

Two Distinct Phonetics Merged into One

In a few cases, because of form simplifications, what were once two dissimilar, unrelated phonetics became exactly identical in form to each other. In each of these cases, the phonetic readings were different from each other, causing a single phonetic to have associated with it two very different sets of readings. Two such phonetics, now identical in form, are shown in the following table. For each of these phonetics, two representative characters are shown as they appeared before simplification, and as they appear today in their standard forms, after simplification. You can see that among the simplified characters, the phonetics now appear identical, despite having different readings.

Original Phonetic Form	Simplified Phonetic Form	Phonetic Readings	Original Form Characters	Simplified Characters
炏	丷	KEI / EI	螢 榮	蛍 栄
臼	丷	KAKU / GAKU	覺 學	覚 学

In the list in this section, such phonetics are grouped together as one item, with the separate sets of *on* readings numbered separately. The phonetic pre-simplification forms are shown in the 'Notes' column, as applicable, referencing these numbers. See P-311 in the list (corresponding to the phonetics just shown) for an example.

Contents of the List

In the list in this section, a standard set of information is given for each phonetic. In the 'Main Reading(s) / Pattern' column, the most common reading or set of readings of each phonetic is listed. The various readings are separated by a slash mark (see, for example, P-002). Relatively uncommon readings are placed in parentheses (see P-009). For phonetics with two or more distinct sets of readings, the readings are numbered separately (see P-157). In some cases, the possible readings are expressed as a pattern; within these patterns, the * symbol identifies that one of several different letters may be located in that position. This symbol may mark a starting consonant (see P-174), a vowel (see P-054), or the presence or absence of a palatalized consonant (see P-176). For example, the pattern *G*N* could fit any of *GAN*, *GIN*, *GUN*, *GEN*, or *GON*. A pattern such as *K*OKU* denotes an optional palatalized consonant; either *KOKU* or *KYOKU* would fit that pattern.

For each phonetic, a few 'Representative Characters' containing that phonetic are listed. Additional characters may also be listed in the 'Notes' section. For each phonetic, all *jōyō* characters which use it in a phonetic role are shown. In a few cases, non-*jōyō* characters are also shown, but only relatively commonly encountered ones (clearly marked as non-*jōyō*). For each character, an *on* reading (or readings) is given. For all *jōyō* characters, these are the principal *on* readings, as identified in the official *jōyō* list. (The official *jōyō* list contains not only a set of official characters, but also official readings for each of these characters.) Non-principal readings are usually not included, but when they are, they are placed in parentheses. *On* readings are all listed using the Latin alphabet, to assist the learner in recognizing patterns among characters. For characters in which no *on* reading is identified in the official list, a *kun* reading from that list is given instead, in hiragana.

In the 'Notes' column, supplemental information is provided, as relevant. This may include information such as additional representative characters, characters which demonstrate exceptional cases, or unrelated but similar characters, such as those which have components similar to—but not identical to—the phonetic. Exceptional cases include characters which contain the phonetic (or appear to contain the phonetic) but which have an *on* reading which is either somewhat different or completely different from the main readings of the phonetic. The latter case (a completely different *on* reading) often occurs when either the character form was simplified and the similarity is coincidental (i.e., the form was originally different and unrelated), or when the phonetic component was used only for its meaning, and not for its reading. Unrelated characters which contain a component similar but not identical in form to the phonetic are shown in order to assist with character recognition.

As mentioned on the previous page, in cases where a phonetic has an older form—in use prior to character simplification—that form is shown in the 'Notes' column. In many cases, older forms still appear in characters outside of the *jōyō* set, and so it is useful to be familiar with some of these.

In some cases, pertinent information does not fit into the 'Notes' column, and is therefore provided in the form of an endnote. Endnotes are listed just after the final page of the tables.

List of Phonetic Components (page 1 of 25)

#	Form	Main Reading(s) / Pattern	Representative Characters			Notes
P-001	士	SHI	士 SHI	仕 SHI	志 SHI	Also: 誌 SHI
P-002	土	TO / DO	土 DO/TO	吐 TO	徒 TO	Exception: 社 SHA 土 is mostly used as a determinative (D-5)
P-003	工	KŌ / KU	工 KŌ/KU	功 KŌ	江 KŌ	Also: 攻, 紅, 項, 貢, 控 KŌ; 虹 にじ² Slight reading variation: 空 KŪ
P-004	丁	CHŌ / TEI	丁 CHŌ/TEI	町 CHŌ	頂 CHŌ	Also: 庁 CHŌ, 訂 TEI; Special reading: 打 DA³ Slight reading variations: 貯 CHO, 灯 TŌ
P-005	于	U	宇 U	迂¹ U		Also: 芋 いも²
P-006	干	KAN	干 KAN	汗 KAN	肝 KAN	Also: 刊 KAN Slight reading variations: 軒 KEN, 岸 GAN
P-007	才	SAI / ZAI	才 SAI	材 ZAI	財 ZAI	
P-008	不	FU / HI / HAI	不 FU	否 HI	杯 HAI	
P-009	行	KŌ (GYŌ)	行 KŌ/GYŌ	衡 KŌ		Also: 桁 けた² 行 is mostly used as a determinative (D-76)
P-010	己	KI (KO)	己 KO/KI	起 KI	記 KI	Also: 紀, 忌 KI; Possibly related: 改 KAI Exceptions: 妃 HI, 配 HAI⁶
P-011	巴	HA / HI	把 HA	肥 HI		
P-012	㔾	HAN	犯 HAN	範 HAN	氾 HAN	Exceptions: 厄 YAKU⁶, 危 KI⁶
P-013	中	CHŪ	中 CHŪ	沖 CHŪ	忠 CHŪ	Also: 仲, 衷 CHŪ
P-014	串	KAN	患 KAN			Also: 串 くし²
P-015	由	YU / YŪ / CHŪ / SHŪ	由 YU/YŪ	油 YU	抽 CHŪ	Also: 宙 CHŪ, 袖 SHŪ Exceptions: 軸 JIKU, 笛 TEKI, 届 とどける⁶
P-016	申	SHIN (JIN)	申 SHIN	伸 SHIN	神 SHIN/JIN	Also: 紳 SHIN
P-017	甲	KŌ / Ō	甲 KŌ	押 Ō		Also: 岬 みさき²; Special reading: 甲 is read as KAN in some compound words
P-018	因	IN / ON	因 IN	姻 IN	咽 IN	Also: 恩 ON Similar form, but unrelated: 囚 SHŪ
P-019	困	KON	困 KON	梱¹ KON		
P-020	菌	KIN	菌 KIN			

List of Phonetic Components (page 2 of 25)

#	Form	Main Reading(s) / Pattern	Representative Characters			Notes
P-021	九	KYŪ	九 KYŪ/KU	究 KYŪ		Also: 尻 しり[2]; Reading variation: 軌 KI Exception: 染 SEN[7]
P-022	十	JŪ / JI' [10]	十 JŪ/JI'	汁 JŪ		Exceptions: 計 KEI[7], 針 SHIN Non-phonetic component in 博 HAKU, 協 KYŌ
P-023	卆	SUI / SAI	粋 SUI	酔 SUI	砕 SAI	Also: 枠 わく[2]; Pre-simplification form: 卒 SOTSU[11]; Similar component in: 雑 ZATSU/ZŌ
P-024	力	RYOKU / ROKU / RIKI	力 RYOKU/RIKI	肋[1] ROKU		Exception: 筋 KIN[7] 力 is mostly used as a determinative (D-49)
P-025	加	KA / GA	加 KA	架 KA	賀 GA	
P-026	刃	NIN / JIN	刃 JIN	忍 NIN	認 NIN	
P-027	刀	TŌ	刀 TŌ			Exception: 辺 HEN[6] 刀 is mostly used as a determinative (D-47)
P-028	分	FUN / H*N / B*N	分 BUN/FUN/BU	貧 HIN/BIN	盆 BON	Also: 粉, 紛, 雰 FUN; 頒 HAN
P-029	方	HŌ / BŌ	方 HŌ	訪 HŌ	放 HŌ	Also: 芳, 倣 HŌ; 防, 坊, 房, 紡, 妨, 傍, 肪 BŌ
P-030	万	MAN / BAN	万 MAN/BAN			Pre-simplification form: 萬 (万 was borrowed long ago to write 萬)
P-031	厉	REI	励 REI			Also: 栃 とち[12] Pre-simplification form: 厲
P-032	王	Ō / KŌ	王 Ō	旺 Ō	皇 KŌ/Ō	Slight reading variation: 狂 KYŌ
P-033	玉	GYOKU / KOKU	玉 GYOKU	国 KOKU		Older form of 国 used phonetic P-189 (was 國) Det. D-33; Non-phonetic component in: 宝 HŌ[13]
P-034	主	SHU / CHŪ / JŪ	主 SHU	駐 CHŪ	住 JŪ	Also: 注, 柱 CHŪ Exception: 往 Ō[6]
P-035	呈	TEI	呈 TEI	程 TEI		聖 SEI may (or may not) contain this phonetic. Regardless, can use phonetic as memorization aid.
P-036	玨	HAN	班 HAN	斑 HAN		
P-037	壬	NIN / CHIN	任 NIN	妊 NIN	賃 CHIN	Similar reading: 淫 IN[14] Exception: 廷 TEI[6] (P-343)
P-038	圭	GAI (KAI / KEI)	街 GAI	涯 GAI	崖 GAI	Reading variation: 佳 KA; Also: 掛 かける[2] Exception: 封 FŪ/HŌ[15]
P-039	丰	HŌ	邦 HŌ	峰 HŌ	縫 HŌ	Also: 蜂 HŌ
P-040	㓞	KEI / KETSU / KITSU	契 KEI	喫 KITSU	潔 KETSU	Pre-simplification form: 韌

List of Phonetic Components (page 3 of 25)

#	Form	Main Reading(s) / Pattern	Representative Characters			Notes
P-041	正	SEI / SHŌ	正 SEI/SHŌ	政 SEI	整 SEI	Also: 征 SEI; 証, 症 SHŌ
P-042	止	SHI	止 SHI	祉 SHI	歯 SHI	Exceptions: 企 KI[7], 肯 KŌ[6], 渋 JŪ[6]
P-043	此	SHI	紫 SHI	雌 SHI		Also: 柴 しば[1]
P-044	旨	SHI	旨 SHI	指 SHI	脂 SHI	Exceptions: 詣 KEI[7], 稽 KEI
P-045	化	KA (KE)	化 KA/KE	花 KA	貨 KA	Also: 靴 KA
P-046	北	HOKU / HAI	北 HOKU	背 HAI		
P-047	比	HI (HEI)	比 HI	批 HI	陛 HEI	
P-048	皆	KAI	皆 KAI	階 KAI	楷 KAI	Also: 諧 KAI
P-049	昆	KON	昆 KON	混 KON		
P-050	氏	SHI	氏 SHI	紙 SHI		
P-051	氐	TEI	低 TEI	底 TEI	邸 TEI	Also: 抵 TEI
P-052	昏	KON	婚 KON			
P-053	民	MIN	民 MIN	眠 MIN		
P-054	艮	KON / G*N	根 KON	限 GEN	銀 GIN	Also: 恨, 痕, 墾, 懇 KON; 眼 GAN Similar in form, but unrelated: 退 TAI[16]
P-055	良	RŌ / RYŌ	良 RYŌ	浪 RŌ	郎 RŌ	Also: 朗, 廊 RŌ; Possibly related: 娘 むすめ[17] Compressed form of phonetic: 良
P-056	郷	KYŌ / GŌ	郷 KYŌ/GŌ	響 KYŌ		
P-057	既	KI / GAI	既 KI	概 GAI	慨 GAI	
P-058	長	CHŌ	長 CHŌ	帳 CHŌ	張 CHŌ	
P-059	辰	SHIN	震 SHIN	振 SHIN	娠 SHIN	Also: 唇 SHIN Exceptions: 農 NŌ (P-060), 辱 JOKU
P-060	農	NŌ	農 NŌ	濃 NŌ		

List of Phonetic Components (page 4 of 25)

#	Form	Main Reading(s) / Pattern	Representative Characters			Notes
P-061	开	KEI (GYŌ)	形 KEI/GYŌ	型 KEI	刑 KEI	Exception: 研 KEN[6]
P-062	井	HEI	併 HEI	塀 HEI	餅 HEI	Special reading: 瓶 BIN[3]
P-063	升	SHŌ	升 SHŌ	昇 SHŌ		
P-064	半	HAN (BAN)	半 HAN	畔 HAN	伴 HAN/BAN	Also: 判 HAN/BAN
P-065	羊	YŌ / SHŌ	羊 YŌ	洋 YŌ	様 YŌ	Also: 養, 窯[14] YŌ; 詳, 祥 SHŌ Exception: 遅 CHI[6]
P-066	平	HEI / HYŌ / BYŌ	平 HEI/BYŌ	評 HYŌ		Also: 坪 つぼ[2]
P-067	乎	KO	呼 KO			
P-068	非	HI / HAI	非 HI	悲 HI	扉 HI	Also: 排, 俳, 輩 HAI Exception: 罪 ZAI[4]
P-069	兆	CHŌ / TŌ	兆 CHŌ	挑 CHŌ	眺 CHŌ	Also: 跳 CHŌ; 逃, 桃 TŌ
P-070	並	HEI / FU	並 HEI	普 FU	譜 FU	
P-071	次	SHI / JI	次 JI/SHI	姿 SHI	資 SHI	Also: 諮, 恣 SHI; 茨 いばら[2] Exception: 盗 TŌ[6]
P-072	央	EI / Ō	央 Ō	英 EI	映 EI	
P-073	夬	KETSU / KAI	決 KETSU	快 KAI		
P-074	太	TAI / TA / DA	太 TAI/TA	駄 DA	汰 TA	
P-075	夫	FU (FŪ)	夫 FU (FŪ)	扶 FU		Exception: 規 KI[6]
P-076	夹	KYŌ	狭 KYŌ	峡 KYŌ	挟 KYŌ	Also: 頬/頰 ほお[2] Pre-simplification form: 夾
P-077	天	TEN	天 TEN	添[18] TEN		Reading variation: 蚕 SAN
P-078	夭	YŌ (SHŌ)	妖 YŌ	笑 SHŌ		Reading variation: 沃 YOKU
P-079	矢	SHI / SHITSU	矢 SHI	疾 SHITSU	嫉 SHITSU	Possible phonetic usage: 知, 痴 CHI Exceptions: 医 I[7], 矣 (used in 挨 AI)
P-080	失	SHITSU / CHITSU / TETSU	失 SHITSU	秩 CHITSU	鉄 TETSU	Also: 迭 TETSU

List of Phonetic Components (page 5 of 25)

#	Form	Main Reading(s) / Pattern	Representative Characters			Notes
P-081	句	KU / KŌ	句 KU	拘 KŌ		Also: 駒 こま²; Character with similar form and same reading: 勾 KŌ
P-082	敬	KEI / KYŌ	敬 KEI	警 KEI	驚 KYŌ	
P-083	旬	JUN (SHUN)	旬 JUN (SHUN)	殉 JUN		
P-084	勺	*AKU / *EKI	約 YAKU	酌 SHAKU	的 TEKI	Exception: 釣 CHŌ
P-085	勻	KIN	均 KIN			
P-086	匊	KIKU	菊 KIKU			
P-087	包	HŌ	包 HŌ	抱 HŌ	泡 HŌ	Also: 胞, 飽, 砲 HŌ
P-088	匋	TŌ / DŌ	陶 TŌ	萄¹ DŌ		
P-089	蜀	*OKU / *AKU	濁 DAKU			Related: 独 DOKU⁵, 触 SHOKU⁵, 属 ZOKU⁵, 嘱 SHOKU⁵ (P-224)
P-090	曷	KATSU	喝 KATSU	渇 KATSU	葛 KATSU	Also: 褐 KATSU; Reading variations: 掲 KEI, 謁 ETSU; Pre-simplification form: 曷
P-091	亡	BŌ / MŌ	亡 BŌ	忘 BŌ	忙 BŌ	Also: 望 BŌ/MŌ; 妄 MŌ/BŌ; 盲, 網 MŌ
P-092	文	BUN / MON	文 BUN / MON	紋 MON		Also: 蚊 か²; Unrelated: 対 TAI / TSUI (form was altered⁶)
P-093	交	KŌ (KAKU)	交 KŌ	校 KŌ	効 KŌ	Also: 絞, 郊 KŌ; 較 KAKU
P-094	市	SHI	市 SHI	姉 SHI		Also: 柿 かき²; Exception: 肺 HAI⁶ Unrelated character with similar form: 師 SHI
P-095	亥	GAI / KAKU / KOKU	該 GAI	核 KAKU	刻 KOKU	Also: 劾, 骸 GAI
P-096	斉	SAI / ZAI / SEI	斉 SEI	済 SAI	剤 ZAI	Also: 斎 SAI Pre-simplification form: 齊
P-097	亢	KŌ	抗 KŌ	航 KŌ	坑 KŌ	
P-098	夜	YA / EKI	夜 YA	液 EKI		
P-099	亦	1. SEKI (EKI) 2. *EN / *AN⁹	跡 SEKI	変 HEN	恋 REN	Also: 湾 WAN, 蛮 BAN #2 Pre-simplification form: 戀
P-100	赤	SEKI / SHA	赤 SEKI	赦 SHA		Character similar in form: 嚇 KAKU

List of Phonetic Components

#	Form	Main Reading(s) / Pattern	Representative Characters			Notes
P-101	介	KAI	介 KAI	界 KAI		
P-102	会	KAI / E	会 KAI/E	絵 KAI/E		Pre-simplification form: 會
P-103	今	K*N / G*N / IN	今 KON/KIN	吟 GIN	陰 IN	Also: 琴 KIN, 含 GAN Exceptions: 念, 捻 NEN; 貪 DON
P-104	令	REI / RYŌ	令 REI	冷 REI	領 RYŌ	Also: 齢, 零 REI; 鈴 REI/RIN Possibly related character: 命 MEI/MYŌ
P-105	全	ZEN / SEN	全 ZEN	栓 SEN	詮 SEN	
P-106	余	*O	余 YO	途 TO	徐 JO	Also: 塗 TO; 除, 叙 JO Reading variation: 斜 SHA
P-107	僉	KEN	検 KEN	険 KEN	剣 KEN	Also: 験, 倹, 鹸[1] KEN Pre-simplification form: 僉
P-108	㐱	SHIN / CHIN	診 SHIN	珍 CHIN		Related: 参 SAN (P-109) originally contained this phonetic, but the form was altered
P-109	参	SAN	参 SAN	惨 SAN/ZAN		
P-110	回	KAI (E)	回 KAI	廻[1] KAI		
P-111	同	DŌ / TŌ	同 DŌ	胴 DŌ	銅 DŌ	Also: 洞 DŌ, 筒 TŌ
P-112	司	SHI	司 SHI	詞 SHI	飼 SHI	Also: 伺, 嗣 SHI
P-113	周	SHŪ / CHŌ	周 SHŪ	週 SHŪ	調 CHŌ	Also: 彫 CHŌ Similar form: P-256 商
P-114	可	KA	可 KA	河 KA	歌 KA	Also: 苛, 何, 荷 KA; Reading variation: 阿 A[1] Similar form: P-081 句
P-115	奇	KI	奇 KI	寄 KI	騎 KI	Also: 綺 KI[1], 崎 さき[2]; Reading variation: 椅 I Special reading: 埼 さい[19]
P-116	内	NAI / NŌ	内 NAI	納 NŌ		Unrelated character with similar form: 肉 NIKU
P-117	丙	HEI / BYŌ	丙 HEI	柄 HEI	病 BYŌ	
P-118	区	KU / Ō	区 KU	駆 KU	殴 Ō	Also: 欧 Ō; Reading variation: 枢 SŪ Pre-simplification form: 區
P-119	凶	KYŌ	凶 KYŌ	胸 KYŌ		
P-120	𡿺	NŌ	脳 NŌ	悩 NŌ		Pre-simplification form: 𦜝

List of Phonetic Components (page 7 of 25)

#	Form	Main Reading(s) / Pattern	Representative Characters			Notes
P-121	冒	BŌ	冒 BŌ	帽 BŌ		
P-122	昌	SHŌ	唱 SHŌ	菖¹ SHŌ		Unrelated, but similar in form, and with same reading: 晶 SHŌ
P-123	曽	SŌ / ZŌ	曽 SŌ	層 SŌ	僧 SŌ	Also: 増, 憎, 贈 ZŌ Pre-simplification form: 曾
P-124	曹	SŌ	曹 SŌ	槽 SŌ	遭 SŌ	
P-125	白	HAKU	白 HAKU/BYAKU	泊 HAKU	迫 HAKU	Also: 舶, 伯 HAKU; 拍 HAKU (HYŌ); 百 HYAKU
P-126	旦	TAN / DAN	旦 TAN/DAN	胆 TAN	担 TAN	Also: 壇 DAN, 但 ただし² Unrelated: 昼 CHŪ (form was altered⁶)
P-127	亘	*EN	宣 SEN	喧¹ KEN		Also: 垣 かき² Exception: 恒 KŌ⁶
P-128	且	SO / JO	租 SO	祖 SO	助 JO	Also: 狙, 粗, 阻, 組 SO; 且 かつ² Reading variation: 査 SA; Unrelated: 宜 GI⁶
P-129	早	SŌ	早 SŌ	草 SŌ		
P-130	卓	TAKU / TŌ	卓 TAKU	悼 TŌ		
P-131	章	SHŌ	章 SHŌ	彰 SHŌ	障 SHŌ	
P-132	単	TAN / DAN / SEN / ZEN	単 TAN	弾 DAN	戦 SEN	Also: 禅 ZEN Pre-simplification form: 單
P-133	里	RI	里 RI	理 RI	裏 RI	Reading variation: 厘 RIN Exception: 埋 MAI
P-134	黒	BOKU / MOKU / KOKU	黒 KOKU	墨 BOKU	黙 MOKU	In 黙, phonetic form is slightly distorted
P-135	童	DŌ / SHŌ	童 DŌ	瞳 DŌ	鐘 SHŌ	Also: 憧 SHŌ
P-136	量	RYŌ	量 RYŌ	糧 RYŌ		
P-137	重	DŌ / CHŌ / SHŌ / JŪ / SHU	重 JŪ/CHŌ	動 DŌ	働 DŌ	Also: 衝 SHŌ; 種, 腫 SHU
P-138	薫	KUN	薫 KUN	勲 KUN		In 勲, phonetic form is slightly distorted
P-139	乗	JŌ	乗 JŌ	剰 JŌ		
P-140	垂	SUI / DA	垂 SUI	睡 SUI	唾 DA	Exception: 郵 YŪ⁷ Unrelated, but similar in form: 華 KA

List of Phonetic Components (page 8 of 25)

#	Form	Main Reading(s) / Pattern	Representative Characters			Notes
P-141	隹	SUI / SAI / TSUI / TAI / YUI / I	推 SUI	椎 TSUI	唯 YUI	Also: 堆 TAI, 催 SAI, 維 I, 誰 だれ [2] Exceptions: 稚 CHI [6], 集 SHŪ, 進 SHIN; Det. D-27
P-142	焦	SHŌ	焦 SHŌ	礁 SHŌ		
P-143	隼	JUN (SHUN)	隼 [1] SHUN/JUN	準 JUN		Related: 准 JUN originated as an abbreviated form of 準
P-144	翟	YAKU / YŌ / TAKU	躍 YAKU	曜 YŌ	濯 TAKU	Pre-simplification form: 翟
P-145	雇	KO	雇 KO	顧 KO		
P-146	蒦	GO / KAKU	護 GO	穫 KAKU	獲 KAKU	
P-147	寉	KAKU	確 KAKU			Also: 鶴 つる [2]
P-148	雚	KAN (KEN)	歓 KAN	観 KAN	勧 KAN	Also: 権 KEN Pre-simplification form: 雚
P-149	泉	SEN	泉 SEN	線 SEN	腺 SEN	
P-150	沓	TŌ	踏 TŌ			
P-151	永	EI	永 EI	泳 EI	詠 EI	
P-152	丞	JŌ (SHŌ)	蒸 JŌ			Related: 承 SHŌ may have also used this phonetic; due to form and reading similarities, best to learn these together
P-153	求	KYŪ	求 KYŪ	球 KYŪ	救 KYŪ	
P-154	录	ROKU / RYOKU	録 ROKU	緑 RYOKU		Exception: 剥 HAKU; Pre-simplification form: 彔 Unrelated, but similar in form: 縁 EN
P-155	桼	SHITSU	漆 SHITSU			Also: 膝 ひざ [2]
P-156	暴	BAKU / BŌ	暴 BŌ	爆 BAKU		
P-157	少	1. SHŌ / SEI 2. BYŌ / MYŌ 3. SA / SHA	少 SHŌ	秒 BYŌ	砂 SA/SHA	Also: 省 SEI/SHŌ, 抄 SHŌ, 妙 MYŌ, 沙 SA Exception: 劣 RETSU [7]
P-158	原	GEN / GAN	原 GEN	源 GEN	願 GAN	
P-159	尞	RYŌ	寮 RYŌ	僚 RYŌ	療 RYŌ	Also: 瞭 RYŌ
P-160	赤	SHUKU / JAKU / TOKU / SEKI	叔 SHUKU	寂 JAKU	督 TOKU	Also: 淑 SHUKU, 戚 SEKI

List of Phonetic Components

#	Form	Main Reading(s) / Pattern	Representative Characters			Notes
P-161	安	AN	安 AN	案 AN		
P-162	要	YŌ	要 YŌ	腰 YŌ		
P-163	娄	RŌ	楼 RŌ			Exception: 数 SŪ Pre-simplification form: 婁
P-164	委	I	委 I	萎 I		
P-165	妻	SAI / SEI	妻 SAI	凄 SEI		
P-166	奴	DO	奴 DO	努 DO	怒 DO	
P-167	女	JO / NYO	女 JO / NYO	如 JO / NYO		Det. D-43; Other phonetics containing 女: 妥 DA, 安 (in 桜 Ō), 妟 (in 宴 EN), and 妾 (in 接 SETSU)
P-168	古	KO	古 KO	固 KO	故 KO	Also: 湖, 個, 枯, 錮 KO Reading variations: 居 KYO (P-221), 箇 KA, 苦 KU
P-169	舌	KATSU / KEI	活 KATSU	括 KATSU	憩 KEI	Special reading: 話 WA³ Exceptions: 舌 ZETSU²⁰, 乱 RAN⁶, 辞 JI⁶
P-170	吉	KICHI / KITSU / KETSU	吉 KICHI / KITSU	詰 KITSU	結 KETSU	
P-171	㕣	EN / SEN	沿 EN	鉛 EN	船 SEN	
P-172	合	1. GŌ / GA'¹⁰ 2. TŌ 3. KYŪ / SHŪ / JŪ	合 GŌ / GA'	答 TŌ	給 KYŪ	Also: 塔, 搭 TŌ; 拾 SHŪ / JŪ
P-173	舎	SHA	舎 SHA	捨 SHA		
P-174	谷	*OKU	谷 KOKU	欲 YOKU	俗 ZOKU	Also: 浴 YOKU Exception: 裕 YŪ
P-175	容	YŌ	容 YŌ	溶 YŌ		
P-176	各	K*AKU / GAKU / R*AKU / RO	各 KAKU	額 GAKU	落 RAKU	Also: 格, 閣 KAKU; 客 KYAKU; 絡, 酪 RAKU; 略 RYAKU; 露, 路, 賂 RO
P-177	召	SHŌ	召 SHŌ	照 SHŌ	招 SHŌ	Also: 昭, 紹, 沼, 詔 SHŌ Slight reading variation: 超 CHŌ
P-178	台	DAI / TAI / JI / CHI / SHI	台 DAI / TAI	怠 TAI	胎 TAI	Also: 治 JI / CHI; 始 SHI Exception: 冶 YA
P-179	占	*EN	占 SEN	点 TEN	粘 NEN	Also: 店 TEN Exception: 貼 CHŌ
P-180	名	MEI / MYŌ	名 MEI / MYŌ	銘 MEI		

List of Phonetic Components

#	Form	Main Reading(s) / Pattern	Representative Characters			Notes
P-181	代	TAI / DAI	代 DAI/TAI	袋 TAI	貸 TAI	
P-182	式	SHIKI / SHI / SHOKU	式 SHIKI	試 SHI	拭 SHOKU	
P-183	武	BU / MU / FU	武 BU/MU	賦 FU		
P-184	伐	BATSU	伐 BATSU	閥 BATSU		
P-185	我	GA	我 GA	餓 GA	蛾[1] GA	
P-186	義	GI	義 GI	議 GI	儀 GI	Also: 犠 GI
P-187	戒	KAI	戒 KAI	械 KAI		
P-188	戠	SHOKU / SHIKI	職 SHOKU	識 SHIKI	織 SHOKU/SHIKI	
P-189	或	WAKU / IKI (KOKU)	惑 WAKU	域 IKI		Old way of writing 国 KOKU: 國
P-190	幾	KI	幾 KI	機 KI	畿 KI	In 畿, the lower left part of the phonetic is removed
P-191	𢦏	SAI	載 SAI	裁 SAI	栽 SAI	Reading variation: 戴 TAI Exception: 繊 SEN[6]
P-192	成	SEI / JŌ	成 SEI	盛 SEI	誠 SEI	Also: 城 JŌ; Similar phonetics include 戊 (used in 茂 MO) and 戉 (used in 越 ETSU)
P-193	咸	KAN / GEN	感 KAN	憾 KAN	減 GEN	
P-194	蔵	ZŌ	蔵 ZŌ	臓 ZŌ		
P-195	戋	SEN / SAN / ZAN	浅 SEN	銭 SEN	践 SEN	Also: 箋 SEN, 桟 SAN, 残 ZAN Pre-simplification form: 戔
P-196	斤	KIN	斤 KIN	近 KIN		Variation: 祈 KI; Exceptions: 析 SEKI, 質 SHITSU/SHICHI, 匠 SHŌ
P-197	斥	SEKI / SO	斥 SEKI	訴 SO		
P-198	兵	HEI / HYŌ / BYŌ	兵 HEI/HYŌ	鋲[1] BYŌ		Exception: 浜 HIN[4] Similar in form, but unrelated: 丘 KYŪ
P-199	折	SETSU / SEI / TETSU	折 SETSU	逝 SEI	哲 TETSU	Also: 誓 SEI
P-200	斬	ZAN / ZEN	斬 ZAN	暫 ZAN	漸 ZEN	

List of Phonetic Components (page 11 of 25)

#	Form	Main Reading(s) / Pattern	Representative Characters			Notes
P-201	果	KA / RA	果 KA	課 KA	菓 KA	Also: 裸 RA Exceptions: 巣 SŌ[6], 彙 I[6]
P-202	楽	*AKU (*EKI)	楽 GAKU/RAKU	薬 YAKU	礫[1] REKI	Pre-simplification form: 樂
P-203	喿	SŌ	操 SŌ	燥 SŌ	藻 SŌ	Also: 繰 くる[2]
P-204	葉	YŌ / CHŌ	葉 YŌ	蝶[1] CHŌ		Top part of phonetic is identical in form to unrelated 世 SEI / SE character
P-205	某	BŌ / BAI	某 BŌ	謀 BŌ	媒 BAI	Top part of phonetic is identical in form to unrelated 甘 KAN character (P-303)
P-206	罙	SHIN / TAN	深 SHIN	探 TAN		
P-207	亲	SHIN	新 SHIN	親 SHIN	薪 SHIN	
P-208	杀	SATSU / SETSU	殺 SATSU	刹 SATSU/SETSU		
P-209	相	SŌ (SHŌ)	相 SŌ/SHŌ	想 SŌ	霜 SŌ	Also: 箱 はこ[2]
P-210	保	HO / HŌ	保 HO	褒 HŌ		
P-211	朿	SHI / SAKU	刺 SHI	策 SAKU		
P-212	未	MI / MAI	未 MI	味 MI	魅 MI	Also: 妹, 昧 MAI
P-213	末	MATSU (BATSU)	末 MATSU/BATSU	抹 MATSU		
P-214	朱	SHU	朱 SHU	殊 SHU	珠 SHU	Also: 株 かぶ[2]
P-215	米	MAI / MEI / BEI	米 BEI/MAI	迷 MEI		Also: 謎 なぞ[2] 米 is mostly used as a determinative (D-59)
P-216	朮	JUTSU	術 JUTSU	述 JUTSU		
P-217	束	SOKU (CHOKU)	束 SOKU	速 SOKU	勅 CHOKU	Exception: 辣 RATSU[7]
P-218	東	1. TŌ 2. REN / RAN [9]	東 TŌ	棟 TŌ	凍 TŌ	Also: 練, 錬 REN; 欄 RAN #2 Pre-simplification form: 柬
P-219	頼	RAI	頼 RAI			Also: 瀬 せ[2] Pre-simplification form: 賴
P-220	陳	CHIN / JIN	陳 CHIN	陣 JIN		陣 likely originated as a variant form of 陳. It is best to learn these two characters together.

List of Phonetic Components (page 12 of 25)

#	Form	Main Reading(s) / Pattern	Representative Characters			Notes
P-221	居	KYO	居 KYO			Also: 据 すえる², 裾 すそ²
P-222	尼	NI / DEI	尼 NI	泥 DEI		
P-223	屈	KUTSU	屈 KUTSU	掘 KUTSU	窟 KUTSU	Also: 堀 ほり²
P-224	属	ZOKU / SHOKU	属 ZOKU	嘱 SHOKU		
P-225	尉	I	尉 I	慰 I		
P-226	辟	HEKI (HEI / HI)	壁 HEKI	癖 HEKI	璧 HEKI	Also: 避 HI
P-227	戻	REI / RUI	戻 REI	涙 RUI		Pre-simplification form: 戾
P-228	倉	SŌ	倉 SŌ	創 SŌ		
P-229	尺	*AKU / *EKI	尺 SHAKU	訳 YAKU	駅 EKI	Also: 釈 SHAKU; 沢, 択 TAKU; Pre-simpl. form: 驛²² Similar in form, but unrelated: 昼 CHŪ²¹, 尽 JIN²¹
P-230	元	GAN / GEN / KAN	元 GEN / GAN	頑 GAN	玩 GAN	Also: 完, 冠 KAN Reading variation: 院 IN
P-231	云	*N	雲 UN	伝 DEN	魂 KON	Also: 転 TEN, 曇 DON
P-232	示	SHI / JI	示 JI / SHI	視 SHI		In 視, abbreviated form of phonetic is used; 示 is mostly used as a determinative (D-44)
P-233	祭	SAI / SATSU	祭 SAI	際 SAI	察 SATSU	Also: 擦 SATSU
P-234	票	HYŌ	票 HYŌ	標 HYŌ	漂 HYŌ	
P-235	奈	NA / NATSU	奈 NA	捺¹ NATSU		
P-236	宗	SHŪ / SŪ / SŌ	宗 SHŪ / SŌ	崇 SŪ	踪 SŌ	
P-237	禁	KIN	禁 KIN	襟 KIN		
P-238	門	MON / BUN	門 MON	問 MON	聞 BUN / MON	門 is mostly used as a determinative (D-63) or a simple meaning component (as in 開 KAI)
P-239	間	KAN	間 KAN / KEN	簡 KAN		Related: 閑 KAN has same reading and similar meaning as 間
P-240	閏	JUN	潤 JUN			

List of Phonetic Components (page 13 of 25)

#	Form	Main Reading(s) / Pattern	Representative Characters			Notes
P-241	貝	BAI / HAI	買 BAI	敗 HAI		Also: 貝 かい², 唄 うた² 貝 is mostly used as a determinative (D-32)
P-242	貞	TEI	貞 TEI	偵 TEI		
P-243	員	IN	員 IN	韻 IN		Exception: 損 SON Related: 円 EN (simplified from 圓)
P-244	貴	KI / I / KAI	貴 KI	遺 I	潰 KAI	Unrelated character with similar component: 遣 KEN
P-245	貫	KAN	貫 KAN	慣 KAN		
P-246	賁	FUN	噴 FUN	墳 FUN	憤 FUN	Possibly related character, with similar form and reading: 奔 HON
P-247	則	SOKU	則 SOKU	側 SOKU	測 SOKU	Possibly related: 賊 ZOKU²³
P-248	頃	KEI	傾 KEI			Also: 頃 ころ²
P-249	立	RITSU / RYŪ / KYŪ	立 RITSU/RYŪ	粒 RYŪ	泣 KYŪ	Special reading: 拉 RA Exception: 位 I⁷
P-250	音	BAI (BŌ / BU)	倍 BAI	剖 BŌ	部 BU	Also: 培, 陪, 賠 BAI
P-251	音	ON / IN / AN	音 ON/IN	暗 AN		Also: 闇 やみ² 音 is also used as a determinative (D-77)
P-252	意	OKU (I)	億 OKU	憶 OKU	臆 OKU	Also: 意 I
P-253	竟	KYŌ (KEI)	鏡 KYŌ	境 KYŌ		Possibly related character, with similar form and same reading: 競 KYŌ/KEI
P-254	竜	RYŪ / RŌ	竜 RYŪ			Also: 滝 たき² Pre-simplification form is P-255 (龍)
P-255	龍	RYŪ / RŌ	龍¹ RYŪ	籠 RŌ		Exception: 襲 SHŪ⁶
P-256	商	TEKI	敵 TEKI	滴 TEKI	適 TEKI	Also: 摘 TEKI; Reading variation: 嫡 CHAKU Unrelated character similar in form: 商 SHŌ
P-257	帝	TEI	帝 TEI	締 TEI	諦 TEI	
P-258	帯	TAI	帯 TAI	滞 TAI		Similar in appearance to component 帚 (C-19)
P-259	呂	RO / RYO	呂 RO	侶 RYO		Exception: 宮 KYŪ/GŪ⁶
P-260	官	KAN	官 KAN	管 KAN	館 KAN	Also: 棺 KAN

List of Phonetic Components

#	Form	Main Reading(s) / Pattern	Representative Characters			Notes
P-261	玄	GEN (KEN)	玄 GEN	弦 GEN	舷 GEN	Also: 牽 KEN [1] (phonetic is partly obscured)
P-262	畜	CHIKU	畜 CHIKU	蓄 CHIKU		
P-263	幺	YŌ	幼 YŌ	擁 YŌ		Exception: 幻 GEN (this character is read as if it contained phonetic P-261)
P-264	兹	JI	滋 JI	磁 JI	慈 JI	
P-265	系	KEI	系 KEI	係 KEI		Exception: 孫 SON [7] (and 遜 SON, which derives from it)
P-266	前	ZEN / SEN	前 ZEN	煎 SEN		
P-267	俞	YU	輸 YU	癒 YU	諭 YU	Also: 愉, 喩 YU Pre-simplification form: 兪
P-268	用	YŌ	用 YŌ	庸 YŌ		Unrelated: 備 BI [6]
P-269	甬	TSŪ / TŌ / YŪ / YŌ	通 TSŪ	痛 TSŪ	勇 YŪ	Also: 湧 YŪ, 踊 YŌ, 樋 TŌ [1]
P-270	甫	HO	補 HO	捕 HO	舗 HO	Also: 哺 HO; 浦 うら [2]
P-271	尃	HAKU / BAKU / BO	博 HAKU	縛 BAKU	簿 BO	Also: 薄 HAKU; Related: 敷 FU [5] Unrelated, but similar in form: 專 SEN [24]
P-272	冊	SATSU / SAKU	冊 SATSU/SAKU	柵 SAKU		
P-273	侖	RIN / RON	輪 RIN	倫 RIN	論 RON	
P-274	扁	HEN	編 HEN	偏 HEN	遍 HEN	
P-275	寸	SUN / SON	寸 SUN	村 SON		Exceptions: 討 TŌ, 酎 CHŪ, 団 DAN [6]
P-276	付	FU	付 FU	府 FU	腐 FU	Also: 附, 符 FU
P-277	寺	JI / SHI	寺 JI	時 JI	持 JI	Also: 侍 JI, 詩 SHI Reading variations: 待 TAI, 特 TOKU, 等 TŌ
P-278	守	SHU	守 SHU	狩 SHU		
P-279	射	SHA	射 SHA	謝 SHA		Left-hand side of phonetic is identical in form to unrelated 身 SHIN character
P-280	寿	JU / CHŪ / TŌ	寿 JU	鋳 CHŪ	祷 TŌ [1]	Pre-simplification form: 壽

List of Phonetic Components (page 15 of 25)

#	Form	Main Reading(s) / Pattern	Representative Characters			Notes
P-281	衣	I	衣 I	依 I		衣 is mostly used as a determinative (D-34)
P-282	表	HYŌ	表 HYŌ	俵 HYŌ		
P-283	袁	EN	園 EN	遠 EN	猿 EN	Pre-simplification form: 袁 (only original jōyō characters 園 and 遠 use the simplified form)
P-284	睘	KAN	還 KAN	環 KAN		Pre-simplification form: 睘
P-285	褱	KAI	壊 KAI	懐 KAI		Pre-simplification form: 褱
P-286	襄	JŌ	嬢 JŌ	醸 JŌ	譲 JŌ	Also: 壌 JŌ Pre-simplification form: 襄
P-287	壮	SŌ (SHŌ)	壮 SŌ	装 SŌ/SHŌ	荘 SŌ	Unrelated, but with similar form and reading: 状 JŌ
P-288	将	SHŌ	将 SHŌ	奨 SHŌ		
P-289	采	SAI	采 SAI	彩 SAI	菜 SAI	Also: 採 SAI
P-290	受	JU	受 JU	授 JU		
P-291	孚	FU	浮 FU	孵¹ FU		Pre-simplification form: 孚 Exception: 乳 NYŪ⁶
P-292	䍃	YŌ	揺 YŌ	謡 YŌ		Pre-simplification form: 䍃
P-293	爰	EN / DAN / KAN	援 EN	暖 DAN	緩 KAN	Also: 媛 EN Pre-simplification form: 爰
P-294	奚	KEI	鶏 KEI	渓 KEI		Pre-simplification form: 奚
P-295	㥯	IN / ON	隠 IN	穏 ON		Pre-simplification form: 㥯
P-296	愛	AI	愛 AI	曖 AI		
P-297	憂	YŪ	憂 YŪ	優 YŪ		
P-298	予	YO / JO (YA)	予 YO	預 YO	序 JO	Also: 野 YA
P-299	矛	MU	矛 MU	務 MU	霧 MU	Exception: 柔 JŪ/NYŪ⁷
P-300	牙	GA / JA	牙 GA	芽 GA	雅 GA	Also: 邪 JA

List of Phonetic Components

#	Form	Main Reading(s) / Pattern	Representative Characters			Notes
P-301	共	KYŌ / KŌ	共 KYŌ	供 KYŌ	恭 KYŌ	Also: 洪, 港 KŌ Unrelated: 異 I, 選 SEN, 殿 DEN / TEN
P-302	昔	SEKI / SHAKU / SAKU	昔 SEKI	借 SHAKU	錯 SAKU	Also: 惜, 籍 SEKI; Reading variation: 措 SO Unrelated character with similar form: 散 SAN
P-303	甘	KAN (KON)	甘 KAN	紺 KON		Unrelated: 某 (P-205)⁶
P-304	其	KI	期 KI	基 KI	旗 KI	Also: 棋 KI; Reading variations: 欺 GI, 碁 GO
P-305	甚	KAN / JIN	甚 JIN	勘 KAN	堪 KAN	Special reading: 堪 can also be read as TAN in some compound words
P-306	圣	KEI (KYŌ)	軽 KEI	経 KEI/KYŌ	径 KEI	Also: 茎 KEI; Pre-simplification form: 巠 Unrelated, but with similar reading: 怪 KAI
P-307	支	SHI / KI / GI	支 SHI	枝 SHI	肢 SHI	Also: 岐, 伎 KI; 技 GI
P-308	友	HATSU / BATSU	髪 HATSU	抜 BATSU		Pre-simplification form: 犮 (simplified form is identical to unrelated 友 YŪ character)
P-309	反	HAN (HEN / BAN)	反 HAN	版 HAN	返 HEN	Also: 坂, 阪, 販, 飯 HAN; 板 HAN/BAN Exception: 仮 KA⁶
P-310	皮	HI / HA (BA)	皮 HI	被 HI	波 HA	Also: 彼, 疲 HI; 破 HA; 婆 BA
P-311	⺍	1. KAKU / GAKU 2. EI / KEI	学 GAKU	覚 KAKU	営 EI	Also: 栄 EI, 蛍 KEI; Exception: 労 RŌ Pre-simplification forms: #1 學, #2 熒
P-312	兴	KYO / YO	挙 KYO	誉 YO		Pre-simplification form: 與 (character 與 was simplified differently: 与 YO)
P-313	龹	KEN (KAN)	券 KEN	拳 KEN	圏 KEN	Also: 巻 KAN
P-314	尚	SHŌ / JŌ / TŌ / DŌ	尚 SHŌ	常 JŌ	党 TŌ	Also: 賞, 償, 掌 SHŌ; 堂 DŌ Related: 当 TŌ⁵
P-315	肖	SHŌ (SAKU)	肖 SHŌ	消 SHŌ	宵 SHŌ	Also: 硝 SHŌ, 削 SAKU Unrelated character similar in form: 鎖 SA
P-316	气	KI (KE)	気 KI/KE	汽 KI		
P-317	乍	SAKU / SA	作 SAKU/SA	昨 SAKU	詐 SA	Also: 搾, 酢 SAKU
P-318	午	GO / GYO / KYO	午 GO	御 GYO/GO	許 KYO	Unrelated: 卸 おろす (on reading: SHA) Unrelated, but similar in form: 牛 GYŪ
P-319	無	MU / BU	無 MU/BU	舞 BU		See note 8
P-320	毎	*AI	毎 MAI	海 KAI	梅 BAI	Also: 悔 KAI; Possibly related: 母 BO Exceptions: 敏 BIN, 繁 HAN, 侮 BU

List of Phonetic Components (page 17 of 25)

#	Form	Main Reading(s) / Pattern	Representative Characters	Notes
P-321	几	KI	机 KI, 飢 KI	Also: 肌 はだ [2] Unrelated: 冗 JŌ [6]
P-322	凡	HAN / BON	凡 BON, 汎 HAN, 帆 HAN	
P-323	処	SHO / KYO / KO	処 SHO, 拠 KYO/KO	
P-324	巩	KYŌ	恐 KYŌ	Exceptions: 筑[1], 築 CHIKU (top element is used as phonetic in these characters)
P-325	弓	KYŪ	弓 KYŪ, 窮 KYŪ	Unrelated, but similar in form: 弔 CHŌ 弓 is mostly used as a determinative (D-52)
P-326	弟	TEI / DAI	弟 TEI, 第 DAI	In 第, top part of phonetic is merged with component above it
P-327	弗	FUTSU / BUTSU / HI	沸 FUTSU, 費 HI	Related: 仏 BUTSU [5] and 払 FUTSU [5] were simplified (however, 私 SHI is unrelated)
P-328	弱	JAKU / DEKI	弱 JAKU, 溺 DEKI	
P-329	鬲	KAKU	隔 KAKU	Exception: 融 YŪ uses component as a determinative, not as a phonetic
P-330	豆	TŌ / ZU	豆 TŌ, 頭 TŌ/ZU, 痘 TŌ	Exceptions: 短 TAN [7], 豊 HŌ [7] Probably unrelated, but with same reading: 闘 TŌ
P-331	登	TŌ / CHŌ	登 TŌ/TO, 澄 CHŌ	
P-332	発	HATSU / HAI (HOTSU)	発 HATSU/HOTSU, 廃 HAI	
P-333	尌	CHŪ / JU	樹 JU, 厨[25] CHŪ	Left-hand part of phonetic also appears in character 鼓 KO and phonetic 彭 (used in 膨 BŌ)
P-334	喜	KI	喜 KI, 嬉[1] KI	
P-335	盾	JUN	盾 JUN, 循 JUN	
P-336	直	CHOKU / JIKI / SHOKU / CHI	直 CHOKU/JIKI, 植 SHOKU, 置 CHI	Also: 殖 SHOKU, 値 CHI
P-337	真	SHIN / CHIN	真 SHIN, 慎 SHIN, 鎮 CHIN	Reading variation: 填 / 塡 TEN Pre-simplification form: 眞
P-338	具	GU	具 GU, 惧 GU	Pre-simplification form: 具
P-339	県	KEN	県 KEN, 懸 KEN	Actual phonetic is 縣 KEN, but due to character simplification, can treat as 県
P-340	首	SHU / DŌ	首 SHU, 道 DŌ, 導 DŌ	

List of Phonetic Components

#	Form	Main Reading(s) / Pattern	Representative Characters			Notes
P-341	及	KYŪ	及 KYŪ	吸 KYŪ	級 KYŪ	Also: 扱 あつかう² Related: 急 KYŪ⁵
P-342	秀	SHŪ / YŪ / TŌ	秀 SHŪ	誘 YŪ	透 TŌ	
P-343	廷	TEI	廷 TEI	庭 TEI	艇 TEI	
P-344	延	EN / (SEN) / TAN	延 EN	誕 TAN		
P-345	建	KEN	建 KEN	健 KEN	鍵 KEN	
P-346	史	SHI / RI (JI)	史 SHI	吏 RI	使 SHI	Related: 事 JI has a similar derivation, and is similar in form; Unrelated: 丈 JŌ
P-347	更	KŌ	更 KŌ	硬 KŌ	梗 KŌ	Exception: 便 BEN / BIN
P-348	定	TEI / JŌ	定 TEI / JŌ	錠 JŌ		Exception: 綻 TAN
P-349	是	TEI / ZE / DAI	是 ZE	提 TEI	題 DAI	Also: 堤 TEI
P-350	従	JŪ	従 JŪ	縦 JŪ		
P-351	足	SOKU	足 SOKU	促 SOKU	捉 SOKU	足 is also used as a determinative (D-20)
P-352	疋	SO	礎 SO	疎 SO		Exceptions: 婿 SEI, 旋 SEN Alternate, compressed forms: 正 and 足
P-353	疑	GI / GYŌ	疑 GI	擬 GI	凝 GYŌ	
P-354	七	SHICHI / SHITSU / SETSU	七 SHICHI	切 SETSU	窃 SETSU	Also: 叱 SHITSU (the form of the phonetic is somewhat altered in this character, though)
P-355	乇	TAKU	宅 TAKU	託 TAKU		
P-356	毛	MŌ	毛 MŌ	耗 MŌ		Special reading: 耗 can also be read as KŌ in some compound words
P-357	也	CHI / JI / TA	地 CHI / JI	池 CHI	他 TA	Reading variation: 施 SHI / SE
P-358	它	JA / DA (TA)	蛇 JA / DA			Also: 舵 かじ¹
P-359	屯	TON / DON / JUN	屯 TON	鈍 DON	純 JUN	Also: 頓 TON
P-360	朔	SO	塑 SO	遡 SO		Unrelated: 逆 GYAKU contains a component identical to the left-hand side of the phonetic

List of Phonetic Components

#	Form	Main Reading(s) / Pattern	Representative Characters			Notes
P-361	苗	BYŌ (MYŌ)	苗 BYŌ	猫 BYŌ	描 BYŌ	
P-362	番	BAN / HAN / HON	番 BAN	藩 HAN	翻 HON	Exception: 審 SHIN
P-363	奄	AN (EN)	庵¹ AN			Also: 俺 おれ²
P-364	禺	GŪ (GU)	偶 GŪ	遇 GŪ	隅 GŪ	Also: 愚 GU
P-365	卑	HI	卑 HI	碑 HI		
P-366	鬼	KI / KAI	鬼 KI	塊 KAI		鬼 is also used as a determinative (D-64)
P-367	耳	JI / CHI	耳 JI	餌 JI	恥 CHI	耳 is mostly used as a determinative (D-67) Exception: 摂 SETSU⁶
P-368	取	SHU	取 SHU	趣 SHU		
P-369	最	SAI / SATSU	最 SAI	撮 SATSU		
P-370	敢	KAN / GEN	敢 KAN	厳 GEN		
P-371	巨	KYO	巨 KYO	距 KYO	拒 KYO	Unrelated character similar in form: 臣 SHIN / JIN
P-372	臤	KEN / KIN	賢 KEN	堅 KEN	緊 KIN	Reading variation: 腎 JIN
P-373	監	KAN / RAN	監 KAN	艦 KAN	鑑 KAN	Also: 濫, 藍 RAN Related: 覧 RAN (part of phonetic removed)
P-374	生	SEI / SHŌ	生 SEI / SHŌ	性 SEI / SHŌ	姓 SEI / SHŌ	Also: 牲, 星, 醒 SEI
P-375	先	SEN	先 SEN	洗 SEN		
P-376	告	1. KOKU 2. ZŌ	告 KOKU	酷 KOKU	造 ZŌ	
P-377	制	SEI	制 SEI	製 SEI		
P-378	青	SEI (JŌ)	青 SEI	静 SEI	情 JŌ	Also: 晴, 清, 精, 請 SEI Pre-simplification form: 靑
P-379	責	SEKI	責 SEKI	積 SEKI	績 SEKI	Also: 漬 つける² Reading variation: 債 SAI
P-380	害	GAI / KATSU	害 GAI	割 KATSU	轄 KATSU	Unrelated character with similar form: 憲 KEN

List of Phonetic Components

#	Form	Main Reading(s) / Pattern	Representative Characters			Notes
P-381	京	KYŌ / KEI / EI GEI / RYŌ	京 *KYŌ/KEI*	景 *KEI*	影 *EI*	Also: 憬 *KEI*, 鯨 *GEI*, 涼 *RYŌ*
P-382	高	KŌ / GŌ	高 *KŌ*	稿 *KŌ*	豪 *GŌ*	In 豪, bottom center part of phonetic is removed
P-383	喬	KYŌ	橋 *KYŌ*	矯 *KYŌ*		
P-384	亭	TEI	亭 *TEI*	停 *TEI*		
P-385	享	1. KYŌ / KAKU 2. JUKU 3. JUN (SHUN / TON)	享 *KYŌ*	郭 *KAKU*	塾 *JUKU*	Also: 熟 *JUKU*, 淳 *JUN*[1]
P-386	卯	1. BŌ 2. RYŪ / RU [9]	柳 *RYŪ*	貿 *BŌ*	留 *RYŪ (RU)*	Vertically compressed form: 卯 Also: 瑠 *RU*, 昴 *BŌ*[1]; Unrelated: 卵 *RAN*
P-387	卬	GEI / GYŌ (KŌ)	迎 *GEI*	仰 *GYŌ (KŌ)*		Exception: 抑 *YOKU*[6] Unrelated character similar in form: 印 *IN*
P-388	却	KYAKU	却 *KYAKU*	脚 *KYAKU*		Similar characters: both 去 *KYO/KO* and 法 *HŌ* contain left-hand side of this phonetic
P-389	即	SOKU / SETSU	即 *SOKU*	節 *SETSU*		
P-390	夗	EN / ON / WAN	怨 *EN/ON*	苑[1] *EN*	腕 *WAN*	Also: 碗 *WAN*[1], 宛 あてる[2]
P-391	心	SHIN	心 *SHIN*	芯 *SHIN*		心 is mostly used as a determinative (D-13)
P-392	必	HI / HITSU / MITSU	必 *HITSU*	秘 *HI*	密 *MITSU*	Also: 泌 *HITSU/HI*, 蜜 *MITSU*
P-393	公	KŌ / SHŌ / Ō	公 *KŌ*	松 *SHŌ*	翁 *Ō*	Also: 訟 *SHŌ*
P-394	悤	SŌ	総 *SŌ*	窓 *SŌ*		In 窓, the phonetic is slightly altered[26] Pre-simplification form: 悤 (also 怱)[27]
P-395	咼	KA	過 *KA*	渦 *KA*	禍 *KA*	Also: 鍋 なべ[2]
P-396	骨	KOTSU / KATSU	骨 *KOTSU*	滑 *KATSU/KOTSU*		骨 is also used as a determinative (D-79)
P-397	五	GO	五 *GO*	語 *GO*	悟 *GO*	Unrelated character similar in form and identical in reading: 互 *GO*
P-398	呉	GO	呉 *GO*	誤 *GO*	娯 *GO*	Also: 虞 おそれ[2]
P-399	丂	KŌ / GŌ	号 *GŌ*	巧 *KŌ*		Reading variation: 朽 *KYŪ*; Unrelated characters with similar component: 汚 *O*, 誇 *KO*, 顎 *GAKU*
P-400	丑	CHŪ / SHŪ (JŪ)	丑[1] *CHŪ*	羞 *SHŪ*		

List of Phonetic Components (page 21 of 25)

#	Form	Main Reading(s) / Pattern	Representative Characters			Notes
P-401	炎	EN / (SEN) / TAN / DAN	炎 EN	淡 TAN	談 DAN	
P-402	朋	HŌ	崩 HŌ			Also: 棚 たな [2]
P-403	劦	KYŌ	協 KYŌ	脅 KYŌ		Also: 脇 わき [2]
P-404	畾	RUI / RAI	累 RUI	塁 RUI	雷 RAI	All three jōyō kanji with this phonetic have been simplified (originally 纍, 壘, 靁)
P-405	争	SŌ / JŌ	争 SŌ	浄 JŌ		
P-406	君	KUN / GUN	君 KUN	郡 GUN	群 GUN	
P-407	唐	TŌ	唐 TŌ	糖 TŌ		
P-408	兼	KEN / REN	兼 KEN	謙 KEN	嫌 KEN	Also: 廉 REN, 鎌 かま [2]
P-409	酉	SHU / SHŪ / YŪ	酒 SHU	醜 SHŪ	猶 YŪ	Det. D-46; Variant form of phonetic: 酋 [28]; Unrelated character with similar form: 西 SEI / SAI
P-410	尊	SON / JUN	尊 SON	噂[1] SON	遵 JUN	
P-411	者	SHA / SHO / CHO / TO	者 SHA	煮 SHA	諸 SHO	Also: 暑, 署, 緒 SHO; 著 CHO; 賭 TO; 都 TO / TSU; 箸 はし [2]; Related: 書 SHO [5]
P-412	耂	KŌ / RŌ / KYŌ / GŌ	考 KŌ	老 RŌ	教 KYŌ	Also: 孝, 酵 KŌ; 拷 GŌ
P-413	利	RI	利 RI	痢 RI		Also: 梨 なし [2]
P-414	列	RETSU / REI	列 RETSU	裂 RETSU	烈 RETSU	Also: 例 REI
P-415	山	SAN / SEN	山 SAN	仙 SEN		山 is mostly used as a determinative (D-9)
P-416	出	SHUTSU / SETSU	出 SHUTSU	拙 SETSU		
P-417	広	KŌ / KAKU	広 KŌ	鉱 KŌ	拡 KAKU	Pre-simplification form: 廣 (see also P-448)
P-418	庄	SHŌ	庄[1] SHŌ	粧 SHŌ		Unrelated character with similar form: 圧 ATSU
P-419	麻	REKI	暦 REKI	歴 REKI		Pre-simplification form: 厤 See note 8
P-420	麻	MA	麻 MA	摩 MA	魔 MA	Also: 磨 MA

List of Phonetic Components (page 22 of 25)

#	Form	Main Reading(s) / Pattern	Representative Characters			Notes
P-421	家	KA (KE)	家 KA/KE	稼 KA	嫁 KA	Unrelated character with component similar in form: 塚 つか
P-422	㒸	TAI / TSUI / SUI	隊 TAI	墜 TSUI	遂 SUI	Unrelated characters with component similar in form: 豚 TON, 逐 CHIKU
P-423	魚	GYO	魚 GYO	漁 GYO		Determinative D-23; Special reading: 漁 can also be read as RYŌ (discussed in Part 1, Section 7.11)
P-424	鳥	CHŌ / TŌ	鳥 CHŌ	島 TŌ		鳥 is mostly used as a determinative (D-24) In 島, part of phonetic is removed
P-425	馬	BA (MA)	馬 BA (MA)	罵 BA		馬 is mostly used as a determinative (D-25)
P-426	為	I / GI	為 I	偽 GI		
P-427	巤	RYŌ / RŌ	猟 RYŌ	蠟[1] RŌ		Pre-simplification form: 獵 Related character: 鼠 (SŌ, ねずみ)[29]
P-428	鹿	ROKU	麓 ROKU			Also: 鹿 しか[2] Exception: 麗 REI[7]
P-429	勿	MOCHI / MOTSU / BUTSU	勿[1] MOCHI	物 BUTSU/MOTSU		
P-430	昜	YŌ / TŌ / CHŌ / SHŌ / JŌ	陽 YŌ	湯 TŌ	腸 CHŌ	Also: 揚, 瘍 YŌ; 傷 SHŌ; 場 JŌ
P-431	易	EKI / I / SHI	易 EKI/I	賜 SHI		
P-432	免	MEN / BEN / BAN	免 MEN	勉 BEN	晩 BAN	Exception: 逸 ITSU[6]
P-433	象	ZŌ / SHŌ	象 SHŌ/ZŌ	像 ZŌ		
P-434	臽	KAN / AN	陥 KAN	餡[1] AN		Pre-simplification form: 臽; Similar phonetic: 舀 (used in 稲 TŌ, with pre-simplification form: 舀)
P-435	奐	KAN	喚 KAN	換 KAN		
P-436	布	FU	布 FU	怖 FU		Unrelated (similarity is coincidental): 希 KI[6]
P-437	左	SA	左 SA	佐 SA	差 SA	In 差, top part of phonetic is distorted
P-438	育	ZUI / DA	随 ZUI	髄 ZUI	堕 DA	Also: 惰, 楕[1] DA; Simplified form of phonetic: 有 (identical, but unrelated, to 有 YŪ/U[30])
P-439	若	JAKU / DAKU / TOKU	若 JAKU	諾 DAKU	匿 TOKU	
P-440	石	SEKI / SHAKU / TAKU / TO	石 SEKI (SHAKU)	拓 TAKU	妬 TO	石 is mostly used as a determinative (D-10)

List of Phonetic Components (page 23 of 25)

#	Form	Main Reading(s) / Pattern	Representative Characters			Notes
P-441	畐	FUKU (FU)	福 FUKU	副 FUKU	幅 FUKU	Also: 富 (and its variant form 冨) FU
P-442	复	FUKU	復 FUKU	複 FUKU	腹 FUKU	Also: 覆 FUKU Exception: 履 RI[6]
P-443	曼	MAN	漫 MAN	慢 MAN		
P-444	㑴	SHIN	侵 SHIN	寝 SHIN	浸 SHIN	
P-445	莫	*AN	漢 KAN	難 NAN	嘆 TAN	Pre-simplification form: 莫
P-446	堇	KIN	勤 KIN	謹 KIN	僅 KIN	Pre-simplification form: 堇
P-447	莫	BO / BAKU / MO / MAKU	墓 BO	模 MO / BO	漠 BAKU	Also: 暮, 募, 慕 BO; 膜 MAKU; 幕 MAKU / BAKU
P-448	黄	KŌ / Ō	黄 KŌ / Ō	横 Ō		Pre-simplification form: 黃; 廣 is simplified as 広 (see P-417); Unrelated, but similar in form: 演 EN
P-449	冓	KŌ	講 KŌ	購 KŌ	溝 KŌ	Also: 構 KŌ Unrelated character similar in form: 再 SAI
P-450	奉	HŌ / BŌ	奉 HŌ	俸 HŌ	棒 BŌ	
P-451	菐	BOKU	僕 BOKU	撲 BOKU		Unrelated character similar in form: 業 GYŌ
P-452	善	ZEN	善 ZEN	繕 ZEN	膳 ZEN	
P-453	坴	RIKU / ROKU	陸 RIKU			Exception: 睦 BOKU
P-454	埶	SEI / NETSU	勢 SEI	熱 NETSU		Related: 芸 GEI[5]
P-455	執	SHITSU / SHŪ / SHI	執 SHITSU / SHŪ	摯 SHI		
P-456	夌	RYŌ	陵 RYŌ	菱[1] RYŌ		
P-457	夋	SAN / SHUN (SA)	酸 SAN	俊 SHUN		Reading variation: 唆 SA
P-458	般	HAN / BAN	般 HAN	搬 HAN	盤 BAN	
P-459	段	DAN / TAN	段 DAN	鍛 TAN		
P-460	叚	KA	暇 KA			Related: 仮 KA once had this phonetic, but its form was simplified (originally 假)

List of Phonetic Components (page 24 of 25)

#	Form	Main Reading(s) / Pattern	Representative Characters			Notes
P-461	兄	KYŌ / KEI	兄 KEI (KYŌ)	況 KYŌ		Exceptions: 祝 SHUKU, 呪 JU; Unrelated, but similar in form: 克 KOKU, 兒 (used in 貌 BŌ)
P-462	兌	*ETSU / *EI	説 SETSU	税 ZEI	鋭 EI	Also: 悦, 閲 ETSU; Reading variation: 脱 DATSU Pre-simplification form: 兌
P-463	見	KEN / GEN	見 KEN	現 GEN		見 is mostly used as a determinative (D-19)
P-464	売	DOKU / TOKU / ZOKU	読 DOKU / TOKU	続 ZOKU		Exception: 売 BAI [31]
P-465	尭	*YŌ	焼 SHŌ	暁 GYŌ		Pre-simplification form: 堯
P-466	冘	CHIN	沈 CHIN			Also: 枕 まくら [2]
P-467	尤	SHŪ / YŪ	就 SHŪ	蹴 SHŪ		Exception: 稽 KEI
P-468	至	SHI / SHITSU / CHI / CHITSU	至 SHI	室 SHITSU	致 CHI	Also: 窒 CHITSU, 緻 CHI
P-469	到	TŌ	到 TŌ	倒 TŌ		
P-470	屋	OKU / AKU	屋 OKU	握 AKU		
P-471	充	JŪ / TŌ	充 JŪ	銃 JŪ	統 TŌ	
P-472	㐬	RYŪ	流 RYŪ	硫 RYŪ		
P-473	㪔	TETSU	撤 TETSU	徹 TETSU		Unrelated: 育 IKU is identical to left-hand side of phonetic
P-474	巟	KŌ	荒 KŌ	慌 KŌ		
P-475	瓜	KO	孤 KO	弧 KO		Non-jōyō 瓜 (うり) means 'melon, gourd' Unrelated character with similar form: 爪 つめ
P-476	秋	SHŪ	秋 SHŪ	愁 SHŪ		
P-477	韋	I / EI	違 I	偉 I	緯 I	Also: 衛 EI Related: 囲 I (simplified from 圍)
P-478	岡	KŌ / GŌ	綱 KŌ	鋼 KŌ	剛 GŌ	Also: 岡 おか [2]
P-479	然	NEN / ZEN	然 ZEN / NEN	燃 NEN		
P-480	敝	HEI	幣 HEI	弊 HEI	蔽 HEI	Pre-simplification form: 敝

List of Phonetic Components (page 25 of 25)

#	Form	Main Reading(s) / Pattern	Representative Characters			Notes
P-481	朝	CHŌ	朝 CHŌ	潮 CHŌ	嘲 CHŌ	
P-482	幹	KAN	幹 KAN			Related: 乾, 韓 KAN (forms are altered [32]) Exception: 斡 ATSU [1]
P-483	朕	SHŌ / TŌ	勝 SHŌ	藤 TŌ	騰 TŌ	Also: 謄 TŌ
P-484	殼	KAKU / KOKU	殻 KAKU	穀 KOKU		See note 8
P-485	虍	KO / KYO / RO / RYO	虎 KO	虚 KYO	慮 RYO	Also: 虜 RYO; Related: 炉 RO [5] Exceptions: 膚 FU, 劇 GEKI, 虐 GYAKU, 戯 GI
P-486	攸	SHŪ / YŪ (JŌ)	修 SHŪ	悠 YŪ		Related: 条 JŌ was simplified (originally: 條)
P-487	庶	DO / TO / SEKI / SHO / SHA	度 DO (TAKU)	渡 TO	席 SEKI	Also: 庶 SHO, 遮 SHA
P-488	面	MEN	面 MEN	麺 MEN		
P-489	坐	ZA	坐 [1] ZA	座 ZA	挫 ZA	The modern meanings of both jōyō 座 and non-jōyō 坐 are 'sit; seat'
P-490	明	MEI / MYŌ	明 MEI / MYŌ	盟 MEI		
P-491	臭	KYŪ / SHŪ	臭 SHŪ	嗅 KYŪ		Pre-simplification form: 臭 (has one extra short stroke)
P-492	軍	1. GUN / UN 2. KI	軍 GUN	運 UN	揮 KI	Also: 輝 KI
P-493	叟	SŌ	捜 SŌ	痩 SŌ		Pre-simplification form: 叟; Similar phonetic: 甹 (used in 挿 SŌ, with pre-simplification form: 臿)
P-494	州	SHŪ (SU)	州 SHŪ / SU	酬 SHŪ	洲 [1] SHŪ / SU	The meanings of jōyō 州 and non-jōyō 洲 are now identical ('administrative district; continent; sandbar')
P-495	冬	TŌ / SHŪ	冬 TŌ	終 SHŪ		
P-496	离	RI	離 RI	璃 RI		
P-497	父	FU	父 FU			Also: 釜 かま [2] (in this character, the phonetic is partly merged with the 金 component below it)
P-498	侯	KŌ	侯 KŌ	候 KŌ	喉 KŌ	Modern form is a corruption of 矦
P-499	宿	SHUKU	宿 SHUKU	縮 SHUKU		
P-500	亜	A / AKU (O)	亜 A	悪 AKU / O		

LIST OF PHONETIC COMPONENTS

Notes:

1. This character is not a *jōyō kanji*, but is nonetheless encountered fairly frequently. It is included in this list to provide additional examples of characters containing the phonetic, and to assist with character and phonetic recognition and comparison.

2. This character contains the phonetic, and has an *on* reading based on the phonetic, but there is no *on* reading for this character in common usage. A common use *kun* reading (in hiragana) is given instead.

3. This character contains the phonetic, but the principal *on* reading shown here came from China at a different time than the most common *on* readings of characters containing this phonetic, and therefore differs from these more common readings.

4. This character used to have a reading which matched the phonetic, but the character was borrowed for use in a different role, and the *on* reading was changed.

5. This character once contained the phonetic, but either as part of a deliberate effort to simplify character forms, or as a side effect of gradual changes to character writing styles, the character was modified in such a way that the full phonetic component no longer appears in it.

6. This character was not intentionally designed with this phonetic component as a discrete element; any similarity with the phonetic is coincidental. Either the character form was altered or simplified at some point, such that it now contains a component identical in form to the phonetic, or the character was designed in a way such that it contains a component or components which coincidentally happen to be identical in form to the phonetic.

7. This character appears to have been created as an ideograph, with the character meaning formed by a combination of the elements in the character—the elements being used only for their meaning and not for their sound. The phonetic component shown here may have been deliberately included in the character, but if so it was used only for its meaning—not to serve as a phonetic indicator.

8. It is mostly likely the case that one of these representative characters was created first, possibly as an ideograph, and then the other was designed based on the first, incorporating one part of it. Therefore, the phonetic component shown here may not be a true phonetic component in the strictest sense. Thinking of it as a phonetic may be helpful for learning the characters listed here, though.

9. Originally, there were two distinct phonetics, separate in form. One or both of them changed, and they are now identical in form. The two sets of readings listed here correspond to the two different phonetics.

10. The ' symbol which appears in a few of the *on* readings in the table corresponds to the small 'tsu' character. For example, the reading GA' corresponds to ガッ in katakana.

11. The pre-simplification form of this phonetic (卒) is also a standalone character, with the principal *on* reading of *SOTSU*.

12. This character is a *kokuji*, and no *on* reading has been assigned to it. It includes the phonetic component as an element, but with no phonetic role. It is listed here for reference.

13. This character has been simplified, with several components removed. In both the older form and the current form, the 王 component is used only as a meaning-indicating component, not as a phonetic.

14. This character was probably not originally designed with the phonetic component intended to be used in a phonetic role. However, since the character does contain the phonetic as a component and its reading is consistent with the phonetic reading, it can be treated as if it were designed that way.

15. This character was originally designed to include phonetic P-039, but its form became corrupted, and the phonetic component was altered.

16. Careful examination of the right-hand side component in this character reveals that it is not identical to the phonetic. Rather, the final stroke (moving down and to the right) is slightly different, curving downward.

17. The *on* reading of this character is not a close match with the phonetic reading, and so it is not clear if this character was originally created as a determinative-phonetic character. Regardless, the *on* reading for this character is not in common use. The character is listed here for reference, with the common use *kun* reading (in hiragana) given.

18. Although this character includes a component closer in resemblance to 夭 (P-078) than to 天 (P-077), from analyzing earlier forms of the character, it appears that it was designed with P-077 as the phonetic. Because the *on* readings of this character and 天 exactly match, and the forms of the components are quite similar, it may be helpful to think of 天 as the phonetic of this character.

19. This special reading originated as a spoken contraction of *saki* (the character is nearly identical in meaning to 崎, which has a *kun* reading of *saki*). This special reading is generally not encountered other than in the place name Saitama.

20. The standalone character 舌 (meaning 'tongue') is unrelated to the phonetic component, which is identical in form. The standalone character once had a slightly different form, but it was altered and now exactly matches the phonetic. This character appears as a component in a few other characters (sometimes as a determinative, such as in 舐 'to lick'), but is not used as a phonetic.

21. Note that the upper component in this character is not identical to the phonetic, as the lower right stroke is shifted to the right (and another component is placed into the open space below it). Characters containing this component with the lower right stroke shifted in this way should be thought of as NOT having this phonetic.

22. Among the characters shown here, two different phonetics have been merged into one. Some of the characters shown here originally used 尺 as a phonetic, while others originally used 睪. The simpler phonetic was used as a replacement for the more complicated one based on a similarity in sound.

23. This character might have originally consisted of this phonetic (則) together with a meaning-indicating component (戈). Whether or not this is true, the phonetic can be used to help remember the character *on* reading.

24. Unlike the phonetic, this component does not have a short, disconnected stroke in the upper right.

25. The most commonly-encountered version of this non-*jōyō* character has been simplified slightly, with the upper left part of the phonetic removed.

26. In the modern version of this character, the top two strokes of the phonetic (念) are merged with the bottom two strokes of the determinative (穴).

27. Non-*jōyō* character 葱 (ねぎ, 'onion') uses one of the older phonetic forms.

28. Components 酉 and 酋 are very similar. Both depict containers of alcohol. The second one also depicts fumes at the top, suggesting an open container. When used in a phonetic role, though, both essentially indicate the same meaning and readings, and so as phonetics can be treated as equivalent to each other.

29. When this phonetic component is used by itself as a standalone character, it acts as a substitute simplified form of the non-*jōyō* character 鼠, meaning 'rat, mouse.' In this case, its main phonetic readings are ignored, and instead it adopts the readings of the character it is replacing.

30. Both the simplified (有) and non-simplified (靑) forms of this phonetic can be seen among the *jōyō kanji*. The simplified form of the phonetic is identical in appearance (but unrelated) to the character 有 YŪ / U.

31. This character is now identical in appearance to the phonetic component. However, that was not the case prior to post-war character simplifications. Both this character and the phonetic component were simplified from much more complicated forms, which, although similar in appearance, were different from each other. The earlier forms can be seen in Chapter 2 (Section 2.11) and in Appendix G (in the Type 6 section).

32. In the first of these two characters, the upper right part of the phonetic is slightly altered in form. In the second, it is removed. However, both can be thought of as containing this phonetic.

Section 3

List of Other Components

3.1 Overview

Among all kanji, there are numerous recurring components—that is, components which are found within a number of different characters. Most commonly, such recurring components have either a determinative or a phonetic role—or possibly even both: used as a determinative in some characters and a phonetic in others. Commonly-encountered components used as determinatives or phonetics are listed in the previous two sections.

There are, though, a small number of recurring components which are not primarily used in either a determinative or phonetic role, and therefore do not belong in either of the previous two sections. This section contains a list of the most commonly occurring of these components. Such components often (but not always) are used in a simple meaning-indicating role, combined with other meaning-indicating components to form ideographic characters (see Part 1, Section 2.4 for a discussion of ideographic characters).

These components are listed in this section simply to assist you in gaining familiarity with them, so that when you encounter them in your studies you can more quickly recognize them and distinguish them from other components similar in appearance. Many of these components have different meanings within different characters. For that reason, meanings are listed in this section for only a few of the components, where most relevant and helpful.

For each component listed here, representative common use characters which include these components are shown, together with the principal *on* (uppercase) and *kun* (lowercase) readings of these characters. The *kun* readings are listed in their entirety, including the portion that would normally be written with okurigana; the division between the kanji portion and the okurigana portion is not marked.

The components are labeled with 'C' followed by a two-digit number (e.g., C-26). Endnotes are listed on the final page of the tables.

List of Other Components (page 1 of 3)

#	Form	Representative *Jōyō* Characters Containing the Component / Notes
C-01	卜	外 *(GAI, GE, soto, hoka, hazusu, hazureru)*, 訃 *(FU)*, 赴 *(FU, omomuku)*, 朴 *(BOKU)*, 掛 *(kakeru, kakaru, kakari)*
C-02	斗	斗 *(TO)*, 科 *(KA)*, 斜 *(SHA, naname)*, 料 *(RYŌ)*
C-03	关	送 *(SŌ, okuru)*, 関 *(KAN, seki, kakawaru)*, 咲 *(saku)*, 朕 *(CHIN)*
C-04	歩	歩 *(HO, BU, aruku, ayumu)*, 渉 *(SHŌ)*, 捗 *(CHOKU)*, 頻 *(HIN)* This component originated as an ideograph of one foot in front of another, suggesting walking.
C-05	井	井 *(SEI, i)*, 丼 *(donburi)*, 囲 *(I, kakomu kakou)*, 耕 *(KŌ, tagayasu)*
C-06	西	価 *(KA, atai)*, 遷 *(SEN)*, 覇 *(HA)*, 慄 *(RITSU)*, 覆 *(FUKU)*, 煙 *(EN)*
C-07	而	耐 *(TAI, taeru)*, 端 *(TAN, hashi, ha, hata)*, 需 *(JU)*, 儒 *(JU)*
C-08	能	能 *(NŌ)*, 熊 *(kuma)*, 態 *(TAI)*, 罷 *(HI)* This component originated as a pictograph of a bear.
C-09	𠂤	追 *(TSUI, ou)*, 帥 *(SUI)*, 師 *(SHI)*, 阜 *(FU)*
C-10	𡗗	春 *(SHUN, haru)*, 奏 *(SŌ, kanaderu)*, 泰 *(TAI)*, and phonetic 奉 *(HŌ / BŌ)* (P-450)
C-11	聿	津 *(SHIN, tsu)*, 書 *(SHO, kaku)*, 筆 *(HITSU, fude)*, 律 *(RITSU)* This component originated as a pictograph of a hand holding a brush.
C-12	隶	逮 *(TAI)*, 康 *(KŌ)*, 隷 *(REI)*
C-13	去	去 *(KYO, KO, saru)*, 法 *(HŌ)*, 蓋 *(GAI, futa)*
C-14	色	色 *(SHOKU, SHIKI, iro)*, 絶 *(ZETSU, taeru, tayasu, tatsu)*, 艶 *(EN, tsuya)*
C-15	丩	糾 *(KYŪ)*, 収 *(SHŪ, osameru, osamaru)*, 叫 *(KYŌ, sakebu)* [1]
C-16	辛	辛 *(SHIN, karai)*, 辞 *(JI, yameru)*, 宰 *(SAI)* Similar but unrelated components appear in: 幸 *(KŌ, saiwai, sachi, shiawase)*, 達 *(TATSU)*
C-17	夫夫	替 *(TAI, kaeru, kawaru)*, 潜 *(SEN, hisomu, moguru)*, 賛 *(SAN)*
C-18	帚	帰 *(KI, kaeru, kaesu)*, 掃 *(SŌ, haku)*, 婦 *(FU)* This component originated as a pictograph of a broom.
C-19	本	本 *(HON, moto)*, 体 *(TAI, TEI, karada)*, 鉢 *(HACHI)*
C-20	微	微 *(BI)*, 徴 *(CHŌ)*, 懲 *(CHŌ, koriru, korasu, korashimeru)*

List of Other Components (page 2 of 3)

#	Form	Representative *Jōyō* Characters Containing the Component / Notes
C-21	叀	専 *(SEN, moppara)*, 恵 *(KEI, E, megumu)*, 穂 *(SUI, ho)*
C-22	圭	素 *(SO, SU)*, 毒 *(DOKU)*, phonetics 青 *(SEI / JŌ)* (P-378) and 責 *(SEKI)* (P-379), and determinative 麦 (D-60)
C-23	广	存 *(SON, ZON)*, 在 *(ZAI, aru)*
C-24	尓	称 *(SHŌ)*, 弥 *(ya)*
C-25	尺	昼 *(CHŪ, hiru)*, 尽 *(JIN, tsukusu, tsukiru, tsukasu)* Similar in form to phonetic 尺 *(*AKU / *EKI)* (P-229)
C-26	𠬝	服 *(FUKU)*, 報 *(HŌ, mukuiru)* [1]
C-27	以	以 *(I)*, 似 *(JI, niru)* [1]
C-28	迷	断 *(DAN, tatsu, kotowaru)*, 継 *(KEI, tsugu)*
C-29	恵	聴 *(CHŌ, kiku)*, 徳 *(TOKU)*
C-30	产	顔 *(GAN, kao)*, 産 *(SAN, umu, umareru, ubu)*
C-31	之	芝 *(shiba)*, 乏 *(BŌ, toboshii)*
C-32	灰	灰 *(KAI, hai)*, 炭 *(TAN, sumi)*; This component, meaning 'ash,' originally depicted a hand over a fire, possibly ideographically suggesting 'fire that can be touched': ash.
C-33	㬎	顕 *(KEN)*, 湿 *(SHITSU, shimeru, shimesu)*
C-34	多	多 *(TA, ooi)*, 移 *(I, utsuru, utsusu)*
C-35	𣎴	派 *(HA)*, 脈 *(MYAKU)* [1] Similar components appear in: 旅 *(RYO, tabi)*, 衆 *(SHŪ)*
C-36	戌	威 *(I)*, 滅 *(METSU, horobiru, horobosu)*
C-37	寒	寒 *(KAN, samui)*, 塞 *(SAI, SOKU, fusagu, fusagaru)*
C-38	素	隷 *(REI)*, 款 *(KAN)*
C-39	帛	綿 *(MEN, wata)*, 錦 *(KIN, nishiki)*
C-40	丘	丘 *(KYŪ, oka)*, 岳 *(GAKU, take)* This component originated as a pictograph depicting hills.

List of Other Components (page 3 of 3)

#	Form	Representative *Jōyō* Characters Containing the Component / Notes
C-41	殳	投 *(TŌ, nageru)*, 役 *(YAKU, EKI)*, 設 *(SETSU, moukeru)*, 殴 *(Ō, naguru)*, 疫 *(EKI)*, 股 *(KO, mata)*, 没 *(BOTSU)*, 毀 *(KI)*, and others
C-42	又	又 *(mata)*, 双 *(SŌ, futa)*, 隻 *(SEKI)*, and others In most characters, this component represents a single hand.
C-43	廾	弁 *(BEN)*, 弄 *(RŌ, moteasobu)*, 算 *(SAN)*, and others In most characters, this component represents a pair of hands holding an object.
C-44	夂	夏 *(KA, natsu)*, 慶 *(KEI)*, 後 *(GO, KŌ, nochi, ushiro, ato)*, and others In most characters, this component represents a single foot, especially one that is dragging.
C-45	舛	舞 *(BU, mau, mai)*, 隣 *(RIN, tonaru, tonari)*, 傑 *(KETSU)*, 瞬 *(SHUN, matataku)* This component depicts two feet: left and right.
C-46	夕	夕 *(SEKI, yū)*, 夢 *(MU, yume)*, 拶 *(SATSU)*, and others; In most characters, this component represents the moon, or, by extension, evening. It is a variant form of 月.
C-47	匚	医 *(I)*, 匠 *(SHŌ)*, 匿 *(TOKU)*, and others; treated as two distinct radicals (R-22 and R-23), but listed here as one component, as the forms are identical within all *jōyō kanji*.
C-48	乚	札 *(SATSU, fuda)*, 礼 *(REI, RAI)*, 乱 *(RAN, midareru, midasu)*, 孔 *(KŌ)*, 乳 *(NYŪ, chichi, chi)*
C-49	巛	巡 *(JUN, meguru)*, 災 *(SAI, wazawai)*, 拶 *(SATSU)*
C-50	釆	釈 *(SHAKU)*, and phonetic 番 *(BAN / HAN / HON)* (P-362)

Note:

1. Based on the loose degree of similarity in the *on* readings of the characters which include this component, it may actually have a phonetic role. That is not certain, however, and so the component is listed in this section instead of in the phonetics section.

Section 4
List of Radicals

4.1 Overview

This section lists all of the 214 character radicals, as specified in this book, together with their alternate forms, where applicable, and their Japanese names. Radicals are described in detail in Part 1, Chapter 4. Further information about radicals, such as how they were named, is provided in Appendix F.

A set of exactly 214 radicals was chosen for this book for consistency with most major kanji dictionaries. The specific components chosen for inclusion were slightly altered from the traditional set of *Kangxi* radicals, though, to reflect the changes that have occurred due to character form simplifications in Japan. These modifications to the radical list ensure that all radicals in the set specified by the Japan Kanji Aptitude Testing Foundation (the creator and administrator of the Kanji Kentei tests) are represented. Furthermore, the ordering of the radicals in this list was revised to reflect modern Japanese character stroke counts. See Appendix F for a more thorough discussion of these changes.

4.2 Example Characters

For each radical listed in the following tables, one example character assigned to that radical is shown. Wherever possible, *jōyō kanji* have been chosen as the example characters. A few radicals do not have any *jōyō kanji* grouped under them, though. (Among all of the *jōyō kanji*, only about 200 of the 214 different radicals are represented.) As a result, some of the example characters that appear in the list are outside of the *jōyō kanji* set.

4.3 Omitted Alternate Forms

For some radicals whose main and alternate forms are only slightly different from each other, only the main form is shown in this list. For example, radical R-167 has the main form 金 (with the radical name かね), but when placed on the left-hand side of a character, it assumes the alternate form 釒 (called かねへん). These two forms, while different, can be easily recognized as being the same component. Thus, the latter has been left off the list. Alternate forms with greater differences, however, are included.

List of Radicals (page 1 of 6)

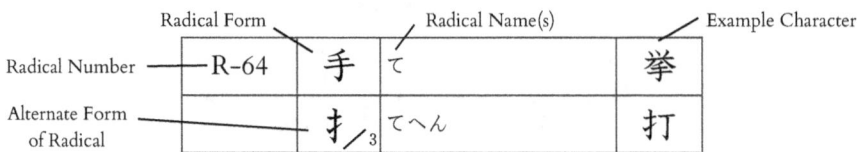

		Radical Form	Radical Name(s)	Example Character
Radical Number →		R-64	手 て	挙
Alternate Form of Radical →		扌/3	てへん	打

Stroke Count of Alternate Form (if different from main form)

		1 stroke		
R-1	一	いち		丁
R-2	丨	ぼう / たてぼう		中
R-3	丶	てん		丼
R-4	丿	の / はらいぼう		久
R-5	乙	おつ / おつにょう		乾
	乚	おつ / おつにょう		乱
R-6	亅	はねぼう		事
		2 strokes		
R-7	二	に		互
R-8	亠	なべぶた / けいさんかんむり		交
R-9	人	ひと		人
	亻	にんべん		仏
	𠆢	ひとやね		企
R-10	儿	ひとあし / にんにょう		元
R-11	入	いる		入
R-12	八	はち / はちがしら		公
R-13	冂	けいがまえ / まきがまえ		円
R-14	冖	わかんむり		写
R-15	冫	にすい		冷
	夂	にすい		冬
R-16	几	つくえ		処

R-17	凵	かんにょう / うけばこ		出
R-18	刀	かたな		切
	刂	りっとう		列
R-19	力	ちから		加
R-20	勹	つつみがまえ		包
R-21	匕	ひ / さじのひ		北
R-22	匚	はこがまえ		匠
R-23	匸	かくしがまえ		区
R-24	十	じゅう		南
R-25	卜	ぼくのと / うらない		占
R-26	卩	ふしづくり		印
	巳	ふしづくり		危
R-27	厂	がんだれ		厚
R-28	厶	む		参
R-29	又	また		友
		3 strokes		
R-30	口	くち		古
	口	くちへん		叩
R-31	囗	くにがまえ		国
R-32	土	つち		圧
	土	つちへん		地
R-33	士	さむらい		声

List of Radicals (page 2 of 6)

R-34	夂	ふゆがしら / すいにょう	冬	R-55	廾	にじゅうあし	弁
R-35	夕	た / ゆうべ	外	R-56	弋	しきがまえ	式
R-36	大	だい	太	R-57	弓	ゆみ / ゆみへん	引
R-37	女	おんな	委	R-58	彑	けいがしら / いのこがしら	彙
	女	おんなへん	好		彐	けいがしら / いのこがしら	彗
R-38	子	こ	存		ヨ	けいがしら / いのこがしら	ヨ
	子	こへん	孫	R-59	彡	さんづくり	形
R-39	宀	うかんむり	安	R-60	彳	ぎょうにんべん	役
R-40	寸	すん	寺			**4 strokes**	
R-41	小	しょう	少	R-61	心	こころ	念
	小	しょうがしら / なおがしら	当		忄₃	りっしんべん	忙
R-42	丷	つかんむり	厳		小	したごころ	恭
R-43	尢	だいのまげあし / おうにょう	就	R-62	戈	ほこがまえ / ほこづくり	成
	尣₄	だいのまげあし / おうにょう	尪	R-63	戸	とだれ / とかんむり	所
R-44	尸	しかばねかんむり / かばね	局	R-64	手	て	挙
R-45	屮	めばえ / てつ	屯		扌₃	てへん	打
R-46	山	やま / やまへん	岳	R-65	支	しにょう / じゅうまた	支
R-47	巛	かわ / まがりがわ	巡	R-66	攴	ぼくづくり / とまた	敍
	川	かわ / さんぼんがわ	州		攵	ぼくづくり / のぶん	放
R-48	工	たくみ / たくみへん	左	R-67	文	ぶん / ぶんにょう	斑
R-49	己	おのれ	巻	R-68	斗	とます / ますづくり	料
	巳	おのれ	巴	R-69	斤	おの / おのづくり	断
R-50	巾	はば / はばへん	席	R-70	方	ほう / かたへん	方
R-51	干	かん / いちじゅう	平	R-71	无	すでのつくり	无
R-52	幺	いとがしら	幼		旡	すでのつくり	既
R-53	广	まだれ	広	R-72	日	にち / ひへん	昨
R-54	廴	えんにょう	建	R-73	曰	ひらび / いわく	最

List of Radicals (page 3 of 6)

Radical Number → R-94	Radical Form → 犬	Radical Name(s) → いぬ	Example Character → 状
Alternate Form of Radical	犭₃	けものへん	独

Stroke Count of Alternate Form (if different from main form)

R-74	月	つき / つきへん	朗
R-75	木	き	条
	木	きへん	村
R-76	欠	あくび / かける	次
R-77	止	とめる	歩
	止	とめへん	此
R-78	歹	がつ / いちたへん	死
R-79	殳	るまた / ほこづくり	段
R-80	毋	なかれ	母
R-81	比	くらべる / ならびひ	比
R-82	毛	け	毯
R-83	氏	うじ	民
R-84	气	きがまえ	気
R-85	水	みず	永
	氺₅	したみず	泰
	氵₃	さんずい	決
R-86	火	ひ	災
	火	ひへん	灯
	灬	れんが / れっか	点
R-87	爪	つめ	爬
	爫	つめかんむり	爵
R-88	父	ちち	爺

R-89	爻	こう / めめ	爽
R-90	爿	しょうへん	牀
	丬₃	しょうへん	爿
R-91	片	かた / かたへん	版
R-92	牙	きば	牙
R-93	牛	うし	牢
	牜	うしへん	物
R-94	犬	いぬ	状
	犭₃	けものへん	独
5 strokes			
R-95	玄	げん	玄
R-96	玉	たま	玉
	王₄	たまへん	球
R-97	瓦	かわら	瓶
R-98	甘	あまい / かん	甚
R-99	生	うまれる / いきる	産
R-100	用	もちいる	用
R-101	田	た / たへん	男
R-102	疋	ひき	疑
	疋	ひきへん	疎
R-103	疒	やまいだれ	病
R-104	癶	はつがしら	発

List of Radicals (page 4 of 6)

R-105	白	しろ / しろへん	百		R-123	羽	はね	習
R-106	皮	けがわ / ひのかわ	皮		R-124	老	おい	老
R-107	皿	さら	益			耂 ₄	おいかんむり	者
R-108	目	め / めへん	盲		R-125	而	しかして / しこうして	而
R-109	矛	ほこ / むのほこ	矛		R-126	耒	らいすき / すきへん	耕
R-110	矢	や / やへん	知		R-127	耳	みみ / みみへん	聞
R-111	石	いし / いしへん	研		R-128	聿	ふでづくり	粛
R-112	示	しめす	祭		R-129	肉	にく	腐
	礻 ₄	しめすへん	社			月 ₄	にくづき	育
R-113	禸	ぐうのあし	禹		R-130	自	みずから	臭
R-114	禾	のぎ / のぎへん	私		R-131	至	いたる	致
R-115	穴	あな	穴		R-132	臼	うす	興
	穴	あなかんむり	空		R-133	舌	した / したへん	舌
R-116	立	たつ / たつへん	端		R-134	舟	ふね / ふねへん	船
6 strokes					R-135	艮	うしとら / こんづくり	良
R-117	竹	たけ	竹		R-136	色	いろ	艶
	𥫗	たけかんむり	笑		R-137	艸	くさ	艸
R-118	米	こめ / こめへん	粉			艹 ₃	くさかんむり	花
R-119	糸	いと / いとへん	紙		R-138	虍	とらがしら / とらかんむり	虎
R-120	缶	ほとぎ / ほとぎへん	缶		R-139	虫	むし / むしへん	蚕
R-121	网	あみ	网		R-140	血	ち / ちへん	衆
	罔 ₅	あみがしら	罔		R-141	行	ぎょうがまえ / ゆきがまえ	術
	罒 ₅	よこめ / あみがしら	罪		R-142	衣	ころも	衰
	罓 ₄	あみがしら	罕			衤 ₅	ころもへん	襟
R-122	羊	ひつじ	群		R-143	襾	かなめのかしら / おおいかんむり	西
	𦍌	ひつじ	義			西	かなめのかしら / おおいかんむり	要
	𦍌	ひつじへん	羚		R-144	瓜	うり	瓜

List of Radicals (page 5 of 6)

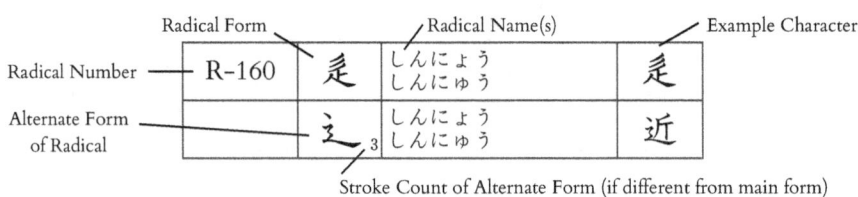

		7 strokes	
R-145	見	みる	親
R-146	角	つの つのへん	解
R-147	言	ことば ごんべん	記
R-148	谷	たに たにへん	谷
R-149	豆	まめ まめへん	豊
R-150	豕	いのこ ぶた	象
R-151	豸	むじな むじなへん	貌
R-152	貝	かい こがい	買
R-153	赤	あか あかへん	赦
R-154	走	はしる そうにょう	越
R-155	足	あし	足
	足	あしへん	路
R-156	身	み みへん	身
R-157	車	くるま くるまへん	転
R-158	辛	からい しん	辞
R-159	辰	たつ しんのたつ	農
R-160	辵	しんにょう しんにゅう	辵
	辶₃	しんにょう しんにゅう	近
	辶₄	しんにょう しんにゅう	逍
R-161	邑	おおざと	邑
†	阝₃	おおざと	郡

R-162	酉	ひよみのとり さけのとり	酒
R-163	釆	のごめ のごめへん	釈
R-164	里	さと さとへん	野
R-165	臣	しん	臨
R-166	舛	ます まいあし	舞
		8 strokes	
R-167	金	かね かねへん	銀
R-168	長	ながい	長
R-169	門	もんがまえ かどがまえ	開
R-170	阜	こざと	阜
†	阝₃	こざとへん	院
R-171	隶	たい れいづくり	隷
R-172	隹	ふるとり	集
R-173	雨	あめ	雨
	雨	あめかんむり	雲
R-174	靑	あお あおへん	青
	青	あお あおへん	静
R-175	非	あらず	非
		9 strokes	
R-176	面	めん	面
R-177	革	かくのかわ かわへん	靴
R-178	韭	にら	韭

†These two radicals have the same form, but appear in different locations within a character.

List of Radicals (page 6 of 6)

R-179	音	おと おとへん	響
R-180	頁	おおがい いちのかい	頭
R-181	風	かぜ	風
R-182	飛	とぶ	飛
R-183	食	しょく	養
	飠	しょくへん	飲
	𩙿	しょくへん	飫
R-184	首	くび	首
R-185	香	かおり	香
	10 strokes		
R-186	馬	うま うまへん	駅
R-187	骨	ほね ほねへん	髄
R-188	高	たかい	高
R-189	髟	かみがしら かみかんむり	髪
R-190	鬥	たたかいがまえ とうがまえ	鬧
R-191	鬯	ちょう においざけ	鬱
R-192	鬲	れきのかなえ	鬻
R-193	鬼	おに きにょう	魅
R-194	韋	なめしがわ	韓
	11 strokes		
R-195	魚	さかな うおへん	鯨
R-196	鳥	とり とりへん	鶏
R-197	鹵	ろ しお	鹼
R-198	鹿	しか	麗
R-199	麥	むぎ ばくにょう	麩
	麦	むぎ ばくにょう	麺
R-200	麻	あさ あさかんむり	靡

	麻	あさ あさかんむり	麿
	12 strokes		
R-201	黃	きいろ	黊
	黄	きいろ	黄
R-202	黍	きび	黎
R-203	黑	くろ	黴
	黒	くろ	黙
R-204	黹	ち ぬいとり	黻
	13 strokes		
R-205	黽	おおがえる	鼇
R-206	鼎	かなえ	鼎
R-207	鼓	つづみ	鼓
R-208	鼠	ねずみ	鼠
	14 strokes		
R-209	鼻	はな	鼻
R-210	齊	せい	齋
	斉	せい	斎
	15 strokes		
R-211	齒	は はへん	齟
	歯	は はへん	齢
	16 strokes		
R-212	龍	りゅう たつ	龍
	竜	りゅう たつ	竜
R-213	龜	かめ	龜
	亀	かめ	亀
	17 strokes		
R-214	龠	やく やくのふえ	龠

Appendices

補

Appendix A
Glossary of Key Terminology

English-language terms

bronze script (*kinbuntai*, きんぶんたい, 金文体): an ancient style of writing the characters, found on bronze artifacts in China—either as part of the mold, imprinted as the item was cast, or etched onto the item after casting. The forms of the characters varied across different regions of China.

character dictionary (*jiten*, じてん, 字典): a dictionary whose entries consist of individual characters, with each listing providing information about the character, such as reading, meaning, and compound words which contain the character. A typical Japanese character dictionary (*kanwajiten*, 漢和辞典) lists more than 10,000 different characters.

character substitution: the replacement of one character with another, such that the replacing character takes on some or all of the roles of the character being replaced. One type of character substitution is called *kakikae* (listed separately in this glossary).

clerical script (*reishotai*, れいしょたい, 隷書体): the way the characters were written just prior to the development of *kaisho*, the standard script. The character forms are similar to *kaisho*, but slightly wider than they are tall, and somewhat less ornate in appearance.

component (*ichibu*, いちぶ, 一部): any part of a character, consisting of one or more elements, or even part of a single element. The terms 'element' and 'component' are quite similar, but are distinguished in this book.

compound word (*jukugo*, じゅくご, 熟語): a fixed word or set phrase consisting of more than one character. Also called a *compound*.

counter word (*josūshi*, じょすうし, 助数詞): a special word, usually written with a single kanji, placed immediately after a number to denote the quantity of a particular type of countable object. Also called a *counter* or a *measure word*.

cursive script (*sōshotai*, そうしょたい, 草書体): a highly stylized way of writing the characters in a loose, quick fashion.

determinative: a component of a character whose purpose is to identify the general category of meaning that the character can be grouped into. There is not a commonly used equivalent term in Japanese; the Japanese term *ifu* (いふ, 意符) refers to any meaning-bearing component within a character, whether or not it is used in a determinative role (in English, such a component could be called a *signific*). The determinative is often confused with the *radical*, as the two concepts are similar.

determinative-phonetic character: a character which was created by combining a determinative component together with a phonetic component. By far the most common type of character, more than 90% of all characters are of this type. Using the terminology of the traditional six methods of character creation, a determinative-phonetic character is called a *keisei-moji* (形声文字). Abbreviated as *D-P character*.

element (*buhin*, ぶひん, 部品): one of the most basic piece parts that a character can be divided into that still has meaning associated with it. The character 休 ('rest'), for example, is made up of two elements: one meaning 'person,' and the other meaning 'tree.' The terms 'element' and 'component' are quite similar, but are distinguished in this book.

etymology (*kaiji*, かいじ, 解字): an explanation of the origin of a character, including why it has the form it has and why it includes the elements it does. Generally speaking, character etymologies are not known with certainty.

extended meaning: a character meaning that is not the original meaning of a character, but rather one that was acquired some time after the character was first created. For some characters, an extended meaning has become the principal meaning of the character.

false etymology: an explanation of the origin of a character which is popularly believed to be true, but in fact is not (or at least is very unlikely to be true).

false phonetic: a component within a character that appears to be the phonetic component of the character, but—for whatever reason—is not. For example, the component 复 is a phonetic component in most characters that contain it, indicating the character *on* reading *FUKU*. However, in the character 履, which has the *on* reading *RI*, the component does not act as a phonetic. So 复 is a false phonetic in 履. (In this particular case, the form of the character 履 changed over time, and now only coincidentally contains a component which resembles the phonetic 复.)

form (*jitai*, じたい, 字体): the composition of a character, including the elements that it is made up of and the strokes used to draw it. Variant characters (such as 氣 and 気) have different forms from each other. A similar term in Japanese, *jikei* (じけい, 字形), refers to the specific, precise shape that a character has when it is written or printed. Two instances of the same character that have the same form, but have minor differences between them in terms of how the strokes are drawn, have different *jikei*.

gothic script (*goshikkutai*, ゴシックたい, ゴシック体): a style of writing the characters similar to regular script, but with lines of equal thickness throughout, and without any type of ornate markings added to the ends of strokes. In English, this character style is called *sans-serif*.

homophone (*dō-on-i-gi-go*, どうおんいぎご, 同音異義語): a word which has the same pronunciation (reading) as another word, but a different meaning. Words which are homophones of each other are written identically in hiragana or katakana, but are written differently when using kanji.

ideograph: a character that was created by using one or more elements not literally, but figuratively to suggest the character meaning. For example, the character 林 means 'grove,' and was developed by using two 'tree' elements to suggest not two, but a relatively large number of trees. (Similarly, the character 森 means 'forest.') Using the terminology of the traditional six methods of character creation, a multi-element ideograph would be called a *kai-i-moji* (かいいもじ, 会意文字).

indicative character: a character that was created using a principle by which line segments are used to help indicate the character meaning. For example, the indicative character 本 consists of a line segment added onto the base (root) of a 'tree' character, marking that part of the character, and thereby suggesting the meaning 'root' or 'origin.' Using the terminology of the traditional six methods of character creation, an indicative character is called a *shiji-moji* (しじもじ, 指事文字).

long vowel sound (*chōon*, ちょうおん, 長音): a spoken vowel sound lasting twice the duration of a basic (short) vowel sound. In Japanese, long vowel sounds occur when a bare vowel mora (a single, short vowel sound with no leading consonant sound) immediately follows another mora having the same vowel sound.

meaning (*imi*, いみ, 意味): the meaning of a character. Characters can have more than one meaning associated with them, and the meaning can differ when the character appears in different words. When reading, the character meaning is determined based on context.

meaning shift: a phenomenon by which a character no longer represents its original meaning, and instead represents (primarily) an alternate, extended meaning that it acquired some time after it was first created.

mora (*mōra*, モーら, plural: morae): one single unit length of sound when speaking. For comparison, a syllable can consist of more than one morae. A short vowel sound has one mora, while a long vowel sound has two. The basic sounds of the Japanese language are all one mora in length.

oracle bone script (*kōkotsu-moji*, こうこつもじ, 甲骨文字): the earliest known way of writing the characters. Characters written in this style were carved onto hard substances, such as ox scapulae (shoulder blades) and turtle plastrons (the mostly flat underside shell), and used in divination: a kind of fortune-telling. After carving a query for the gods (regarding future weather, crop yields, battle outcomes, the monarch's health, etc.), a heat source—such as a hot poker—was applied to pits which were chiseled into the back side of the bone or shell, and the resulting cracks were analyzed to determine the answer to the query.

palatalized consonant (*yōon*, ようおん, 拗音): a consonant sound that is spoken as if it is immediately followed by a /y/ sound, with no intervening vowel sound between the two. When written in hiragana or katakana, palatalized consonants are represented with small versions of the *ya*, *yu* or *yo* characters, paired with and placed after a single hiragana character which, when written in *rōmaji*, ends in *i*.

phonetic borrowing: the borrowing of a character, based on its sound, to represent a word different in meaning from that already represented by the character.

phonetic component (*onpu*, おんぷ, 音符): a component of a character whose purpose is primarily to indicate the reading of the character (specifically, the *on* reading, in the case of Japanese). Also called a *phonetic*.

pictograph: a character that was created as a picture of the thing that it represents. For example, the character 魚 means 'fish,' and the form of the character originated as an image of a fish (oriented with the head at the top and tail fin at the bottom). Using the terminology of the traditional six methods of character creation, a pictographic character is called a *shōkei-moji* (しょうけいもじ, 象形文字).

prefix word (*settōji*, せっとうじ, 接頭辞): a partial word attached to the beginning of a root word, used to modify the meaning of that root word. For example, the prefix 未 (*mi*), meaning 'not yet,' when added to 完成 (*kansei*), meaning 'complete,' produces 未完成 (*mikansei*), meaning 'incomplete.'

principal reading: the most commonly used reading of a character. A single character can have both a principal *on* reading and a principal *kun* reading. A few characters have more than one of either of these.

radical (*bushu*, ぶしゅ, 部首): a specially-designated component of a character by which the character is organized within character dictionaries. For characters containing a determinative, the determinative component is usually designated as the radical.

reading (*yomikata*, よみかた, 読み方): how a character (or compound word, etc.) is pronounced / spoken.

regular script (*kaishotai*, かいしょたい, 楷書体): the most recent of the major historical different styles of writing the characters, still in use today. This script, called *kaisho* in Japanese, had become standard by the seventh century AD. It is based on a calligraphic representation of the characters (i.e., drawn with a brush and ink), and has significantly influenced most other character writing and printing styles in use today.

related readings: two different but similar *on* readings which both apply to the same character or phonetic component, and share a common derivation.

script (*shotai*, しょたい, 書体): a general style in which the characters as a set are written. Common scripts in use today include *kaisho*, *minchō*, and gothic.

seal script (*tenshotai*, てんしょたい, 篆書体): an old style of writing the characters in use as the main system of writing in China primarily during the Qin dynasty (221-206 BC). By the time of the succeeding Han dynasty, the seal script had already been reduced in role, primarily used only in the design of decorative name seals, from which the modern name of this script derives.

semi-cursive script (*gyōshotai*, ぎょうしょたい, 行書体): a way of writing the characters in a loose, quick fashion. The basic structure of a character (such as the elements it contains) is usually still visible.

stroke (*hikkaku*, ひっかく, 筆画): when writing a character, a single drawn line. More specifically, a line drawn from the time the writing instrument contacts the writing surface, to when it leaves the writing surface.

stroke count (*kakusū*, かくすう, 画数): the total number of strokes which make up a character.

stroke order (*hitsujun*, ひつじゅん, 筆順): the order in which strokes are drawn as a character is written.

stroke order diagram: a diagram which demonstrates the proper order in which strokes are drawn as a character is written.

suffix word (*setsubiji*, せつびじ, 接尾辞): a partial word attached to the end of a root word, used to modify the meaning of that root word. For example, when the character 化 (*ka*), which means 'change,' is appended to the word 国際 (*kokusai*), meaning 'international,' it produces the word 国際化 (*kokusaika*), meaning 'internationalization.'

syllabic /n/ sound (*hatsuon*, はつおん, 撥音): a sound in the Japanese phonology consisting only of a nasal /n/ sound, with no accompanying vowel sound. This sound is expressed in hiragana with the ん character, and in katakana with the ン character.

textbook script (*kyōkashotai*, きょうかしょたい, 教科書体): a character writing style very similar to regular script, but easier for students to emulate when learning to write characters.

traditional Japanese (*jōdai-nihongo*, じょうだいにほんご, 上代日本語): a version of the Japanese language spoken long ago, prior to the adoption of words from Chinese. The phonology (set of spoken sounds in the language) of traditional Japanese is different from that of modern Japanese.

typeface (*katsuji-shotai*, かつじしょたい, 活字書体): a complete set of characters in a specific, consistent design style, used when printing or displaying, such as on a computer monitor. Typefaces are made up of sets of fonts of various sizes.

variant character (*itaiji*, いたいじ, 異体字): an alternate way of writing a character that is identical with the standard form of the character in terms of meaning(s), reading(s), and usage. Simply put, another way to write the same character. Also called a *variant*.

Japanese-language terms

ashi (あし, 脚): a character region name, denoting the bottom part of a character. When appended to a component name, this term identifies that the component is commonly located at the bottom of a character.

ateji (あてじ, 当て字): the use of characters solely for their reading, with no regard for character meaning. This term also describes the characters themselves, when used in this way. In modern Japanese, *ateji* are used primarily to write words of native Japanese origin.

boinkōtai (ぼいんこうたい, 母音交代): a sound phenomenon found mostly in traditional Japanese in which the vowel sound in the final syllable (mora) of a noun changes when the noun is used as the first part of a compound word.

furigana (ふりがな, 振り仮名): small characters (usually hiragana, but sometimes katakana or *rōmaji*) placed near a word written with kanji, used to indicate the way the word is intended to be read.

hen (へん, 偏): a character region name, denoting the left side of a character. When appended to a component name, this term identifies that the component is commonly located on the left-hand side of a character.

hiragana (ひらがな, 平仮名): one of two 'syllabaries' used in the writing of Japanese. Used primarily for writing the equivalent of English prepositions and other small helper words, as well as *okurigana* and *furigana*.

hyōgaiji (ひょうがいじ, 表外字): characters not among the *jōyō kanji* (and, depending on the context, also not among the *jinmeiyō kanji*).

jinmeiyō kanji (じんめいようかんじ, 人名用漢字): a designated set of characters which can be used in assigning given names to newborn children.

jōyō kanji (じょうようかんじ, 常用漢字): a set of characters established by the Japanese government, considered to be the most essential characters for daily life. Following revisions to the set in 2010, there are a total of 2136 characters designated as *jōyō kanji*.

***jūbako* reading** (*jūbako-yomi*, じゅうばこよみ, 重箱読み): the reading of a two-character compound word which is read using the *on* reading of the first character and the *kun* reading of the second character. Compare with *yutō* reading.

jukujikun (じゅくじくん, 熟字訓): a compound word in which the characters are used only for their meaning, with no regard for either the *on* or *kun* readings of the individual characters in the word. For example, the word *otona* ('adult,' おとな, 大人) is written with characters meaning 'large' and 'person,' but the individual *on* and *kun* readings of these characters cannot be found within any part of the word *otona*. Such a compound word can be thought of as a multi-character *kun* reading.

***kaisho* script** (*kaishotai*, かいしょたい, 楷書体): (*see* regular script)

kakikae (かきかえ, 書き換え): a type of character substitution where one character is phased out of usage and another character takes on all the meanings of that phased out character (as well as retaining its own meanings). For example, the character 暗, meaning 'dark,' took over the role of the character 諳, meaning 'to memorize.' Today, the character 諳 is phased out of usage, and 暗 is used in compound words with both the 'dark' and 'memorize' meanings.

kamae (かまえ, 構 [also 構え]): a character region name, denoting any outer, enclosing part of a character comprising two or more sides (other than the two such regions with separate designations: *nyō* and *tare*). When appended to a component name, this term identifies that the component is located along two or more sides of a character.

kango (かんご, 漢語): a word imported from China, or a word read in the same way as a word imported from China, using the *on* reading of each character in the word.

kanji (かんじ, 漢字): Chinese writing characters.

kanmuri (かんむり, 冠): a character region name, denoting the top part of a character. When appended to a component name, this term identifies that the component commonly occupies the top of a character. The term *kashira* is also sometimes used for this region.

katakana (かたかな, 片仮名): one of two 'syllabaries' used in the writing of Japanese. Used primarily for writing words of foreign origin, and representing onomatopoeic sounds.

kokuji (こくじ, 国字): a kanji character (or characters) created in Japan.

***kun* reading** (*kun-yomi*, くんよみ, 訓読み): the reading of a character, compound word, etc., when it is used to write a word of Japanese origin.

kyōiku kanji (きょういくかんじ, 教育漢字): the set of characters taught to Japanese children during elementary school. Currently, there are a total of 1006 characters designated as *kyōiku kanji*.

mazegaki (まぜがき, 混ぜ書き): the writing of a word in such a way that some, but not all, of the kanji in it are replaced with hiragana.

***minchō* script** (*minchōtai*, みんちょうたい, 明朝体): a style of writing the characters similar to regular script, but with thin horizontal lines, thicker vertical lines, and triangular serifs. Named for the Ming Dynasty of China, the period during which the style became popular.

nanori (なのり, 名乗り): a special character reading, distinct from a character's *on* and *kun* readings, which is found almost exclusively in Japanese personal names.

nyō (にょう, 繞): a character region name, denoting the (combined) left and bottom sides of a character. When appended to a component name, this term identifies that the component is commonly found occupying the left-hand and bottom sides of a character.

okurigana (おくりがな, 送り仮名): the hiragana characters that appear within a word when it is written using kanji. For example, the word *atarashii* is usually written as 新しい. In this way of writing the word, the hiragana characters し and い are *okurigana*.

***on* reading** (*on-yomi*, おんよみ, 音読み): the reading of a character based on the way it was spoken in China.

rendaku (れんだく, 連濁): a sound phenomenon in Japanese in which the initial consonant sound of a word appearing within a compound word, in other than the starting position, changes from an unvoiced to a voiced sound. For example, when the words *mizu* and *ki* are put together to make a compound word, the reading becomes *mizugi*, with the unvoiced /k/ sound changing to a voiced /g/ sound. The occurrence of *rendaku* does not strictly obey a set of rules; whether or not a given compound word is affected by this phenomenon is somewhat unpredictable.

renjō (れんじょう, 連声): a sound phenomenon in Japanese in which the initial vowel sound of a word appearing within a compound word, in other than the starting position, changes by acquiring a starting consonant sound, the sound of which is the same as or similar to the ending sound of the preceding word in the compound. For example, when the characters *han* (反) and *ō* (応) are put together to make a two-character compound word, the reading becomes *hannō*, with an additional /n/ sound added onto the beginning of the second part of the compound. This sound change appears infrequently in modern Japanese.

rōmaji (ろーまじ, ローマ字): the characters of the Latin (Roman) alphabet.

sokuon (そくおん, 促音): a sound phenomenon in Japanese in which the final sound (mora) of the first part of a compound word is dropped out and replaced with an elongation of the initial consonant sound of the second part of the compound. For example, when the characters *ketsu* (欠) and *seki* (席) are put together into a compound word, the final mora of *ketsu* (*tsu*) is dropped, and replaced with an elongation of the /s/ sound of *seki*, resulting in a compound word reading of *kesseki* (けっせき). When preceding the consonant sounds /t/, /k/, or /p/, the *sokuon* sounds like an inaudible pause of one beat. Preceding /s/, it sounds like a one-beat hold of the start of the /s/ sound. When written in hiragana or katakana, the *sokuon* is expressed with a small version of the *tsu* character (the second character in けっせき), which itself is also called a *sokuon*.

tare (たれ, 垂): a character region name, denoting the (combined) top and left sides of a character. When appended to a component name, this term identifies that the component is commonly found occupying the top and left sides of a character.

tsukuri (つくり, 旁): a character region name, denoting the right side of a character. When appended to a component name, this term identifies that the component is located on the right-hand side of a character.

wago (わご, 和語): words of native Japanese origin.

yamato kotoba (やまとことば, 大和言葉): (see *wago*)

***yutō* reading** (*yutō-yomi*, ゆとうよみ, 湯桶読み): the reading of a two-character compound word which is read using the *kun* reading of the first character and the *on* reading of the second character. Compare with *jūbako* reading.

Appendix B
Japanese Romanization Styles

In Japanese, the term *rōmaji* (ローマ字; literally: 'Roman characters') refers to the letters of the Latin (also called Roman) alphabet. The entire Japanese language can be written in *rōmaji*. To do so, it is necessary to transliterate the Japanese sounds into the Latin alphabet. As some sounds in Japanese do not exactly match sounds made in English and other languages that use the Latin alphabet, there are multiple ways this can be done.

Today, there are two principal ways to 'romanize' the Japanese language: the Kunrei method and the Hepburn method. The Kunrei method, called *kunreishiki* (訓令式) in Japanese, is simpler and more consistent, and is the method first taught to Japanese schoolchildren. When reading text transliterated by this method, though, some sounds are not produced correctly by speakers of English and other foreign languages who are not familiar with Japanese pronunciation. The Hepburn method, called *hebonshiki* (ヘボン式) in Japanese, attempts to resolve this problem by using special forms for these sounds which would result in them being pronounced more accurately by speakers of English. One criticism of the Hepburn method, though, is that when studying the Japanese language using Hepburn romanization, it is harder to understand Japanese grammatical inflection, as patterns are obscured.

Kunrei and Hepburn Differences

The following table shows the basic (single mora) sounds of Japanese that are represented differently using the Kunrei and Hepburn methods. For each sound, the hiragana representation is shown, together with both the Kunrei romanization and the Hepburn romanization.

Hiragana	Kunrei	Hepburn	Hiragana	Kunrei	Hepburn
し	si	shi	ちゃ	tya	cha
ち	ti	chi	ちゅ	tyu	chu
つ	tu	tsu	ちょ	tyo	cho
ふ	hu	fu	じゃ	zya	ja
じ	zi	ji	じゅ	zyu	ju
ぢ	zi	ji	じょ	zyo	jo
しゃ	sya	sha	ぢゃ	zya	ja
しゅ	syu	shu	ぢゅ	zyu	ju
しょ	syo	sho	ぢょ	zyo	jo

Vowels

With both the Kunrei and Hepburn methods, individual vowels are romanized in the same way. In modern Japanese there are only five basic vowel sounds, all short in duration. (These vowels can be grouped together to create more complex vowel sounds, though.) Written in *rōmaji*, these vowels are represented with the letters *a, i, u, e,* and *o*, but these letters were assigned based on a pronunciation corresponding with romance languages such as Italian, not with English. They are pronounced as follows (all spoken with a very short duration):

Hiragana	あ	い	う	え	お
Rōmaji	*a*	*i*	*u*	*e*	*o*
Pronunciation	'ah'	'ee'	'ooh'	'eh'	'oh'

Long Vowels

There is some variability in how long vowel sounds (two of the same vowel sound spoken consecutively) are romanized. The most common ways are to:

- Use the same vowel twice, written consecutively.

- Use a single vowel, but one with a special symbol placed on top of it to indicate that it is a long vowel, such as ō or ô. The first of these symbols (the straight line) is called a macron, and the second is called a circumflex.

- Use only a single vowel to represent the full long vowel sound.

- Use two consecutive vowels, but ones which are different from each other. This method is only used with the *e* and *o* long vowel sounds, writing the long vowel forms as *ei* and *ou*, respectively.

The city name Kyoto (きょうと, 京都), whose first syllable is spoken with a long vowel sound, would be written in each of the above ways as follows:

Kyooto   (repeat the vowel)

Kyōto   (use the macron form of the vowel)

Kyoto   (use only a single vowel)

Kyouto   (use two different vowels, written consecutively)

The third one of these, Kyoto, is how the city is commonly romanized for a foreign audience.

Other ways of representing long vowels are sometimes used when writing certain people and place names. For example, the long *o* vowel sound is sometimes written as *oh*. Using this style, the city name Osaka (おおさか, 大阪), which begins with a long vowel sound, would be written as Ohsaka. This name is most commonly written with just a single vowel, though: Osaka.

Appendix C

Principles of Stroke Order

This appendix describes some of the principles governing the order in which strokes are drawn when writing characters. The proper stroke orders for most characters follow the principles described herein, although there are some exceptions.

This set of principles is not fully comprehensive; it does not explain how to draw every stroke of every single character. Rather, it includes some of the most commonly used principles, found in the writing of a number of different characters. Ultimately, the proper stroke order of each character must be learned individually, but being familiar with these principles will help you to remember the proper stroke order for many characters, and speed up the memorization process.

To master drawing characters using the proper stroke order it is best to practice drawing them repeatedly as you learn them. Doing so will help you to develop a kind of 'muscle memory' that helps you to continue to draw the characters correctly as you write them later.

Although some of these principles may seem complicated at first, after repeated practice writing characters with these principles in mind, they will begin to make sense and will not seem so complicated.

The principles described herein are divided into two groups: general principles which apply to a wide variety of characters, and principles for drawing specific components found within a number of different characters.

Stroke order (and direction) is indicated in the example characters by means of small numbers which mark the starting point of each stroke in a character.

A. General Principles

1. Stroke Direction

Generally, vertical strokes are drawn from the top to the bottom, and horizontal strokes are drawn from the left to the right:

Most slanted or curved strokes are drawn from the higher endpoint to the lower endpoint. (See stroke #1 in the first character below, and strokes #3 and #4 in the second.)

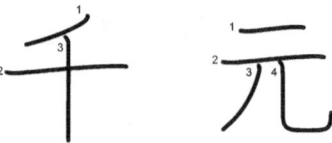

2. Top to Bottom, Left to Right

Characters are generally drawn in an order such that strokes in the upper part of a character are drawn before strokes in the lower part, and strokes on the left side of a character are drawn before strokes on the right. In other words, characters are generally drawn in a top-to-bottom, left-to-right order:

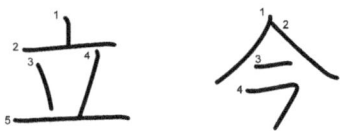

3. Bends within a Single Stroke

Note that stroke #4 in the character on the right above has a sharp bend in it. Single strokes are allowed to bend when drawn, but only a bend downward when moving to the right (as in the above example), or a bend to the right when moving downward. The following three characters each contain a stroke with bends. Specifically, they are: stroke #1 in the first character (bending downward), stroke #3 in the second character (bending to the right), and stroke #6 in the third character (first bending to the right, and then bending downward).

Note that the following character:

could be physically drawn with a single stroke without the pen leaving the paper—starting in the upper left and ending with the hook at the bottom. Doing so, though, would violate this principle in two places: bending to the left when moving down, and bending down when moving to the left. This character is properly drawn with a total of three strokes, two of which have bends in them (stroke #1 and stroke #3).

APPENDIX C

4. Diagonal Crossing Strokes

In characters in which two diagonal strokes cross each other, the stroke moving down from the right to the left is drawn before the one moving down from the left to the right:

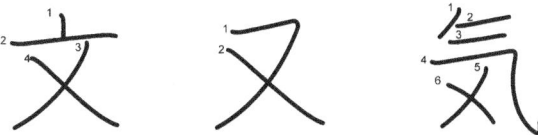

5. Downward Left Stroke

A stroke moving downward to the left that exactly ends at a point along another stroke moving straight downward or down to the right will be drawn immediately before that other stroke. See stroke #1 in the first character below, and stroke #5 in the second, for examples.

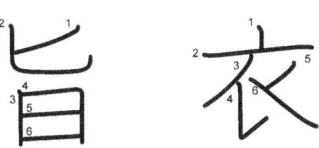

6. Short, Angled Strokes

Short, angled strokes not connected to any other stroke of a character are usually drawn in the normal top-to-bottom, left-to-right order when in symmetric pairs:

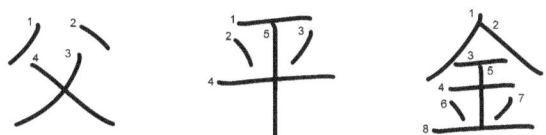

but single short, angled strokes (i.e., not part of a pair) are usually drawn last when located in the bottom part of a character or in the upper right:

When located in any other part of a character, these single strokes are usually drawn in the normal top-to-bottom, left-to-right order:

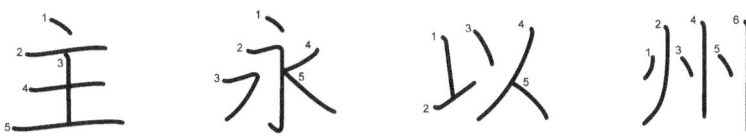

7. Four-sided Enclosure

A four-sided, box-shaped component is drawn with three strokes: the first down the left side, the second across the top and down the right side (as a single, bending stroke), and the third along the bottom. If this component encloses other elements within it, then its left, top, and right sides are drawn first, followed by the internal contents, and then finally the bottom side of the enclosure, as in the final two examples below.

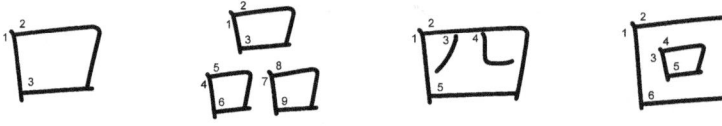

8. Three-sided Enclosures

a. A three-sided enclosure consisting of a left side, top, and right side is drawn before the contents it encloses. The left side is drawn first, and then the top and right side are drawn as a single stroke. Examples:

b. For a three-sided enclosure consisting of top, left, and bottom sides, the top is drawn first, followed by the interior contents, and finally the left side and bottom are then drawn as a single stroke. Example:

c. For a three-sided enclosure consisting of left, bottom, and right sides, the interior contents are drawn first, followed by the left and bottom sides (as a single stroke) and then the right side. Example:

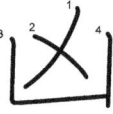

9. Strokes Crossing into Enclosure Top

Strokes which cross from above into either a four-sided enclosure or a three-sided left-top-right enclosure are drawn immediately after the top and sides of the enclosure are drawn:

10. Vertical Centerline Strokes

For long vertical strokes which pass through the center of a character, the order in which the stroke is drawn depends on several factors.

a. If the stroke is disconnected at both the top and bottom, draw it last:

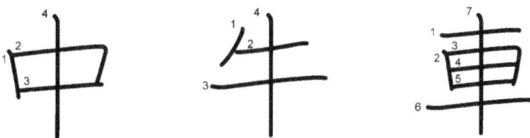

unless there are strokes which originate somewhere along that vertical center stroke. In that case, those strokes are drawn *after* the vertical center stroke:

b. If the vertical center stroke is connected to a horizontal stroke at the top but disconnected at the bottom, extending down below all horizontal strokes, draw it last:

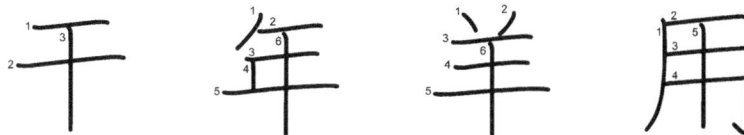

c. If the vertical center stroke exactly meets up with a horizontal stroke at the bottom, regardless of whether or not it is connected at the top, it is always drawn *before* the bottom horizontal stroke:

In most such characters, the vertical stroke(s) is/are drawn just after the first horizontal stroke:

There are exceptions, though, where the vertical stroke is drawn later:

Regardless, though, the vertical stroke is always drawn at some point prior to the bottom horizontal stroke.

11. Separable Elements Drawn Individually

When a character is separable into a set of clearly distinct elements, the character is usually drawn in a way such that each element is drawn completely before moving on to the next one. For example, the character 'forest' (below left), which consists of three tree elements, is drawn one tree at a time, starting with the top element and then the lower left one and finally the lower right one. The character 'cry; call out' (below right) consists of a mouth element and a bird element, side-by-side. First the left element is drawn completely, and then the right one.

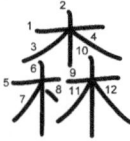 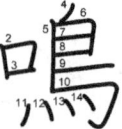

A few elements, though, are special in that the drawing of their strokes is mixed together with the drawing of other nearby elements. For example, with the four-sided enclosure that we already saw (item #7), if the enclosure contains elements within it, the left, top and right sides of the enclosure are drawn before the interior contents, but the bottom stroke is drawn after the interior contents. In the next section, two more examples of such special elements are given (see item #15).

12. Complete Left-Right or Top-Bottom Separation

If an imaginary perfectly horizontal line can pass all the way through a character without touching any part of it (i.e., the character can be cleanly divided into upper and lower parts), the components above the imaginary line are all completely drawn before any of the components below the line.

Similarly, if an imaginary perfectly vertical line can pass all the way through a character without touching any part of it (i.e., the character can be cleanly divided into left and right parts), the components to the left of the imaginary line are completely drawn before the components to the right of the line.

With the character on the left below, a horizontal imaginary line can pass clear through the character (near the bottom), but a vertical line cannot. So the top components are drawn first, and then the bottom component. With the character on the right, a vertical line can pass all the way through, but not a horizontal line. Thus, the left component is drawn first, followed by the components on the right.

If you look carefully at the following character, you can see that an imaginary vertical dividing line can pass straight through from top to bottom, but there is no point within the character where an imaginary horizontal line can pass straight through from left to right without touching part of a component. Accordingly, with this character the components on the left-hand side are drawn completely before the components on the right-hand side.

This character can be divided into four distinct, separate components, each of which does not touch any other (厶, 月, ヒ, and ヒ). When writing this character, per this and the previous principle, each of these components is drawn completely, one at a time, and in this order: upper left, lower left, upper right, and finally lower right.

B. Specific Components

In this section are principles unique to particular components which can be found within a number of different characters.

13. *Shinnyō* and *Ennyō* Elements

The *shinnyō* (辶) and *ennyō* (廴) elements are drawn after the components that appear to their upper right. Examples:

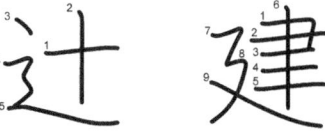

Note that both the *shinnyō* and *ennyō* elements above *could* be drawn with two strokes, but the official stroke count for each of these elements is three.

14. 'Can' / 'Allowed' Component

The 'can' / 'allowed' component (below) is written with a stroke order such that the top stroke is drawn first, followed by the box element, followed by the downward stroke. Note that the two strokes which form the upper right of the character are not drawn consecutively.

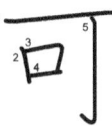

Also note that the similar-looking 'official' / 'govern' character is drawn differently (the upper right portion consists of only a single stroke):

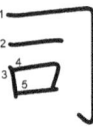

15. 'Pike' and 'Stringed Arrow' Elements

The similar-looking elements:[1]

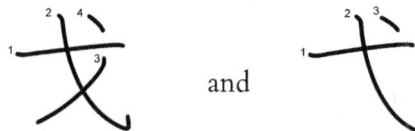

are drawn non-continuously if another component is placed within the lower left part of the element. In that case, the horizontal stroke is drawn first, followed by the other component in the lower left, and finally the remaining parts of the element. Examples:

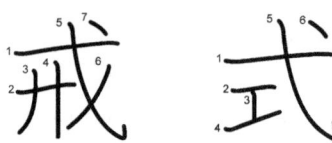

16. *Kabane* Component

The *kabane* component, which resembles a capital P in the Latin alphabet:

is drawn in the following order: top and right side (as a single stroke), lower horizontal stroke, left side. Examples:

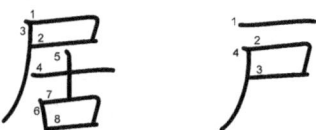

There are other unrelated components which contain the same strokes as this element, but with an extra interior vertical or horizontal stroke as well. In these cases, the interior stroke is drawn just before the lower horizontal stroke:

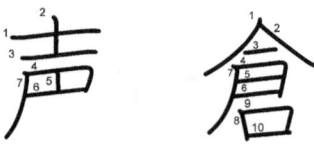

This principle also applies to some other similar-looking characters, such as:

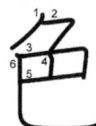

---

[1] The first of these two elements is used in characters related to warfare, and is believed to represent a type of long, bladed spear, similar to a pike. The origin of the second element is less clear; it may depict either an arrow with string attached (used for hunting birds), or a type of stake used for tethering animals.

17. 'Cliff' Component

For characters including a 'cliff'-like component (a pair of strokes, one on top and one on the left, which resemble a cliff in shape):

the top stroke is usually drawn before the left-side stroke, as in the following examples:

This is true even for characters containing a similar component in which the top stroke includes a downward, hooked portion:

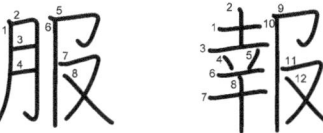

An exception to this principle occurs when another stroke passes through (or appears as if it almost passes through) the top stroke. In that case, the left-side stroke is drawn first:

When the top stroke is not horizontal, but is actually a stroke moving down to the left, it is always drawn first:

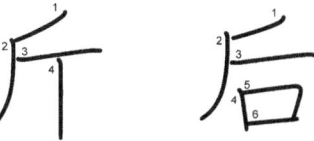

18. 'Water'-like Components

In characters containing the 'water' element:

or an element similar in appearance, the center downward stroke is drawn first, followed by the strokes to the left and then the strokes to the right:

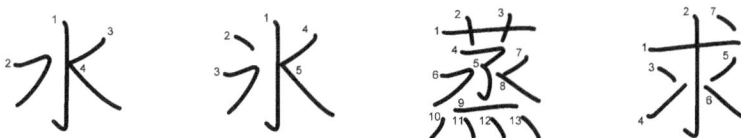

19. 'Person'-shaped Component Crossed by Horizontal Strokes

If a character includes a pair of strokes which resemble those of the 'person' element:

with one or more horizontal strokes passing through it, the 'person'-like pair of strokes is drawn *after* the horizontal crossing stroke(s):

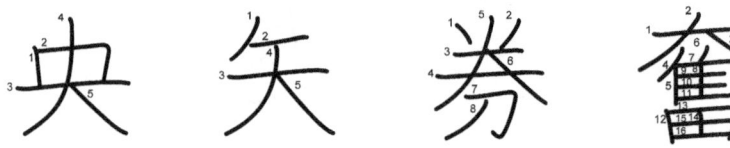

In the final example above, the two strokes resembling the 'person' element are separated, not touching each other. The same principle still applies, though.

Similarly, the strokes resembling the 'person' element within the 'fire' character:

are drawn last, after the two short strokes.

20. 'Left Hand' Element

The order in which the two strokes of the 'left hand' element:

are drawn varies from character to character. There are two different general principles, either one of which could be used to determine the proper order of drawing these strokes, but both are a bit complicated. Use either one of these principles if it helps you to remember the stroke order.

1. The first stroke of the 'left hand' element is drawn in the same direction as the first stroke of the component to its lower right.

2. If the component appearing to the lower right of the 'left hand' element has vertical strokes on each side, then the downward stroke of the 'left hand' element is drawn first. Otherwise, the horizontal stroke is drawn first.

Examples:

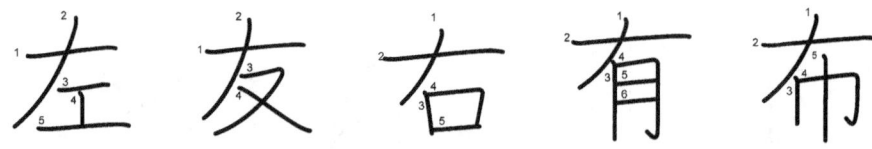

APPENDIX C

21. 'Tare' / 'Hana' Component

When the following set of strokes appear within a character:

they are drawn in the following order: topmost horizontal stroke, second horizontal stroke, short vertical strokes (left then right), bottom horizontal stroke, and finally centerline vertical stroke. Examples:

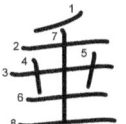  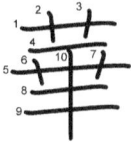

Note that in each of these cases, the centerline vertical stroke follows the earlier principle for such strokes (#10), and so, for example, is drawn last in the third character above.

Appendix D

The Traditional Six Principles of Character Creation

Many modern texts which discuss the etymology of Chinese characters refer to a set of six different principles by which the characters were created. The six principles concept has reached an iconic status since being first described approximately 2000 years ago. It has become well known primarily because of its inclusion in the classic and influential early character dictionary *Shuowen Jiezi*, published in the second century AD in China.

The six principles concept has its origin in the ancient text (likely third or second century BC) *Zhou Li* ('*Rites of Zhou*'). Within that work, among the duties listed of a particular government official is teaching children of nobility and bureaucrats the 六書, a term consisting of characters meaning 'six' and 'writing.' Although the exact meaning of this term is unclear, and no further explanation was given in that text, later scholars took this to mean the six principles of character creation, several of them going so far as to propose what they believed to be those six principles. The six principles described in the *Shuowen Jiezi* are the most influential set, and continue to be frequently referenced to this day.

Today, we know there were not precisely six principles that governed the creation of all characters. However, because the six principles concept continues to be referenced (most Japanese kanji dictionaries still utilize it), and the principles identified generally correspond to actual methods of character creation, familiarity with these principles may be worthwhile for some kanji learners. The version of the six principles as described in the *Shuowen Jiezi* is therefore briefly described in this appendix.

Note that the first four of these six principles are actual principles of character creation, but the final two appear to involve characters whose meanings have changed, and so are not really principles of creation, but rather principles of how a character obtained its eventual main meaning. Furthermore, the description of these principles in the *Shuowen Jiezi* itself is extremely brief and not perfectly clear, which has resulted in much confusion and debate. Differing interpretations of these six principles, especially the last two, abound.

Within the *Shuowen Jiezi*, for each of the six principles cited, the following information was provided:

- The name of the principle. Exactly two kanji characters are used in each name.

- A very brief description of the meaning of the principle.

- Two examples of characters that were created using the principle.

Following is the author's interpretation of the six principles as described in the *Shuowen Jiezi*. Note that the names of the principles given here (both the *rōmaji* and hiragana versions) are based on Japanese readings of the characters.[1]

1. *shiji* (しじ, 指事, 'indicated thing') These are characters which use special marks to help *indicate* the character meaning. Examples given: 上 and 下. The 上 character in an earlier form was simply a small line (or sometimes a dot) above a longer horizontal line, suggesting the meaning 'above,' while the 下 character consisted of a small line below a larger line, indicating 'below.' This is equivalent to the **indicative** type of character in this book.

2. *shōkei* (しょうけい, 象形, 'image form') These are characters created based on a drawing that *resembles* the object depicted. The example characters given are 日 and 月, which in their earliest forms resembled the sun and moon, respectively. This is equivalent to the **pictographic** type of character in this book.

3. *keisei* (けいせい, 形聲, 'form and sound') These are characters in which one component indicates the *category of meaning* of the character, while another component indicates the *phonetic*, or pronunciation of the character. Examples given: 江 ('inlet') and 河 ('river'). In each of these two characters, the left-hand element indicates that the character has to do with water, and the right-hand component indicates the overall pronunciation of the character. This is equivalent to the **determinative-phonetic** type of character in this book.

4. *kai-i* (かいい, 會意, 'assembled meaning') These are characters created based on *combining the meanings* of individual elements to suggest the overall meaning of the character. Examples given: 武 and 信. 武 is a combination of a pike (a long, bladed thrusting spear)[2] and a foot, and is thereby believed to represent a weapon and a foot soldier together, suggesting the character meaning 'military.' 信, meaning 'trust,' is a combination of a person and words, perhaps suggesting that a man's word is his trust. Characters in this category are sometimes referred to as *associative* characters. This category is equivalent to a multiple-component version of the **ideographic** type of character in this book.

5. *tenchū* (てんちゅう, 轉注, 'transfer – annotate') This is easily the least understood of the six categories. Various theories exist for the meaning of this category. The example characters given are 考 and 老, which, when the *Shuowen Jiezi* was compiled, had approximately the same meaning as each other: elderly person. (考 now means 'ponder; consider.') From the brief description in the *Shuowen Jiezi*, this category may have to do with characters having a **mutually shared meaning**. However, this is not fully clear, and this category is interpreted in various ways in modern textbooks.

6. *kashaku* (かしゃく, 假借, 'borrow – loan') The meaning of this category is unclear, but may refer to characters that were *borrowed for their sound* to represent secondary meanings distinct from the original. The new meaning could be an extended meaning that is related to the original, or could have no connection to the original meaning other than having the same sound. Examples given: 令 and 長, which today mean 'command; order' and 'length,' respectively. Nowadays, this principle is most often explained as **phonetic borrowing**.

---

[1] As character meanings have changed over time, some of the intended meanings of the characters used in the names of these principles may differ from the modern meanings of those characters. In the above English translations of the principle names, the intended meanings are inferred.

[2] The pike element within this character is drawn differently than in most other characters containing the equivalent element (戈).

Appendix E
The Origin of *Kana*

In addition to kanji, the Japanese written language consists of two phonetic writing systems: ***hiragana*** (平仮名) and ***katakana*** (片仮名). Together, these systems are referred to as ***kana***.

Unlike the Latin alphabet, in which vowel sounds and consonant sounds are represented separately with different symbols, each *kana* character represents a complete spoken syllable.[1] For that reason, these writing systems are referred to as 'syllabaries,' rather than 'alphabets.'

Hiragana and katakana were developed separately, but they are duplicates of each other in that they each contain a set of characters which correspond to the same sounds in the Japanese language. Any spoken sounds in Japanese can be written in either hiragana or katakana. The only difference between the syllabaries is how they are typically used in the writing of Japanese.

Because there are characters to represent every possible spoken syllable in the language, hiragana and katakana contain many more characters than does a typical alphabet. There are presently 46 unique characters in each syllabary. Some of them can be modified by adding special marks (called *dakuten* and *handakuten*), and some of them have smaller versions with special purposes.[2]

The term *kana* developed as a contraction of *kari-na* (仮字), meaning 'borrowed character.'[3] It is now written as 仮名, as the *na* reading of the 字 character has become obsolete.

Representation of Sounds

To be precise, the hiragana and katakana syllabaries each contain characters for all of the different possible basic syllables that could be spoken in an earlier form of the Japanese language. Consistent with that version of the language, each character represents either just a short vowel sound (V), or the combination of an initial consonant sound and a short vowel sound (CV). A few additional sounds were incorporated into the language later and still exist in the language today: the *sokuon*, the palatalized consonant, and the syllabic /*n*/ sound. The *sokuon* is represented by a small form of the *tsu* character (っ/ッ). Palatalized consonants are represented by pairing smaller forms of the *ya*, *yu*, and *yo* characters (ゃ/ャ, ゅ/ュ, and ょ/ョ) with another character. The syllabic /*n*/ sound is represented by the later addition of another character to the syllabaries: ん/ン.

---

[1] Technically, as discussed in Part 1, Chapters 7 and 8, it's more accurate to say that each character represents a single spoken *mora*.
[2] The reader is assumed to be familiar with the basic composition and usage of the kana syllabaries; those topics will not be discussed here in detail.
[3] This term reflects the origin of the kana as kanji which were borrowed for their sound and simplified in form (see next page). The term was used in contrast to the ma-na (真字) or 'true characters,' which were the full kanji themselves, used for their meaning.

Originating from Kanji

Kanji were the first written characters to be used in Japan. Later, both hiragana and katakana were developed in Japan, each deriving from kanji. The forms of the individual characters have the appearance they do because of the kanji characters they were modeled after.

Development of the syllabaries grew out of a method of using kanji for their phonetic value (i.e., sound) to write words in the native Japanese language. Specifically, when native Japanese sentences were first written using kanji, many of the characters chosen were used primarily just for their sound (i.e., *on* reading); only a small number were used for their meaning. Only a limited subset of all known kanji were used in this phonetic role, but sometimes more than one different character was chosen to represent the same sound.

The oldest known surviving Japanese poetry collection: the *Manyōshu* (万葉集), is one of the early written works to use kanji in this way. From its title, the subset of kanji which were used phonetically to write Japanese sentences became known as the *manyōgana*. From this limited subset of characters, both hiragana and katakana were born, in roughly the ninth century AD, with katakana predating hiragana.

The name 'katakana,' with 'kata' meaning 'part,' refers to the fact that only parts of kanji, not whole characters, were used. Specifically, only from one to four strokes were taken from the *manyōgana* characters (from either the standard or the cursive forms)—most often the initial or final strokes. In some cases, an entire character was used when its total stroke count was small.

Hiragana were based on the simplified, cursive script forms of the *manyōgana* characters, and were initially used primarily by women, who were not taught kanji. The origin of the 'hira' part of the term 'hiragana' is unclear; it may derive from the 'common' or 'ordinary' meanings of the 平 character, so named to contrast the characters with katakana.

Originally, many spoken syllables could be represented by more than one hiragana character, but in the year 1900 the redundant hiragana characters were purged, with one standard character chosen to write each of the then 48 sounds. These redundant, purged hiragana characters are now referred to as *hentaigana* (変体仮名), and some can still be seen on shop signs, product packaging, and in other places where a traditional look is desired. The syllabic /n/ sound was not recognized as a proper sound in Japanese writing until this 1900 reform, and so, not previously having its own character, was assigned a *hentaigana* for the /mu/ character: ん, a sound which it often replaced in colloquial Japanese.

The specific source kanji (more specifically, *manyōgana*) used to create the kana syllabaries are not all known with complete certainty, and so there is some slight disagreement among different sources; the most commonly cited source characters are listed in the table on the next page. In many cases, as you can see in the table, the same kanji was the source of both the hiragana and the katakana form. Note that most of the source characters were used for their *on* reading, but a few, such as 江 and 女, were used for their *kun* reading.

Two pairs of characters, appearing in the table under /wi/ and /we/, have been purged from the official set by orthography reforms, but are still included in the table for completeness. These characters are now mostly obsolete, but are sometimes still encountered in certain contexts. When used, they are sometimes pronounced as /i/ and /e/, or /yi/ and /ye/, due to sound changes which have taken place in Japanese.

Characters are listed in the table using the modern standard order, called *gojūon*. In each cell, the hiragana character is on the left and the katakana equivalent is on the right. Immediately below them the source kanji characters are shown. Where the source kanji is the same for both the hiragana and katakana characters, only that one character is shown.

Source Kanji for Hiragana and Katakana

A		I		U		E		O	
あ	ア	い	イ	う	ウ	え	エ	お	オ
安	阿	以	伊	宇		衣	江	於	(於)
KA		**KI**		**KU**		**KE**		**KO**	
か	カ	き	キ	く	ク	け	ケ	こ	コ
	加		幾		久	計	介		己
SA		**SHI**		**SU**		**SE**		**SO**	
さ	サ	し	シ	す	ス	せ	セ	そ	ソ
左	散		之	寸	須		世		曽
TA		**CHI**		**TSU**		**TE**		**TO**	
た	タ	ち	チ	つ	ツ	て	テ	と	ト
太	多	知	千		川		天		止
NA		**NI**		**NU**		**NE**		**NO**	
な	ナ	に	ニ	ぬ	ヌ	ね	ネ	の	ノ
	奈		仁		奴		祢		乃
HA		**HI**		**FU**		**HE**		**HO**	
は	ハ	ひ	ヒ	ふ	フ	へ	ヘ	ほ	ホ
波	八		比		不		部		保
MA		**MI**		**MU**		**ME**		**MO**	
ま	マ	み	ミ	む	ム	め	メ	も	モ
末	万		美	武	牟		女		毛
YA				**YU**				**YO**	
や	ヤ			ゆ	ユ			よ	ヨ
	也				由			与	與
RA		**RI**		**RU**		**RE**		**RO**	
ら	ラ	り	リ	る	ル	れ	レ	ろ	ロ
	良		利	留	流		礼		呂
WA		**WI**				**WE**		**WO**	
わ	ワ	ゐ	ヰ			ゑ	エ	を	ヲ
	和	為	井				恵	遠	乎
N									
ん	ン								
无	尓								

Appendix F
Radicals in Depth

F.1 Introduction

This appendix provides a detailed explanation of many aspects of character radicals. A total of 214 different radicals are designated in this book. A complete list of these radicals (numbered R-1 through R-214) is provided in Part 2 of the book. Radicals are also discussed in Part 1, Chapter 4.

This book does not place much emphasis on the radical, so it is recommended that the content of this appendix, and radicals in general, be studied only by those interested in specifically learning about character radicals. Do note, though, that knowing radical names (and element names in general) can help with learning and remembering kanji. The naming of radicals is explained in this appendix, and radical names are included in the radical list in Part 2 of the book.

F.2 Radical Designations

Even though most characters consist of two or more elements, by definition each character has only one radical. It is based on that radical that characters are ordered in kanji dictionaries.

As explained in Part 1, Chapter 4, for many characters the choice of component to be the radical is an obvious one. But for some characters, any of several elements could be designated as the radical, and the choice is rather arbitrary. For a small number of characters, there is disagreement among different character dictionaries as to which component is the radical. In cases of disagreement, the author recommends following the standard established by the Japan Kanji Aptitude Testing Foundation, which administers the Kanji Kentei test.

F.3 The Set of Radicals

Most character dictionaries identify exactly or approximately 214 different character radicals, assigning each character in the dictionary to one of those radicals. The quantity 214 has become standard because of the influential *Kangxi Zidian* dictionary published several centuries ago in China. The particular set of 214 radicals defined in that dictionary is still used by many dictionaries today.

In some modern Japanese kanji dictionaries, though, the set of radicals used varies slightly from the '*Kangxi* radicals.' This is mostly because of changes that have been made in the forms of some characters since the *Kangxi Zidian* was issued.

For example, as part of the effort in Japan to simplify the forms of characters, some complicated components in some characters were removed and replaced with a new, simpler component called *tsu kanmuri*:

ハノ

which did not previously exist in any character. In many of the characters which now contain this component, the part that it replaced included what had been the character radical, making it necessary to choose a different radical for the character. In response, many dictionaries established the *tsu kanmuri* component as a new radical, and assigned some of those characters to it.[1]

With this component added as a radical, then, to keep the total number of radicals at the traditional quantity of 214, another radical needed to be purged. This was done in some dictionaries by combining what were once two distinct radicals:

夂 and 夊

into one. This choice is sensible, as among all *jōyō kanji* which contain the second radical (夊), its form has been altered and it now appears identical to the first one (夂).

Other than small changes such as these, the list of 214 radicals in Part 2 of this book closely follows the set of *Kangxi* radicals. (There are also some minor stroke count differences, discussed later in this appendix.)

Note that within character dictionaries the distribution of characters among the various radicals is uneven. For example, some of the 214 radicals have hundreds of characters grouped under them, whereas others have only a few. The set of radicals was chosen so that all known characters could be categorized into the smallest possible number of groups. But for characters consisting of only uncommon components, it was often necessary to place them in a category with only a few other characters sharing one of those components. Additionally, some characters consisting of only a single, complex component were categorized based on only a portion of the character, grouped with a few other characters sharing that same piece part (as discussed in Part 1, Chapter 4).

F.4 Radical Names

The Japanese have given their own names to all the standard radicals. In fact, many of the radicals have been assigned more than one name, and so can be referred to in one of several ways. In the Part 2 radicals list, the most commonly used names for each radical are shown.

---

[1] This component was also adopted as part of the character simplification effort in mainland China, but was applied to fewer characters than in Japan.

Some of the radical names contain within them a reference to a character region, such as *hen* or *kanmuri*. Generally, the region is included in the radical name when the radical is predominantly or exclusively located in that region of a character.

If the form of the radical is altered when it is located in a particular region, that altered form of the radical will usually have its own special name, which usually includes the region name as part of it. For example, when the 'hand' component on the left below appears on the left-hand side of a character, it assumes the altered form shown below on the right:

That altered form of the radical, appearing in characters such as 打, is called *te hen*. When appearing in a character in the original (above left) form, such as in 挙, the radical is simply called *te*.

In addition to the possible appending of a region name, which indicates where within a character the radical is usually located, radical names were in most cases derived using one of the following ten principles.

1. The radical's individual piece parts are described by using the names of katakana or kanji characters they resemble. Examples:

    - The radical *tsu kanmuri* (ᅟ) resembles a vertically compressed katakana *tsu* character (ツ). (*Kanmuri* is a character region name, and indicates that this component usually appears at the top of characters.)

    - The radical *ichita* (歹) resembles the kanji *ichi* (一) on top of the katakana *ta* character (タ).

    - The radical *rumata* (殳) resembles the katakana *ru* character (ル) (with a connecting line at the top) on top of the kanji read as *mata* (又).

    - The radical *nogi* (禾) resembles the katakana *no* character (ノ) on top of the 'tree' kanji (木), read as *ki* (changed to *gi* via the *rendaku* process).

2. The radical is named for an object that it resembles. Examples:

    - The radical *tatebō* (｜) gets its name from the fact that it looks like an upright (*tate*) pole or stick (*bō*). This radical is also simply called *bō*.

    - Both names of the *nabebuta / keisan kanmuri* radical (亠) describe what it looks like. *Nabebuta* means 'pot lid,' and *keisan* means 'paperweight.'

3. The radical's name is its reading when it is used by itself as a standalone character. Either the character's *on* reading or *kun* reading may be used. Examples:

    - The radical *sun* (寸), as a standalone character, has an *on* reading of *sun*.

    - The radical *tsuchi* (土), as a standalone character, has a *kun* reading of *tsuchi*.

In some cases, rather than just the reading of the character by itself, the radical name is a word that is written in part using the character. Examples:

- The radical *tomeru* (止), as a standalone character, is part of the word *tomeru*, written in kanji and hiragana as 止める.

- The radical *arazu* (非) is named for an archaic Japanese expression meaning 'it is not so.' This expression is written as 非ず.

4. The radical is identified by referring to a particular character that contains it as one part. Usually, a region term is also used to refer to the specific part of the source character where the radical is located. Examples:

- The radical *ito gashira* (幺) consists of the upper part (*kashira*) of the *ito* character (糸: 'thread').

- The radical *gan dare* (厂) consists of the upper and left-hand parts (*tare*) of the *gan* character (雁: 'goose').

Rather than specify a region within the source character, the particular component can be identified in other ways, such as by its meaning. Example:

- The radical *furutori* (隹) appears within the character 舊 (now written 旧), which has the meaning 'old; former' and is read as *furu* in the Japanese word 舊い (*furui*). The meaning of the radical is 'bird' (*tori*).

5. The radical is a modified or abbreviated form of a character. Its name includes the reading of that character and also describes in what way it is modified. Examples:

- The radical *sanzui* (氵) is an abbreviated form of the 'water' character (水: *on* reading *sui*), and consists of three (*san*) strokes.

- The radical *yokome* (𭃂) is identical in form to the 'eye' character (目: *kun* reading *me*), but oriented horizontally (*yoko*).

- The radical *rittō* (刂) is a modified form of the 'sword' character (刀: *on* reading *tō*), used when the element is compressed to the right-hand side of a character. Reflecting that the compressed form is narrow and tall, as if standing upright, the radical name consists of parts meaning 'stand' (立, *ritsu*) and 'sword' (刀, *tō*).

6. The radical name indicates the meaning of the radical in characters that contain it. Examples:

- The radical *kemono hen* (犭) is used in characters having to do with animals (*kemono*). (This radical is a modified form of the 犬 [*inu*] character.)

- The radical *kotoba* (言) is so named because its meaning in characters which contain it has to do with words and language (*kotoba*). (This radical is usually located on the left-hand side of a character, with a slightly altered form: 訁. This version of the radical is called *gonben*.)

7. The radical's meaning and character reading are combined in the name to distinguish the radical from other similar radicals. Examples:

- The radical *nikuzuki* (月), an abbreviated form of the radical 肉 (*niku*), has the same form as the character *tsuki* (月 : 'moon'). The radical's meaning (*niku*) and (apparent) reading (*tsuki*) are combined in its name. (Some dictionaries group the *tsuki* and *nikuzuki* radicals together, while others treat them as separate.)

- The radical *munohoko* (矛) has the meaning *hoko* (a type of long weapon similar to a pike). As a full, standalone character, the *on* reading of this component is *mu*.

8. The radical is named to contrast it with another radical similar in appearance. Examples:

- The radical pair *kogai* (貝) and *ōgai* (頁) literally mean 'small shell' and 'large shell,' respectively, but only the first has to do with seashells. The *ōgai* radical has to do with parts of the face and head.

- The radical pair *kozato hen* (阝) and *ōzato* (阝) literally mean 'small village' and 'large village,' respectively, but only the second character has to do with villages. The *kozato hen* radical has to do with hills or mounds of earth.

9. The radical is named after a word that it can be used to write informally (for example, as an abbreviation of, or a former version of, the proper character). Examples:

- The radical *haba* (巾) gets its name from its use in Japan as an abbreviation of the character 幅, read as *haba* and meaning 'width.'

- The radical *fudezukuri* (聿) depicts a hand holding a brush (*fude*). Long ago, this is how the character 'brush' was written. (The proper form used today is 筆.)

10. The radical name reflects a particular, special usage of the character. Example:

- The radical *hiyomi no tori* (酉) depicts a container for alcohol. However, the radical is named from the usage of the character 酉 as one of the 12 divisions of the Chinese zodiac (*hiyomi*), where it is represented by a bird (*tori*). In this case, even though the original meaning of the element is 'alcohol container,' the radical name derives from an unrelated usage with a different meaning.

Conclusion

Some radical names are very common and known by most Japanese people. Others are not well known. It is not necessary to memorize radical names, but sometimes it is helpful to remember some of the more commonly used ones. Remembering the names formed using the first method can even help in remembering how to write those radicals.

In the radical list in Part 2, the names of all radicals are provided, but the derivations of the names are not. Note that for radicals which are known by more than one different name, the separate names may have been constructed based on different principles. Finally, do not assume that the name of a radical directly relates to its meaning in the characters that contain it, as this is often not the case. (Radical meanings are discussed later in this appendix.)

F.5 Radical Form and Stroke Count Variations

Some radicals can appear within characters in one of several different forms, such as the variations 手 and 扌 which we saw in the last section. For such multi-form radicals, each of the various forms is shown in the list of radicals in Part 2, grouped together and assigned the same radical number.[2] Radicals most commonly have multiple forms due to either element compression or character simplification.

Element Compression

In Part 1 of the book, we saw numerous examples of how some components undergo form change when compressed into a certain part of a character. 手 and 扌 are one such example; the component 手 takes the form 扌 when compressed to the left-hand side of a character. The 手 form and the 扌 form have each been designated as character radicals. Both are listed in Part 2 under radical number R-64, with the full-character form (手) as the principal form.

Each of these variations of the 'hand' component are common and can be found within many characters. For a few other characters, though, only the compressed form is common; the full-character form is almost never encountered. This is true of characters meaning 'grass; herbs' and 'movement (along a road),' which, in their full, standalone character forms, appear this way, respectively:

艸　　　辵

These forms are quite rare. Whenever these characters are placed as elements into other characters, they take on the simpler forms shown below, with the 'grass' element placed at the top of a character, and the 'movement' element placed in the lower left.

These compressed forms have both been designated as character radicals. It is standard, though, in radical lists for the full-character versions of components to be treated as the principal form of the radical. Thus, although both are rare, 艸 and 辵 have been designated as the principal forms of these radicals; it is under these forms that the radicals are listed in most character dictionaries. Furthermore, by convention radicals are ordered within the radical list using the stroke counts of the principal forms. Thus, even though the simplified forms above —written with three strokes each—are much more common, both are listed in most radical lists under the stroke counts of the full-character forms: six for 艸, and seven for 辵.

The list of radicals in Part 2 of this book follows this convention. Specifically, radicals are ordered using the stroke count of the full-character principal form, and all the variations of a given form are listed immediately below it, using the same radical number. See R-64, R-137, and R-160 in the Part 2 list (corresponding to the above three characters) for examples.

As should be clear from this discussion, to be able to efficiently use a Japanese character dictionary, it is very useful to have familiarity with the principal, full-character forms of radicals, even when they are not that commonly encountered within characters.

---

[2] Some radical forms which are only slightly different from the main form are not separately listed in Part 2.

APPENDIX F

Character Simplification

Character simplification resulted in simpler forms of some characters and components. One such simplification occurred with the character *mugi* ('wheat' / 'barley' / 'oats'), which was simplified from the form on the left below (consisting of eleven strokes) to the form on the right (seven strokes):

Another simplification occurred with the element *shoku hen*, the compressed form of the *shoku* character (食, 'food') found on the left-hand side of characters. This element was simplified from the form on the left below (with nine strokes) to the form on the right (eight strokes):

㣇 → 飠

With characters and components whose forms have been simplified, such as *mugi* and *shoku hen* above, as a general rule the simplified versions were only applied to *jōyō kanji*, while characters outside of the *jōyō kanji* were not simplified, and therefore still use the older, more complex forms.³

Character dictionaries typically include many more characters than just the *jōyō kanji*. Thus, non-simplified versions of characters and components also appear in a character dictionary. Some of these have been designated as character radicals, including the pre-simplification versions of both *mugi* and *shoku hen* (the versions on the left above). Therefore, the pre-simplification forms of these components also need to be included in radical lists.

By convention, it is the non-simplified, full-character versions of radicals that are treated as the principal form. Thus, in the case of the *mugi* character, the 麥 version is treated as the principal form in most radical lists. The Part 2 radicals list follows that convention; the *mugi* radical is located in the 11-stroke radicals section, with 麥 as the principal form (see R-199).

Revised Stroke Counts

The traditional 214 '*Kangxi* radicals,' are ordered based on radical stroke count, from smallest to largest. This is standard for radical lists in character dictionaries. The radicals in Part 2 of this book are ordered that same way, as well. However, the ordering in Part 2 is slightly different from the *Kangxi* set. This is due to revisions that have taken place in Japan of the stroke counts of a few radicals.

Take, for example, the following component:

舛

This component originated as an image of two feet: left and right. It has been designated as a radical, but only a few characters are assigned to that radical. It also appears as a component in several *jōyō kanji*, including 舞 ('dance'). Per the official stroke counts of all *jōyō kanji* which contain it, the above component is drawn with exactly seven strokes.

---

³ There are some exceptions to this rule, but it is true in most cases. One exception has occurred with the component 攴 → 攵. This particular form change was made so long ago that even many non-*jōyō* characters use the simplified form.

The specific strokes and their proper order in those *jōyō* characters are shown in the following stroke order diagram:

舛

The traditional stroke count of this component is different, though. Traditionally, in China, the above strokes #5 and #6 were drawn together as a single stroke, resulting in a total stroke count of six. The component is still drawn that way in China.

Although in all *jōyō kanji* which contain this component it is written using seven strokes, the same is not necessarily true of non-*jōyō* characters which contain it. Similar to how character simplifications generally were not applied to non-*jōyō* characters, in some character dictionaries revised stroke counts were also not applied to non-*jōyō* characters. According to such dictionaries, then, the above component is written with six strokes in non-*jōyō* characters. Other character dictionaries treat revised stroke counts differently, applying them to *jōyō* and non-*jōyō* characters alike. In such dictionaries, the above component is drawn with seven strokes even in non-*jōyō* characters which contain it.

The handling of radicals themselves is inconsistent, too. In the case of the 舛 radical, some dictionaries group it with six-stroke radicals, and others with seven-stroke radicals.[4]

Several other components are affected in the same way. When appearing as components within *jōyō kanji*, 牙, 瓜, 臣, and 韋 each have an official stroke count one greater than the traditional value. These components are also all radicals, and could be ordered in a radical list based on the traditional stroke count or the revised stroke count. For such radicals, this book follows the standard of the Japan Kanji Aptitude Testing Foundation. Accordingly, the 舛 radical is treated as having seven strokes—one stroke greater than the traditional *Kangxi* value. The 瓜, 臣, and 韋 radicals are treated similarly.[5]

F.6 Radical Meanings

Many, but not all, components used as character radicals have meaning associated with them. However, radical meanings are not included in the list of radicals in Part 2. This is because radicals do not consistently indicate only a single meaning.

A number of radicals consist of only a partial element, and have no clear meaning on their own. The characters grouped under such radicals do not share a meaning connection with each other. For example, the radical *nabebuta* (亠) has many characters listed under it, but by analyzing early forms of those characters, it can be seen that the two strokes of this radical

---

[4] Some dictionaries list the radical in both places, in order to assist users. Even in such dictionaries, though, each radical is assigned a principal stroke count, and the pages of the dictionary are ordered using these principal stroke counts.
[5] The radical 牙 is a special case. In 2010, when 牙 was added to the *jōyō* list as a full, standalone character, the original (non-revised) stroke count of four was established as standard (with a five-stroke version as an acceptable alternate). This differed from all previously-added *jōyō* characters containing 牙 as a component, each of which treat the 牙 component as having five strokes, per their official stroke counts. In the Part 2 list, the 牙 radical is grouped with four-stroke radicals, to match the standard full-character stroke count.

originally represented a variety of different, unrelated objects. For example, in the character for 'mix' / 'exchange': 交 (which we learned in Part 1, Chapter 2), the 亠 part of the character was originally the head and arms of a person with crossed legs. In another character, it was the roof of a building, and in another it was originally the head of an animal. There is not one single meaning associated with this radical.

But even with radicals that do have meaning associated with them, there are numerous cases where characters are grouped under the same radical even though the shared radical component originally had several different forms and meanings among the characters. One such example is the radical 玉, with its variant form 王. In most characters grouped under this radical, the component is a determinative, based on a pictographic image of a jewel, and identifying characters having to do with jewels or precious stones. But in some other characters, the meaning of the radical component is 'king.' And in still others, it is 'musical instrument.' These unrelated meanings were each originally written with components having different forms, but all the various forms transformed in a way such that they are now all identical. The form similarity was a factor in these diverse characters being grouped together under the same radical.

As these examples show, it can't be assumed that all characters which are assigned to the same radical are related in meaning to each other. The main purpose of assigning radicals was to efficiently organize the characters in as few groups as possible. This goal greatly affected radical assignment among the characters.

For the reasons just discussed, radical meanings are not included in the Part 2 radicals list. The most commonly used radicals are also determinatives, though, and determinative meanings are described in detail in the Part 2 list of determinatives.

Appendix G

Character Simplifications and Variant Forms

For some characters, in addition to the standard, common form, there exist one or more alternate forms that are still sometimes encountered. In most such cases, the standard form is a simplified version of the alternate form, having a simpler design and usually consisting of fewer strokes. In this appendix, we look at such character simplifications, as well as other types of variant character forms.

G.1 Character Form Simplifications

Throughout their history, simplifications have been made to many characters, both in Japan and in China, usually with the purpose of simplifying the writing of the characters. Many of these simplifications were used only informally, but some became quite popular, and widely used.[1] Just after World War II, the Japanese government officially established a set of common use characters (originally called the *tōyō kanji*, now called the *jōyō kanji*). As part of this effort, the official forms of many of the common use characters were simplified, in many cases adopting the informal simplifications that had been in popular use up until that time.

When needing to distinguish between different character forms, the newer, simplified form is referred to as the *shinjitai* (新字体, literally: 'new character form'), and the older form as the *kyūjitai* (旧字体, 'former character form'). The older forms of characters, in addition to being called *kyūjitai*, can also be considered variant characters: *itaiji* (異体字). That is, the older version can be thought of as a variant of the newer, standard version.

Most of the older forms of the characters appearing in this section were the principal versions used in documents produced in Japan prior to 1945. Today, many of these older forms are almost never encountered anymore. But some are still relatively common. For example, the older version of the 'dragon' character (龍) is still commonly seen—perhaps even more often than the modern simplified version (竜).

Most character modifications were made deliberately, with the purpose of making the characters easier to read and write. With fewer strokes and a simpler form, characters can be written faster and are less complicated to decipher when reading. A few of the modifications, though, were apparently based on mistakes that became so widely adopted that it was decided to make the mistaken version the official version.

---
[1] Popularly-spread, but non-standard ways of writing characters are called *zokuji* (俗字).

There are a variety of methods by which characters were simplified. For example, some characters were simplified by removing strokes determined to be excess and unnecessary. Other characters were simplified by replacing a rarely seen component with a more common one similar in appearance. Still others were simplified by replacing all or part of them with strokes derived from the *cursive* form of the character. The cursive style, described in more detail in Appendix N, is a roughly drawn style which contains fewer strokes than the standard form.

Some simplifications were applied to individual character components. In those cases, most characters containing the same component were usually modified in the same way. In Japan, though, the simplifications were only officially applied to characters included in the *jōyō kanji* list, and so the standard forms of characters not on the list do not incorporate the equivalent simplifications.[2] For consistency, though, the makers of some computer typefaces have chosen to also simplify some of these non-*jōyō* characters using the same principles.

Many of the simplified forms were in use unofficially for a long time, in both Japan and China, and also became the official versions in mainland China when they issued their own set of character simplifications.[3] Other simplifications were unique to Japan. This has resulted in a different appearance of some characters between Japan and China. For example, the character 歴 ('history; experience') was only slightly simplified in Japan, as 歴, but was more significantly simplified in China: 历. In Taiwan and Hong Kong, most of the older character forms are still the standard forms, as the mainland China character simplifications were not formally adopted.

The extent to which the older forms of characters are able to be represented in Japanese computer typefaces varies depending on the typeface and the character. For example, some older form characters that are still commonly used in many people and place names appear in all or most computer typefaces, whereas others that are extremely rare are represented in only the largest, most comprehensive typefaces.

There is no need to memorize any of the older character forms shown herein, but do realize that some of these forms will still be encountered periodically in various contexts, and so at least being somewhat familiar with them can be helpful when reading Japanese. Furthermore, having an understanding of and familiarity with the principles used in these simplifications will aid in the recognition of non-simplified characters not included in the *jōyō* list.

If you are considering learning some of these older forms, keep in mind that it is not as cumbersome as learning new characters. This is because the older forms, just like any other variant characters, have the same readings and meanings as the standard forms. So it is not necessary to learn any new readings or meanings, it is only necessary to mentally associate the older, variant character with its modern standard form.

About the List

The characters are grouped in this section based on the type of modification that was made. Overall, the types of changes are divided into six major categories. Some characters were

---

[2] It was intended that characters not on the *jōyō* list would be phased out of usage, and so these characters were not altered from their traditional forms.

[3] The simplification of characters in mainland China, beginning in 1956, was larger in scope than that in Japan, with many more characters affected.

simplified using more than one of the principles described. Those characters are listed only once: in the section which is most relevant. It is not possible to know with certainty the reasons behind each of the simplifications, so assumptions are sometimes made in the category classifications.

The older form of each character is shown first, followed by the modern, standard form. Many of the characters are marked with one or more numbers. These numbers correspond to the notes listed at the end of the section. For some of the simplified characters (specifically, the ones labeled with note #5), the simplified form is identical to that of a separate, unrelated character that existed prior to the simplification and had a different meaning associated with it. As a result of the simplification, the old meaning, in essence, became purged, replaced with that of the character being simplified (or is now treated as an alternate, uncommon, meaning). Some of these characters even had a completely different, unrelated *on* reading which was replaced with the *on* reading of the character being simplified (as explained in Section 2.11 in Part 1 of the book, using the characters 体 and 洪 as examples).

Note that some of the older forms shown here appear in a different typeface from the corresponding modern form, and therefore in addition to stroke differences may exhibit other minor differences in appearance. These appearance differences are only due to the different typefaces being used, and should be ignored.

Finally, note that this list is not fully comprehensive, but instead is intended merely to show sufficient examples in order to demonstrate each the various principles of simplification that have been used. In particular, some component changes affected a large number of common use characters, but it is not practical to list all affected characters.

Type 1: Character Cleanup

Description: The character is 'cleaned up' by means of simple aesthetic changes. These changes result in a cleaner, simpler look with only minor changes to the character appearance.

A. 'Straightening out' angled lines: taking two small angled line segments and merging them into one long horizontal or vertical stroke:

練 → 練[1]　鍊 → 錬[1]　欄 → 欄[1]　黑 → 黒
默 → 黙[2]　墨 → 墨　薫 → 薫　勳 → 勲[2]
毒 → 毒　毎 → 毎　海 → 海　梅 → 梅
悔 → 悔　敏 → 敏　侮 → 侮　繁 → 繁
來 → 来　峽 → 峡　挾 → 挟　狹 → 狭
頰 → 頬　從 → 従　縱 → 縦　溫 → 温[1]

B. Altering of the orientation of the vertical strokes in the downward facing 'hand' element:

探 → 採　彩 → 彩　乳 → 乳　暖 → 暖

C. Inverting a pair of angled strokes, changing the orientation:

平 → 平　牛 → 半　判 → 判　益 → 益
送 → 送　隊 → 隊　消 → 消　鎖 → 鎖
說 → 説　稅 → 税　銳 → 鋭　尊 → 尊
曾 → 曽　增 → 増　僧 → 僧　層 → 層
憎 → 憎　贈 → 贈

D. Modifying the component resembling a capital 'E' (facing either forward or backward), making the horizontal lines aligned and equal in length (this modification was only applied to characters in which a separate vertical stroke is *not* passing through this component):

雪 → 雪　急 → 急　侵 → 侵　浸 → 浸
婦 → 婦　虐 → 虐

E. Adding a single stroke to give a more balanced look and to create an appearance consistent with the commonly encountered 少 component:

步 → 歩　頻 → 頻　涉 → 渉　賓 → 賓

F. Making small, subtle changes to the way strokes are drawn, including changes to stroke length and stroke direction, as well as the splitting of one stroke into two, and the merging of two strokes into one. There are many characters which underwent these minor changes; only a small fraction of them are shown here. The examples shown are representative of all the types of changes made, though. Note that in some computer typefaces, a few of the older forms shown here may still be encountered.

  1. Slightly shortening a stroke to end precisely at a another stroke:

  周 → 周　告 → 告　契 → 契　唐 → 唐
  虜 → 虜[1]　構 → 構　非 → 非　博 → 博
  成 → 成　灰 → 灰　巨 → 巨　寧 → 寧
  具 → 具

  2. Slightly extending a stroke:

  鼻 → 鼻　冒 → 冒　亡 → 亡　叫 → 叫

  3. Slightly repositioning a stroke:

  舍 → 舎　捨 → 捨

4. Removing one small segment of a stroke:

包 → 包   抱 → 抱   港 → 港   選 → 選
全 → 全   內 → 内   八 → 八   貧 → 貧
使 → 使   建 → 建   及 → 及

5. Changing the direction / angle of a stroke:

主 → 主   食 → 食   商 → 商   所 → 所
程 → 程³   冬 → 冬   次 → 次   率 → 率
羽 → 羽   曜 → 曜   前 → 前   服 → 服

6. Replacing a longer, single curved or bending stroke with two shorter strokes very similar in appearance:

晚 → 晚   卑 → 卑   雅 → 雅

7. Replacing two shorter strokes with one longer stroke:

花 → 花

G. Performing other kinds of minor alteration to components in a way that does not significantly alter character appearance. These changes were made to speed up character writing or to make characters easier to draw. In some cases, the total stroke count is reduced.

飯 → 飯   飼 → 飼   館 → 館   飲 → 飲
青 → 青   清 → 清   精 → 精   晴 → 晴
輸 → 輸   諭 → 諭   愉 → 愉   癒 → 癒
負 → 負   危 → 危   免 → 免   絕 → 絶[1]
黃 → 黄   橫 → 横   漢 → 漢   難 → 難
嘆 → 嘆   勤 → 勤   謹 → 謹   僅 → 僅
眞 → 真   愼 → 慎   鎭 → 鎮   塡 → 填
倂 → 併   塀 → 塀   瓶 → 瓶   餅 → 餅
研 → 研[1] 册 → 冊   柵 → 柵   歲 → 歲
述 → 述   術 → 術   吳 → 呉   誤 → 誤
敎 → 教   煙 → 煙   恆 → 恒[1] 旅 → 旅
顏 → 顔   產 → 産   兼 → 兼 → 兼

Type 2: Component Abbreviation

Description: Strokes are eliminated from the character to reduce the total stroke count. Often, a complex portion of a character is replaced with a simpler form. The cursive script form of a component is sometimes used as the basis for the simplified form. The character appearance is relatively unchanged.

A. Removing minor strokes that don't contribute significantly to character appearance, enhancing simplicity in reading and writing, and avoiding clutter:

返 → 返　近 → 近　殼 → 殻　穀 → 穀
德 → 徳　聽 → 聴　徴 → 徴　懲 → 懲
郞 → 郎　朗 → 朗　廊 → 廊　寬 → 寛
專 → 専　惠 → 恵　穗 → 穂　騷 → 騒
隨 → 随[1]　髓 → 髄[1]　墮 → 堕[1]　隆 → 隆
者 → 者　緒 → 緒　諸 → 諸　都 → 都
穩 → 穏　隱 → 隠　藏 → 蔵　臟 → 臓
器 → 器　突 → 突　戾 → 戻　淚 → 涙
臭 → 臭　類 → 類

B. Removing a pair of identical elements, replacing them with four simple strokes in a 'water splatter' pattern:

樂 → 楽　藥 → 薬　澁 → 渋　攝 → 摂
壘 → 塁

C. Removing a complicated or cluttered portion located at or near the top of the character and replacing it with a component similar in appearance to the katakana *tsu* character (ツ):

榮 → 栄　營 → 営　螢 → 蛍　勞 → 労
覺 → 覚　學 → 学　擧 → 挙　譽 → 誉
單 → 単　戰 → 戦　禪 → 禅　彈 → 弾
獸 → 獣　嚴 → 厳　櫻 → 桜　巢 → 巣

D. Removing one part of the character, and replacing it with a component similar in appearance to the katakana *me* character (メ):

氣 → 気　區 → 区　驅 → 駆　歐 → 欧
毆 → 殴　樞 → 枢

E. Performing other types of stroke reduction that do not significantly alter character appearance, in order to simplify the forms of elements and to make the character easier to draw.

祥 → 祥　神 → 神　福 → 福　社 → 社
儉 → 俭　劍 → 剣　險 → 険　檢 → 検
壤 → 壌　孃 → 嬢　讓 → 譲　釀 → 醸
勸 → 勧　歡 → 歓　觀 → 観　權 → 権
壞 → 壊　懷 → 懐　屬 → 属　囑 → 嘱
綠 → 緑　錄 → 録　剝 → 剥　緣 → 縁
麥 → 麦　麵 → 麺　燒 → 焼　曉 → 暁
兩 → 両　滿 → 満　參 → 参　慘 → 惨
棧 → 桟　殘 → 残　淺 → 浅　踐 → 践
錢 → 銭　兒 → 児　陷 → 陥　稻 → 稲
插 → 挿　搜 → 捜　瘦 → 痩　繩 → 縄
亞 → 亜　惡 → 悪　乘 → 乗　剩 → 剰
壯 → 壮　莊 → 荘　裝 → 装　狀 → 状
寢 → 寝　將 → 将　獎 → 奨　謠 → 謡
搖 → 揺　惱 → 悩　腦 → 脳　竝 → 並
豐 → 豊　艷 → 艶　帶 → 帯　滯 → 滞
渴 → 渇　揭 → 掲　謁 → 謁　褐 → 褐
喝 → 喝　爭 → 争　淨 → 浄　靜 → 静
爲 → 為　僞 → 偽　冰 → 氷　樣 → 様
旣 → 既　槪 → 概　慨 → 慨　卽 → 即
節 → 節→ 節　　鄕 → 鄉 → 郷
響 → 響 → 響　　強 → 强

Type 3: Component Substitution

Description: A complicated or rare component within a character is replaced with a simpler, more recognizable component, based on similarity of appearance. Replacement components were chosen without regard to meaning. Also included in this section are characters in which one component has been mistakenly replaced with another similar-looking component.

A. Making a minor change to turn a rarer component into a more commonly occurring component quite similar in appearance:

盜 → 盗　　拜 → 拝　　鬪 → 闘　　屆 → 届
拔 → 抜　　髮 → 髪　　賴 → 頼　　瀨 → 瀬
沒 → 没　　逸 → 逸　　殺 → 殺　　塚 → 塚
卷 → 巻　　圈 → 圏　　擊 → 撃　　襃 → 褒
延 → 延

B. Redesigning one or more components of the character, removing cluttered or rare elements and replacing them with more common elements having a roughly similar overall appearance. In some cases, the character's cursive script form influenced the choice of replacement component:

奧 → 奥　　斷 → 断　　繼 → 継　　齒 → 歯
齡 → 齢　　數 → 数　　樓 → 楼　　肅 → 粛
獻 → 献　　辭 → 辞　　亂 → 乱　　遲 → 遅
碎 → 砕　　粹 → 粋　　醉 → 酔　　雜 → 雑
齊 → 斉　　濟 → 済　　齋 → 斎　　劑 → 剤
徑 → 径　　莖 → 茎　　經 → 経　　輕 → 軽
曆 → 暦　　歷 → 歴　　贊 → 賛　　潛 → 潜
戲 → 戯　　顯 → 顕　　濕 → 湿　　纖 → 繊
虛 → 虚　　靈 → 霊　　溪 → 渓　　鷄 → 鶏
對 → 対 [4]

C. Replacing one component with another very similar-looking component, possibly due to widespread confusion over which is correct:

效 → 効　　敕 → 勅　　收 → 収　　敍 → 叙
霸 → 覇　　祕 → 秘　　隷 → 隷　　閒 → 間
眾 → 衆

Type 4: Component Removal

Description: One or more significant components of the character are removed. In some cases, the remaining parts of the character are slightly altered or relocated.

絲 → 糸　蟲 → 虫　疊 → 畳　處 → 処
醫 → 医　聲 → 声　壓 → 圧[6]　應 → 応[6]
藝 → 芸[5,6]　團 → 団[6]　條 → 条　餘 → 余[5]
豫 → 予[5]　縣 → 県　號 → 号　罐 → 缶[5,6]
價 → 価　覽 → 覧　點 → 点[2]　貳 → 弐[7]
濾 → 沪　獨 → 独[6]　觸 → 触[6]　衞 → 衛[8]
犧 → 犠

Type 5: Phonetic Replacement

Description: The phonetic component of the character is replaced with an alternate phonetic component which has the same or a similar reading, but a simpler form. (In some cases, the replacement phonetic component is actually a closer match to the modern Japanese character *on* reading.)

國 → 国　傳 → 伝　轉 → 転　爐 → 炉
驛 → 駅　釋 → 釈　擇 → 択　澤 → 沢
譯 → 訳　廳 → 庁　燈 → 灯　證 → 証[5]
擔 → 担　膽 → 胆　竊 → 窃　蠶 → 蚕[5]
總 → 総　窗 → 窓[9]　鐵 → 鉄　圍 → 囲[10]
懼 → 惧　癡 → 痴

Type 6: Character Overhaul

Description: A significant change is made to the appearance of the character, appreciably reducing the total stroke count. Complicated components within the character are replaced with entirely different components simpler in form.

A. Merging the character together with a simpler, already existing character with the same *on* reading (and in some cases a similar meaning):

辨 → 弁[5]　瓣 → 弁[5]　辯 → 弁[5]　臺 → 台[5]

B. Borrowing a different, unrelated already existing character only for its ease of writing, even though it has a different (but similar) *on* reading. The reading of the borrowed character is changed to match that of the character being simplified:

缺 → 欠[5,6]　濱 → 浜[5,6]

C. 'Reinventing' the character in a whole new form, representing the meaning in a completely different way:

雙 → 双　　嶽 → 岳[11]　　萬 → 万　　勵 → 励
體 → 体[5,11]

D. Removing one or more parts of the character, and further redesigning or altering the remaining portion:

龍 → 竜　　瀧 → 滝　　寶 → 宝[6]　　舊 → 旧
畫 → 画　　據 → 拠[12]　　寫 → 写[13]　　與 → 与[14]

E. Significantly redesigning one part or all of the character, simplifying it so that a cluttered, complex portion is replaced with a much simpler part, written with many fewer strokes. For some of these characters, the altered elements have been changed using the cursive script form of the character as a model:

壽 → 寿　　鑄 → 鋳　　獵 → 猟　　龜 → 亀
發 → 発　　廢 → 廃　　遞 → 逓　　關 → 関
續 → 続　　讀 → 読　　賣 → 売　　壹 → 壱
會 → 会　　繪 → 絵　　歸 → 帰　　鹽 → 塩
圓 → 円　　圖 → 図　　盡 → 尽　　晝 → 昼
蠻 → 蛮　　變 → 変　　戀 → 恋　　灣 → 湾
實 → 実　　邊 → 辺[15]　　當 → 当[6]　　黨 → 党
廣 → 広[16]　　擴 → 拡　　鑛 → 鉱　　拂 → 払
佛 → 仏　　假 → 仮[6]　　禮 → 礼 → 礼
彌 → 弥　　稱 → 稱 → 称[17]

Notes:

1. Following this change, the character now appears to contain a component which is identical in form to an already existing, unrelated component found in other characters. (Technically, therefore, this character could also be grouped under Type 3: Component Substitution.)

2. The arrangement of the components within this character was also slightly altered.

3. Although difficult to see, the topmost stroke of the lower right-hand component is changed from slightly slanted downward to straight across.

4. The simplified left-hand side of this character is based on 文, but the form is slightly altered to fit in the narrow space, resulting in slight differences (e.g., the downward stroke to the right is shortened).

5. The simplified form of this character is identical in appearance to a different character that already existed prior to the simplification. In other words, the character was simplified to a form that was already being used to represent some other meaning. The old meaning was either purged, or is now considered to be an alternate meaning.

6. With this character, the simplification resulted in the removal (or loss) of the phonetic component.

7. An additional stroke was also added to the upper left.

8. In this case, the middle lower portion was removed, and then the full form of the center part—which had been abbreviated—was restored.

9. In the modern, simplified version of this character, the top two strokes of the replacement phonetic (公) are merged with the bottom two strokes of the top component (穴).

10. Interestingly, the new component chosen to be the phonetic was chosen for its *kun* reading instead of its *on* reading. This is uncommon.

11. As a result of the changes, this character went from being a determinative-phonetic character to an ideographic character.

12. The simplified form most likely came about based on similarities (or confusion) between the right-hand side of 據 and the character 處, which was simplified to 処.

13. The simplified form likely derives from an alternate way of writing the old form, where the lower part is drawn this way: 舄.

14. This character was simplified differently from other common use characters containing the same component: 擧 (→挙) and 譽 (→誉).

15. Several other variations of the old form of this character, slightly different from the one shown in the table, are still in existence, and can be found in family names.

16. The simplified version of this component may have been chosen for similarity with other characters that have a similar meaning to 廣 (namely, 宏 and 弘).

17. The original character (the leftmost of the three) was first confused with the similar-looking middle character. Subsequently, the character was simplified in a way consistent with other characters having the same right-hand side phonetic component as the middle character (such as the character appearing on the far left of the row).

G.2 *Ryakuji* – Handwritten Simplified Forms

The simplified forms shown in the previous section of this appendix have become the standard versions of those characters. There are also a small number of other characters for which alternate, simplified, unofficial forms can sometimes be seen. For the most part, these simplified forms are not included in Japanese computer-based typefaces, and so are only encountered in handwriting. These variants are called *ryakuji*, which means 'abbreviated character,' because they are almost always written with fewer strokes than the standard forms.

As an example, the character for 'fish' is shown here in both the standard form, and two alternate *ryakuji* forms:[4]

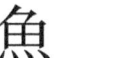

    Standard Form   *Ryakuji* Form 1   *Ryakuji* Form 2

The bottom four strokes of the standard form are replaced in the *ryakuji* forms, in one case with the 大 element (three strokes), and in the other case with just a single horizontal line (one stroke).

Ryakuji handwritten variant forms are infrequently encountered and entirely unofficial, and are not discussed elsewhere in this book.

---

[4] For clarity, the *ryakuji* forms are shown here as they would look if represented in a computer-based typeface. However, *ryakuji* characters are typically handwritten variants only, and are generally not represented within computer-based typefaces.

G.3 Other Variant Character Forms

The older versions of the characters shown in the first section of this appendix (that is, the versions in existence prior to character simplification and modification) can now be thought of as variant versions of the modern, standard versions.

There are also other kinds of variant character forms in existence that are not an older form of the standard character, but rather just a different version that has coexisted together with the standard version over time.

A few examples of this kind of variant character are provided in this section, organized based on the type of variation. The more common, standard form is listed first, followed by the less common form in parentheses. These alternate ways to write characters (in parentheses) are sometimes seen in people and place names. When encountering the non-standard forms, they should be treated as equivalent to the standard form version.

This list is not comprehensive; only a few examples of each type are shown.

Type 1 - Essentially the same form, but with a slightly different way of writing:

高 (髙)

Type 2 - The same components, but in a different arrangement:

島[1] (嶋, 嵨)　峰 (峯)　裏 (裡)[2]

Type 3 - An ideographic representation, rather than the standard D-P representation:

涙 (泪)[3]

Type 4 - Confusion as to which element is correct:

恥 (耻)[4]

Type 5 - Using an alternate determinative (but one which still identifies the same category of meaning):

翻 (飜)　坂 (阪)[5]

Notes:

1. In the standard form of this character, four strokes of the 'bird' component are removed.
2. The constituent elements of this character are the same in each case, but the form of the 'clothing' element is different between these two characters. See Part 1, Section 6.7 for further discussion.
3. In the non-standard form, the meaning 'tear' (as in from crying) is represented by the elements 'water' and 'eye.'
4. The form on the left is standard in Japan, while the alternate form (in parentheses) is standard in China.
5. Technically, the version in parentheses is an alternate way to write 坂, and can be thought of as a variant. However, because the alternate form is well known (most notably being used in the name of the city of Osaka, but also used in many other people and place names) it is no longer considered a variant character, and is now treated as a full, separate character from 坂. In fact, it was added to the *jōyō kanji* list in 2010.

Appendix H
Common *Kokuji*

This appendix contains a list of *kokuji* (kanji created in Japan) that may be periodically encountered. For each character, the common readings are given; *on* readings are in katakana and *kun* readings are in hiragana (with okurigana placed after the ・ mark). A simple character meaning is also provided.

Not all *kokuji* are listed—only some of the more common ones. The characters listed on the first page are all *jōyō kanji*; the first two of these are also *kyōiku kanji*. These characters are all labeled with either K or J, denoting whether they are *kyōiku kanji* or *jōyō kanji*, respectively.

The characters on the second page are not as commonly encountered as those on the first page, but may still be seen from time to time by frequent readers of Japanese. These characters were chosen, in part, to demonstrate the variety of characters that were created by the Japanese.

Note that for some of the *kun* readings in the list, there are alternate ways to write the same word, with an identical or similar meaning, using non-*kokuji* kanji.

Character	Reading(s)	Meaning	Category
畑	はたけ、はた	cultivated field	(K)
働	はたら・く、ドウ	to work	(K)
込	こ・む、こ・める	to enter; to be put in	(J)
峠	とうげ	mountain pass	(J)
塀	ヘイ	fence	(J)
搾	しぼ・る、サク	to squeeze	(J)
枠	わく	frame (such as a door frame)	(J)
栃	とち	horse chestnut	(J)
腺	セン	gland	(J)
匂	にお・う、にお・い	to be fragrant; to give off an odor	(J)

Character	Reading(s)	Meaning
笹	ささ	bamboo grass
辻	つじ	crossroads
鰯	いわし	sardines
躾	しつけ	discipline
凧	たこ	kite
鋲	ビョウ	thumbtack; rivet
俣	また	crotch; groin; fork (such as in a road)
鱈	たら	fish of the family Gadidae (cod, haddock, etc.)
榊	さかき	*Cleyera japonica* evergreen (sacred to shrines)
凪	なぎ	calm at sea; a lull
樫	かし	evergreen oak
麿	まろ	affectionate suffix used with boys' names
杢	もく	woodworker
籾	もみ	unhulled rice
喰	く・う、く・らう	eat; drink; suffer (a scolding, a punch, etc.)
鳰	にお	little grebe; dabchick (a type of water bird)
硲	はざま	ravine; gorge
噺	はなし	talk; speech; chat; negotiations
凩	こがらし	cold, wintry wind
裃	かみしも	traditional ceremonial outfit
癪	シャク	spasms; convulsions
梺	ふもと	base of a mountain
鉃	ぶりき、ブ	tin plate

Appendix I
Kun Readings That Fit the Pattern of Valid *On* Readings

As discussed in Chapter 7 (Section 7.4), a valid character *on* reading follows a well-defined set of rules. Most *kun* readings do not fit these rules, and so are not difficult to distinguish from *on* readings, once the rules have been learned. For *kun* readings which do fit the rules, though, it could be easy to confuse them with *on* readings. In this appendix is a list of characters with common *kun* readings that happen to fit the pattern of valid *on* readings, and therefore might be easily mistaken for *on* readings.

Although some of the characters listed here may have more than one *kun* or *on* reading, only the relevant *kun* reading(s) and the principal *on* reading(s) are shown in the list. To help distinguish the readings, the *kun* readings are all listed in hiragana (and lowercase Latin letters), and the *on* readings are all listed in katakana (and uppercase Latin letters).

This list is not comprehensive. The *kun* readings listed here are primarily those of simple nouns, as such words are the easiest to confuse with *on* readings. There are also a number of verbs of native Japanese origin which, when inflected in certain ways, could satisfy the rules of a valid *on* reading, but with an understanding of verb inflection such words can be relatively easily recognized as *kun* readings.[1] Verb forms, therefore, are not included in the list.

The list is sorted by *kun* reading, using the standard Japanese order (called *gojūon*). For characters with more than one *kun* reading which fits the pattern of an *on* reading, each reading is listed separately. (For example, the character 家 is listed under both the *uchi* and *ya* readings.)

---

[1] Verbs read with a *kun* reading can fairly easily be recognized as such because they usually are written with okurigana. Perhaps the verbs that might most easily be confused with *on* readings are the Group 2 verbs, which, in certain inflected forms, do not include okurigana. For example, the verb *miru* (見る, 'see'), when in its noun or combining form, simply becomes *mi* (written as 見), as seen in compound words such as *hanami* (花見, 'flower viewing') and *mitsukeru* (見付ける, 'find'). In these words, the character 見 is read as *mi*, a *kun* reading, but one which fits the pattern of a valid *on* reading. Being aware of patterns of verb inflection will help avoid mistaking such readings as *on* readings.

Character	*Kun* Reading	Principal *On* Reading(s)
秋	あき (*aki*)	シュウ (*SHŪ*)
息	いき (*iki*)	ソク (*SOKU*)
市	いち (*ichi*)	シ (*SHI*)
内	うち (*uchi*)	ナイ (*NAI*)
家	うち (*uchi*)	カ / ケ (*KA / KE*)
江	え (*e*)	コウ (*KŌ*)
尾	お (*o*)	ビ (*BI*)
御	お (*o*)	ゴ (*GO*)
沖	おき (*oki*)	チュウ (*CHŪ*)
奥	おく (*oku*)	オウ (*Ō*)
貝	かい (*kai*)	バイ (*BAI*)
木	き (*ki*)	モク / ボク (*MOKU / BOKU*)
黄	き (*ki*)	コウ (*KŌ*)
口	くち (*kuchi*)	コウ (*KŌ*)
毛	け (*ke*)	モウ (*MŌ*)
子	こ (*ko*)	シ (*SHI*)
先	さき (*saki*)	セン (*SEN*)
崎	さき (*saki*)	キ (*KI*)
幸	さち (*sachi*)	コウ (*KŌ*)
巣	す (*su*)	ソウ (*SŌ*)
背	せ (*se*)	ハイ (*HAI*)
関	せき (*seki*)	カン (*KAN*)
田	た (*ta*)	デン (*DEN*)
滝	たき (*taki*)	ロウ (*RŌ*) (rarely used)
龍 / 竜	たつ (*tatsu*)	リュウ (*RYŪ*)
千	ち (*chi*)	セン (*SEN*)
津	つ (*tsu*)	シン (*SHIN*)

Character	*Kun* Reading	Principal *On* Reading(s)
月	つき (tsuki)	ガツ / ゲツ (GATSU / GETSU)
土	つち (tsuchi)	ド / ト (DO / TO)
手	て (te)	シュ (SHU)
戸	と (to)	コ (KO)
時	とき (toki)	ジ (JI)
名	な (na)	メイ (MEI)
菜	な (na)	サイ (SAI)
夏	なつ (natsu)	カ (KA)
荷	に (ni)	カ (KA)
新	にい (nī)	シン (SHIN)
音	ね (ne)	オン (ON)
値	ね (ne)	チ (CHI)
根	ね (ne)	コン (KON)
野	の (no)	ヤ (YA)
之	の (no)	シ (SHI)
軒	のき (noki)	ケン (KEN)
羽	は (ha)	ウ (U)
歯	は (ha)	シ (SHI)
葉	は (ha)	ヨウ (YŌ)
場	ば (ba)	ジョウ (JŌ)
灰	はい (hai)	カイ (KAI)
初	はつ (hatsu)	ショ (SHO)
日	ひ (hi)	ニチ / ジツ (NICHI / JITSU)
火	ひ (hi)	カ (KA)
匹	ひき (hiki)	ヒツ (HITSU)
辺	へ (he)	ヘン (HEN)
部	へ (he)	ブ (BU)

Character	Kun Reading	Principal On Reading(s)
間	ま (ma)	カン (KAN)
真	ま (ma)	シン (SHIN)
牧	まき (maki)	ボク (BOKU)
町	まち (machi)	チョウ (CHŌ)
街	まち (machi)	ガイ (GAI)
松	まつ (matsu)	ショウ (SHŌ)
身	み (mi)	シン (SHIN)
実	み (mi)	ジツ (JITSU)
御	み (mi)	ゴ (GO)
幹	みき (miki)	カン (KAN)
道	みち (michi)	ドウ (DŌ)
目	め (me)	モク / ボク (MOKU / BOKU)
女	め (me)	ジョ / ニョ (JO / NYO)
家	や (ya)	カ / ケ (KA / KE)
矢	や (ya)	シ (SHI)
屋	や (ya)	オク (OKU)
湯	ゆ (yu)	トウ (TŌ)
夕	ゆう (yū)	セキ (SEKI)
雪	ゆき (yuki)	セツ (SETSU)
世	よ (yo)	セ / セイ (SE / SEI)
夜	よ (yo)	ヤ (YA)
宵	よい (yoi)	ショウ (SHŌ)
四	よん (yon)	シ (SHI)
我	わ (wa)	ガ (GA)
輪	わ (wa)	リン (RIN)
枠	わく (waku)	(kokuji - no on reading)

Appendix J
Boinkōtai Noun Inflection

Traditional Japanese made heavy use of inflection: the changing of word endings to express different meanings. Some types of inflection are still seen regularly today in modern Japanese, such as the different inflections made to verb endings to express different moods, tenses, etc. But some types of inflection have been largely phased out of the language, and only traces of them can still be found today, used only in particular words.

One type of inflection that has been mostly phased out of the language is the changing of the endings of some simple Japanese nouns when they are used as the first part of a compound word. For example, as described in Part 1, Section 8.10, the word *me* ('eye') is sometimes changed to *ma* when it is used as the first part of a compound word. This can be seen in the compound word for 'eyelid': *mabuta*. This compound word is made up of *me* (altered to *ma*) and *futa*, meaning 'lid' (altered to *buta* by the *rendaku* process).

In Japanese, this type of inflection is called *boinkōtai* (母音交代), which literally means 'vowel exchange.' Compound words affected by *boinkōtai* can still be found in the language today, although the number of them is relatively small. The vowel changes follow several different patterns. By far, the most common of these is the alteration of an ending *e* sound to an *a* sound, such as in *me* → *ma*.

On the following page, several examples of compound words affected by *boinkōtai* are shown. The words are organized by inflection type.

Note that for some compound words of this type, when written with kanji, the fact that the word is actually a compound word can be hidden. See Chapter 8 (Section 8.9) for a discussion of how kanji can hide the fact that a word is actually a compound word. The list which follows includes two hidden compound words.

Examples of *Boinkōtai* Noun Inflection

Character	Sound change	Example word using inflected form
e → a inflection:		
目	*me → ma*	目蓋 *mabuta* ('eyelid')
手	*te → ta*	助ける *tasukeru* † ('help, assist')
船	*fune → funa*	船酔い *funayoi* ('seasickness')
稲	*ine → ina*	稲妻 *inazuma* ('lightning')
胸	*mune → muna*	胸板 *munaita* ('chest; breast')
雨	*ame → ama*	雨雲 *amagumo* ('raincloud')
風	*kaze → kaza*	風車 *kazaguruma* ('windmill; pinwheel')
上	*ue → uwa* ‡	上履き *uwabaki* ('indoor shoes')
苗	*nae → nawa* ‡	苗代 *nawashiro* ('rice plant nursery')
i → o inflection:		
木	*ki → ko*	木霊 *kodama* ('an echo; spirit of a tree')
黄	*ki → ko*	黄金 *kogane* ('gold')
火	*hi → ho*	火影 *hokage* ('firelight')
e → o inflection:		
背	*se → so*	背く *somuku* † ('rebel; disobey; betray')
o → a inflection:		
白	*shiro → shira*	白菊 *shiragiku* ('white chrysanthemum')

† This is a hidden compound word: a word originally created as a compound, but which is written today with only a single kanji. In the case of *tasukeru*, the character for the original inflecting word (手) does not appear in the modern form of the word.

‡ The inflected mora has a different starting consonant sound due to sound changes which occurred in Japanese. See Part 1, Section 8.10 for further explanation.

Appendix K
Common Compounds with Special Readings

This appendix lists common compound words which have readings that cannot be exactly obtained from the readings of the individual characters in them. There are many more such words; these are among the more commonly encountered and are provided here as examples.

With some of these words, the unusual reading came about due to the fact that one or more of the characters now used to write the compound were not originally part of the word, but were substituted later based on similarity of reading and relevance to word meaning. For each word listed here an explanatory note is added, providing information such as how the character readings differ from their principal forms.

Group A – Slightly Altered Readings: the compound readings are closely related to the *on* or *kun* readings of the individual characters in them, but with some slight differences.

Compound	Reading	Notes
時計	*tokei*	see Chapter 9, Section 9.10 discussion
景色	*keshiki*	see Chapter 9, Section 9.10 discussion
登山	*tozan*	first character more commonly read as *TŌ*
文字	*moji*	first character more commonly read as *MON*
今年	*kotoshi*	first character more commonly read as *KON*
夫婦	*fūfu*	first character more commonly read as *FU*
上手	*jōzu*	second character commonly read as *SHU* or *SU*
相撲	*sumō*	both characters differ from standard *on* readings
三味線	*shamisen*	first character (read *SAN*) used for meaning
笑顔	*egao*	first character reading shortened from *emu*
尻尾	*shippo*	modified form of readings *shiri* and *o*

Group B – Unexpected Readings: the compound reading bears little or no relation to the readings of its individual kanji. In many words like these, characters are used only for their meaning, not their reading (i.e., *jukujikun*).

Compound	Reading	Notes
昨日	*kinō*	possibly an abbreviation of *saki no hi*
今朝	*kesa*	likely derives from *kono asa / ke asa:* 'this morning'
今日	*kyō*	likely derives from *kono hi:* 'this day'
明日	*asu*	may derive from *akasu* (明かす): 'greet the dawn'
果物	*kudamono*	see Chapter 8, Section 8.10 discussion
大人	*otona*	see Chapter 9, Section 9.10 discussion
風邪	*kaze*	see Chapter 5, Section 5.3 discussion
田舎	*inaka*	word origin unclear
七夕	*tanabata*	see Chapter 5, Section 5.3 discussion
梅雨	*tsuyu*	may derive from 露 (*tsuyu*): 'dew'
お土産	*o-miyage*	word origin unclear
息子	*musuko*	see Chapter 9, Section 9.10 discussion
眼鏡	*megane*	may derive from *me wo kaneru:* 目を兼ねる
浴衣	*yukata*	derives from *yukatabira*, a type of bathrobe
下手	*heta*	word origin unclear
一人	*hitori*	*ri* is an old counter word for people

Appendix L

Mixed *On-Kun* Compounds

Most two-character compounds are read using either the *on* reading of each character or the *kun* reading of each character. Some, though, use a mix: one of each. Compounds that have an *on-kun* reading, in that order, are said to have a *jūbako yomi* (重箱読み), while compounds that have a *kun-on* reading are said to have a *yutō yomi* (湯桶読み). Note that the compound words *jūbako* and *yutō* themselves have the type of reading for which they are named; that is, they are each a member of their own category. A *jūbako* is a set of stacked, usually lacquered, food boxes. A *yutō* is a wooden container for holding and serving hot liquids.

In this appendix, several common compound words of each type are listed. The reading of each word is shown in both *kana* and *rōmaji*. In each *kana* reading, the *on* portion is written in katakana, and the *kun* in hiragana. In the *rōmaji* readings, the *on* reading is in uppercase letters, and the *kun* in lowercase. For each word, a brief definition is also given. This is not a comprehensive list; only a few examples of each type are given.

Common *Jūbako* Readings

(first character read with *on* reading, second with *kun* reading)

Word	Reading (*kana*)	Reading (*rōmaji*)	Meaning
台所	ダイどころ	DAIdokoro	kitchen
番組	バンぐみ	BANgumi	(TV) program
毎年	マイとし	MAItoshi	every year
職場	ショクば	SHOKUba	workplace
茶色	チャいろ	CHAiro	the color brown
蛇口	ジャぐち	JAguchi	faucet
本棚	ホンだな	HONdana	bookshelf
肉屋	ニクや	NIKUya	butcher
仕事	シごと	SHIgoto	job; occupation
試合	シあい	SHIai	match; bout

Note that in the final two words above, the first part (シ, *SHI*) actually comes from the combining form of the native Japanese word する. Thus, the compound as a spoken word is fully *kun*, or native Japanese, but in the written form a different character is substituted (as a kind of *ateji*), creating an *on-kun* compound.

Common *Yutō* Readings

(first character read with *kun* reading, second with *on* reading)

Word	Reading (*kana*)	Reading (*rōmaji*)	Meaning
場所	ばショ	baSHO	location
荷物	にモツ	niMOTSU	luggage
切符	きっプ	kipPU †	ticket
値段	ねダン	neDAN	price
泥棒	どろボウ	doroBŌ	thief
見本	みホン	miHON ‡	sample
手順	てジュン	teJUN	procedure
夕食	ゆうショク	yūSHOKU	dinner
焼肉	やきニク	yakiNIKU ‡	grilled meat
中味	なかミ	nakaMI	contents

† The *kun* portion of this word is abbreviated (final sound replaced with *sokuon*).
‡ The *kun* portion of this word is in its combining form.

Note that the final word above is an alternate way to write the all-*kun* compound word 中身 (なかみ, *nakami*), which also means 'contents.' The alternate form above is often used when referring specifically to food.

Appendix M

Four-Character Compounds

In English, many sayings and figurative expressions have become firmly established in the language. Some of these expressions can be classified as proverbs or adages, which relate pieces of wisdom or useful advice. Examples are 'a stitch in time saves nine,' 'the squeaky wheel gets the grease' and 'loose lips sink ships.' Many of these expressions, including these three, are also idioms: expressions in which the words used are not meant to be taken literally, but rather represent a larger concept. Other examples of English idioms include the phrases 'going out on a limb' and 'beating around the bush.'

As you would expect, all languages have proverbs and idioms. In Chinese, many such expressions came to be commonly expressed with a short phrase consisting of exactly four characters. Many of these expressions were subsequently adopted into the Japanese language.

In Japanese, four-character compound words and phrases are called *yojijukugo* (四字熟語, よじじゅくご), a term which literally means 'four character compound word.' Used in its broadest sense, the term includes any word or phrase written with exactly four characters. But this term has also come to denote figurative expressions (such as idioms and proverbs), because so many of these expressions are written as four-character compounds.

Hundreds of four-character compound figurative expressions can be found in the Japanese language. Some are very common and well known, others less so. Some of these expressions were created in Japan, in imitation of the Chinese style.[1] In this appendix, we'll take a look at *yojijukugo*, including studying how these expressions were formed, and learning about some common patterns seen among them.

Formation

Although not true of all *yojijukugo*, many were composed by combining two two-character words together. For example, the expression 試行錯誤 (しこうさくご, *shikō-sakugo*) is made up of the two compound words 試行 (*shikō*), meaning 'a trial; a test run,' and 錯誤 (*sakugo*), meaning 'mistake; error.' The four-character compound means 'trial and error.'

Some four-character compounds were formed by abbreviating a longer expression, taking just four characters from it which could be used to represent the whole expression. We saw an example of this in Chapter 9 (Section 9.2), where the English expression, 'kill two birds with one stone' has been converted into a four-character compound, using characters with the meanings 'one,' 'stone,' 'two,' and 'bird(s),' in that order: 一石二鳥. In Japanese, this four-character phrase represents the meaning of the full expression; other words appearing in the English version of the expression, such as 'kill,' are omitted.

---

[1] There are also idioms and proverbs in Japanese that do not follow the four-character format; most such expressions are native to Japanese, not originating in China.

In Japan, one of the most well known *yojijukugo* is *ichi-go-ichi-e* (いちごいちえ), written in kanji like this:

一期一会

This expression can roughly be translated as 'one meeting in a lifetime.' The expression is Japanese in origin, and was molded into the four character form in imitation of the Chinese style; the four characters are an abbreviated form of a longer expression, which had its origins in Japanese tea ceremony. The expression (both the short and long versions) conveys the notion that any one gathering between people will be the only such gathering in their lives, never again to be repeated exactly, and so the moment should be cherished.

Character Reading

Although all the characters in *ichi-go-ichi-e* are read using *on* readings, the second and fourth characters are read not with their principal *on* reading, but with a less common reading. Specifically, 期 is most commonly read as KI, but is read here as GO, and 会 is most commonly read as KAI, but is read here as E. It is not uncommon for *yojijukugo* to be read with less common *on* readings. The reason for this is that many of these expressions are rather old, and tend to use the first style of *on* reading brought to Japan: the *go on* reading, whereas for many everyday compound words a later reading: the *kan on* reading, is now the most common. (See Part 1, Section 7.9 for a description of the various types of *on* readings.)

Meaning

Sometimes the meaning of a *yojijukugo* is fairly obvious from the four characters in it, but other times it is not. For *yojijukugo* which are idioms, the figurative meaning is not always easily determined from the literal meaning, and must be learned. Following are a few examples of idiomatic *yojijukugo* whose figurative meanings may not be immediately obvious based on their literal meanings.

Expression: 大器晩成 (たいきばんせい, *taiki-bansei*)

    Literal meaning: large containers are completed in the evening
        (i.e., it requires time to fabricate a large container)

    Figurative meaning: great talent matures late

Expression: 危機一髪 (ききいっぱつ, *kiki-ippatsu*)

    Literal meaning: danger, one strand of hair

    Figurative meaning: barely avoiding a calamity (by "a hair's breadth")

Expression: 三日坊主 (みっかぼうず, *mikka-bōzu*)

    Literal meaning: three-day monk

    Figurative meaning: a person who quickly tires of new things tried

Similarity to English Expressions

Some Japanese *yojijukugo* have very close counterparts in English. Each of the following expressions has a close English equivalent.

Expression: 十人十色 (じゅうにんといろ, *jū-nin-to-iro*)

    Literal meaning: ten people, ten colors

    Figurative meaning: each person has their own tastes and disposition

    English equivalent: different strokes for different folks

Expression: 二束三文 (にそくさんもん, *ni-soku-san-mon*)

    Literal meaning: two bundles, three 'mon' (an old unit of money)

    Figurative meaning: very inexpensive; can be bought cheaply, and therefore not special

    English equivalent: a dime a dozen

Expression: 自業自得 (じごうじとく, *ji-gō-ji-toku*)

    Literal meaning: own deeds, own benefit

    Figurative meaning: you receive the results of your own actions
        (most commonly used in reference to bad deeds)

    English equivalent: you reap what you sow

Patterns

Often, certain patterns can be found within *yojijukugo*, occurring within many different compounds. Two common patterns are using numbers in the first and third positions, and using words meaning the opposite of each other in the first and third positions.

We have already seen four examples of the first of these patterns (numbers in the first and third positions):

        一石二鳥   一期一会   十人十色   二束三文

Two examples of the other common pattern (opposites) are shown below.

Expression: 同床異夢 (どうしょういむ, *dō-shō-i-mu*)

    Literal meaning: same bed, different dream

    Figurative meaning: people who are in the same situation, but have different ways
        of thinking and different objectives

Expression: 内剛外柔 (ないごうがいじゅう, *nai-gō-gai-jū*)

    Literal meaning: inside strong, outside soft

    Figurative meaning: tough on the inside, but gentle on the outside

Appendix N

Semi-cursive and Cursive Scripts

At the start of Section 2.11 in Part 1, we learned the five principal (known) writing styles that the characters passed through during their development: oracle bone, bronze, seal, clerical, and regular scripts. Other historical styles of writing the characters have also been developed, some of which have played a peripheral role in character development by influencing the overall look of the characters, but only to a limited extent. For a few characters, though, these other styles have had a large influence on the modern form. Most notable among these other historical writing styles are semi-cursive script and cursive script.

Semi-cursive script and cursive script both originated from clerical script; both were faster, rougher, less precise ways to write the characters using a brush and ink. Unlike clerical script (and regular script), where the brush leaves the paper after each stroke, with both semi-cursive and cursive scripts multiple strokes are drawn without the brush leaving the paper. In some writing, even consecutive characters are sometimes joined together.

With **semi-cursive script** (*gyōshotai* in Japanese)—also referred to as 'running script' based on a direct translation of its Chinese name—the basic structure of a character (such as the elements it contains) is still visible for most characters. This script (or variations of it) has long been used as a shorthand handwriting style.

With **cursive script** (*sōshotai* in Japanese)—also referred to as 'grass script' based on a direct translation of its Chinese name[1]—the writing is even faster and looser than with semi-cursive script. As a result, the basic structure of the character can barely be seen. It is difficult to recognize characters written in this style without special training and experience.

---

[1] Although one of the meanings of the first character in the name of this style is 'grass,' the intended meaning in this word is 'rough,' so this translation is not wholly accurate.

Following are examples of characters drawn in the regular, semi-cursive, and cursive styles, for comparison. Although the regular style was developed after the semi-cursive and cursive styles, it is listed first here to make clear which characters are being shown. There is a large degree of variability in how characters can be drawn in the semi-cursive and cursive styles. The forms shown here are only representative examples.

	Script		
	Regular	Semi-cursive	Cursive
mountain	山	山	山
ear	耳	耳	耳
elephant	象	象	象
woman	女	女	女
rain	雨	雨	雨
origin / source	本	本	本
foot / leg	足	足	足
listen	聞	聞	聞
distant / far	遠	遠	遠
flag	旗	旗	旗
storehouse	蔵	蔵	蔵
crime	罪	罪	罪

The cursive script forms of certain kanji formed the basis of the hiragana characters. This can be seen here with the 'woman' character, whose cursive script form was the basis for the hiragana *me* character (め). Some cursive script character forms also influenced the modern, standard simplified forms of some characters (see Appendix G).

Appendix O
Special Non-Kanji Characters

In addition to kanji, hiragana, and katakana (and rōmaji, standard punctuation marks, etc.), a small number of additional characters with unique roles are sometimes used in the writing of Japanese. This appendix lists some of these special characters, along with a brief description of how each is used.

Character	Usage
¥	Symbol used to denote Japanese yen. Placed prior to the amount.
ヶ	Used in two ways: (1) as part of a counter word for certain items, such as months (e.g., 2 ヶ月) and places (e.g., 3 ヶ所), where it is read as *ka* (or, rarely, *ko*); and (2) as a substitute for the grammatical particle が (*ga*), when used in its old-style possessive role. This latter usage is primarily seen in place names (e.g., 袖ヶ浦, そでがうら, *Sodegaura*). Identical in form to the katakana /ke/ character, but when used in the above roles, a half-height version is most commonly used. Originated as an abbreviation of the 箇 character.
〆	Symbol used in place of the character pair しめ (can take the place of several different kanji). Seen primarily in certain words, most notably しめきり (〆切). Originated as a mark placed on a sealed letter.
※	Symbol used to mark an important note. Similar to an asterisk.
〒	Symbol representing the Japanese post office. Placed at the start of a postal code when addressing a letter.
々	Kanji repeating mark. Used to indicate that the preceding character should be repeated (e.g., 色々 = 色色).
ゝ ゞ	Hiragana repeating marks. Repeats the immediately preceding character. With the second mark, the preceding character is repeated, but with a *dakuten* sound added (e.g., さゞ = さざ).
ヽ ヾ	Katakana repeating marks. Repeats the immediately preceding character. With the second mark, the preceding character is repeated, but with a *dakuten* sound added (e.g., タヾ = タダ).
〳	Another type of repeating mark, similar to the ones above.
仝	Another type of repeating mark, meaning 'same as the above.'

Appendix P
The 100 Most Common Japanese Surnames

This appendix lists the 100 most common Japanese surnames. The kanji in many surnames can be read in multiple ways; in the following list, only the most common ways of reading each name are shown. Name readings are all expressed in katakana.

Rank	Name	Reading
1	佐藤	サトウ
2	鈴木	スズキ
3	高橋	タカハシ
4	田中	タナカ
5	渡辺	ワタナベ
6	伊藤	イトウ
7	山本	ヤマモト
8	中村	ナカムラ
9	小林	コバヤシ
10	加藤	カトウ
11	吉田	ヨシダ
12	山田	ヤマダ
13	佐々木	ササキ
14	山口	ヤマグチ
15	松本	マツモト
16	井上	イノウエ
17	斎藤	サイトウ
18	木村	キムラ
19	林	ハヤシ
20	清水	シミズ

Rank	Name	Reading
21	山崎	ヤマサキ
22	池田	イケダ
23	阿部	アベ
24	森	モリ
25	橋本	ハシモト
26	山下	ヤマシタ
27	石川	イシカワ
28	中島	ナカシマ・ナカジマ
29	前田	マエダ
30	藤田	フジタ
31	小川	オガワ
32	岡田	オカダ
33	後藤	ゴトウ
34	長谷川	ハセガワ
35	村上	ムラカミ
36	近藤	コンドウ
37	石井	イシイ
38	坂本	サカモト
39	遠藤	エンドウ
40	青木	アオキ

Rank	Name	Reading
41	藤井	フジイ
42	西村	ニシムラ
43	福田	フクダ
44	太田	オオタ
45	三浦	ミウラ
46	藤原	フジワラ
47	岡本	オカモト
48	松田	マツダ
49	斉藤	サイトウ
50	中川	ナカガワ
51	中野	ナカノ
52	原田	ハラダ
53	小野	オノ
54	竹内	タケウチ
55	田村	タムラ
56	金子	カネコ
57	和田	ワダ
58	中山	ナカヤマ
59	石田	イシダ
60	上田	ウエダ
61	森田	モリタ
62	原	ハラ
63	柴田	シバタ
64	酒井	サカイ
65	工藤	クドウ
66	横山	ヨコヤマ
67	宮崎	ミヤザキ
68	宮本	ミヤモト
69	内田	ウチダ
70	高木	タカギ
71	安藤	アンドウ
72	谷口	タニグチ
73	大野	オオノ
74	今井	イマイ
75	丸山	マルヤマ
76	高田	タカダ
77	河野	コウノ・カワノ
78	藤本	フジモト
79	小島	オジマ
80	武田	タケダ
81	村田	ムラタ
82	上野	ウエノ
83	杉山	スギヤマ
84	増田	マスダ
85	菅原	スガハラ
86	平野	ヒラノ
87	小山	コヤマ
88	大塚	オオツカ
89	久保	クボ
90	千葉	チバ
91	松井	マツイ
92	岩崎	イワサキ
93	野口	ノグチ
94	松尾	マツオ
95	木下	キシタ・キノシタ
96	菊地	キクチ
97	野村	ノムラ
98	佐野	サノ
99	渡部	ワタナベ
100	新井	アライ

Data courtesy of Suzaki Haruo (http://www2s.biglobe.ne.jp/~suzakihp).

Index

abbreviations,
    ateji-derived, 114
    in character transformation, 56, 284-285
    in compounds, 113-114, 173, 183-184
    in elements, 123-124
    in handwritten characters, 289
agglutinative language, 160
ateji, 30, 104, 105-107, 109, 132
    defined, 105, 245
    used in abbreviations, 114
boinkōtai, 168-169, 297-298
    defined, 168, 245
bronze script, 48, 241
calligraphy, 7, 116, 117-118
Cangjie, 21, 22
character dictionary, 82, 89, 182
    defined, 89, 241
    typical characteristics, 5, 90, 92, 95, 116, 141, 182, 269, 270, 273-276
character substitution, 59, 60-63, 183, 246, 301
    defined, 60, 241
Chinese language, 4, 11, 12, 69, 141, 303
    character readings, 13, 18, 28, 114, 140, 152
    influence on *on* readings, 143
    loan words, 108, 109, 131-132, 144, 154
    phonology, 11, 29, 68
    use of *ateji*, 105
clerical script, 48, 49, 307
    defined, 49, 241
common use characters
    see *jōyō kanji*
component, 8
    defined, 37, 241
composition, character, 126-129
compound, 9-11
    defined, 9, 241
    four-character, 175, 303-305
    hidden, 167-168, 298
    native Japanese (*kun*-based), 160-162
    three-character, 174
    two-character, 171-174
    with special reading, 182-183, 299-300
consolidation, of characters
    see *kakikae*
consonant cluster, 136, 152
consonant elongation, 111, 154, 178
counter words, 109-111
    defined, 110, 241
cursive script, 48, 58, 241, 266, 280, 307-308
dakuten, 43, 145, 180, 265, 309
derived words, 165

determinative, 32-35
    breadth of meaning, 33-34
    connection to character meaning, 41, 43, 46-47
    defined, 32, 241
    difference with radical, 93-95
    quantity of, 95
determinative-phonetic character, 40-44
    as percentage of all kanji, 40, 44, 65
    defined, 40, 242
element, 8-9
    contrasted with component, 37
    defined, 8, 242
    repeated, 25
    variations in form, 24, 122-124
etymology,
    character, 16-17, 26, 43, 68-69, 77-79, 87
        defined, 17, 242
        false, 78-79
    compound, 176-178
extended meaning, 27-32
    defined, 27, 242
false phonetic, 151-152
    defined, 151, 242
form, character, 6-7, 115-129
    defined, 6, 242
furigana, 15, 72
    defined, 15, 245
gemination, 178, 179
gothic script, 119-120
    defined, 119, 242
haiku, 136
handakuten, 180, 265
hanzi, 105
hentaigana, 266
Hepburn-style romanization, 249
hiragana, 4, 15
    defined, 246
    guidelines for usage, 15
    origin, 154, 265-267, 308
    usage as annotation, 85
    usage as grammatical modifier, 132
    usage as *okurigana*, 156-161
    usage in *mazegaki*, 184-185
    usage with auxiliary verbs, 103
    usage with *jukujikun*, 109
    usage with *kun* readings, 42
    words written in, 76, 83, 102-104
homophone, 28, 75-76, 242
    kun-based, 75-76, 103, 165
    on-based, 76, 152
hyakushō yomi, 141

hyōgaiji, 100, 246
ideograph, 23-26, 44, 63, 264, 290
　defined, 23, 242
　single object, 24-25
indicative character, 26, 264
　defined, 26, 243
inflection, word, 13, 101, 102, 103, 132, 156-162
　defined, 13
　noun, see *boinkōtai*
Japanese language,
　phonology, 154-155, 169, 265
　plain form, 14, 16
　polite form, 14, 135
　sentence structure, 14-16, 110
jinmeiyō kanji, 73, 99
　defined, 99, 246
jōyō kanji, 18, 98, 102
　additions to, 85, 199
　character simplifications and, 57, 59, 198, 275, 277, 278
　defined, 18, 246
　total number of, 18, 86, 246
jūbako reading, 301
　defined, 175, 246
jukugo
　see compound
jukujikun, 75, 107-109, 182, 300
　defined, 108, 246
kaisho script, 117-120
　defined, 117, 246
kakikae, 61-62
　defined, 62, 246
kango, 131-132
　adjective modifiers, 133-134
　adverb modifiers, 134
　conversion into, 185-186
　defined, 131, 246
　nouns, 132
　verb modifiers, 132-133
Kangxi radicals, 90, 231, 269, 270, 275, 276
kanji, 3-4
　as symbols, 69, 77-78
　defined, 3, 246
　frequency of usage, 5, 81-85
　history, 4
　quantity, 5, 82-83, 85
katakana, 4, 15
　defined, 247
　guidelines for usage, 15
　origin, 154, 265-267
　usage as phonetic, 15
　usage with *on* readings, 42
　words written in, 101-102, 106, 107, 114, 144
keiyōdōshi
　see *na*-adjective
kokuji, 4, 12, 63-64
　defined, 63, 247
　list of common characters, 291-292

kun reading, 11-13, 44, 106, 107, 131
　defined, 12, 247
　distinguishing from *on* reading, 137
　multiple readings, 162-164
　number of syllables in, 13
　origin, 12
　standard way of expressing, 42
kunreishiki romanization, 249
kyōiku kanji, 18, 70, 98-99
　defined, 18, 247
　total number of, 18
Latin alphabet, 4, 16, 81, 121, 265
　comparison with kanji, 64
long vowel sound, 16, 135-136, 145, 155, 250
　defined, 155, 243
macron, 16, 144-145, 250
manyōgana, 266
mazegaki, 103, 184-185
　defined, 103, 247
meaning,
　character, 4, 7-8, 68, 79
　　defined, 7, 243
　　learning, 87-88
　　multiple, 74-75
　compound, 9-11, 113-114, 176-178
meaning shift, 30, 243
minchō script, 118-119, 121
　defined, 118, 247
mixed *on* and *kun* compound, 175, 301-302
　see also *jūbako* reading, *yutō* reading
mora, 135-137, 153-155, 265
　counting, 136
　defined, 135, 243
na-adjective, 133
nanori reading, 169
　defined, 169, 247
nesting, character, 45-47
non-*kanji* characters, 309
okurigana, 14, 156-159, 161, 163, 175
　defined, 14, 247
on reading, 11-13, 44
　defined, 11
　distinguishing from *kun* reading, 137
　multiple readings, 39, 138-139, 140-141
　number of syllables in, 13
　origin, 11, 131
　principal reading, 139
　standard way of expressing, 42
　types, 141-144
　use in prefixes and suffixes, 111
　valid readings, 135-138
onomatopoeia, 15
oracle bone script, 48
　defined, 48, 243
palatalized consonant, 136, 154-156, 199
　defined, 154-155, 243
　in related readings, 146, 149
　representation in *kana*, 265

INDEX

particles, grammatical, 15, 16, 110, 164, 169
phonetic
    see phonetic component
phonetic alphabet, 4, 15
phonetic aspect of characters, 17, 44, 65, 68
phonetic borrowing, 28-30, 264
    defined, 28, 243
phonetic component, 17, 36-40, 195-199
    connection to character meaning, 41, 43, 46
    defined, 36, 243
    loss of phonetic role, 59, 61, 151
    multiple readings, 138, 140-141
pictograph, 22-23, 44, 64, 67, 264
    defined, 22, 244
polite modifier, 135
predicate, 133
prefix, 111-113
    defined, 111, 244
    grammatical usage, 160
    negation, 173-174
    polite, 135
radical, 89-93, 269-277
    choice of component for, 91-92
    defined, 89, 244
    difference with determinative, 93-95
    meanings, 276-277
    names, 97-98, 270-273
reading, character, 7
    defined, 7, 244
    learning, 86-87
    multiple, 75
regions, character, 96-98
    in radical names, 271, 272
regular script,
    see *kaisho* script
related readings, 39, 144-149
    defined, 39, 244
rendaku, 75, 97-98, 179-181
    defined, 180, 247
renjō, 181-182
    defined, 181, 247
rōmaji, 16, 249-250
    defined, 16, 247
    kunrei and Hepburn differences, 249
    vowel representation, 249-250
Roman alphabet
    see Latin alphabet
ryakuji, 289
script (writing), 48
    defined, 244
seal script, 48-49
    defined, 49, 244
semi-cursive script, 48, 244, 307-308
Shang Dynasty, 4
Shuowen Jiezi, 47, 90, 263-264
simplification, character, 57-60, 279-289
    in China, 280
    radical re-designation, 92

six principles of character creation, 47, 263-264
sokuon,
    character, 136, 155, 178-179
        counting mora, 136
    defined, 154, 178, 248
    representation in *kana*, 265
    sound change phenomenon, 111, 178-179
    vocal sound, 154-156
South Korea, use of kanji, 4
spaces, in sentences, 15, 16
standard script
    see *kaisho* script
stem, word, 13, 14, 15
stroke, 6-7, 115
    defined, 6, 244
    types, 117-118
    variations, 9, 24, 120-122
stroke count, 7, 89-90, 115-116, 120
    defined, 7, 244
    of radicals, 275-276
stroke order, 6-7, 115-116
    defined, 7, 245
    principles, 251-261
stroke order diagram, 6, 116, 245
suffix, 111-113, 174
    defined, 111, 245
    grammatical usage, 160
surnames, most common, 311-312
syllabary, 4, 101, 154, 265-266
    see also *hiragana*, *katakana*
syllabic /n/ sound, 154-156
    counting mora, 136
    defined, 154, 245
    representation in *kana*, 265, 266
syllable, 4, 135
taboo character, 60-61
tense, grammatical, 13, 156
    expressed with *okurigana*, 14, 16
    non-standard form, 164
textbook script, 119-120
    defined, 119, 245
tōyō kanji, 98, 279
traditional Japanese, 27, 154-156, 297
    defined, 154, 245
transformation, character form, 47-60
transliteration, 16, 249-250
typeface, 117, 119-122, 124, 245
unrelated readings, 150
variant character, 60, 82-83, 99, 124-126, 279-290
    defined, 60, 245
verbs, transitive and intransitive, 158-160
Vietnam, use of kanji, 4
wago, 132, 248
Xu Shen, 90
yamato kotoba
    see *wago*
yutō reading, 301-302
    defined, 175, 248

List of Book Illustrations

Front Cover – Combination lock. The five dials contain the characters from the second verse of the Tang Dynasty poem 憫農 ("Sympathy for Peasants") by Li Shen (?-846). Setting the second line of the verse on the dials allows the lock to be opened. In the personal collection of Yip Fat-chi. Photograph by Mr. Yip.

Chapter 1 Title Page – Seal imprint. Seal reads 長安獄丞: Chang-an Prison Deputy. (Chang-an is a former name of Xian.) Imprint made from replica of original seal. In the collection of China Seal Museum, Hangzhou City, China. Photograph courtesy of China Seal Museum.

Chapter 2 Title Page – Replica of Shang Dynasty oracle bone. This replica is of a tortoise plastron (the underside shell). The engraved characters were used in fortune-telling. In the personal collection of Ta-Chen and Sheue-Hwa Mo. Photograph courtesy of Ta-Chen Mo.

Chapter 3 Title Page – Bamboo slat book. Sun Tzu's *The Art of War* (孫子兵法). Commissioned by the Qianlong Emperor of Qing Dynasty (r. 1735-1796 AD). University of California, Riverside Special Collections & Archives. Composited photo illustration based on original photography by Vlasta Radan.

Chapter 4 Title Page – Folding fan. Calligraphy is of Tang Dynasty poem 同王徵君洞庭有懷 by Zhang Wei (720-770). Photograph by the author.

Chapter 5 Title Page – Chinese spade coin. Circa Xin Dynasty (9-23 AD). Molded with the characters 貨布 (*huo bu*), meaning 'money spade.' In the personal collection of Dr. Gary Lee Todd. Photograph by Dr. Todd.

Chapter 6 Title Page – Decorative ceramic roof tile end cap (*onigawara*). Formerly mounted on the roof of a small hot-spring bath building in Beppu, Oita, Japan. The single character on the tile (熱; *netsu*), meaning 'heat,' marks the name of the bathhouse. In the collection of Miyuki-ya inn in the Kannawa district of Beppu. Photograph by Daniel Dupriest.

Chapter 7 Title Page – Replica of bronze cooking vessel known as *da ke ding*. The original *da ke ding* was made during China's Western Zhou Dynasty (1046-771 BC), and weighs approximately 200kg (440 pounds). The inner wall contains an inscription of 290 characters, divided into two parts: a eulogy for the owner's grandfather, and a confirmation of the owner's commission. Photograph courtesy of Thomas Leung.

Chapter 8 Title Page – Tea brick. Loose tea compressed into a brick and depicting the image of and character for horse. Photograph courtesy of Bliss Dake, Mighty Leaf Tea Company.

Chapter 9 Title Page – Mahjongg tiles. The eight wan and south wind tiles are shown. In the personal collection of Doi Hideko. Photograph by Ms. Doi.

About the Author

Steve Thenell (pronounced *tuh-NELL*) first went to Japan in 2004 to teach English. Not knowing Japanese at all, he quickly started studying the *hiragana* and *katakana* syllabaries, and then began to prepare for the monumental task of learning *kanji*. Seeking advice from many sources on learning strategies, he did his best to learn the characters, but only with much effort. When he finally became comfortable with the characters, he looked back and realized that learning them could have been much easier if he had known some key information earlier on. That's the inspiration for this book.

About the creation of this book, he says, "I did all of this because I felt it needed to be done. But it was truly a labor of love."

www.ingramcontent.com/pod-product-compliance
Lightning Source LLC
Chambersburg PA
CBHW080423230426
43662CB00015B/2192